"Glenn's thoroughly researched work on feminism and rhetoric crystalizes issues, resolves many theoretical incompatibilities, provides a spectrum of methodologies for analysis and criticism, and offers an emotionally elegant plea of hope for the future of rhetorical feminism. Without question, the most coherent, thorough, and insightful treatment of the subject that I have read."—Richard Leo Enos, author of *Greek Rhetoric before Aristotle*

"Cheryl Glenn's latest opus is a book rhetoricians engaged in public life have been waiting for, a work by a distinguished scholar anchored in both rhetoric and feminism. In eight eloquent chapters Glenn develops a compelling argument for moving rhetorical feminism from highbrow scholarship into its larger transformative virtue, or 'hope.' This is engaged scholarship at its most luminous and destined to be a reference work for many years to come."—Philippe-Joseph Salazar, author of *Words Are Weapons: Inside ISIS's Rhetoric of Terror*

"*Rhetorical Feminism and This Thing Called Hope* serves two important functions: it provides readers a historical account of how the field of feminist rhetoric emerged within rhetoric and composition studies; it also provides a new concept and theory, *rhetorical feminism*, which Glenn offers as a means for working toward 'equality, social justice, coalition across differences, inclusion, representation, and ever-developing rhetorical effectiveness.'"—Krista Ratcliffe, coeditor of *Rhetorics of Whiteness: Postracial Hauntings in Popular Culture, Social Media, and Education*

"When you open the pages of *Rhetorical Feminism and This Thing Called Hope* you are in for an invigorating ride. From Glenn's meticulous overview of the relationship between feminism and rhetoric to her framework for and exploration of what she identifies as "rhetorical feminism," to her transformative discussion of methods and methodologies, to her wise (and often witty) advice about teaching, mentoring, and administering—this book speaks eloquently and passionately to the work we must do to inhabit and perform rhetorical feminism. Best of all, it gives reasons to trust in "this thing called hope."—Andrea A. Lunsford, author of *EasyWriter*

Studies in Rhetorics and Feminisms

Series Editors, Cheryl Glenn and Shirley Wilson Logan

RHETORICAL FEMINISM AND THIS THING CALLED HOPE

CHERYL GLENN

SOUTHERN ILLINOIS UNIVERSITY PRESS
CARBONDALE

Southern Illinois University Press
www.siupress.com

Copyright © 2018 by Cheryl Glenn
All rights reserved
Printed in the United States of America

21 20 19 18   4 3 2 1

Cover illustration: still from Sigalit Landau's 2005 video *DeadSee* (eleven-minute, thirty-nine-second loop); used with the artist's permission.

Library of Congress Cataloging-in-Publication Data
Names: Glenn, Cheryl, author.
Title: Rhetorical feminism and this thing called hope / Cheryl Glenn.
Description: Carbondale : Southern Illinois University Press, [2018] | Series: Studies in rhetorics and feminisms | Includes bibliographical references and index.
Identifiers: LCCN 2017060239 | ISBN 9780809336944 (paperback : alk. paper) | ISBN 9780809336951 (e-book)
Subjects: LCSH: Feminism and literature.
Classification: LCC PN56.F46 G54 2018 | DDC 808.0082—dc23 LC record available at https://lccn.loc.gov/2017060239

Printed on recycled paper. ♻

*To rhetorical feminists,
especially those I'm lucky enough
to call my friends*

We cannot wait to speak until we are perfectly clear and righteous.
—Adrienne Rich, "Split at the Root"

CONTENTS

Preface xi

Introduction: Rhetorical Feminism—Definitions, Terms, Parameters 1

1. Activism 5
2. Identities 24
3. Theories 49
4. Methods and Methodologies 96
5. Teaching 124
6. Mentoring 149
7. (Writing Program) Administration 174
8. This Thing Called Hope 193

Notes 215
Works Cited and Consulted 237
Index 261

PREFACE

Rhetorical Feminism and This Thing Called Hope introduces the theory of *rhetorical feminism* and clarifies how our feminist rhetorical practices have given rise to this tactic (or theoretical stance). The book elucidates distinctions and overlap between *feminist rhetoric* and rhetorical feminism in ways that equip our field for a more expansive dialogue.

Rhetorical Feminism and This Thing Called Hope is broken into eight chapters that define the parameters of rhetorical feminism and demonstrate the role it plays. To that end, I focus on the understanding and application of rhetorical feminism within a variety of specific contexts of feminist rhetorical interactions, research, and embodiment.

- "Activism" (chapter 1) charts the relationship of feminism, rhetoric, coalition, and activism, from the nineteenth-century push for women's suffrage to the 2017 Women's March on Washington, tracing deployments of rhetorical feminism as a way to gain a historical sense of the term.

- "Identities" (chapter 2) focuses on the theoretical and practical progress feminist rhetoricians have made in order to move beyond the monolithic identity of "woman" and on the ways they have used rhetorical feminism to consider all identities (our own as well as those of Others) as intersectional and epistemic resources.

- "Theories" (chapter 3) outlines transformative feminist engagements with mainstream rhetorical theory,[1] engagements anchored in hope that demonstrate tenets of rhetorical feminism, including progress toward greater representation and inclusivity of everyday rhetors, disidentification with traditional rhetorical practices, transformation of rhetorical transactions, reconsideration of the rhetorical appeals, and appreciation for alternative means of delivery.

- "Methods and Methodologies" (chapter 4) acknowledges that separating theory from research applications is nearly impossible yet offers an attempt to do just that. Researchers are tapping the features of rhetorical feminism to transform both rhetorical research methods (ways to obtain information) and methodologies (ways to analyze that information).

- "Teaching" (chapter 5) returns to rhetoric's roots as a teaching tradition. Rhetorical feminism is evidenced in teaching rhetorical transactions beyond that of the persuasive argument that accommodate and account for the positionalities, experiences, and identities of students.

- "Mentoring" (chapter 6) connects feminism with yet another rhetorical tradition. The feminist intervention into the traditional hierarchical master-apprentice model of mentoring points to a model that supports mentees through the process of becoming part of, being in, and belonging to a profession, a model that works to shape the *next* generation of mentors.

- "(Writing Program) Administration" (chapter 7) examines the work that has opened up to women leaders, many of whom bring feminist politics and rhetorical training to the post. In this role of administrator, they not only analyze the hierarchical scene of administration but couple rhetorical power with the teaching of writing.

- Finally, "This Thing Called Hope" (chapter 8) illuminates our present political moment, a gloomy moment of restricted environmental policies, international relations, health care, and social programs that affect the most vulnerable of our citizens. Rhetorical feminism's emphasis on hope (Cornel West's "leap of faith" kind of hope) continually reminds us that we must trust that change will come and pro/actively pursue positive change. Now, more than ever, in this new, amped-up, masculinist order, we need the powers of rhetorical feminism as we teach, mentor, administer, write, and live productively and hopefully with one another.

This brief exploration into rhetorical feminism (which holds the promise that is hope) reminds us what it means to work in our field, to be a feminist, rhetorician, researcher, teacher, mentor, administrator—even mentee and student.

PREFACE

Rhetorical Feminism and This Thing Called Hope came into being with substantial support from colleagues, students, and friends. At Penn State, I am grateful to Susan Welch, dean of the College of Liberal Arts, and Mark Morrisson, English department head, for recognizing the hope that is this book and allowing me the time to realize it. I am thankful for Gregg Rogers for serving as interim director of the Program in Writing and Rhetoric during my absence and to research assistant extraordinaire Greg Coles for tracking down the most obscure poems, articles, and chapters. Each time I sent Greg on a wild goose chase, he returned with a golden egg. I am also indebted to the research findings of Heather Adams, Sarah Adams, Laura Brown, John Smilges, Shannon Stimpson, and Sarah Summers.

Happy Valley colleagues and friends Robin Becker, Kendra Boileau, Jim Brasfield, Veronica Burk, Charlotte Holmes, Joan Richtsmeier, Marie Secor, Jack Selzer, Sandy Spanier, and Sandy Stelts, and the Rhetorichicks (Ebony, Anne, Rosa, Pamela, Debbie, Michele, and Mary) provided diversions as well as support, as did my feminist rhetorical colleagues and friends beyond Happy Valley, including Lisa Ede, Anders Eriksson, Marie Gelang, Lori Gray, Anita Helle, Claire Hogarth, Debra Hughes, Laura Kaye Jagles, Karl Kageff, Berit von der Lippe, Alfredo Lujan, Marianne and Maynard Makman, Joyce Irene Middleton, Roxanne Mountford, Brigitte Mral, Char Rosen, Char de Vazquez, the Coalition of Feminist Scholars in the History of Rhetoric and Composition, and, of course, the Green Camp girls. C. Jan Swearingen died the day I submitted this manuscript. How I miss her.

Greg Coles, Jessica Enoch, Shirley Wilson Logan, Andrea Lunsford, Krista Ratcliffe, and an anonymous reader read and responded perceptively to drafts of this project, giving generously of their time and expertise. Acquisitions editor Kristine Priddy provided me with expert guidance, along with project editor Wayne Larsen, production manager Linda Buhman, copy editor Julie Bush, and the rest of the team at Southern Illinois University Press. For their insightful reads, invaluable criticisms, corrections, and suggestions, I remain infinitely grateful. The shortcomings of this book are solely my own.

I'm also grateful to visionary feminist Israeli artist Sigalit Landau, who generously allowed me to use a still from her 2005 *DeadSee* video for the cover of this book.

Of course, my greatest debt is to my family, all of whom have grown accustomed to my work schedule and writing life. How fortunate I am to spend my life with Jon, Anna, Bill, Edward, Helen, Imogen, Krysta, Miguel, Mom, and Terry, whose spirits buoy my own.

RHETORICAL FEMINISM AND THIS THING CALLED HOPE

INTRODUCTION: RHETORICAL FEMINISM—DEFINITIONS, TERMS, PARAMETERS

Our past is seeding in our present and is trying to become our future.
—Adrienne Rich, *Arts of the Possible*

Feminist rhetoric is a case in point. This subfield slowly came into focus in the late 1980s and early 1990s when rhetoric and feminism were beginning to connect, using the past to seed our present and build our future. At that time, nearly all the rhetoricians were men (think Aristotle to Kenneth Burke), and rhetoric was a wholly masculinized field, with a scholarly focus on rhetoric that was political, agonistic, aristocratic, and persuasive. Studies of rhetoric operated as "terministic screens" (Burke, *Language* 45), reflecting our institutional focus on the discursively powerful while deflecting the rhetorical contributions of everyone else (women, people of color, the disabled, those of various sexualities or cultural-ethnic groups). Thus, accounts of rhetoric at the time (Bizzell and Herzberg, Corbett, G. Kennedy) were written from an epistemological position of alleged gender neutrality and truth, chimeras for those who already inhabited hegemonic ideology.

Yet even back then, a number of us were imagining a new field of study. We hoped that rhetorical study would come to embrace such foundational feminist concepts as openness, authentic dialogue and deliberation, interrogation of the status quo, collaboration, respect, and progress—and vice versa. The feminist values of inclusivity and representation could be realized, if only rhetoricians would learn how to appreciate the vast variety of people and practices that actually embody rhetoric every single day. Feminists, on the other hand, would come to appreciate traditional rhetorical understandings and tools such as public performance, audience

INTRODUCTION

analysis, argument, artistic appeals, exigence, and kairos. I do not think feminist rhetoricians have been expecting too much. Still, the mutual transformation of the disciplines has been slow.

Once feminism was firmly established as an academic discipline, recovering and recuperating women's contributions in the broad history of culture-making across the disciplines, feminist *rhetorical* recovery work started up in earnest, to the point that studying the rhetorical accomplishments of women (many of them feminists) is no longer exceptional; rather, it is the norm. Whether the woman under analysis is Kathy Acker, Gloria Anzaldúa, Aspasia, Anna Julia Cooper, Margery Kempe, Victoria Earle Matthews, Ida Burnett Wells, or Zitkála-Šá (Gertrude Simmons Bonnin), and whether she is on the platform, at her desk, onstage, on a screen, in the parlor, or in the streets, she is nearly naturalized at the scene of rhetoric.[1] Now, rhetoric and feminism are slowly transforming each other. This feminist rhetorical recovery work has laid the groundwork for building our field as one of hope, where rhetorical recognition and appreciation take into consideration the place, culture, ethnicity, class, ability, movements, and orientations of human beings throughout time.

One such early endeavor to spark a connection between rhetoric and feminism was "Border Crossings: Intersections of Rhetoric and Feminism." In this 1995 essay, Lisa Ede, Andrea Lunsford, and I argue that

> rhetoric offers feminism a vibrant process of inquiring, organizing, and thinking, as well as a theorized place to talk about effective communication; feminism offers rhetoric a reason to bridge differences, to include and to empower, as well as a politicized sphere to discuss rhetorical values. (401)

Although I had been working at this confluence for several years, the essay helped crystallize the ideology of feminist rhetoric and moved our thinking toward supporting such an ideology. This book provides a stance for doing just that.

To that end, *Rhetorical Feminism and This Thing Called Hope* serves as a guide. Although rhetoric and feminism have yet to coalesce into a singular recognizable field, the outline of such a field displays prominent features, which I identify throughout this book. I feel sure these features will help move our feminist rhetorical project forward, yet I realize that they are not the only ones that will arise (as I explain in the concluding chapter). Nor will the feminist rhetorical researchers I cite be the only active researchers in our field. After all, much feminist recovery work remains to be undertaken with regard to how concerns for culture, ethnicity, race (including whiteness), gender, age, ability, and status reflect feminist concerns in the United States as well as around the globe. Layers of theory must be plumbed in order to locate the core theories of both fields—rhetoric and feminism—and determine the rich and complex ways both fields can productively interanimate each other. More important, at this point, is the synergy released as these features and researchers slowly merge. This coalescence continues to generate feminist rhetorical scholarship that moves us beyond a singular, steady focus on the recovery of rhetorical women. We feminist rhetoricians are now investing in rhetorical theories and practices that challenge traditional antagonistic rhetorical performance, and we open ourselves to new tactics and value-laden theories such as rhetorical feminism.[2]

Throughout this book, I reference two terms: *feminist rhetoric* and *rhetorical feminism*. Feminist rhetoric is, first and foremost, a set of long-established practices that advocates a political position of rights and responsibilities that certainly includes the equality of women and Others. Throughout this book, the term *Others* resonates with women, people of color, or people disenfranchised on the basis of their race, gender, sexuality, ethnicity, religion, ability, language, or all the possible intersections of these identity markers. There are occasions when I refer to the *subaltern* or the *marginalized,* fully aware that these terms—like Others—are fraught and provisional (particularly given that Gayatri Spivak's initial postcolonial use of "subaltern" referred to those people *completely* separated from societal discourses of postcolonial power).

Feminist rhetoric also focuses on the rights, contributions, expertise, opportunities, and histories of marginalized groups and supports coalitions across and among these groups. It relies on rhetorical concepts and practices, including a response to an exigence, attention to audience, arguments based on reason and evidence, purposeful and appropriate language, and, of course, the rhetorical appeals of ethos, logos, and pathos. It uses and respects traditional, alternative, and contemporary rhetorical deliveries, ranging from the pen, platform, pulpit, petition, and demonstration to digital genres and rhetorics, manifestos, books, articles, and more. In short, feminist rhetoric indicates a fusion and evolution of rhetoric and feminism. "Feminist rhetoric" is common parlance in rhetorical studies, what with a book series, a biennial conference, articles, and conference presentations bearing that term.

INTRODUCTION

Rhetorical feminism, on the other hand, is a tactic (actually a set of tactics)—a theoretical stance—that is responsive to the ideology that is feminism and to the key strategy that is feminist rhetoric. Anchored in hope, rhetorical feminism offers ways to disidentify with hegemonic rhetoric, with the dominant rhetorical histories, theories, and practices articulated in Western culture.[3] As a tactic, then, rhetorical feminism is in a constant state of response, reassessment, and self-correction. Rhetorical feminism enacts goals that are dialogic and transactional rather than monologic and reactional and attends to (provisionally) marginalized audiences that may or may not have the power to address or resolve the exigence. Rhetorical feminism employs and respects vernaculars and experiences, recognizing them as sources of knowledge. And rhetorical feminism also shows us ways to reshape the rhetorical appeals, including a reshaped logos based on dialogue and understanding, a reshaped ethos rooted in experience, and a reshaped pathos that values emotion. Finally, rhetorical feminism uses and respects alternative delivery systems, especially those long considered feminine, such as silence and listening. The key features of rhetorical feminism are threaded throughout this book. Rhetorical feminism is a conceptual action, a trope that can be used to help negotiate cross-boundary mis/understandings and reconciliations; illuminate rhetorical theories; advance feminist rhetorical research methods and methodologies; energize feminist teaching, mentoring, and administration; and secure our hope for the future. In these ways, rhetorical feminism works in the service of and to advance feminist rhetoric.[4]

After all, the stubborn belief to which rhetoricians seem to hold fast is that rhetorical practices should *do* something, that rhetorical inquiry should make a difference in the world. Rhetorical feminists steadfastly believe that human lives are equal in value—and that we must continue to work to make that so in our world. Although *agency* is a contested term, both rhetoric and the feminists who employ it do, indeed, have agency, the power to take efficacious action. And even if that agency is always contingent, it can be adopted strategically (echoing Spivak), as well as rigorously, to redefine rhetorical history, theory, and praxis to the end of representing and including more users and uses of rhetoric; to represent more ethically and accurately the dominant and the marginalized alike (even as we rethink this metaphor); and to prepare the next generation of rhetorically empowered scholars, feminists, teachers, and citizens. We can use our feminist rhetorical agency, our rhetorical feminism, to realize our hope.

ONE: ACTIVISM

I have met brave women who are exploring the outer edge of possibility, with no history to guide them and a courage to make themselves vulnerable that I find moving beyond the words to express it.
— Gloria Steinem, "Sisterhood"

Public, political, activist women—those Sister Rhetors who speak, write, and theorize their activism in the private, pedagogical, and public spheres—embody the best of feminist rhetoric, a set of long-established practices that advocates a political position of rights and responsibilities that certainly include the equality of women and Others.[1] And their work is effective, embodying as it does the feminist principles of equality, respect, and coalition building. Some Sister Rhetors also enact the tactic of rhetorical feminism, a set of practices that includes disidentification with hegemonic rhetoric; goals that are dialogic and transactional; attention to marginalized audiences; respect for vernaculars, experiences, and emotion; a reshaping of the rhetorical appeals; and uses of alternative delivery systems—all anchored in hope. Both feminist rhetors and rhetorical feminists respond to power, their responses including speaking, silence, listening, or action of some kind.

All the women rhetors I feature in this chapter have employed the strategy of feminist rhetoric to intervene into the rhetorical-political-social sphere and establish themselves as activist leaders. Some of them have embodied the tactic of rhetorical feminism. These women demonstrate the ways that public and private language use can be a means to create a different kind of world characterized by a different set of practices and values, ones that establish *eudaemonia*, the greatest good for all human beings.

Sister Rhetors have been active in the United States since the 1880s, with the last three decades (beginning in the 1990s), in particular, bringing incredible attention to their rhetorical effectiveness all around the globe. Sister Rhetors speak, write, listen, and contemplate their way into the public sphere, where they inaugurate politics, practices, and shared understandings (fraught as that phrase may be) that benefit the dispossessed and the disenfranchised (rather than reinforce the status quo for the benefit of the already powerful and privileged). Thus, their ultimate goal reaches far beyond so-called equality with men.

The changes they effect are good—if not always welcome. Though often excluded from the public sphere,[2] women activists (Sister Rhetors, no less) enter and work to transform that public sphere by chronicling their own history, capturing their own present, revising effective rhetorical participation, and working to legislate a future of equal protection and opportunity—the future they want to inhabit and the one they want for future generations. For all of these reasons, this chapter is devoted to the activism of Sister Rhetors; it moves beyond an appreciation of their work to argue for the importance of developing and using rhetorical feminism.

I begin this chapter with a snapshot of the contemporary feminist-political moment, one that captures the stronghold that patriarchy continues to enforce and provides the exigence for rhetorical feminism. Then, I provide a brief overview of white and free black Sister Rhetors in the United States, women who valiantly and for decades struggled to obtain the right to speak publicly and to vote, often using the set of tactics that constitute rhetorical feminism.[3] These women represent feminism's first "wave" (a problematic yet efficient term). Even now, in the second decade of the twenty-first century, women's status as full citizens, public rhetors, and political leaders remains abridged, contested. After examining the rhetorical-political reach of such early Sister Rhetors as Maria W. Miller Stewart, Angelina Grimké, Lucretia Mott, Sojourner Truth, and Frances Harper, I chart the extent of their influence, the measure of their rhetorical-political success. Then I provide a second snapshot, that of the contemporary global political moment, to illustrate the continued restrictions on women, including the many ways that women's right to vote, their so-called legal equality, has not yet accorded them social, political, or economic—let alone legal—equality.[4] To bring home that point, I provide examples of US women's political status. I close the chapter with the example of Hillary Rodham Clinton, who leverages the power of rhetorical feminism for her feminist political work. Despite two agonizing defeats for the presidency, Clinton continues to work on the behalf of women and children, in the hope that all US citizens may eventually become equal.[5]

Legal Rights but Not (Yet) Equal Rights

"The right of citizens of the United States to vote shall not be denied or abridged by the United States or by any State on account of sex"—so says the Nineteenth Amendment to the US Constitution, which was ratified by Congress on 18 August 1920, after some seventy years in the making. This seventy-year struggle was stalled when white and free black suffragists diverted their political support to such monumental issues as the emancipation of slaves, the Union army's role in the Civil War, African American men's enfranchisement, and war efforts for the Great War (World War I). Yet despite those historic pauses and their own rhetorical failures, US women eventually mounted arguments that proved to be pivotal in their securing the right to vote.

Even following the passage of the Nineteenth Amendment in 1920, the US political climate has remained profoundly chilly for women both politically and rhetorically. US women have been consistently thwarted in their attempts for political and legal equality. For example, in 1923 Alice Paul introduced the Equal Rights Amendment, which reads, "Equality of rights under the law shall not be denied or abridged by the United States or any state on account of sex." That proposed amendment has yet to be passed. Thus, despite having the vote, US women continue to be hindered in their attempts to participate in, contribute to, and influence US politics in the public sphere. In the 2017 US Senate, for instance, with a membership of 100, only 21 senators are women (21 percent). Of the 435 members of the US House of Representatives, only 85 are women (19.5 percent). Over the course of American history, women "historically account for only a small fraction—about 2 percent—of the approximately 12,000 individuals who have served in the US Congress since 1789" ("Women in National Parliaments"). As governors of our fifty states, only six women are serving in 2017 (12 percent). And despite the fact that women constitute 54 percent of voters in the United States, the nation comes in ninety-ninth place (behind Saudi Arabia) out of 186 countries in the number of women participating in our national legislature ("Women in National Parliaments"). In 2017, no woman has yet to be president or vice president of the United States, but then only twenty-nine women serve as head of government or head of state of their countries (from Germany and Grenada to Iceland and Barbados) and only two women rule as queen (in the United Kingdom and Denmark) worldwide. Only three women have ever served as US secretary of state—Madeleine Albright, Condoleezza Rice, and Hillary Rodham Clinton—and these three were appointed in the late twentieth and early twenty-first centuries, by three recent presidents.[6]

I rehearse these numbers and percentages for two reasons: to consider whether equal representation in government would actually equal democratic equality, and to show that the push for authentic democratic equality is far from over, despite the fact that the US Constitution is based on "We the people" forming "a more perfect union" and "establishing justice." Such a democracy has not yet formed, not one that illustrates the democratic ideals handed down to us by the ancient Athenians, who promoted "the importance of everyone having a voice, being listened to carefully, and [being] heard with respect" (Gilligan, *Joining* 24). Of course, "everyone" was a land-owning citizen man.

Self-proclaimed as the most powerful democracy in the world, the United States continues to silence women's rhetorical performance in the public sphere of political participation, as the 2016 presidential campaign demonstrated so well.[7] In terms of being heard with respect, women in the United States suffer the effects of a nation that maintains marked inequalities based on race, sexuality, ability, ethnicity, income, and gender. Despite popular propaganda, gender discrimination is still prominent, rooted in the nearly universally perceived sexual differences that continue to constitute inequality. Feminist historian Joan Wallach Scott underscores this disconnect: "The formal rights of the citizen for women did not translate into social and economic equality. . . . They might gain formal political equality, but substantively—in the family, the marketplace, and the political arena—they were hardly equal" (100). Despite the crucial importance of equality under the law, legal equality alone cannot decree social equality. Somehow, legal and social equality need to converge—but they do not, not in the United States, maybe not anywhere. As political theorist Wendy Brown reminds us, "Women's formal political equality is neither the sign nor the vehicle of their integration" (36). Thus, the mistaken idea held by many, particularly suffragists, is that the "right to vote" trips the mechanism that releases voice, power, and equality.

Both US women *and* men must travel down a circuitous path together before every US citizen is truly equal. The history of the vote in the United States—for landless men, African American men, women, American Indians, and eighteen-year-olds—provides a sequence of convincing cases in point. Legal rights have not yet translated into authentic equal rights—not socially, politically, or culturally, which is the reason feminist rhetorical activists still have so much more work to do.

True equality manifests itself when a person's political, civic, rhetorical words or actions are accepted, heard, and acted on (positively or negatively) by an engaged audience. Thus, intersecting categories of sexuality, status, race, and so on are neither mutually exclusive to nor constantly overlapping with power and equality. After all, sexual and racial identities have long been used to justify and exploit such power differentials or inequality. Rather than abiding in those categories of so-called difference, power and equality actually and invariably abide in rhetorical fundamentals. To wit, women's enfranchisement was a formidable step toward greater equality between the sexes; however, it represents only one step in an uneven and slow movement within a rhetorical ecology that regulates who speaks, who remains silent, who listens, and who acts responsively.

But I do not want to get ahead of myself, so I will start with an early moment in US women's efforts to obtain political voice as a means of demonstrating the early power of rhetorical feminism.

Taking Up the Cause of Suffrage (by Way of Abolition and Public Speaking)

When the North American colonies were coalescing in separation from England, women went *unmentioned* in our Declaration of Independence. The collaborators on the Declaration (all men) wrote, "We hold these truths to be self-evident, that all men are created equal." Despite the fact that women qua women are never mentioned in our foundational governing document, some people have argued that the word *men* actually meant "men *and* women." Such an argument might have stood if, at the time, African American or Native American men had been considered "men," if landless white men or women of any socioeconomic class or race were deemed to be "men." None of these Others could cast a vote or speak out in a way to legally effect public change, save for the freeborn men of African slave descent who lived in New Hampshire, Massachusetts, New York, New Jersey, and North Carolina.[8]

Daughters, wives, and sisters of already enfranchised men constituted one of the earliest disenfranchised groups to take on the cause of suffrage in an organized way, initially giving little thought to the legal status of Others.[9] After all, upon marriage, women gave up varying measures of financial and legal rights they might have had as single women. All of

ACTIVISM

a "free" woman's personal property and real estate holdings (whether brought into or accumulated during the marriage) belonged to her husband, for him to do with as he would.[10] Divorce was nearly impossible for a woman (whether hers was a case of a husband's abandonment, cruelty, incurable mental illness, impotence, or adultery). If she were ultimately successful in divorcing him, she relinquished all her personal and real property as well as, in most cases, the custody of her children. If a woman worked outside the home, she received shockingly less pay than her counterparts who were men; in addition, she had no right to her own wages. Educational opportunities for women were rare. "No people," states Ellen Carol DuBois, "with the exception of chattel slaves, had less proprietary rights over themselves in eighteenth-century and early nineteenth-century America than married women" (45).

Notwithstanding the hardships and legal constraints within the domestic sphere, both white and free black women were encouraged (and sometimes required by their jobs) to attend church, where their rhetorical-activist talents went mostly unrecognized—but were not always forbidden. In the quasi-public sphere of the nineteenth-century church, women responded to the world around them, organizing, speaking out, and effecting change. They used the venue of the church to enact their rhetorical feminism as well, attending to the marginalized by organizing assistance leagues for the education of children, promoting temperance, supporting orphans, and so on. These church-based efforts allowed women to develop the ability to run meetings, speak in public, and raise money for charity or petition the government on behalf of others, as representatives of activist groups or as individuals. Their rhetorical feminism allowed them to leverage the powers of silence and listening as well as the epistemic value of experience.

The Religious Society of Friends (that is, Quakers) created a hospitable scene for women to develop these rhetorical-political skills, given the fact that Quaker women were expected to "minister" (to speak during a Quaker meeting) and to travel (sometimes alone), preach, and publish from the very beginning of the movement. Yet Quaker women were "discouraged from mingling with outsiders in the reform movements" (Bacon 94) and "barred . . . from participating in the . . . abolition societies of the day" (101). These church-honed public skills resulted in women's work in both the antislavery and women's suffrage movements (with many Quaker women deeply involved in both undertakings, despite church prohibition). In fact, the women's rights movement had its roots in the campaign to end slavery.

Suffragist and antislavery activists Maria W. Miller Stewart, a free black woman living in Boston, and Angelina Grimké, a white Quaker from a wealthy Charleston, South Carolina, family, were among the first Sister Rhetors (with Stewart believed to be the very first) to speak publicly on contemporary political issues, to address "promiscuous" audiences composed of men and women alike, and to call out racism and sexism as interlocking evils. Theirs was a feminist rhetoric advocating for the equality of women and Others, to be sure, also inflected by a rhetorical feminist commitment to judicious speaking, listening, and silence—but mostly to hope and possibility.

The idea for what would become the Nineteenth Amendment was propelled in 1848, when a few hundred white Sister Rhetors (including Elizabeth Cady Stanton and Lucretia Mott) and forty men (including Frederick Douglass, the only African American in attendance) gathered at the first Woman's Rights Convention in Seneca Falls, New York. There these suffragists collaborated on their Declaration of Sentiments, listing eighteen rights in the US Declaration of Independence that were explicitly denied to women, white women being the focus of their concern.[11]

It is important to note that men and women of color influenced the development of this convention. For instance, Douglass, a lifetime supporter of women's rights, advertised the 1848 Seneca Falls meeting in his newspaper, the *North Star*. One of the few men present at the historic meeting, he did not speak, feeling as he did that women—not prominent men—should speak for the movement.[12] Furthermore, some of the early white suffragists (Stanton, Mott, and Matilda Joslyn Gage, in particular) were inspired to pursue women's rights by the example set by the Iroquois, whose women were central to the culture, workings, and power structure of the Iroquois Confederacy.[13]

Despite the fact that the US Constitution referred only to "people" and "citizens" (never "men" or "women"), white women used the Declaration to argue for eighteen specific rights, which would accord them equal treatment under the law. Such rights included speaking in public, testifying in court, preaching from a pulpit, pursuing education, obtaining civil existence after marriage, controlling personal wages and property, holding legal custody of children, and entering into professions. White women also sought to earn wages equal to those of men doing the same jobs—and the right to vote, the most difficult of those rights to achieve.[14]

Although none of their performances were successful at the time, such nineteenth-century legends as Maria W. Miller Stewart, Angelina Grimké,

ACTIVISM

Lucretia Mott, and Sojourner Truth[15] called out gendered and raced discriminatory issues, unfair processes, and glaring disparities, some of which continue to endure in public events ranging from police responses and immigration policies to political demonstrations and presidential debates.

Maria W. Miller Stewart

In her 1833 "Farewell Address to Her Friends in the City of Boston," Stewart, who herself had long endured constant criticism for speaking publicly on political issues, admonished women—black and white—to remain active, public, and outspoken, following the precedents set by their foremothers (hers was a strategy also employed by Lucretia Mott, discussed below). Stewart was best known for her 1832 "Lecture Delivered at Franklin Hall" in Boston. Her notorious outspokenness on issues of employment restrictions based on sex and race, constraints on free Northern blacks, women's limited legal status, and black men's silence and passivity had all translated into her reputation as an aggressive, activist rhetor and someone (a black woman, no less) who should not be on a public platform in the first place. Her rhetorical-political stance was considered uncompromising and confrontational—masculinist attitudes that always met with some measure of opposition, even among friends. In her "Farewell," Stewart announced her retirement from public speaking, ironically submitting to social pressure to do just that but not before blasting her promiscuous audience one final time for their own inaction, tapping such rhetorical feminist tactics as disidentification, attention to the marginalized, and respect for emotion and experience.

As she rose to the platform to bid farewell, however, she invoked the humility topos, a traditionally feminine rhetorical strategy for excusing, ahead of time, her blatant social transgression. She opened her valediction with a story about the transitory nature of life, the power of her religious conversion, and her closeness with Jesus, who "for wise and holy purposes, best known to himself," had "unloosed" her tongue and put his words in her mouth (qtd. in M. Richardson 67). Fortuitously, Jesus spoke through her, she said, "to confound and put to shame" all those who had risen up against her (67). In these ways, Stewart was conciliatory (but only to a measure), identifying her Christian ways with the interests of her Christian audience (as Kenneth Burke would have her do; see *Rhetoric of Motives* 55).

Her leading question, then, responds to the age-old exigence of womanhood, beautifully capturing the spirit of assured, sanctified defiance with which she took the stage, daring her promiscuous audience to challenge her rhetorical and political right to do so:

> What if I am a woman; is not the God of ancient times the God of these modern days? Did he not raise up Deborah, to be a mother, and a judge in Israel? Did not queen Esther save the lives of the Jews? And Mary Magdalene first declare the resurrection of Christ from the dead? Come, said the woman of Samaria, and see a man that hath told me all things that ever I did, is not this the Christ? St. Paul declared that it was a shame for a woman to speak in public, yet our great High Priest and Advocate did not condemn the woman for a more notorious offence than this; neither will he condemn this worthless worm. (qtd. in M. Richardson 68)

Though purposefully provocative, invoking the rhetorical feminist strategy of disidentification, Stewart's tone was also appeasing to her audience in that she invoked biblical women as her models, strong, holy women who fulfilled God's will and did God's work. She used the occasion of her retirement strategically, knowing that (although prohibited) women's participation in public discourse and civic action—as public speakers and active, responsive listeners—was the best way to commence women's suffrage and halt slavery. Women must establish themselves as Sister Rhetors invested in the public good, women who can effect change.

Angelina Grimké

Angelina Grimké was also proscribed from taking the platform as a Sister Rhetor, but called as she was to be a Quaker minister, she felt it her duty to speak out publicly on the political issue of slavery as well as on the status of women (despite church policy to the contrary), disidentifying, in the process, with hegemonic rhetorical expectations and leveraging experience and emotions—all tactics tethered to hope. Of course, she could neither vote nor run for office, but her status as a woman did not hold her back from admonishing the 1838 Massachusetts state legislature:

> [B]ecause slavery is a political subject, it has often been said that women had nothing to do with it. Are we aliens because we are women? Are we bereft of citizenship because we are mothers, wives, and daughters of a mighty people? Have women *no* country—no interests staked in public weal—no liabilities in common peril—no

partnership in a nation's guilt and shame? . . . This dominion of women should be resigned—the sooner the better; in the age which is approaching she should be something more—she should be a citizen. (qtd. in Lerner 7)

Despite the fact that she was not welcomed to the legislature (in fact, she was harassed), Grimké distinguished herself by being the first woman to address a US legislative body. She and her sister, Sarah, had already scandalized themselves by publicly speaking out against slavery, which they had witnessed firsthand back in South Carolina; consequently, Angelina had little to lose by appearing before a legislature that was packed with white men and women eager to witness the words of a brazen, "unsexed" white woman.[16]

The members of Grimké's audience were not surprised to hear her antislavery message, but they were stunned by her claims for women's political, legal, and human rights. A rhetorical feminist, she attended to the needs of the marginalized (slaves and women) and publicly valued the knowledge that comes with experience—in this case, that of women and slaves. As such, she was one of the first US women to coalesce women's rights with the abolitionist movement, using rhetoric persuasively, publicly, and politically. At the time, her speech was considered a rhetorical failure, given that she carried little immediate influence with legislative decisions. Yet time has proved her speech to be a success. This rhetorical feminist addressed an audience uninterested in resolving the exigence at that time. But by constructing arguments based on reason, evidence, and experience that could be taken up by other women and men, Grimké managed to pave the way for the normalization of women's rhetorical activism, if not their eventual legal equality.

Lucretia Mott

It was within this climate of women's rhetorical activism that Quaker minister Lucretia Mott entered the public, political arena by supporting Grimké's and Stewart's claims of the interlocking evils of racism and sexism. Mott went even further than other white abolitionist feminist rhetors at the time by extending the definition of what it means to be a *woman*,[17] a term that legislators, public speakers, and preachers (all men) were handily using to prohibit "naturally" weak and dependent women from the responsibility of political participation.[18]

One popular speaker at the time was literary critic, poet, and essayist Richard Henry Dana Sr., who had been touring the country lecturing on "woman," a human being he described as different from "man" in every mental, physical, and social way, using literary and religious support for his sentiment.[19] For Dana, men were naturally public beings, just as women were naturally domestic beings.

Immediately after hearing Dana's lecture in December 1849, Mott attempted to discuss with him their differing views on the topic but was dismissed, save by sympathetic Philadelphians who invited her to deliver a response to Dana's sentiments. Just a few days later, Mott gave what would come to be her most famous lecture, "Discourse on Woman." In repudiation of Dana's sentiments, Mott delivered an anti-patriarchal reading of society, law, and religion, creatively wrapped in Quaker principles, biblical interpretation, and rhetorical feminism. Her response was not only reasonable and logical but also powerful and transactional.

In her "Discourse," Mott (like Stewart) addresses gender inequalities by invoking powerful biblical women (following the tradition of many women platform speakers), a move that bolstered her authority before her Christian audience and perhaps softened their unwillingness to listen to her. Her allusions to Miriam (Exod. 15:20), Deborah (Judg. 4, 5), Huldah (2 Kings 22:14), Anna (Luke 2:36), Priscilla (Acts 18:2), and Phebe (Rom. 16:1), as well as to the four daughters of Philip (Acts 21:8–9), enact women's equality, capability, and potential—and with God's blessing.[20] These historical women, along with the many women who prophesied (Acts 21:9), who were the companions of Jesus (Matt. 27:55), and who were "fellow workers in Christ Jesus" (Rom. 16:1–12), provide scriptural authorization of women's rhetorical participation in the public sphere.[21]

Perhaps as a rhetorical strategy, Mott alleges reluctance for making "the demand for the political rights of women" (36) and aims, instead, to fulfill the rhetorical feminist transaction of shared understanding. Nevertheless, she argues that woman seeks "not to be governed by laws, in the making of which she has no voice. She is deprived of almost every right in civil society, . . . except in the right of presenting a petition"[22] (36). Given that women's current legal status is "unworthy of a Christian nation," women want "nothing as favor, but as right" (36). Antithetical to Dana's definition of "woman" is Mott's, which is an act of rhetorical feminist disidentification with masculinist thought. She describes "woman" as a human being, fully sentient and capable of taking her rightful, legal place as a voting citizen, with rights equal to those of white property-owning men. Such rights would allow her to speak out on abolition and speak up in making all laws in the land. Mott's work as a Sister Rhetor, as an abolitionist feminist rhetor, continued.[23]

Abolitionist societies, like the church, afforded white women the opportunity to develop skills in organizing and holding public meetings and gathering petitions. In addition, activist rhetorical women, black and white, extended their influence by establishing literacy, literary, and educational societies that served African American men and women of all ages as well as white women.[24]

The African American women's clubs (or the National Association of Colored Women's Clubs)[25] coalesced around urgent social issues: the killing of innocent black men; the education of children; the feeding, clothing, and sheltering of those in need. Many of these clubs were mutual aid societies, while others were Bible, literary, leadership, abolitionist, and suffrage societies. White women's societies, for the most part, were dedicated to social reform: suffrage, abolition, educational opportunities, temperance, health, and welfare. In concert with their ongoing initiatives, these women planned a series of meetings in order to publicize their demands and to organize for action, noteworthy among which was the Woman's Rights Convention, held in Akron, Ohio, in 1851.

Sojourner Truth

What would make the Akron convention famous was the recalled appearance of African American antislavery activist Sojourner Truth, a former slave who was spending her life as a Sister Rhetor, agitating for social justice (suffrage and freedom for all, black and white, regardless of socioeconomic class). As a rhetorical feminist, she disidentified with hegemonic rhetoric, leveraged the vernacular, spoke to and from the margins, emphasized experience and emotion, and reshaped the rhetorical appeals. According to various secondhand reports of her appearance, a six-foot tall, dignified black woman made her way to the pulpit, despite the hissing from the spectators and the active discouragement of her white counterparts, and electrified the audience. A longtime champion of African American rights and abolition, Truth used this occasion to support women's rights as well, considering "both causes as essentially the denial of natural rights" (Fitch 425).

In "Aren't I a Woman," Truth crafts a logical appeal that cleverly exposes the lies and distortions in the conception of "womanhood," knowing that her detractors, many of whom were slaveholders, were using the term to signify *white* womanhood, exemplified by land-owning-class white women who were thought to be too weak and helpless to be entrusted with the vote.[26]

> That man over there says that women need to be helped into carriages, and lifted over ditches, and to have the best place everywhere. Nobody ever helps me into carriages, or over mud puddles or gives me any best place (*and raising herself to her full height and her voice to a pitch like rolling thunder, she asked*), and aren't I a woman? Look at me! Look at my arm! (*And she bared her right arm to the shoulder, showing her tremendous muscular power.*) I have plowed, and planted, and gathered into barns, and no man could head me—and aren't I a woman? I could work as much and eat as much as a man (when I could get it), and bear the lash as well—and aren't I a woman? I have borne thirteen children and seen them almost all sold off into slavery, and when I cried out with a mother's grief, none but Jesus heard—and aren't I a woman? Then they talk about this thing in the head—what's this they call it? (*"Intellect,"* whispered someone near.) That's it honey. What's that got to do with woman's rights or Negroes' rights? . . .
>
> Then that little man in black [a clergyman] there, he says women can't have as much rights as man, 'cause Christ wasn't a woman. Where did your Christ come from? (*Rolling thunder could not have stilled that crowd as did those deep, wonderful tones, as she stood there with outstretched arms and eye of fire. Raising her voice still louder, she repeated,*) Where did your Christ come from? From God and a woman. Man had nothing to do with him. (*Oh! What a rebuke she gave the little man.*)
>
> . . .
>
> 'Bliged to you for hearing on me, and now old Sojourner hasn't got anything more to say. (qtd. in Campbell, *Man Cannot* 2: 100–01)

When Truth finished, the crowd went wild, many of them crying, so moved were they by Truth's eloquence, insight, and truths. Hers was a rhetorical success, no doubt achieved by her masterful delivery, experiential and vernacular reasoning, and witty question-and-answer with regard to the origins of Jesus—all accompanied by bodily proof.

Like Mott and Stewart, Truth drew on familiar biblical texts that she used to advance unfamiliar ends and overcome their trained incapacities.

Truth managed to demonstrate not only that black women were, indeed, women and mothers but also that they could also be extraordinarily gifted rhetorically and politically, despite their slavery, illiteracy, and lack of land.

Given the import of this Woman's Rights Convention in Akron, Ohio, and its mixed audience, Truth's rhetorical display might have served as a turning point in the fight for suffrage for all free Americans, black as well as white. While suffrage and antislavery activism often worked hand in hand and could be argued for simultaneously, abolition became the primary exigence once the Civil War began. Women like Truth were gaining the right to speak publicly before a willing-to-listen (even if not always compliant) audience, yet their arguments for women's suffrage[27] were temporarily set aside as the country engaged in the Civil War, a savage internecine battle over the economy, states' rights, and slavery.

Securing Abolition—but Not Yet the Vote

The leading suffragists were divided among themselves with regard to what role to play vis-à-vis the war. Many of the women's rights activists were white Northerners as well as abolitionists, and they contributed to the abolitionist movement as though they were full citizens. They hoped that their contributions to the war effort would evince their political capacity, rational rhetoric, and, therefore, their fitness to vote. Unfortunately, neither women nor free blacks would be granted the vote as a reward for patriotism.

After the defeat of the Confederate army by the Union army, all blacks were emancipated. Within a few years, African American men, as a result of the Fourteenth and Fifteenth Amendments, would be granted citizenship and the right to vote, a goal the abolitionist feminists had long supported. But the Fourteenth Amendment explicitly excluded women by referring only to "male inhabitants" and "male citizens."

Many free African American women spoke from and to the margins as rhetorical feminists in favor of women's suffrage.[28] Yet these women were conflicted over whether to support the Fifteenth Amendment awarding suffrage to black men only or to insist upon the primacy of a universal suffrage that included women of all races. (See Terrell.) Rather than being perceived as a universal right, the right to vote was, to some, a zero-sum game with the possibility of only one winner and one loser (both sides doubling down protection of their own possibility). The controversies among black and white men and women would endure, with most (white) men continuing to believe that no woman (regardless of race) was suited for the vote, and most white abolitionist women unwilling to oppose the enfranchisement of black men, even if it "came at a cost to themselves" (Frost-Knappman and Cullen-DuPont 166). Part of the tactic of rhetorical feminists is to support the marginalized.[29] Rhetorical feminists also work to move their projects forward by dialogic (rather than monologic) means, as these rhetorical feminists continued to do until they gained the right to vote.

The American Equal Rights Association

In an effort to resolve these suffrage-related conflicts, postbellum activist women, along with some abolitionist-feminist men, established the American Equal Rights Association.[30] Together, black and white, men and women, they began the formal struggle to "secure Equal Rights to all American citizens, especially the right of suffrage, irrespective of race, color, or sex" (Frost-Knappman and Cullen-DuPont 167). Still, conflicts remained, even as many of them performed rhetorical feminism.

Frances Harper, a prominent African American antislavery author and speaker, ultimately ranked race above sex in this debate, articulating the complexities of intersectionality (a term that postdates her), as the rhetorical feminist she was.[31] But at that convention, Harper lectured on all the ways "we are all bound up together," coalescing the rights, responsibilities, and hopes of the franchised and disenfranchised alike. As related in *History of Woman Suffrage,* Harper argued at the 1869 American Equal Rights Association Convention that when "it was a question of race she let the lesser question of sex go. . . . If the nation could handle only one question, she would not have the black woman put a single straw in the way" (Stanton, Anthony, and Gage 2: 391–92).[32] It was at that convention that the three-year-old organization split over this very issue, eventually falling apart. Yet for the rest of the nineteenth century, suffragists continued to work—unsuccessfully—on the vote for women, in a state-by-state effort as well as on the national front.

Finally, when the United States entered World War I in 1917, the leaders of the Woman Suffrage Party knew the time had come for them to press the hardest they had ever pressed. They remembered well the lessons of the Civil War: women were not rewarded with the vote for their wartime efforts, nor were they awarded the vote for waiting their turn after the African American man. So even during the "war to end all wars," Sister

Rhetors continued to wage a forceful, unrelenting campaign. In *Alice Paul and the Suffrage Campaign,* Katherine Adams and Michael Keene describe Paul's nonviolent yet militant verbal rhetorical strategies for gaining social justice (that is, suffrage) as "strong, positive, and energetic" (32). Among this rhetorical feminist's eventually successful demonstrations were hunger strikes, White House picketing, and a national boycott, all for the purpose of pressing President Woodrow Wilson for a federal suffrage amendment (Frost-Knappman and Cullen-DuPont 326).

Finally, Success, Albeit Mitigated Success

The following year (1919), both houses of the US Congress passed the Nineteenth Amendment, the federal woman suffrage amendment. As my much-compressed review of the US women's suffrage movement indicates, women's right to vote was envisioned as sparking Cicero's *vita activa,* the active, equal political participation of women as citizens. But such has not been the case, not in any country that has awarded women the right to vote. Socially constructed gender roles and expectations continue to render woman less capable—and her contributions less valuable—in the public sphere of acting and speaking. The dialectic relationship between those who speak and those who (are willing to) listen is a nuanced dynamic, always configured within a delicate triangulation of possibility, compliance, and ir/resolution. Where women and men are concerned, women still and regularly speak and listen at a disadvantage.

Even Now

Even in 2017, as illustrated earlier in this chapter, woman's public, political participation remains limited, her activism and resistance still necessary. For instance, most of the 105 women serving in the 114th US Congress were elected in the 1992 ("Year of the Woman") elections and after or in special elections, which means that women as a coalition lack the leadership possibilities that come with significant seniority.[33] Our foremothers, feminist rhetorical activists (some of whom were rhetorical feminists), fought hard for the right to vote, and contemporary women are, indeed, reaping benefits, despite the significant barriers we still face. Yet, as Sister Rhetors, we continue to hope, asking, as Maria Stewart did nearly two hundred years ago, *What if we are women?*

Very often my hope has appeared in the form of Hillary Rodham Clinton, the most visible of twenty-first-century US Sister Rhetors (with

ACTIVISM

Elizabeth Warren close behind) and the most successful *un*successful presidential candidate in the history of the United States.[34] Since taking the political stage, she has worked for the rights of women and children, both in the United States and around the world, often exercising such precepts of rhetorical feminism as speaking to the margins, respecting experience and emotion, valuing silence and listening—and holding onto hope.

Clinton first demonstrated her power as a rhetorical feminist when she announced that her 2000 run for the US Senate seat from New York would be anchored in a "Listening Campaign," a rhetorical trope—deliberately disidentifying and feminine—that successfully sustained her throughout her first official foray into elected politics and her two-term service as senator. She committed herself to listening *to* the concerns and recommendations of her constituents rather talking *at* large groups of them. Clinton focused on listening *to* people in one-on-one conversations, small-group meetings, and coffee klatches. Her goal was to build community across differences and difficulties.[35]

She resumed her "Listening Tour" when she entered what would be her first bruising and unsuccessful presidential race. Although she did not win, this Sister Rhetor succeeded in earning over eighteen million votes.[36] And during her second presidential campaign, which won her sixty-six million votes and the majority of the popular vote by over three million votes,[37] she continued to speak up and out knowledgeably and eloquently on issues that affect all Americans (not just the rich and powerful), issues including Medicare and Medicaid, the Affordable Care Act, the Paris Climate Change Accord, reproductive rights, renewable energy, tuition costs, and voter registration (all the while carefully effacing her once-hawkish stance on the war in Iraq and her views toward defense and national security).[38] But eloquent policies and a majority vote were not enough to win her the election. A poorly run campaign, an exhausted candidate, and enduring sexism are all reasons offered for her loss.[39]

In her gracious, unyielding, and widely televised concession speech, Clinton revealed yet controlled her emotions. She did not argue about the past but rather challenged her audience—and girls, in particular—to join her in shaping a better future: "To all the little girls who are watching this, never doubt that you are valuable and powerful and deserving of every chance and opportunity in the world to pursue and to achieve your own dreams."

Throughout her public, political, rhetorical career, Clinton has come to demonstrate the power of traditionally feminine traits filtered through rhetorical feminism: reaching out (and working through a problem together), productive silence (thoughtful consideration), respectful listening (so she is sure she understands), judicious speaking (rather than mere exhortation), learning from past experience (whether national, personal, or that of her audience), and a deep commitment to hope and possibility. In other words, she has participated in areas of focus that have been documented for many successful rhetorical feminists: the use of emotion and experience, silence and listening, risk taking, conflict resolution, and strategic vision.

Clinton has not been alone in embodying rhetorical feminism. Around the world, more than thirty Sister Rhetors have been elected into powerful leadership positions, as president, prime minister, governor-general, chancellor, or state counselor of their nations,[40] while countless others have been self-appointed.

All around the globe, these self-appointed women have strategized to institute appropriate outlets for their political platforms: speaking out, writing up, and demonstrating, whether loudly or silently. For example, Code Pink works to end US-funded wars and occupations; Women in Black,[41] inspired by the South African anti-apartheid Black Sash movement and the Argentinian Madres de la Plaza de Mayo, mobilizes against wars of *any* kind, *any*where. Baring Witness, another global network of antiwar protesters, merits further mention because its participants *embody* their cause: on International Women's Day (8 March), from Santa Fe, New Mexico, to Cape Town, South Africa, and from Antarctica to Hiroshima, Japan, these women meet in groups large enough to create words of peace with their *naked* bodies, forming them into the international peace sign or into letters that spell out "PEACE," "PAZ," "NO WAR," or "WHY?" Liberian Women in White (now known as the Liberian Mass Action for Peace), the first Christian-Muslim alliance consisting *wholly* of women, helped end both Charles Taylor's bloody dictatorship and Liberia's civil war. One Billion [Women] Rising, founded by Eve Ensler of *Vagina Monologues* fame, strives to eradicate violence against girls and women.[42] American lawyer and politician Reshma Saujani founded Girls Who Code, an organization that seeks to increase the number of women in computer science and related fields.[43] Of course, there is the Black Lives Matter movement, founded by Alicia Garza, Patrisse Cullors, and Opal Tometi in response to the repeated killings of black men by police officers, the twice-as-high unemployment for blacks as for whites, and the sustained apartheid-like nature of our public schools. And, finally, there was the Women's March on Washington, purposefully scheduled for the day after Donald Trump's inauguration, 21 January 2017. This nonviolent protest march sent a "bold message to our new administration on their first day in office, and to the world that women's rights are human rights. We stand together, recognizing that defending the most marginalized among us is defending all of us" (womensmarch.com).

By demonstrating (and I do mean demonstrating) new ways of being rhetorical (being accessible, invitational, inclusionary, networked, silent, thoughtful, resistant, active) and new ways of being feminist (attentive to audience, to understanding, to silence, to negotiation), these Sister Rhetors, these rhetorical feminists, have been envisioning a world that is rounder, more humane, and more future-oriented. Sister Rhetors around the globe continue to guide us into our field of hope, a place of eudaemonia for us all.

TWO: IDENTITIES

With whom do you believe your lot is cast?
From where does your strength come?

I think somehow, somewhere
every poem of mine must repeat those questions

which are not the same. There is a *whom*, a *where*
that is not chosen that is given and sometimes falsely given

in the beginning we grasp whatever we can
to survive
—Adrienne Rich, "Sources, IV"

For how long has my lot been cast with feminism? For how long have I tapped the strength that is feminism? As Adrienne Rich teaches us, these questions are not the same, for any answers are predicated on what is given, "sometimes falsely given," on what is "not chosen," and on what "we grasp" in order to survive ("Sources, IV" 6). Was I turning to feminism when I told my high school guidance teacher that I would become an English teacher, though if I had been a boy, I could have become a doctor? Was I turning to feminism when, early on, I realized that my first marriage was built on an immovable foundation of sexism? Was I turning to feminism when I asked my rhetoric professor (a man) if there were any women in the history of rhetoric? Not consciously, that is for sure. But as I look back, I feel certain that my younger days were filled with feminist moves that at the time I could imagine only as moves to survive.

But now my life is consciously anchored in feminism—as well as in rhetoric—a life that far exceeds mere survival. Now, as I regularly return to the variables of the rhetorical equation (who can/not speak, what can/not be said, who can/not listen, who will/not be listened to, and what those listeners can/not do), I am most troubled by the variable of who will be listened to. Whose identity is such that they always/already merit an audience, listeners who are willing to consider doing something in response? After all, too often, one's identity—whether cultural-ethnic, racial, religious, political, gender, sexual, generational, or whatever—serves as the deciding factor in the rhetorical equation, as though one's presented, professed, or presumed identity dominates the rhetorical transaction.[1] Some identities are initially presented visibly or physically (age, race, sometimes gender and religion), but all identities are constructed through rhetorical transactions, what Kenneth Burke describes as "words about words" (*Rhetoric of Religion* 1). And just as important to my study is the fact that all identities carry with them experiential knowledge, which rhetorical feminists acknowledge and respect, along with such tactics as emotion, the vernacular, and alternative means of delivery (among others).

Given the overall feminist objective of my research agenda—to make rhetorical studies more representative and inclusive of all the people who use rhetoric ethically and effectively—I naturally knit together the threads of rhetoric and feminism, foregrounding the strand of identity for its generative capacity. How much stronger, more invitational, might rhetoric, feminism, and rhetorical feminism be when identity is woven with them? As the field of feminist rhetoric has developed in the academy, it has been influenced by different so-called waves of feminism, each one modeling new ways for us to theorize the concept of identity so that in our contemporary moment we can acknowledge the intersectional power or weakness (however provisional) of an individual's being, experience. Rather than seeing anyone in terms of a single feature (race, gender, sexuality, or status, for instance), we now understand identities to be experiential, emotional, rich, complex, even fluid, in ways that can help explain who speaks, who listens, who does not—and when.

Consequently, in this chapter I interrogate the power that is identity, teasing out its strengths and complications—all with regard to its function in transactions of rhetorical feminism. I move through discussions of how identity determines who may speak, who merits an audience, and who can speak for whom—rhetorical situations that can easily result in success or failure. Three theories in particular—Burke's identification, Kimberlé Crenshaw's intersectionality, and Gayatri Chakravorty Spivak's strategic essentialism—offer possibilities for healing the fissures among feminists. Finally, I explain identity as an epistemic resource that can enhance the transactions and understandings of rhetorical feminism as we speak across difference and disagreement with a commitment to hope and possibility.

Meriting a Rhetorical Audience

Who merits a listening audience, and who is willing to consider the rhetor's message?[2] Those immutable questions undergird every rhetorical transaction. After all, if no one is listening, where does rhetorical power actually lie? Current rhetorical scholarship helps us understand the seeming powerlessness of those who cannot speak—those who have no agency, no listening audience, or both. I have written at length about productive silence and imposed silencing, about people who use their agency to remain silent or feel silenced (intimidated, in fact). Krista Ratcliffe and Jacqueline Jones Royster have accounted for the critical importance of listening, of the benefits for the rhetor and audience alike; and Pat Belanoff, Susan Cain, Anne French Dalke, Anne Ruggles Gere, George Kalamaras, Mary M. Reda, Katherine Schultz, and Lois Weis and Michelle Fine have explained issues of agency and audience in the classroom, as they identify the generative qualities of silence and listening. All this scholarship thoroughly penetrates issues of who can/not speak and who is/not willing to listen.

However, none of this aforementioned scholarship isolates the friction at the specific nexus of rhetoric, feminism, and identity as well as *Who Can Speak? Authority and Critical Identity* does. In their edited collection of essays, Judith Roof and Robyn Wiegman include variegated examinations of agency, identity, and speaking, all of which strive to resolve the issue of "Who can speak?" Andrew Lakritz, for example, determines who has the authority to "pass unmolested through the significant passageways of our culture" (4), readily admitting that "he has routinely existed within the dominant power structure in the United States" and that he is, "despite the small difference of being Jewish, a part of the ruling establishment" (5). For a well-educated white man, then, authority is a given, already a priori.

With frequent allusions to Gayatri Spivak and her postcolonial insights, Lakritz and the other contributors to the collection (including Linda Martín Alcoff; see below) probe the parts of the rhetorical equation. The issue of who can speak, of who has the *authority* to speak, is anchored in identity, to be sure, with those already and always in power considered agents worth listening to, whose words are heeded. Parsing an answer to the question of whether those with rhetorical agency are self-empowered, empowered by circumstances, or authorized by others is nigh impossible, though some scholars attempt to enact this work in their rhetorical analyses. Regardless of the rhetor's measure of agency or authority vis-à-vis identity, that rhetorical agent must efficiently negotiate resources and constraints within the rhetorical context to proceed with any successful action.

Spivak's 1985 "Can the Subaltern Speak?" moors the kaleidoscopic triangulations of voice, identity, and agency (or power). Spivak charges Western academic culture, particularly then-current scholarship on identity, as a kind of "openly ethnic," "nostalgic . . . third-worldism" ("Political Commitment" 281). And when she poses her groundbreaking question, "Can the subaltern speak?," she performs a critique of the rhetorical power most Others (including the subaltern) find inaccessible. The rhetorical disadvantage Spivak identifies within subalternity is also present in varying degrees among women, people disabled in some way (including age), or members of cultural-ethnic-racial-religious groups (even if the members of these groups are linguistically or geographically isolated from a [colonial] power discourse). From that position, either they cannot speak or, when they do, they are not heard.

After all, identity politics reads the differences and hierarchies that society has created and continues to enforce. Somehow, then, the effect of an oppositional identity politics is the reification of difference, and these continual instances of power and power-over continuously form us, according to Judith Butler.[3] Thus, even if a member of a subaltern group exercises the agency to speak, will anyone listen? Will this speaking agent have a receptive or rhetorical audience? Of course, Spivak tells us that once the subaltern subject has the agency to speak, to occupy hegemonic discourse, then he or she is no longer a subaltern subject. These issues of agency, audience, identity, and status have long colored rhetorical studies, hence the newfound epistemological value of cultural-ethnic and other identity-related rhetorics now so evident on panels, in publications, and at conferences.[4]

Questions of who can speak and who will listen justify the attention of rhetorical and feminist scholars, to be sure, given that the interests, experiences, and opinions of the so-called subaltern subject are too often represented by those who already enjoy a position of power. Men speak for women; whites speak for people of color; academics speak for non-academics; legislators speak for "the people"; and so on. The powerful speak for and about those subaltern subjects and their plight, securing a listening audience while simultaneously (and sometimes inadvertently) suppressing the subaltern subject's own opportunity to speak, be heard, be heeded, and, thus, be translated from that identity.

In "The Problem of Speaking for Others," Alcoff explains how the relationship between the speaker and the audience affects influence, even persuasion: "Who is speaking to whom turns out to be as important for meaning and truth as what is said; in fact what is said turns out to change according to who is speaking and who is listening" (102). In other words, the relationship (and the identities of the people in that relationship) at this transactional moment affects "whether a claim is taken as a true, well-reasoned, compelling argument or significant idea" (103). Why else do students want letters of recommendation from established professors (rather than from their TAs), those established professors from even more illustrious ones, interns from elected officials, clerks from corporate lions? Customarily, the more renowned the rhetor, the more readily his or her words are endorsed—even when the rhetor does not speak from firsthand experience but rather serves as a ventriloquist for those occupying the subaltern.

Given the rhetorical limitations of any subaltern group, what can those individuals hope to accomplish among themselves without a powerful rhetor to speak for them? Yes, they have solidarity, lived experience, even eloquence, as Malala Yousafzai, Gloria Anzaldúa, and Sojourner Truth have proved. Yet the possibilities of such rhetorical resources often deteriorate in the corrosive presence of poverty, illiteracy, physical weakness, social insignificance. Many subaltern subjects place their hope in an advocate, someone already privileged by his or her identity.

Consider the case of Academy Award winner Angelina Jolie, whose current mission is to undertake advocacy on behalf of refugees.[5] In her role as Goodwill Ambassador for the Office of the United Nations High Commissioner for Refugees, this widely recognized celebrity exercises her sociocultural power—her identity—to mobilize humanitarian efforts among powerful people and their organizations for the benefit of the subaltern people for whom she advocates. Ever since she was a teenager, Malala Yousafzai has advocated in speeches, in radio and television interviews, in her blogs, and by her example for human rights and especially for the rights of girls and women to be educated. When the Pakastani teenager was shot in the head by Taliban militants (her punishment for her outspoken support of women's education), Malala (as she is called) became the focus of international attention. Her recovery and recuperation in England allowed her to prepare an even stronger case for women's educational rights, to the point that she received the 2014 Nobel Peace Prize. She is now a student at Oxford. Like Jolie, Malala is an international celebrity—and advocates for those without sociocultural power, agency, and voice.

Little wonder, then, that identity plays such a crucial role in rhetorical feminist relationships in terms of who (thinks she) has agency and who does not have agency but mostly in terms of comparative agency (who has more power in this relationship). Identity conditions rhetorical relationships: who speaks, who listens, and what those listeners can and will do. Thus, the status of who speaks and who-speaks-for-whom invites close examination, especially given that speaking for others long ago created deep fissures in feminism. Alcoff describes such fissures as the "strong, albeit contested, current within feminism which holds that speaking for others—even for other women—is arrogant, vain, unethical, and politically illegitimate" (97–98). That is, who speaks—and how—for herself, to others, and for others are concerns of rhetorical feminism, rooted as those concerns are in such rhetorical feminist precepts as disidentification,[6] dialogue, marginalization, vernaculars, experience, and, of course, hope.

Cleaving Identity

A pivotal rhetorical concept for understanding rhetorical relationships is Kenneth Burke's "identification," the primary strategy for bridging division between rhetor and audience, "since it is so clearly a matter of rhetoric to persuade a man by identifying your cause with his interests" (*Rhetoric of Motives* 24). Burke goes on to advise, "You persuade a man only insofar as you can talk his language by speech, gesture, tonality, order, image, attitude, idea, *identifying* your ways with his" (55). Identification, then, has served as an efficient means for building group identification between rhetor and audience as well as among members of a group or an audience. Such group identification has worked for many (but not all) feminists across the waves who have experienced identification as a nonagonistic move (despite the limitations of Burke's masculinist theory).[7]

Equal political, social, workplace, and educational rights and opportunities; patriarchy; sexism, sexuality, and gender presentation; racism; elitism; motherhood and reproduction (or not!); harassment (which was not yet conceptualized, let alone named)—these are the issues and ideals to which feminists have long cleaved,[8] coalescing those who identify with one another and separating others who do not. For instance, in an effort to identify women's equality with that of men for the purpose of gaining full citizenship, first-wave white feminists attempted to fit all women into the universal category of *citizen,* thereby neglecting the interests of many black women. Second-wave white feminists, on the other hand, worked to distinguish women *from* men and framed a universal (essentialized) category of *woman* that erased, in the process, the gender identification, sexualities, and cultural-ethnic identities of far too many Others who also claimed the identity of woman.[9] Despite intentions of unity and inclusion across these feminist waves, not all women identified with the white heterosexual, citizen-class spokeswomen who were cresting the waves. Many women in the movement felt excluded on the basis of their race, culture, socioeconomic class, or sexuality, exclusions that now seem obvious but were not obvious to the white women leaders at the time—hence, the problems in building a single feminist coalition.

Working to create strong group identification—through gender alone—during the first and second waves was in some ways straightforward: women enumerated grievances, proposed resolutions to those grievances, and organized processes for collective action. Taking advantage of various opportunities for change, those feminists with the socioeconomic means and time to network, advertise, and mobilize did just that. With most of these second-wave women representing Betty Friedan's college-educated, middle-class white heterosexual women of means, the mainstream movement mostly reflected the demands of those mainstream women—to the exclusion of nearly everyone else.

Identities, rights, and concomitant movements of every kind—civil rights, Black Power, Stonewall and LBGTQ rights, the American Indian Movement, affirmative action, equal opportunity, the United Farmworkers—were major concerns of many second-wave feminist activists, nonmainstream and mainstream alike. Still, the mainstream second-wave movement remains best identified with the campaign for the Equal Rights Amendment, which states, "Equality of rights under the law shall not be denied or abridged by the United States or by any State on account of sex." Although the ERA would have benefited all women, it became a divisive issue among feminists.

Despite their best intentions, middle-class white heterosexual feminists failed rhetorically, as they did not consistently attend to the petitions of feminist activists not working in and for mainstream feminist issues, those women who acknowledged what would come to be called "intersectionality." The ERA appeared to be the primary and exclusive concern of better-funded white women rather than an important issue for all feminists. Such a twofold perception of "primary" and "exclusive" diverted media attention and the movement itself from the range of needs experienced by so-called Others—nonwhite, working poor, lesbian, bisexual, and non-Western women (and men). By investing their energies in the ERA, these second-wave activists shortchanged the petitions of nonmainstream feminist activists. Given their identities, many of these Others were speaking out in a parallel rhetoric of collective action (from civil rights to farmworkers' rights) but doing so without the media attention, visible presence, and financial support of the white women activists, who should have been by their sides or in their audience.[10]

Instead, these second-wave feminists used their rhetoric (without giving much thought to their "identities") to speak and write publicly on behalf of "the" feminist movement (as they so often did and were expected to do). Despite their self-identification as antiracist, antisegregationist, proto-intersectional feminists, both Gloria Steinem and Betty Friedan, for instance, were called out for not using rhetoric that explicitly addressed the concerns of women of color and lesbians, who were working within racial, educational, class, or legal constraints of their own. The fissures within the second-wave feminist movement offered perfect opportunities for rhetorical feminists to disidentify with hegemonic feminist rhetoric, speak to and from the margins, invite dialogue, lift up vernaculars and experiences of all participants, and foreground hope and possibility. The time was ripe for feminism—and feminist rhetoric—to leave its homogenizing tendencies behind. Women of color, working-class women, and nonheterosexual women would speak back, up, and out.

Feminist Rhetoric and Dis/Identification

By the late 1960s and early 1970s, women of color were re/considering their relationship with the (white) women's movement, establishing the 1974 Combahee River Collective and issuing a 1977 "Black feminist" statement to that same effect:

> One issue that is of major concern to us and that we have begun to publicly address is racism in the white women's movement. As Black feminists we are made constantly and painfully aware of how little effort white women have made to understand and combat their racism,

> which requires among other things that they have a more than superficial comprehension of race, color, and Black history and culture. Eliminating racism in the white women's movement is by definition work for white women to do, but we will continue to speak to and demand accountability on this issue. (Combahee River Collective 21)

Members of the collective connected themselves with the "second wave of the American women's movement beginning in the late 1960s" yet enumerated the reasons black feminists could not merge with that movement: "both outside reactionary forces and racism and elitism within the movement itself have served to obscure our participation" (14). Nor could they merge with the various strands of Black Liberation (which some perceived as sexist), despite admitting that they were "greatly affected and changed by [Black Liberation's] ideology, . . . goals, and the tactics used to achieve [those] goals" (14).

The goal of this collective was to "develop a politics that was antiracist, unlike those of white women, and antisexist, unlike those of Black and white men" (14). And the genesis of participants' political work was their personal identity: "We believe that the most profound and potentially the most radical politics come directly out of our own identity, as opposed to working to end somebody else's oppression" (16). For the black women of this collective, their cause had already realized that identity-inflected politics and rhetoric expanded the feminist principle that the personal is political: "We have in many ways gone beyond white women's revelations because we are dealing with the implications of race and class as well as sex. . . . No one before has ever examined the multilayered texture of Black women's lives" (17).[11] That "no one" (read "none of the white women activists'") had examined the texture of black women's lives became a divisive rallying cry—a resistant, critically instructive feminist rhetoric—in the women's movement.

The complex relationships among difference, identity, language, and power are fixed in the political arena in which identities position themselves. Therefore, the critical import of identity politics—of individual, lived experience—undermines any ideal of a universal women's movement, a universal feminist voice.[12] Third-wave feminists have tried to learn from the mistakes of the second wave, consciously disrupting the inevitable influence of previous waves, continuously pointing to the intersectional diversity within the category of *woman*, diversity that plays out in economics, education, cultural-ethnic self-affiliation, sexuality, ability, and gender presentation but most of all in individual choice. None of these differences should constrain one's identity as a free human being or as a feminist. Identity matters, as the controversy between second-wave feminist rhetorical leaders Audre Lorde and Mary Daly makes so clear. Theirs is an abiding controversy—still now in the twenty-first century.

Speaking—and for Whom?

During the second wave, identity began to merge with politics explicitly and vice versa. The issue of who can speak for whom became heated—and essentialized. As uncomfortable as white feminist activists may have felt at the time, the push back from women of color was critical to how feminism might move forward as a unifying force. In the early 1990s, June Jordan spoke up: "There is difference and there is power. And who holds the power decides the meaning of difference" (197). The 1979 public rhetorical exchange between white feminist theologian Mary Daly and black feminist literary great Audre Lorde serves as a prime example of rhetorical power (and failure). I stop to consider their exchange because of its contemporary resonance and long-lasting implications and lessons.

Lorde initiated the exchange by sending Daly a personal letter in May 1979, charging her with a lack of feminist awareness in thinking that "all women suffer the same oppression simply because we are women" ("Open Letter" 67). After reading Daly's *Gyn/Ecology*, Lorde believed that Daly had lost "sight of the many varied tools of patriarchy," including "how those tools are used by women without awareness against each other" (67).[13] Four months later, having received no response from Daly, Lorde published "An Open Letter to Mary Daly," unleashing a torrent of white-feminists-are-racist sentiment from many of Lorde's supporters.

In the letter, Lorde describes how she finds much of *Gyn/Ecology* "full of import, useful, generative, and provocative" (66), explaining that it is in such a spirit that she is writing to Daly, "hoping" to share with her the benefits of her own insight just as Daly had shared hers with Lorde (66). Lorde analyzes *Gyn/Ecology*, rhetorically engaging in Daly's vision of myth, mystification, and the Goddess—that is, until she realizes that Daly's goddess images are limited to "white, western European, judeo-christian" examples only, with no mention of "Afrekete, Yemanje, Oyo, and Mawulia" (67). Puzzled, Lorde asks Daly point-blank if she has ever really read the work of black women or of Lorde herself—or if she "merely finger[ed] through them for quotations" that might "valuably support an already conceived idea concerning some old and distorted connection between us" (67).

In other words, without deep knowledge of black women's experience, Daly should not be speaking for all women. Doing so was using a tool of patriarchy against Other women. Doing so "serves the destructive forces of racism and separation between women—the assumption that the herstory and myth of *white* women is the legitimate and sole herstory and myth of all women" (69; emphasis added). Having had her say, Lorde closes by explaining why she changed her mind about "never again" speaking to "white women about racism":

> I felt it was wasted energy because of destructive guilt and defensiveness, and because whatever I had to say might better be said by white women to one another at far less emotional cost to the speaker, and probably with a better hearing. But I would like not to destroy you in my consciousness, not to have to. So as a sister Hag, I ask you to speak to my perceptions. Whether or not you do, Mary, again I thank you for what I have learned from you.
>
> This letter is in repayment. (70–71)

Until 2004, few scholars or activists realized that Daly had, indeed, responded—and in just a little *over* four months and just after Lorde had published her letter.[14] On 22 September 1979, Daly had written:

> First, I want to thank you for sending me *The Black Unicorn*. I have read all of the poems, some of them several times. Many of them moved me very deeply—others seemed farther from my own experience. You have helped me to be aware of different dimensions of existence, and I thank you for this. . . .
>
> . . . You have made your point very strongly and you most definitely have a point. I could speculate on how *Gyn/Ecology* would have been affected had we corresponded about this before the manuscript went to press, but it doesn't seem creativity-conducing to look backward. There is only now and the hope of breaking barriers between us—of constantly expanding the vision.

Before signing off, Daly invites Lorde to meet with her, hoping to see and talk with her soon, inviting dialogue, invoking hope, and wishing her "the strength of all the Goddesses."

Whether Daly wrote back to Lorde is not the primary issue here. Nor is it one of deep-seated racism on the part of Daly (though covertly and overtly, racism continues to circulate widely in American culture and the American subconscious). Rather, the issue is an even larger one of unconscious, unacknowledged privilege, power, and responsibility—of one feminist rhetorical identity over another.

In *Gyn/Ecology,* Daly strives to speak for all women—and fails on several levels: (a) she implicitly writes for and to white women only; (b) she uses examples from nonwhite culture only to support her points rather than to develop those examples in the context of nonwhite culture; and (c) she admittedly does not recognize, let alone understand, some of the nonwhite experiences that she used or that she was later given by Lorde (poems in *The Black Unicorn,* for instance). Of course, Daly was writing before it was fashionable to declare one's subject position, one's standpoint, one's limitations. As her letter makes clear, she wished she had spoken to Lorde about these issues of identity, feminism, and rhetoric before the publication of the book.

But she had not.

Daly continues to serve as an example of the white feminist rhetor who did not know enough about nonwhite issues to address them. Does such a charge equate with racism? Not necessarily.[15] Still, a white person, a white feminist rhetorical activist, can unconsciously benefit from white privilege by not thinking about, not studying, and not learning from the material conditions and lived experiences of nonwhite women. Rhetorical feminism expects its practitioners to open up dialogue, in the way Lorde does and in the way Daly extends that dialogue. It speaks to those at the edges of mainstream discourse (even when those at the edges are famous, established). And rhetorical feminism values emotions and experience as authentic sources of knowledge, as features of rational argument. It is Lorde's charge of "white privilege" that sticks. And in that charge, the so-called subaltern does, indeed, speak.

Strategic Identification à la Spivak's Strategic Essentialism

Long considered the leading expert on subaltern status, Spivak has reworked her definition of the "subaltern" over the years.[16] Revising both the category itself and the terms of analysis, Spivak offers a wide definition: the subaltern as woman, who is "to a rather large extent the support of production" (*Critique* 67), and the subaltern as a "word reserved for the sheer heterogeneity of decolonized space" (310). Her conception, however temporary, also encompasses "women's global subalternity" (89). Working across and through the complexities of diversity-in-identity, subaltern women can employ what Spivak terms "strategic essentialism." Although women may not share specific characteristics or experiences, strategic essentialism is politically efficacious when its proponents tacitly (and temporarily) presume that women share a common social position, a mode of treatment, or constraints of gender structures into which intervention is required. Strategic essentialism is about the need to accept an essentialist position in order to coalesce temporarily, to leverage group agency. Doing so allows groups to speak out and act together rhetorically—despite their different agendas, backgrounds, experiences, politics, and causes. (The 2017 Women's March on Washington provides a case in point, despite its not having one singular message.)

Rebecca Walker, credited with inventing the term "third wave," writes about the ways a strategic essentialism might work across disparate feminist identities:

> To be a feminist is to integrate an ideology of equality and female empowerment into the very fiber of my life. It is to search for personal clarity in the midst of systemic destruction, to join in sisterhood with women when often we are divided, to understand power structures with the intention of challenging them. . . .
> I am not a postfeminist. I am the Third Wave. ("Becoming" 41)[17]

Variously fueled by individual choices; engagement with popular culture, politics, and social justice; public-sphere rhetoric; online activism; intersectional support; and, yes, identity—contemporary feminism (be it third wave, fourth wave, or power feminism) ultimately disrupts. To maintain any momentum, these individual supporters of women's rights must continue to try to forge some means of working together, some shared essentialized identity—across their generations, differences, identities, and rhetorics. In their *Manifesta: Young Women, Feminism, and the Future*, Jennifer Baumgardner and Amy Richards write about the crucial role of an activist feminist self in every community and the importance of diverse, cross-generational, intersectional feminist knowledge and appreciation. Regardless of what such a calculated coalition might be called or called for, a kind of workable strategic essentialism must be conceivable and achievable—even if minimally acceptable. Such a coalition is designed to be fragile and temporary. Furthermore, any change has to be envisioned as a possibility—on the basis of rhetorical feminist hope—before it can even begin.

The goals of the third-wave movement, anchored as it is in "historically feminist concerns" (Sanders 5–6), and of the fourth wave, with its online, international grassroots activism, are to establish connections among feminists, connections that simultaneously emphasize the diversity of women's experience. Fourth-wave rhetorical feminists have expanded that diversity to include women of faith and spirituality; women of all sizes, nations, and sexualities; online activism; and support of intersectionalities of every kind. Universalism and easy essentialism are resisted, as are the hierarchical feminist-generational logics of race, sexuality, economic status, culture, ability, and geographic location. Still, strategic, temporary essentialism—strategic coalition—is possible.[18] According to Lise Shapiro Sanders, emphasizing "feeling" over "identity" enables strategic (essentialist) alliances without ignoring the conflicts rendered by "power and hierarchy in the historical relations among women" (11). The conflicts between white middle-class feminists and women of color during the fight for suffrage and the ERA serve as historical-rhetorical lessons for us all, as does the Lorde-Daly struggle for recognition, to be recognized and respected by an Other.

Despite their designated distancing from, their rich critiques of, and their professed appreciation for the second wave of feminism, the successive feminist waves serve as powerful tools for energizing, validating, and coalescing the ever more internally diverse women's movement that has followed. Nonetheless, third-wave feminists experience internal conflicts, whether about participants, theories, or practices.[19] When Sojourner Truth addressed the first annual meeting of the American Equal Rights Association in 1867, she spoke to the same kinds of conflicts: "I am for keeping the thing going while things are stirring; because if we wait till it is still, it will take a great while to get it going again."

Of course, the central obstruction to keeping the feminist "thing going" is unsuccessful, unproductive rhetorical interactions and transactions—an essential point that is usually elided. Rhetorical feminism's principles of hope, dialogism, and respect of vernaculars, marginalization, and experience could constitute the common ground necessary for identification, for bridging division, and for moving forward. Though not a unity, all feminists can be strategically assembled "through their location within activist history into a determinate social group amenable to collective mobilization on a coalitional [however ephemeral] basis" (Stone 27).

The Power of Intersectionality: Cutting Both Ways

Identities, divisions, and systems of oppression are not new, nor are their intersections. Kimberlé Crenshaw's theory of intersectionality explains how racism, religious bias, economic deprivation, and LGBTQ-phobia intensify the effects of sexism, racism, and other prejudices directed toward categories of identity.[20] In academic parlance, the theory of intersectionality is now frequently invoked whenever a person knowingly speaks from multiple self-identified categories, as many people (Spivak and Roxane Gay, for example) are now doing.

Conversely, the theory is wielded against those, like the uninformed Patricia Arquette, who speak obliviously to multiple categories and oppressions as though they are just one—in her case, the oppression of gender. Arquette's widely viewed 2015 Academy Award acceptance speech serves as an example of feminist rhetorical activism, to be sure, as well as of the ways one (white) woman's essentialism can sabotage strategic essentialism—and set off a firestorm:

> It's time for women. Equal means equal.... The truth is, even though we sort of feel like we have equal rights in America, right under the surface, there are huge issues at play that really do affect women. It's time for all the women in America, and all the men that love women, and all the gay people, and all the people of color that we've all fought for to fight for us now.

Clearly, Arquette's final sentence struck a chord, in person and online. Blogger Mikki Kendall's campaign #SolidarityIsForWhiteWomen provided rich soil for a fast-growing commentary by women of color, white women, gays, lesbians, transgender people, bisexuals—seemingly every self-identified group within feminism. The commenters all seemed to subscribe to equality, that basic tenet of feminism, and yet they questioned Arquette's position on equality. Most of the commenters, bloggers, and tweeters charged Arquette with prioritizing the rights of white women over those of the LGBTQ community and of people of color. If that was the case, so they argued, feminist solidarity (strategic essentialism) was reserved only for white heterosexual women—not for the likes of them.

Although faulted online and in the press for remarks that seemed to ignore intersectional experience, Arquette herself may not be wholly to blame for her lack of academic and rhetorical knowledge. As Akiba Solomon assures her blog readers,

> intersectionality becomes common sense if you've heard of it. But if you haven't had the privilege of taking women's studies courses, haven't been exposed to the black feminist canon, or you haven't had the time or tech to consume the online cultural products of young feminist thinkers, that term might not be that hot in your streets. (par. 14)

And Crenshaw herself admits that the concept of "intersectionality is not easy," particularly since it is a legal concept originally conceived to challenge the ways antidiscrimination law separates race and gender (par. 6): "Intersectionality draws attention to invisibilities that exist in feminism, in anti-racism, in class politics" (par. 7). She admonishes, "The challenge is to remain sensitive to power differentials we ourselves don't experience" and stresses that it has always been the project of black feminism to draw "attention to the erasures, to the ways that 'women' of course are invisible in plain sight" (par. 7).

Indeed, Crenshaw's theory of intersectionality explains the effect and intensity of multiple oppressions while simultaneously clarifying the firestorm following Arquette's remarks, which were described by the conversants as unquestionably "anti-intersectional." When pressed into service, however, intersectionality also points to the feminist rhetorical failure to talk across differences and the refusal to transcend those differences (even temporarily) in order to coalesce into strategic essentialism. Intersectionality might also explain why traditional rhetorical transactions continue to fail feminism: such traditional transactions are hierarchical and persuasion-oriented rather than collaborative, dialogic, and understanding-oriented.

In an NPR-sponsored roundtable about Twitter, Gay spoke to the powers and limits of intersectionality, which she described as an "awkward word representing an important idea," right before she coupled it with feminism:

> No one assumes only one identity. We cannot consider the needs of women without also accounting for race, ethnicity, gender, citizenship, class, sexuality, ability, and more. Such nuanced awareness, such intersectionality, is the marrow within the bones of feminism. Without it, feminism will fracture even further. ("Looking," par. 6)

In short work, Gay reveals that contradiction that is a unified feminism. Just as identity forges coalitions at the same time that it severs them, so, too, does feminism, which is fractured by the very same identities that hold it together. Gay states, "Feminists are individuals who ideally share the belief that the rights of women are as inalienable as the rights of men" (par. 3).[21] But despite that shared belief (or fantasy) in a singular feminism, "feminism as a global movement meant to unite all women . . . has failed at one of the most basic; it has not been welcoming to all women" (Kendall, par. 4). White feminists try not to speak for others, but they often do. Therefore, a reinvention of a singular feminism is exactly what nonwhite feminists are refusing. They have been there. They too often are there.

Gay's interrogation of contemporary feminism includes a bell-hooks-like yearning for that "elusive *real* feminist, the most authentic feminist, the feminist who best captures what feminism is and should be" ("Looking," par. 1), a yearning based in the hope and possibility of rhetorical feminism, committed as it is to dialogism, the marginalized, vernaculars, and the knowledge gained from personal experience. Even if many of us yearn for instructions for how to be that real feminist, Gay's real feminist is actually a "convenient fantasy," existing only to delude us into thinking there might be a "handy checklist advising us how to be the best possible feminists"—or that an intersectional, unified feminism might be possible (pars. 1, 2). The schisms among feminists are indeed divisive, but they are also generative, for they can open up dialogue, spark self-questioning, and provide opportunities for productive silence and listening. And so these schisms remain, even among the most committed of feminists.

A Feminist Failure to Communicate

Too many white middle-class, heterosexual women trust that gender trumps race, believing themselves always/already allied with other feminists or standing ready to coalesce. In response, many nonwhite feminists view the white feminist stance of alleged openness as suspect, pointing to the ways it "erases the experiences of women of color, [alienating] many from a movement that claims to want equality for all" (Kendall, qtd. in "Twitter Sparks," par. 3).[22] In the face of the monolith, Other feminists "are obliged to suppress their needs in defense of white prerogatives" (Kendall, qtd. in Ross, par. 3). Mainstream white feminists too often have no conception of how their rhetorical stance of openness is actually a stance-without-a-view. Shan tweets, "Privileged people have a terrible time recognizing when It's Not All About Them."[23]

Not surprising, then, that when confronted with accusations of using essentializing rhetoric, of overstepping, ignoring, not listening, not seeing, or not analyzing, many of those same white feminists respond defensively, as though any critique of their rhetoric is exceptional, off the mark, wrongheaded. Too often their response is a closed one, even when they are bombarded by "black and brown and Asian people, trans folk and those with preferred pronouns or identity gripes and aspirations, the angry disenfranchised and the outsider aspirants" (Kendall, qtd. in Ross, par. 22).

And if they apologize, they still do not seem to get it. Or maybe they are just not very good at it.

Indeed, apologizing, untangling facts and feelings, is tough and so takes courage and understanding. However, "sometimes . . . those in power [the apologizers] frame themselves as being tremendously disempowered by critique" (Crenshaw, qtd. in Adewunmi, par. 11). They are defensive. They do not seem to realize that a critique of their rhetoric is not the silencing, ignoring, or annihilation of that same voice, as it would be for so many Others. It is a critique, talking back, a way to stake a claim in the dialogue, a way to participate and contribute. Yet however edifying and ultimately productive such dialogues might be, they are often painful, embarrassing, and angry. They may be important dialogues, but they are rarely easy.

Accordingly, it is especially important for hopeful feminists to consider how they might use rhetorical feminism more effectively. In "Five Ways White Feminists Can Address Our Own Racism," Sarah Milstein admonishes feminists to assume the other person is saying something "especially true" when you feel "defensive" (par. 8), an assumption that should help us all identify ways that we are unconsciously racist rather than ways to prove we are not (par. 13). Still, it is difficult to hear what seems like anger-induced accusation rather than the criticism-intended-for-education that it often is. Too many mainstream feminists who assume feminism to be an inclusive (or nearly inclusive) coalition cannot seem to translate their conception into substantive coalitional rhetoric, practices, and accountability.[24] So how might all the privileged-feminists-with-a-platform establish common ground in an impasse, even as we privileged academic feminists recognize the dangers of common ground? How might we do so with those without a platform? How might all of us prepare a scene of mutual identification? These are questions I address below.

Feminist Options

In terms of successful, bridge-building communication, rhetorical feminism attends to two major feminist problems. The first issue (complex as it is) can be addressed by respecting (collaborating with when necessary) the audience to which Others speak out and up for themselves (which I discussed above). The second issue might be addressed most easily if those in privileged positions took seriously the rhetorical feminist precepts of silence and listening to Others, which is the subject of this section. In "Twitter, Feminism, and Race: Who Gets a Seat at the Table?," blogger Mikki Kendall reminds us all that "the way equality is defined by the women in the forefront can be incredibly problematic, especially if those leaders lack a connection to ethnically and racially diverse communities" (par. 7). Kendall rightly focuses on women in the "forefront," women who already have a platform, an audience. But the problem of speaking and listening to Others cuts much deeper, through intersecting identities (of race, culture, ability, sexuality, or other features), multiple political stances, theoretical dispositions, and waves, all of which are strung on a commitment to equality.

Kendall is right: an underlying issue has always been about how *equality* is defined. The women in the forefront invoked by Kendall are privileged feminists, who from her viewpoint always/already have seats at the table. Do these feminists need connections with "ethnically and racially diverse communities"? Yes—but they need more than that: sometimes they need to get out of the way so Other feminists can take a seat. They also need to develop authentic relationships with Other feminists. They need mutually informing rhetorical relationships forged on common ground (however tenuously), rhetorical relationships that emphasize Burkean identification[25] and assume (as Chaim Perelman and Lucie Olbrechts-Tyteca would have them) the *"existence of intellectual contact"* (14). The goal of such rhetorical feminist transactions must be that of conscientious understanding if ever feminists—from all subject positions—can hope to coalesce, to strategize among and across differences.

The rhetorical goal of understanding provides a marked divergence from the traditional rhetorical goal of persuasion, from what Perelman and Olbrechts-Tyteca describe as *"gaining the adherence of minds"* (14). Rather than delivering a tattoo of claims powerful enough to influence (if not overpower) an audience, a rhetorical feminism of understanding is multifaceted and multiphased, allowing time for all sides to listen, keep silent, consider, and weigh. Thus, the goal of understanding is predicated on a process of invitation that encourages mutual participation, as Karen Foss, Sonja Foss, and Cindy Griffin have taught us with their theories of invitational and transformational rhetorics, Krista Ratcliffe with her theory of rhetorical listening, and I with my theory of rhetorical silence.

Not enough feminists are employing invitation, let alone enjoying the transformation that accompanies the successful reach across divisions. Instead, too many feminists of every identity category register frustrations with intramovement communications (most of them recorded online), which they describe as one-sided salvos, defensive explanations, not-very-thought-out calls to action, stonewalling, bickering, and, of course, STFUs (shutthefuckups).

Because productive face-to-face rhetorical engagements are so very difficult to establish, far more cross-difference communications occur online, where people too often post with anonymity and abandon. Feminist blogger Jill Filipovic outlines some of the problems with online rhetorics: "When it comes to feminism in media and online, it's fairly easy to use the right words to prove you're on the right side of things; it's harder to step back and make sure you aren't drowning out others" (qtd. in "Twitter . . . : A Roundtable," par. 3).[26]

Whether cross-cutting communication is face-to-face or online, successful or not, feminist participants and bystanders from all sides manage to agree on one thing: unsuccessful rhetorical interactions are missing an intersectionalist viewpoint and understanding. They are also missing the establishment of common ground and strategic yet temporary coalition building.

In *Hearing the Other Side,* Diana C. Mutz catalogs the alleged benefits of exposure to conflicting views, which include developing greater self-understanding, understanding of others, and tolerance (69). Mutz never goes so far as to argue that these three benefits are always realized, stating instead that "it is *not* important that they learn about the rationales for one another's political views" (68; emphasis added). Much more significant to the establishment of successful interpersonal communication, according to Mutz, is the development of "close relationships with those [who] hold quite different political viewpoints" (68); otherwise, we live and work in an echo chamber of our own beliefs and words. In other words, it is important to learn from personal experience that those different from oneself are not necessarily bad people. For rhetorical feminists, experience is a source of epistemic knowledge, as are emotions, both of them freighted with ethos and pathos, with the politicized internalized.

IDENTITIES

Mainstream rhetoricians have yet to give sustained attention to the powerful effect of positive emotions on a communicative transaction, save to speak to the rhetorical appeals. But rhetorical feminists have, indeed. To that end, Mutz nudges us to reflect on the role of familiarity, the ways that trust, affection, and personal respect enhance communicative and deliberative success across difference and through thorny issues—as does hope. And emotions fill the gaps between our instinct and our reasoning, providing a way for us to pay attention to the world, especially when we need to decide what to do and what or whom to believe. Even if we are not sure about what to do, Ratcliffe encourages us to take the risk of listening rhetorically from a position of identification, disidentification, even nonidentification—especially if our doing so produces a rhetoric of invention, of the open hand (*Rhetorical* 77).

Until the Trump campaign and presidency, diversity was lauded as one of America's strengths. But even then, private individuals did little on their own to realize that goal of communicating with people who embodied values, opinions, and lived experiences markedly different from their own. Nonetheless, the potential for positive consequences from communication across lines—and from and into the margins—of difference is immeasurable. Such communication remains elusive for most people, including feminists. Ironically, the more diverse and broad-ranging feminism becomes, the more like-minded feminists within the movement stay together in segregated networks and clusters of familiarity, and the less people within those self-identified categories will initiate cross-contact and reveal their opinions.[27] Even in the face of the fact that cross-cutting contact eventually reduces prejudice, prejudice (whether conscious or unconscious) lessens the amount of intergroup contact people have in the first place.

Thus, we need to employ a practical, workable theory of cross-cutting conversation that addresses the rich and complex issue of diversity, whether the theory is anchored in formal rules of engagement, calibrated levels of acceptable risk taking, or balanced attention (and respect) to speaker and audience alike—a theory such as invitational rhetoric, rhetorical listening, or rhetorical silence. After all, successful rhetorical feminist transactions occur when feminists work to establish authentic connections with members of more diverse, often marginalized but sometimes centralized feminist communities, and vice versa. Authentic dialogic rhetorical connections can also succeed when rhetorical feminists analyze and strive to reach their intended audience as well as when they are willing to recognize or consider themselves as the target audience. Just as an online STFU can be a rhetorical refusal (or a call to remain silent and listen), so is a feminist message of exclusion, whether sent or received. Regardless of intention.

Mutuality is key to any cross-cutting understanding and political coalition in rhetorical feminism. Ideally (as in "not realistically"), a rhetorical feminist and her rhetorical audience willingly participate in a two-way communication, taking turns talking and listening, both trying to establish good reasons for identifying with each other, both trying to reach each other, both trying to consider a broader range of concerns, even if only temporarily. Any hierarchy of leadership, participation, or values must be suspended, even if only temporarily. Of course, real humans, not ideals, are the participants in such occasions. We must risk getting it wrong.

Kendall's blog posts serve to remind feminists of the power of online (Tumblr, Twitter, blog) and face-to-face communications to influence the people who participate in them as well as those who read and listen to them. In urging individual responsibility for the sake of group possibility, Kendall writes,

> We cannot lose sight of those people who need us to do the work to educate ourselves, to reach them, to help them achieve their goals. And, no, that's not an endorsement of speaking for anyone, or of trying to play savior. It's an endorsement for doing the intellectual work and getting our collective hands dirty in the trenches. This is an endorsement of listening, of not always trying to be the leader, and instead of handing the proverbial reins over to others even if we don't know them well and aren't sure the favor will ever be reciprocated. ("Twitter Sparks," par. 9)

Kendall's sage advice expands upon that of Ratcliffe and Foss, Foss, and Griffin, with all of them arguing for dialogic, transactional rhetorical exchanges among equals who speak with invitation and listen with consideration.

So, what might a rhetorical feminist do? "No one tactic will heal the factures in feminism," writes Gay. "Creating long-lasting and necessary change requires committed and sustained effort on many fronts. [But] until we put our ideas into practice, that change cannot begin" ("Looking," par. 17). Gay's caution is spot-on: there is no one surefire cure to the fractures within feminism, yet there are at least two ways that a fractured feminism can draw on its internal intersectional strength: those fractures can be braced to withstand pressures internal and external, and they can be strengthened with the hope and possibility that is rhetorical feminism.

Experience, research, and good sense tell us to move out of our feminist comfort zones, initiate hard talks with feminists who hold values and experiences different from our own, and work together to keep the feminist agenda above the lines of division, putting hope in play, making a leap of faith beyond the evidence.[28] We rhetorical feminists must strive toward ethical, safe, and yet sometimes painful dialogue, from the margins to the center, from margin to margin, if ever rhetorical feminists are to come together in their advocacy of human rights and social justice. We must, in good faith, do this, despite the fact that "we're all humans, all operating with feet of clay and our own personal biases" (Kendall, qtd. in "Twitter . . . : Who Gets a Seat?," par. 11).[29] We must do this, staying alert to the toll these interchanges might have on us and making time to take care of ourselves and others. When all is said and done, feminist solidarity is a short phrase for a broad concept: we may not always share the same goals or the same concept of community, let alone the same idea of how to achieve those goals or that concept, but we are all feminists—and feminists who use rhetoric at that. That one shared feature can serve as an experiential and emotional epistemic resource for our strategic coalitions.

Identities as Epistemic Resources

Discussions of identity and the politics thereof are not new, but in combination with feminism and rhetoric, the old discussion takes a new turn. The objectives of the rhetorical feminist project (inclusivity; dialogue; respect for the languages, emotions, and experiences of all people) align beautifully with that of identity studies (recognition and respect of all people), especially when identities are also tapped for their knowledge-generating potential as they are in the practice of rhetorical feminism. In addition, feminism and identity studies come together in a struggle with issues of exclusion, inclusion, alliances, power relations (including agency and social positioning), essentialism, and representation. Taken together, then, feminism, identity studies, and rhetoric can coalesce to move forward the democratic ideal of equality at the same time that the coalition undermines the ideologies and practices that unfairly dis/advantage some people at the expense of others. Such a coalition holds great promise, including the potential to realize the epistemic power of any identity (what with its vernacular and lived experience) to produce real knowledge of the systemic workings of power in society. The marginalized already know this to be true. The mainstream needs to learn it.

After all, who we actually understand ourselves to be and not be, with whom we self-identify and do not, has consequences for how we experience and understand the world, how we see ourselves participating or not in public affairs, how we speak and listen (and to whom), what we think we deserve (or not), and what we do/not take for granted. And given that our identity can be constructed or realized only in the presences of Others (regardless of our positionality), our identity automatically equals a comparison and contrast about our own social, physical, economic, intellectual, cultural—that is, rhetorical—position vis-à-vis that of Others. In short, we can—and should—recognize our own positions in systems of power even if we do not directly experience those systems as oppressive. Identity has an epistemic cognitive component, as rhetorical feminism reminds us.

"Whether cultures are inherited or consciously and deliberately created" is not the point, argues Satya P. Mohanty. Rather, the point is that "'personal experience' [itself] is socially and 'theoretically' constructed, and it is precisely in this mediated way that it yields knowledge" (33). Our experiences are "crucial indexes" of our specific relationships to history, the social world, and ourselves. Our experiences also help us compare reality and possibility—what is to what could and ought to be (Mohanty 38, 41). In these ways, our identity realistically serves as a lens through which we can gauge power relations, privileges and entitlements, potential and possibility for change—and initiate promising rhetorical feminist transactions. When we pay attention to the experiential accounts of Others (those in the mainstream and those on the margins), when we listen to the knowledge and insights they have gained from their own grounded experience of identity, we can learn how fundamental features of our society work, things beyond our own experiential capacity.

In so many cases, those inhabiting the subaltern, fully cognizant of social hierarchy and their own domination, can contribute "more objective knowledge" about the world that is constitutively defined "by relations of domination" than can those who are not always/already dominated (Mohanty 58). Such subjective perspectives can provide information and knowledge that regularly elude those in the mainstream—unless they take the initiative to learn. Our capacity to know ourselves, make sense of the world, and know and learn from Others is further enhanced when we realize how the power of our social location (that is, our individual and collective cultural identity) regulates our ability to know things, to make insights, and to speak and listen to Others with respect and sensitivity. Our identity can inhibit what we know and understand or can enable our capacity to recognize, analyze, and change. In these ways, identity is a knowledge-accruing location, a hermeneutic horizon from which we attempt to know—and change—the world. That is to say, identities—our own and Others'—are epistemic resources that we feminists and rhetoricians are too often leaving untapped. Rhetorical feminism shows us how to tap them.

So what might these accounts of identity teach us? They bring to life the argument that identity is always created in the presence of complex Others—and, largely, through speech, action, and, often, skin. Our relationships with Others (whether they reside in the center or on the margins) offer us a twofold opportunity to recognize—and speak to—our situatedness in oppressive or advantageous systems of power as well as to acknowledge the epistemic privilege of Others who have experienced those systems as oppressive.

Surely, those in power could listen and learn before speaking, could engage in authentic dialogue (as rhetorical feminism suggests)—but only if they take the time to consider the human effects of their un/conscious superior worldview, only if they take the time to know someone unlike themselves, to realize that difference and deficiency are not the same. To listen first and then speak. For subaltern subjects, their identity helps them make sense of their experiences in the world they share with those who feel superior, helps them read the world in specific ways, helps them calculate the risks and possibility for change through speech and action. They already understand life on the margins. It is up to those in the center to make the same leap of understanding.

As I have argued throughout this chapter, when identities serve as epistemic resources for rhetorical transactions rather than as sources of contention, they can be readily tapped for the diverse perspectives they provide. Paula Moya reminds us that "the texts and lived experiences... of marginalized people are rich sources of frequently overlooked information about our shared world" (3). As such, they enrich our standpoint, helping us *re*consider how we communicate across differences; how we might establish common ground in an impasse; why we must employ conscientious listening, silence, and speaking; and how, together, we rhetorical feminists might collaborate in the analysis and transformation of our social worlds—the rhetorical work that sustains our hope.

THREE: THEORIES

> It was an old theme even for me:
> Language cannot do everything.
> —Adrienne Rich, "Cartographies of Silence"

Feminist rhetorical scholars have been proposing and illustrating new theoretical positions since the 1970s (see Campbell; Donawerth; Ede and Lunsford; Moraga and Anzaldúa; Spitzack and Carter; and Trinh, for instance). As Sonja K. Foss and Cindy L. Griffin explained to us a quarter of a century ago,

> The primary goal of feminist scholarship is to discover whether existing rhetorical theories account for women's experiences and perspectives and to construct alternative theories that acknowledge and explain women's practices in the construction and use of rhetoric. ("Feminist Perspective" 331)

When I stop to consider the roots of some of these feminist theoretical moves, the alternative (that is, collaborative) perspectives—and practices—of Lisa Ede and Andrea Lunsford come to mind. Early on, Ede and Lunsford's scholarship nudged us toward working out ways to cooperate without submission; to respect and work with our mutual strengths and perceptions; to overcome (or, at least, set aside) our mutual differences and vulnerabilities; and, thereby, to stimulate the formulation of new ways of being productively rhetorical, new ways of expanding the discipline.

Even into the twenty-first century, the early feminist theoretical goal remains in place, one of expanding the realm of rhetorical possibility and democratizing rhetorical studies. As such, the tactic of rhetorical feminism accommodates greater representation and inclusivity of everyday rhetors by encouraging disidentification with those elitist and exclusive traditional rhetorical practices; transformation of rhetorical transactions, particularly at the scene of argument; adjustment of the rhetorical appeals so that emotion and experience balance logic and reason; and appreciation for the power of alternative means of delivery, especially those long considered to be feminine or passive: silence and listening. All of these tactical features (or moves) originate in the canon of invention—and in the hope and possibility that anchor rhetorical feminism.

Despite their potential to reinvigorate rhetorical studies, feminist rhetorical theories have had only modest influence on the discipline at large, where the rhetorical tradition—what with its influential men, millennia-old theories, and generative practices—dominates an irregular, sometimes contradictory rhetorical frame of reference. Maurice Charland asks, "If tradition is neither coherent nor harmonious, why gesture toward it?" (121). His answer is simple:

> Rhetoric's gesture is to tradition which posits "rhetoric"' as a transhistorical object that is knowable.... "Tradition"... implies historical continuity, and hence a legitimation narrative. To speak of rhetoric's tradition is to allude to gifts from a distant past, from ancient and wise teachers, and their ongoing validation and preservation. (121)

Some feminist rhetorical theories acknowledge a connection (however fraught) with "rhetoric," but mainstream rhetorical theories remain mostly untouched by feminism.[1]

What seems to generate the most scholarly fruit is feminist rhetorical theory written by and aimed exclusively at women and other subaltern groups (based on race, ethnicity, religion, gender, status, ability, or other identity features). Feminist theorizing itself is an act of resistance, a way to uncover and discover the sites of oppression and repression, but it also maps until-now unmarked strengths and contributions—all the while creating an inventional space for women in all their intersectionalities. Writing this theory fulfills the need to continue the struggle to be heard, and this writing enables theorists to rethink and create new approaches—rhetorical feminism, for instance—for disidentifying and dismantling antagonism, competitiveness, and domination, too often the features of so-called traditional rhetoric.[2]

Employed in the service of feminism, rhetorical feminism offers a tactic that can be used to stimulate ephemeral coalitions across underrepresented groups, to establish a rhetorical audience (who, like the rhetor, may be marginalized), and to speak to those who want to listen and listen to those who want to speak. Rhetorical feminism is anchored in the possibilities for coalition, inclusion, and diversity. Renowned feminist theorists Gloria Anzaldúa, bell hooks, Mary Daly, Starhawk, and Trinh T. Minh-ha are included in this chapter, their work diversifying rhetorical theory. These women have been recovered and recuperated as rhetoricians, as Patricia Bizzell ("Opportunities"), Jacqueline Jones Royster ("Disciplinary Landscaping"), and I ("Remapping") have called for, as have others. They also serve as examples of feminist rhetors/rhetoricians whose work can be identified by extrapolation (see Ratcliffe, *Anglo-American Challenges*). All the women featured in this chapter can be considered rhetorical theorists who employ the tactic (the theoretical stance) of rhetorical feminism.

This chapter maps out some of rhetorical feminism's most prominent conceptual actions: disidentification, transformation and transaction (at the scene of argument), reconceptualization of the rhetorical appeals, and expanded notions of delivery (to include silence, listening, and emotion), each of which facilitates resistance. The chapter also offers the example of several theorists in each category. Rather than a neat taxonomy of theorizing and a fixed set of theorists, I offer a set of permeable categories that allows for easy movement among and across them, including overlapping features, and the inclusion of women whose work illustrates one or several distinctive features of rhetorical feminism. Throughout this chapter, I refer to both feminist rhetoric and rhetorical feminism (see introduction and chapter 1 for definitions). Because her writing so clearly exemplifies all the features of rhetorical feminism, I devote the first part of this chapter to the writings of Gloria Anzaldúa before moving on to the rhetorical feminist writings of hooks, Daly, Starhawk, and Trinh and then on to the work of recognized rhetorical scholars who specialize in feminism.

Rhetorical Feminism and Disidentification

21 mayo 80
Dear mujeres de color, companions in writing—
I sit here naked in the sun, typewriter against my knee trying to visualize you. Black woman huddles over a desk in the fifth floor of some New York tenement. Sitting on a porch in south Texas, a Chicana fanning away mosquitos and the hot air, trying to arouse the smouldering embers of writing. Indian woman walking to school or work lamenting the lack of time to weave writing into

> *your life. Asian American, lesbian, single mother, tugged in all directions by children, lover or ex-husband, and the writing.*
>
> —Gloria Anzaldúa, "Speaking"

Never self-identified as a rhetorician, Anzaldúa nonetheless provides one of the most compelling examples of rhetorical feminism, starting with disidentification, her stance of self-conscious, purposeful rhetorical individuality. Her 1981 "Speaking in Tongues: A Letter to 3rd World Women Writers" fulfills all the requirements of a successful rhetorical transaction while transcending traditional rhetorical theory and long-established models. The letter moves into the future, fueled by the hegemony, racism, and Anglo-mainstream silencing that continue to propel feminist rhetorical concerns. In her letter, Anzaldúa decries any necessary rhetorical tutelage and defies comparison to traditional rhetorical deliveries. Hers is a strategy of disidentification, a term coined by José Esteban Muñoz to describe an intentional subversion of dominant expectations for being in the world.[3]

An analysis of Anzaldúa's letter reveals the power of disidentification in rhetorical feminism. Anzaldúa disidentifies with those traditional practices that could (even temporarily) marginalize her or her audience, refuses to adjust her writing for an allegedly more-prestigious-than-she-is academia, and establishes and speaks from a center of her own making. Unwilling to allow the problematic center-margin metaphor to dictate either her positioning or her performance, Anzaldúa speaks from a position of her own choosing, addressing the powerful "third-world"[4] women with whom she shares the space:

> It is not easy writing this letter. It began as a poem, a long poem. I tried to turn it into an essay but the result was wooden, cold. I have not yet unlearned the esoteric bullshit and pseudo-intellectualizing that school brainwashed into my writing.
>
> How to begin again. How to approximate the intimacy and immediacy I want. What form? A letter, of course. ("Speaking" 165)

Anzaldúa's letter provides an expansive preview of the changes rhetorical feminism could bring to our discipline. First of all, Anzaldúa disidentifies with and will not "bow down to the sacred bull, form" (167). Hers is not a traditional argumentative essay but rather a multigenre—and multilingual—letter, weaving quotations, poems, and Spanish into it, offering a "counterweight to the discipline's focus on the finished speech as the primary subject of study" (Palczewski, "Bodies" 10). Her transformation of the argument serves as a model for third-world women. Anzaldúa continues:

> My dear *hermanas,* the dangers we face as women writers of color are not the same as those of white women though we have many in common. We don't have as much to lose—we never had any privileges. I wanted to call the dangers "obstacles" but that would be a kind of lying. We cannot *transcend* the dangers, can't rise above them. We must go through them and hope we won't have to repeat the performance. ("Speaking" 165)

Unlike the traditional, monologic finished speech, which "achieve[s] distance" from (167) or offers "correction" to an audience, the epistolary genre that Anzaldúa employs invites dialogic connection and response. A rhetorical adaptation to the exclusion of women from the public podium, her letter exemplifies the value of third-world women's writing at the same time that it initiates a dialogue among her readers and herself.

Second, the traditionally marginalized status of the Chicana writer is one Anzaldúa capitalizes on, positioning herself as actively resistant to the mainstream. If she is marginal, then she is purposefully, radically marginal. As a rhetorical theorist, Anzaldúa identifies the invisibility and silences of people who are not in the white masculinist mainstream or the white feminist world; she excavates a rhetorical space for Other women. Her separatism empowers her and her audience, indicating her agency as a rhetorical being who speaks and listens to Others in the languages and genres that best suit their needs:

> Unlikely to be friends of people in high literary places, the beginning woman of color is invisible both in the white male mainstream world and in the white women's feminist world, though in the latter this is gradually changing. The *lesbian* of color is not only invisible, she doesn't even exist. Our speech, too, is inaudible. We speak in tongues like the outcast and insane. ("Speaking" 165)

Like Gayatri Spivak teaches us, author and agency are anchored in identity, and Anzaldúa embraces her own, speaking up—and out.

Third, Anzaldúa's letter addresses a very specific audience (third-world women writers) and the expectations of a response; after all, epistolary form (often described as "feminine") is dialogic, participatory, expectant. But she invokes an even broader audience, perhaps non-third-world women who (like me) eavesdrop in ways that will help them educate themselves. (See Ede and Lunsford's "Audience Addressed" and Ratcliffe's "Eavesdropping.") She poses questions to her audience, writing with expectations of response, immediacy, and intimacy among women:

> How hard is it for us to *think* we can choose to become writers, much less *feel* and *believe* that we can. What have we to contribute, to give? Our own expectations condition us. Does not our class, our culture as well as the white man tell us writing is not for women such as us? ("Speaking" 166)

The letter itself, the language, the details all signal that her rhetorical audience is third-world women writers—not the so-called mainstream, not middle-class straight white women, and certainly not academic Anglo men. Third-world women writers are those who can identify with poverty, long working hours, physical labor, calloused hands, and "being fucked by the Man *a la* La Chingada" (167). Only third-world women writers will understand that followers of "the white feminist establishment" are "notorious for 'adopting' women of color as their 'cause' while still expecting us to adapt to *their* expectations and *their* language" (167).

And fourth, Anzaldúa writes in her multilingual vernacular:

> The Third World woman revolts: *We revoke, we erase your white male imprint. When you come knocking on our doors with your rubber stamps to brand our faces with* DUMB, HYSTERICAL, PASSIVE PUTA, PERVERT, *when you come with your branding irons to burn* MY PROPERTY *on our buttocks, we will vomit the guilt, self-denial and race-hatred you have force-fed into us right back into your mouth.* (167)

Although she has "strung credentials and published books around [her] neck like pearls," she will not use the kind of language that contributes to the "invisibility" of her "sister-writers" (167).

In these four basic ways, Anzaldúa disarms the mainstream rhetorical community, speaks to her rhetorical audience, and critiques argumentative, academic posturing to be nothing more (or less) than hegemonic discourse that wrongly claims to be "universal," "humanitarian," and "eternal" (170). Clearly, hegemonic theory is not any of those things, for Anzaldúa's "Letter" offers rhetorical feminism, which converges on experience, the vernacular— what she describes as the "particular and the feminine and the specific historical moment" (170)—reaching an entirely different, and much broader and much more diverse, audience.[5]

Because she is determined to be heard by her clearly identified rhetorical audience (rather than by those academics invested in what Barbara Christian calls "the race for theory"), Anzaldúa directly critiques those first-world men and women who would otherwise overlook or silence her:

> The white man speaks: Perhaps if you scrape the dark off of your face. Maybe if you bleach your bones. Stop speaking in tongues, stop writing left-handed. Don't cultivate your colored skins nor tongues of fire if you want to make it in a right-handed world. ("Speaking" 166)

Furthermore, Anzaldúa handily addresses the issue of being heard, valued, and published by those Christian refers to as "having the power" (52). These are the men (mostly) who control the presses and the journals, determining which ideas are valuable, publishable. Thus, both Anzaldúa and Christian speak to the issue of mainstream control and circulation of theoretical ideas, the exclusion of women's contributions, and the vital importance of those excluded contributions, given the fact that feminist rhetorical theorizing is always coupled with practice.

Despite obstacles and overt discouragement, Anzaldúa claims the right to be a writer, the right to be heard, the right to energize the intellectual achievements of herself and Other women, the right to theorize, and, especially, the right to ground theory in everyday practice and to gather knowledge from everyday experience. Anzaldúa's theoretical writing is real, embodied, experimental, decidedly nonmainstream, thus not likely to be embraced by those in control. But then those in control are not her intended audience.

Just as she actively ignores that too-often invoked (but decidedly nonexistent) "general audience of educated readers," Anzaldúa actively disidentifies with those in control, actively removing herself and those like her from their consideration. Her rhetorical feminist moves of self-exclusion paradoxically represent a rhetoric of self-substantiation, for she writes herself and her world into being. Hence, hers is an authenticating act of Otherness through separation, a substantiation without justification: *"Why should I try to justify why I write? Do I need to justify being Chicana, being woman? You might as well ask me to try to justify why I'm alive"* ("Speaking" 169).

Those allegedly in power usually initiate exclusion, but in this case, Anzaldúa employs her own agency to initiate separation from those in control, thereby creating a space for herself and Others to center their rhetorical feminism in the reality of life's practices: "*There is no separation between life and writing*" ("Speaking" 170). For Anzaldúa and third-world women, life and writing consolidate into agency, warding off a sense of muteness, alienation, or marginalization, advancing them, instead, toward voice, self-actualization, even survival: "The act of writing is the act of making soul, alchemy. It is the quest for the self, for the center of the self, . . . the dark, the feminine" (169). Rhetorical feminism, what with recognition of and respect for so-called Others, for their vernaculars, for their experience, works for Anzaldúa. She is not concerned with acceptance in academia—such is not important. Anzaldúa emboldens herself and her audience, "Find the muse within you. The voice that lies buried under you, dig it up. Do not fake it, try to sell it for a handclap or your name in print" (173). She and other third-world women recalculate the center, thus becoming the subjects of their own sphere, not the objects of another's. Their disidentification from hegemonic rhetoric is complete.

The significance of Anzaldúa's rhetorical feminism lies in the strength and inspiration it brings, not only to herself but to Others like her. Christian echoes that sentiment when she states that writing like Anzaldúa's is not in the service of "discourse among critics but is necessary nourishment for their people and one way by which they come to understand their lives better" (53). In these ways, the purpose of Anzaldúa's disidentification is experimentation, clarity (demystification), dialogue, and inclusiveness as opposed to the exclusive, monologic, hegemonic theory that Christian describes as "one which mystifies rather than clarifies our condition, making it possible for a few people who know that particular language to control the critical scene" (55).

The goal of Anzaldúa's rhetorical feminism is twofold: to make the struggles, alliance building, and healing of third-world women more accessible to them and thereby confront the racism of Western imperialism in general and the white feminist movement in particular ("Haciendo caras" xvi, xviii). As such, Anzaldúa's rhetorical feminism is authentic, practical, plausible, and portable. Third-world women can theorize—can write. And when they do, Anzaldúa asks that they "[w]rite of what most links us with life, the sensation of the body, the images seen by the eye, the expansion of psyche in tranquility: moments of high intensity, its movements, sounds, thought"

("Speaking" 172). Third-world women, "tugged in all directions by children, lover or ex-husband," will theorize their lives from all their various standpoints, limitations, and experiences. Whether the schools they attended racialized, discouraged, or educated them, these women can theorize and write. Whether they are educated or whether they sit naked in the sun with a typewriter, huddle over a desk in New York City, fan away mosquitoes on a South Texas porch, or walk to school or work in India, these women can compose in their heads ("Speaking" 165–66). They can write in the kitchen, on the bus, in the welfare line, on the job, during meals—even on the john. They can write by hand or on a keyboard—it does not matter.

What matters is that they respect their personal experience, their language, and their writing, that they enrich the lives of their third-world sisters at the same time that they enrich their own. Paramount, Anzaldúa admonishes her audience, is that "[y]our skin must be sensitive enough for the lightest kiss and thick enough to ward off sneers" ("Speaking" 172).

A few years later, Audre Lorde would speak similarly to the crucial import of women's writing to her survival "within living structures defined by profit, by linear power, by institutional dehumanization" ("Poetry" 39). Like Anzaldúa and Christian, Lorde challenges third-world women "to see, to feel, to speak, and to dare":

> For there are no new ideas. There are only new ways of making them felt—of examining what those ideas feel like being lived on Sunday morning at 7 a.m., after brunch, during wild love, making war, giving birth, mourning our dead—while we suffer the old longings, battle the old warnings and fears of being silent and impotent and alone, while we taste new possibilities and strengths. (39)

These rhetorical feminists lay the foundation for a rhetorical future of change rooted in embodied experience, what Lorde describes as "a bridge across our fears of what has never been before" (38).

bell hooks

Since the 1970s, public intellectual hooks has offered rhetorical feminism in a new key, actively disidentifying with traditional theories of masculinist, democratic deliberation, linking herself instead with concepts of civil rights and of speaking up and out, which she believes to be the responsibilities of every human being. Like Anzaldúa's, hooks's rhetorical feminism encourages everyone in her audience to embrace their rhetorical agency, regardless of how they are raced, classed, gendered, abled, sexualized, aged, or otherwise identified. Hooks translates her theory into an attention to audience members, many of whom are from underrepresented groups. Following Anzaldúa, hooks—throughout all her writings—makes her ideas widely accessible. And following Christian, hooks confirms that it is lack of accessibility that "diminishes our work's power to make meaningful interventions in theory and practice" (hooks, "Critical Reflections" 100). For these reasons, hooks purposefully uses down-to-earth language (the vernacular), unadorned prose (she eschews footnotes, which signal "for academic readers only"), and homely anecdotes (personal experience) as she grapples with thorny and complex sociocultural issues, such as pedagogy, education, and visual culture. Her theoretical goal is one of resistance, pushing her ideas to the point of dismantling "white supremacist capitalist patriarchy," a phrase that appears repeatedly throughout her work. Resisting and overthrowing domination is the through-line of her writings and the core of her feminist rhetorical theory.

Unlike the goal of traditional rhetoric, hers is not to dominate. Instead, her goal is to think critically together with her audience about their context and standpoint, take seriously their rhetorical agency, confront their domination, and, thereby, change their world. She transforms her rhetorical theories into spoken, written, and embodied rhetorical deliveries that inspire her audience to name and intervene into the dominating forces in their daily lives.

In *Teaching to Transgress: Education as the Practice of Freedom,* for instance, hooks speaks to the ways feminist theory is a liberatory practice (another echo of Anzaldúa):

> I find writing—theoretical talk—to be most meaningful when it invites readers to engage in critical reflection and to engage in the practice of feminism. To me, this theory emerges from the concrete, from my efforts to make sense of everyday life experiences, from my efforts to intervene critically in my life and the lives of others. This to me is what makes feminist transformation possible. Personal testimony, personal experience, is such fertile ground for the production of liberatory feminist theory because it usually forms the base of our theory-making. While we work to resolve those issues that are most pressing in daily life (our need for literacy, an end to violence against women and children, women's health and reproductive rights, and

> sexual freedom, to name a few), we engage in a critical process of theorizing that enables and empowers. (70)

And the reason she commits herself to accessible (vernacular) prose is her continued amazement

> that there is so much feminist writing produced and yet so little feminist theory that strives to speak to women, men and children about the ways we might transform our lives via a conversion to feminist practice. Where can we find a body of feminist theory that is directed toward helping individuals integrate feminist thinking and practice into daily life? (70)

She continues by speaking to the racism that separates white women from women of color and by reminding her readers that it is white women's "inability to listen to black women that impedes feminist progress" (102):

> Many of the black women who were actively engaged with the feminist movement were talking about racism in a sincere attempt to create an inclusive movement, one that would bring white and black women together. We believed that true sisterhood would not emerge without radical confrontation, without feminist exploration and discussion of white female racism and black female response. Our desire for an honorable sisterhood, one that would emerge from the willingness of all women to face our histories, was often ignored. Most white women dismissed us as "too angry," refusing to reflect critically on the issues raised. By the time white women active in the feminist movement were willing to acknowledge racism, accountability, and its impact on the relationships between white women and women of color, many black women were devastated and worn out. We felt betrayed; white women had not fulfilled the promise of sisterhood. That sense of betrayal continues and is intensified by the apparent abdication of interest in forging sisterhood, even though white women now show interest in racial issues. It seems at times as though white feminists working in the academy have appropriated discussions of race and racism, while abandoning the effort to construct a space for sisterhood, a space where they could examine and change attitudes and behaviors towards black women and all women of color. (102–03)

Speaking from and to a standpoint of marginality vis-à-vis hegemonic rhetoric, hooks contributes to a theory of rhetorical feminism by collapsing the role of theorist and rhetor as well as by closing the traditional distance between the rhetor and her audience: she purposefully uses "we" and "our" to place herself alongside her audience, sharing with them a sense of betrayal and exhaustion.

Hooks understands listening to be a much-valued feature of rhetorical feminism, one instrumental to any rhetorical transaction, especially one aimed at healing division or opening up dialogue. Yet listening is too often dismissed as "feminine" or passive. Her purpose is to liberate her audience, to free them from responsibility for the failed interracial sisterhood, for white women's inability to listen. Revising the role of theorist and the relationship between the rhetor and her audience, adjusting for a purpose that liberates rather than dominates, and employing theory rooted in personal experience are among the contributions hooks has made to rhetorical feminism as she simultaneously disidentifies with exclusionary, traditional rhetorical theories and practices.

Mary Daly

Feminist theologian Daly also disidentifies with traditional rhetoric, describing its practices within the habitual realm she calls the "foreground." In the masculinist foreground, rhetors routinely dominate and control one another, and women police, dominate, and disrespect themselves as well.[6] For Daly, the foreground encompasses a sphere of the ideologically sanctioned oppression of women, whereas the parallel realm she refers to as the "Background" stimulates women's rhetorical agency and practices, promoting the development of Spinsters (those who Spin Background truths to expose foreground lies) as well as of Hags and Crones (whose age is privileged). Hags and Crones are distinguished by their courage, strength, wisdom, and emancipatory language, which sustain all women in the life-loving and affirming Background, a sphere of rhetorical feminism. Daly's emphasis on the actions of and relationships between women brings the Lesbian/lesbian dimensions of her work into the realm of the habitual, the normal, and into a foreground without sexual oppression.[7]

Unlike Anzaldúa's and hooks's plain, clear language, Daly's rhetorical language can be hard to follow, replete as it is with playful metaphors that transform foreground (or habitual) ways of being and doing in the world. Daly's is a rhetorical feminism of disidentification with/in that foreground, and she deliberately uses metaphors that redefine and transcend customary logic and meaning. She also plays with capitalization and spelling, all in the cause of disrupting the foreground and focusing on the powers emerging from the Background.

In *Websters' First New Intergalactic Wickedary of the English Language*, Daly ("in cahoots with" Jane Caputi) redefines the term *mystery* and, in the process, punctures the power it carries in the foreground:

> *Webster's* [*Third New International Dictionary*] serves up several definitions of *mystery*, each more unappetizing than the next. Thus, for example, we read that it means "a religious truth revealed by God that man cannot know by reason alone and that once it has been revealed cannot be completely understood." ... It is Crone-logical to point out that one possible reason why a "religious truth" said to be revealed by god continues to be unintelligible is simply that it makes no sense. Mystified believers are of course commanded to deny their own intellectual integrity and blindly believe the babbling of men to whom god purportedly has revealed the nonsensical mystery. (5–6)

In short, Daly disidentifies with men's religious mysteries (and with the worship of manlike gods), which make no sense to her—not theoretically, practically, or theologically. She continues with her critique of religious men who, she suspects, fear the possibility of their exposure:

> Hoping to distract from his own stupendous senselessness and to prevent women from Seeing through ... his illusions/delusions ... , man cloaks himself in ever murkier mysteries ... all-male clubs and secret societies—those manifold priesthoods of cockocracy, marked by mumbo-jumbo, ridiculous rituals, and cockaludicrous costumes. (6)

Daly's confrontation and disidentification with the foreground emphasizes her resistance to the traditional rhetorical practices of domination. *Gyn/Ecology*, perhaps her best-known work, inspires her mostly women readers to bond in friendship in order to overthrow domination by the patriarchy of the church, state, home, and public sphere and by patriarchal rhetoric itself:

> The rulers of patriarchy—males with power—wage an unceasing war against life itself. Since female energy is essentially biophilic, the female spirit/body is the primary target in this perpetual war of

> aggression against life. Gyn/Ecology is the re-claiming of life-loving female energy. This claiming of gynergy requires knowing/naming the fact that the State of Patriarchy is the State of War. . . . Furies/Amazons [women in the Background] must know the nature and conditions of this State in order to dis-cover and create radical female friendship. . . . [W]e must understand that the Female Self is The Enemy under fire from the guns of patriarchy. We must struggle to dis-cover this Self as Friend to all that is truly female, igniting the Fire of Female Friendship. (355)

Daly's epideictic rhetorical feminism merges with the deliberative: she revs up the emotion and looks to a possible future where women join together, systematically ignore men, and make the world a better place. The tactic of rhetorical feminism offers Daly hope and supports her as she reenvisions rhetorical principles, methodically excises patriarchal power, and replaces it with feminine cooperation and agency, knowing full well that she has made the world a better place.

Starhawk

Finally, Starhawk offers another rhetorical feminist example of disidentification, distinguishing her rhetorical practices by their unequivocal subversion of hegemonic ones. For instance, she rejects some of the "basic tenets" of rhetorical theory, as established in Kenneth Burke's "Definition of Man," one being that we humans are "goaded by the spirit of hierarchy (or moved by the sense of order)" (*Language* 16). For her, participation in hierarchy brings only disappointment and disempowerment, for, in such a mindset, individuals must continually "earn" their worth (and their self-worth) through status, material objects, and "power over" others. Experiencing power-over another and sensing another's power-over oneself are conditions evident in traditional rhetorical practices, conditions that perpetuate a feeling of estrangement. But perhaps more pernicious for Starhawk is the fact that "power-over" also resides within our individual selves where it mal/functions as the "self-hater" (Starhawk, *Truth* 16). While earning status is a never-ending process of estrangement, recognizing, and honoring, each individual's inherent worth is an ever-nourishing process of interconnection and mutual commitment. For these reasons, one transactional goal of Starhawk's rhetorical feminism is to affirm the unique spirit that resides in each individual, the life force that binds all humans—and all living things—together. With self-conscious, self-aware rhetorical feminism, she advocates for the integrity and rights of every person.

Starhawk actively disidentifies with the public patriarchal rhetorical world of power-over, aligning, instead, with the often more private world of power-from-within, which she refers to as the spirit world, the world of the Goddess. She knows full well that the word *Goddess* makes many people uneasy, because the word "can be mistaken for the worship of an external being" and "smacks of Paganism, of blood, darkness, and sexuality, of lower powers" (*Dreaming* 4). Nevertheless, she moves ahead with the concept in order to emphasize how "power-from-within *is* the power of the low, the dark, the earth; the power that arises from our blood, and our lives, and our passionate desire for each other's living flesh" (4).

In actively disidentifying with, resisting, and rebelling against traditional rhetorical practices, Starhawk argues for the life-giving qualities of a spiritual rhetorical orientation:

> The political issues of our times are . . . issues of spirit, conflicts between paradigms or underlying principles. If we are not to survive the question becomes: how do we overthrow, not those presently in power, but the principle of power-over? How do we shape a society based on the principle of power-from-within? (*Dreaming* 4)

In these ways, Starhawk's rhetorical feminism is one of power-from-within and power-with-others—decidedly not power-over.

After all, she writes, the history, experience, and presence of women and people of color are negated daily by power-over: "We lose our own sense of self-worth, our belief in our own content" (*Dreaming* 6). And we feel estranged—from one another as well as from the rest of the natural world. Unlike the hegemonic patriarchal sphere, the allegedly marginalized Goddess sphere nurtures "immanence," "the awareness of the world and everything in it as alive, dynamic, interdependent, interacting, and infused with moving energies" (9). Unlike Burke's man, who is "separated from his natural condition by instruments of his own making" (*Language* 16), Starhawk's language-users and language-misusers self-consciously "choose to take this living world, the people and creatures in it, as the ultimate meaning and purpose of life, to see the world, the earth, and our lives as sacred" (*Dreaming* 9). And unlike Burke's man who is "striving for perfection" (*Language* 16), Starhawk's rhetor realizes that "to be human is to be imperfect" (*Dreaming* 42), yet another reason power-from-within and power-with are so important.

A commitment to power-with transforms the rhetorical goal of persuasion, of power-over, into something "more subtle, more fluid and fragile than authority. [Power-with] is dependent on personal responsibility, on our own creativity and daring, and on the willingness of others to respond," a willingness that is respect, "not for a role, but for each person" (Starhawk, *Truth* 11, 10).[8] In *Dreaming the Dark*, Starhawk assures us that "there is a certain element of daring in resistance," all the more reason to rely on one's power-from-within (99). Power-with, power-from-within, immanent worth—these are the concepts Starhawk uses to translate dominating (sometimes oppressive) rhetorical practice into nonhierarchical, mutually respectful communication that honors the Goddess, who "represents the divine embodied in nature, in human beings, in the flesh" (*Dreaming* 9). And it is that divine that supplies our immanent value—and our power.

These rhetorical feminists—who actively disidentify with hegemonic rhetorical theories and write, instead, to and for the provisionally yet systematically marginalized with whom they do identify—offer us a way to cross into a more inclusive and more representative rhetorical future. Like theories, the set of tactics constituting rhetorical feminism are multiple, sometimes even contradictory, but they all represent expansiveness. After all, as Anzaldúa writes, "If we [women] have been gagged and disempowered by theories, we can also be loosened and empowered by theories" ("Haciendo caras" xxv). The many other feminists who follow in this chapter have crossed that bridge as well, establishing new ways of being rhetorical. In addition to successfully executing disidentification, rhetorical feminism works to revise and reinvigorate rhetorical principles, reestablishing the rhetorical appeals and reforming the rhetorical canons of invention and delivery, as the following sections will demonstrate.

Transformations and Transactions

> If the mind were clear
> and if the mind were simple   you could take this mind
> this particular state   and say
> *this is how I would live if I could choose:*
> *this is what is possible.*
>
> —Adrienne Rich, "What Is Possible"

Rhetorical feminists conceive of new possibilities for conceptualizing and delivering their message, whether from the pulpit and platform or from the realms of silence and cyberspace. To do so, they often must remodel, even transform traditional rhetorical practices, purposes, and transactions, as the theorists in this section do so very well. Filmmaker, musician, and theorist Trinh T. Minh-ha serves as the lead example, perhaps because she has not been totally acculturated to Western ways of thinking, having lived in Asia and Africa as well as in the United States. Her unique conceptualization of rhetorical theory provides insight into the true plasticity of the art of rhetoric, the elasticity of language, argument, and "objectivity." Still, Trinh[9] is not the only theorist who transforms rhetorical theory, just as transformation is not the only contribution she makes.

Trinh T. Minh-ha

In some ways, Vietnam-born Trinh is in a class by herself, for she believes that all language—regardless of the source or the destination—is completely hegemonic. Nonetheless, her self-conscious, purposeful transformative theory speaks explicitly to the status of women, people of color, and non-Westerners, rhetorical beings for whom "disrupting the grand narratives of the human sciences becomes a means of survival" (qtd. in Parmar 70). "A straight oppositional discourse," Trinh avers, "is no longer sufficient" (qtd. in Parmar 70). As such, her theory removes itself from hegemonic rhetorical theory by being neither confrontational nor resistant nor disidentifying. For Trinh, disruption works best; accommodation is outside the realm of possibility. Her goal is a transformation of feminist theory, and such transformation "requires a certain freedom to modify, appropriate, and re-appropriate without being trapped in imitation" (*When* 161). Hers is a version of rhetorical feminism, directed to the marginalized, dialogic and transactional, and deeply committed to possibility.

Trinh's theory confounds some academics—what with its exposure of hegemony and intellectual colonizing, its outright dismissal of objectivity, and its acknowledgment that feminism has always been heterogeneous. When questioned about the ways her scholarly work conforms to or resists academic expectations, she replies,

> Academics, infatuated with their own normalization of what constitutes a "scholarly" work, abhor any form of writing that exceeds academic language and whose mode of theorizing is not recognizable,

> hence not classifiable as "theory" according to their standard of judgement. (qtd. in Parmar 68)

Trinh accepts the marginal status of her theory vis-à-vis mainstream feminist thought and surely with regard to the "male-is-norm world" that is "taken for granted as the objective, comprehensive societal world" (*When* 103).

She describes the status of those for whom the stance of objectivity remains so readily available—and assured:

> Highly privileged are those who can happily afford to remain comfortable in the protected world of their own, which neither seems to carry any ambiguity nor does it need to question itself in its mores and measures—its utter narrowness despite its global material expansion. (*When* 159)

"There is necessarily a subjectivity in every objectivity," Trinh argues (qtd. in Penley and Ross 96), thereby joining the ranks of many feminist intellectuals who agree that any illusion of objectivity, ideological neutrality, or gender-neutral epistemology is available only to those who already espouse the dominant ideology. Trinh dismisses outright any illusions of objectivity.

In terms of the rhetorical transaction, Trinh dismantles such familiar components as objectivity as well as instrumentality, clarity, language, truth, meaning, identity, and audience. She even undoes the authenticity of the transaction itself, given what she considers the corruption of thought by patriarchy and hegemony. Patriarchy may hobble intellectual nimbleness, but hegemony

> is most difficult to deal with because it does not really spare any of us. Hegemony is established to the extent that the world view of the rulers is also the world view of the ruled. It calls attention to the routine structures of everyday thought, down to common sense itself. (*When* 148)

"*Rhetoric,* whose aim was to order discourse so as to *persuade,*" writes Trinh, becomes unraveled in the hands of theorists who recognize the power of theory to "upset rooted ideologies," to shake up "established canons" and question "every norm validated as 'natural' or 'human'" (*Woman* 16, 42).

So far as the components of any rhetorical transaction are concerned, Trinh casts off received ideas of the instrumentality of language (or rhetoric) in the first place, acknowledging as she does that even though clarity and correctness ("two old mates of power") have long been equated with that instrumentality, they do not guarantee it (*When* 17). After all, clarity is always ideological and reality always adaptive. Therefore, the demand for clear communication that allegedly reflects reality proves to be nothing else but an intolerance for any language other than the one approved by the dominant ideology. Such is not the case with rhetorical feminism.

Trinh explains, "Language has been reduced to a 'mere vehicle of thought,'" a linguistic act "*used* to orient toward a goal or to sustain an act, but it does not constitute an act in itself" (*When* 16). And she continues to decouple language from rhetoric (from persuasion or communication), for language "only communicates itself *in* itself" (31). Language itself is a hegemonic discourse with hegemonic mechanisms—it is language, nothing more. For these reasons, writing as a woman is "simultaneous engagement and disengagement with master discourses," with entry into the "master's house" a "forced entry" (qtd. in Parmar 71). As such, this task of writing, of using rhetoric, of "releasing oneself from external censorship," though difficult for men, "demands even more from a woman for whom the margin of social acceptability remains minimal" (*When* 130)—unless, of course, they purposefully disidentify with the master discourse, as rhetorical feminists so frequently do.

Her views on truth and meaning, two crucial elements in a rhetorical transaction, also merit attention. Truth and meaning, Trinh tells us, "are likely to be equated with one another. Yet, what is put forth as truth is often nothing more than *a* meaning"[10] (*When* 30). We cannot conjoin meaning with truth, for "truth is produced, induced, and extended according to the regime in power" (30). And the "truth of reason [logos] is not necessarily a lived truth" (qtd. in Penley and Ross 100), especially for women and people of color whose truth and meaning are not recognized by that regime. For Trinh, only destabilized meaning, "at once plural and utterly singular," is authentic, nonhegemonic meaning that does not rely on "any single source of authority" but, rather, "empties it, or decentralizes it" (*When* 41). And such destabilized meaning might actually be truth, for "truth does not make sense; it exceeds meaning and exceeds measure. It exceeds all regimes of truth" (*Woman* 123).

If received notions of truth and meaning can be disregarded, what is the role of the audience in Trinh's rhetorical theory? Once again, Trinh breaks away from the dominant Western system of thought, writing that "meaning can neither be imposed or denied" on or by an audience (*When* 49).

So whether the audience receives, let alone understands, the rhetor's purpose and meaning is beside the point. Furthermore, when rhetors reach for an audience, they most often relate to that audience as though it is a "consumer" of the rhetor's so-called truth and meaning rather than as actual individuals who could—and *should*—productively participate in the resolution of problems, the making of meaning, the consideration of truth.

And as for the rhetor herself? Well, the rhetor's role, complicated by the traditional will to persuade and to displace another's meaning or truth with her own, does not actually rely on logos, on reason, or even on the participation of the audience at all. Traditionally, the rhetor has been monologic, her words complete, rather than dialogic, her thoughts open and unfinished. In most cases, communication is a one-way street with a rhetor driving headlong toward closure. The rhetor, "left intact in its [the rhetor's] positionality and its fundamental urge to decree meaning," considers herself "both as key and as transparent mediator," someone who is "likely to turn responsibility into license" (*When* 48). Driving fast with such a license, traditional rhetors do not always stop to unpack the ideological underpinnings of their stance, let alone of the actual meaning of their communication.

Any discussion of communication and rhetoric circles right back to the rhetorical exigence itself, a term not used by Trinh. She refers, instead, to "conflicts" or "differences" predicated on division, which not only define identities but also are thought to launch communication. To understand difference is to understand a shared responsibility, which requires—at the very least—a willingness on the part of the rhetor to reach out to the Other, to the unknown, with the unfinished message. Difference can move forward a narration, whether it includes sameness or separateness, and it can accommodate a multiplicity of identities, meanings, and truth. Only if the rhetor is able and willing to deal with the unfamiliar can the rhetorical transaction offer language in the service of "an extremely important site of struggle . . . of social change" (qtd. in Parmar 70). Trinh's rhetorical feminism offers us ways to do just that.

Sonja K. Foss and Cindy L. Griffin

A sustained focus on the interaction of women rhetors, feminism, and feminist rhetorical theories and practices has resulted in one of the most influential transformations of the rhetorical transaction itself: Foss and Griffin's 1995 proposal for an "invitational rhetoric." In their proposal for invitational rhetoric, Foss and Griffin build upon the scholarship of many feminist scholars (from Jean Bethke Elshtain and Sally Miller Gearhart to Cheris Kramarae and Sonia Johnson) to propose a new, feminist framework for rhetorical transaction, one that gingerly disidentifies with persuasion, the traditional transaction. Foss and Griffin acknowledge "the patriarchal bias that undergirds most theories of rhetoric," summing up such bias as defining rhetoric in terms of its "persuasive, influential power" ("Beyond Persuasion" 2).

This sustained focus on persuasion, on influencing others, however, has blinded scholars and laypeople alike to the myriad other ways that rhetoric could be successfully used every day. They cite Gregory J. Shepherd, who writes that "interaction processes have typically been characterized essentially and primarily in terms of persuasion, influence, and power" (qtd. in "Beyond Persuasion" 2), building on his definition to expand the parameters of such a process. However, given their commitment to such feminist principles as equality, immanent value, and self-determination, Foss and Griffin propose an alternative to the traditional rhetorical transaction: "Although we believe that persuasion is often necessary, we believe an alternative exists that may be used in instances when changing and controlling others is not the rhetor's goal; we call this rhetoric *invitational rhetoric*" ("Beyond Persuasion" 5).

For Foss and Griffin, invitational rhetoric is a natural outgrowth of feminist rhetorical theory, a "means to create a [mutually informing] relationship" and an "invitation to understanding" (5). The authors continue:

> Invitational rhetoric constitutes an invitation to the audience to enter the rhetor's world and to see it as the rhetor does. In presenting a particular perspective, the invitational rhetor does not judge or denigrate others' perspectives but is open to and tries to appreciate and validate those perspectives, even if they differ dramatically from the rhetor's own. Ideally, audience members accept the invitation offered by the rhetor by listening to and trying to understand the rhetor's perspective and then presenting their own. When this happens, rhetor and audience alike contribute to the thinking of an issue so that everyone involved gains a greater understanding of the issue in its subtlety, richness, and complexity. Ultimately, though, the result of invitational rhetoric is not just an understanding of an issue. Because of the nonhierarchical, nonjudgmental, nonadversarial framework established for the interaction, an understanding of the

> participants themselves occurs, an understanding that engenders appreciation, value, and a sense of equality. (5)

Although written for feminists and rhetoricians, Foss and Griffin's theory of invitational rhetoric is highly accessible, another example of rhetorical feminism. First of all, they disidentify with the traditional focus on persuasion as the *sole* transactional goal of rhetoric both in their writing and in their theory. (*Sole* is the operative term here.) Second, they use simple language in order to reach people on the margins of academia and beyond, demonstrating respect for all readers. And, finally, their belief in the generative qualities of an invitational rhetoric that is dialogic and mutually transformative illustrates their deep commitment to and hope for the power of rhetorical transactions that are based in understanding rather than in persuasion, dominance, and control.

Rather than serving solely as a venue for establishing power over another, invitational rhetoric readily offers other communicative options, rhetorical transactions based on the offering of perspectives, the re-sourcement of energy (particularly negative energy), and the recognition of immanent value, that of the audience and rhetor alike.[11] Thus, the transactional goal of invitational rhetoric is understanding, a goal that can stand alone or complement the goal of persuasion.

Sally Miller Gearhart

Gearhart's 1979 "The Womanization of Rhetoric" was perhaps the first feminist essay to challenge—and vehemently disidentify with—rhetoric's key principle of persuasion, launching a powerful salvo that declared, "Any intent to persuade is an act of violence" (195):

> Of all the human disciplines, [rhetoric] has gone about its task of educating others to violence with the most audacity. The fact that it has done so with language and metalanguage, with refined functions of the mind, instead of with whips or rifles does not excuse it from the mindset of the violent. (195)

By so doing, her work might easily slip under the rubric of "argument," but her insightful transformation of rhetoric's long-held transactional goal makes her work more fitting here. Gearhart's theory unloosened the age-old notion that successful rhetoric equates with winning, dominating, conquering only, for

> [c]ommunication can be a deliberate creation or co-creation of an atmosphere in which people or things, if and only if they have the internal basis for change, may change themselves; it can be a milieu in which those who are ready to be persuaded may persuade themselves, may choose to hear or choose to learn. With this understanding we can begin to operate differently in all communicative circumstances, particularly those wherein *learning* and *conflict encounter* take place. (198)

She argues that rhetoric's goal of persuasion regularly goes so far as to violate the "other" in order to fashion that person in one's own image. In sharp contrast to those classic rhetorical methods of persuasion, Gearhart's confrontational feminist reconceptualization of the rhetorical transaction calls for reimagining the conventional contract between the rhetor and the audience, for thinking of rhetorical practices—transactions—as collaborative, negotiable, cooperative, and based on a willingness "on the deepest level to yield his/her position entirely to the other(s)" (199).

Gearhart prompts innovative, feminist ways to reconsider the transaction between rhetor and audience when she writes, "The change in the discipline of speech from the concentration on speaker/conqueror to an interest in atmosphere, in listening, in receiving, in a collective rather than in a competitive mode—that change suggests the womanization of that discipline" (200–01). For Gearhart, then, authentic change happens only from within—not from an outside force, a rhetorical transaction that disidentifies with the tradition. In addition, her rhetorical feminism relies on personal experience and emotion as sources of knowledge and power, gateways for changing ourselves, the only truly significant contribution we can make to the world around us:

> I'm approaching daily encounters with totally different assumptions that *trying to change other people doesn't work,* that such agitation only muddies the waters and usually makes me feel rotten, particularly when I fail; second, I'm assuming that *cleaning up my own act is the best contribution I can make to any cause;* third, I'm assuming that *what I put out into the world returns to me in like quantity.* . . . I'm astounded at the changes that are taking place in my life as a result of these assumptions. [*Whether the world is changing or not is still an open question, in case that matters.*] ("Notes" 8)

Finally, Gearhart demonstrates her willingness to embrace alternative delivery systems, especially those long considered feminine, another feature of rhetorical feminism. She closes "Notes from a Recovering Activist" with a meditation: "May All That Is grant me the serenity to acknowledge that I cannot change others, the courage to change myself, and the wisdom, in any conflict, to find a third path" (11). In other words, while rhetoric continues to be the study of persuasion, conquest, and conversion of others to the rhetor's ideals, rhetorical feminists know that we can change only ourselves.

Karlyn Kohrs Campbell

Karlyn Kohrs Campbell's 1971 "The Rhetoric of Women's Liberation: An Oxymoron" pushed scholars to recognize the transformation of the discipline itself, what with its being embodied and employed by women—by feminists, no less. At a time when few academics were considering the various fractures and divisions among the various women's liberation activists, Campbell acknowledged yet transcended those internal divisions to concentrate on the second-wave movement holistically, describing its discourse and rhetoric as so disjunctive, so substantively different from traditional rhetorical practices, that "feminist rhetoric" itself was, at the time, an oxymoron:

> Insofar as the role of rhetor entails qualities of self-reliance, self-confidence, and independence, *its very assumption is a violation of the female role.* Consequently, feminist rhetoric is substantively unique by definition, because no matter how traditional its argumentation, how justificatory its forms, how discursive its method, or how scholarly its style, it attacks the entire psychosocial reality, the most fundamental of values, of the cultural context in which it occurs. . . . [C]onsider the apparently moderate, reformist demands by feminists for legal, economic, and social equality, demands ostensibly based on the shared value of equality. . . .
>
> The demand for legal equality arises out of a conflict in values. Women are not equal to men in the sight of the law. ("Rhetoric" 126)

Campbell continues to explain the theoretical and practical ways that the rhetoric of women's liberation actually transforms any concept of a traditional rhetorical transaction:

It seems to me that any audience of such argumentation confronts a moral dilemma. The listener must either admit that this is not a society based on the value of equality or make the overt assumption that women are special or inferior beings who merit discriminatory treatment. (126)

Campbell disidentifies holistic feminist rhetorical practices from traditional masculinist ones on the grounds that the feminist rhetorical practices focus on the contributions of a woman rhetor, whose "social position is [always/already] at odds with fundamental democratic values" of "self-reliance, self-confidence, and independence" embodied by the rhetor, who is, "naturally," a man (126). In short, any woman rhetor, speaking on any subject, is perpetually at odds with the traditional masculinist, aristocratic, public, political rhetor—yet, at the same time, each woman rhetor represents a transformation, a unique instantiation of the discipline. Feminist rhetoric, which asks only that women be considered equal to men—a "moderate, reformist demand"—is considered to be "revolutionary and radical in the extreme" because such rhetoric, just by existing, is perceived to confront if not "attack the fundamental values underlying this culture. The option to be moderate and reformist is simply not available to women's liberation advocates" (127). Disidentification, however, is available.

Twenty-seven years later, in "'The Rhetoric of Women's Liberation: An Oxymoron' Revisited," Campbell critiques her earlier scholarship by updating it. She does not, however, revise her basic argument that rhetorical feminism disidentifies with hegemonic rhetorical practices in one foundational way: women are the rhetors, the actors, the agents in a culture that benefits men. The personal may be political, but the difficulties for women that feel personal are actually systemic: "Feminism is so threatening for women and for men because it involves change in personal relationships as well as systemic changes" ("Rhetoric ... Revisited" 141). For rhetorical feminists to move their agenda ahead, they must recognize and value personal experience, emotion, and mutual understanding as they self-consciously advocate for human rights and social justice. Feminist rhetors' demands for "equality of opportunity in education, professions, and pay [are] assertions of quality and personhood" that fly in the face of traditional masculinist rhetorical and democratic ideals (140). Women have spoken to and from the margins, gradually developing an authentic sense of agency and possibility—despite repeated rhetorical failures in terms of gaining legal and social equality. "Women's willingness to breach decorum remains important, illustrated in more recent times by the activities of the Guerilla Girls" (141). Rhetorical feminists continue to transform rhetorical transactions.

Rhetorical Feminism at the Scene of Argument

Effective argument has long been considered the linchpin of successful persuasion, thought to be the only valid transactional goal of rhetoric. Reasoned discourse, or logic, was believed to be part and parcel of persuading one's opponent. For the most part, any measure of persuasion continues to be calculated according to the effectiveness of the argument's logos, a fifth century BCE term for the artistic appeals (rhetorical or persuasive) that give shape to an argument with good moral, practical, and aesthetic reasons as well as with supportive evidence. Rhetorical feminists, however, have reformulated the artistic appeals as well as expanded the concept of evidence, with experience and emotion given full consideration as such. In rhetorical feminism, ethos and pathos are every bit as important as logos.

In "Beyond Argument in Feminist Composition," Catherine E. Lamb, foreshadowing much of the feminist work to come, maintains that there are many other and more fruitful rhetorical methods than the adversarial, so-called logical method, which privileges "certain forms and language" (13). Rather than depending on monologic argument, she suggests using the practices of negotiation, mediation, invitation, and productive counterargument as well—after all, she writes, argument is the *means,* not the *end.* The end is a fair and satisfying resolution of conflict (11).[12]

Foss and Griffin's invitational rhetoric also expands that singular transactional goal of persuasion to include invitation and understanding, neither of which is solely dependent upon logos. And Gearhart revises that singular goal from winning by violent means (through agonistic and manipulative aims) to co-creation, self-persuasion, often self-initiated change. Using "re-sourcement" (framing the issue differently) and "offering" (freely providing one's vision, one's understanding of the world), she straightforwardly alters the traditional rhetorical goal to accommodate difference and cooperation. These two compelling views on persuasion point to the work of Ellen W. Gorsevski, whose *Peaceful Persuasion: The Geopolitics of Nonviolent Rhetoric* takes us directly into the heart of argument culture, where the power has, for too long, resided solely in the rhetor, whose charge has been to wield logic (or reason) for the sole purpose of changing someone else.[13] Rhetorical feminists, on the other hand, value dialogue, listening, and productive silence.

Gorsevski extends the concept of rhetorical feminism by showcasing the advantages of peaceful persuasion, a process of argumentation in which power, interrelatedness, and inimitable dignity are distributed equally among all participants, rather than resting solely with the monologic logos of the rhetor. Unlike the power-over of traditional argument, understanding and insights are the two major components of peaceful persuasion, components that Gorsevski aligns with the Isocratean "vision of community and influence exerted in the public sphere for the good of all" (50). She argues for the value of such persuasion, particularly in the twenty-first century, with migrations, diasporas, and mobility of all kinds requiring effective communication across cultures, ethnicities, nationalities, and all other axes of difference—and conflict. The expansiveness of peaceful persuasion seems also significant, for the process focuses less on the individual rhetor than on "situational elements inviting reaction on the part of . . . many people" (122). Furthermore, taking into consideration the "rhetorical climate" of peaceful persuasion is also significant, acknowledging, as it does, the emotions and experiences of the people involved.

Gorsevski describes a version of experience—experience-, emotion-, and silence-respecting rhetorical feminism:

> In a rhetorical climate, total *experience* supersedes oratorical texts and unique or socially privileged individuals as the foremost fonts of rhetoric. However inarticulate they may be, involuntary bodily and emotional expressions of frustration, anger, and fear or joy, hope, and kinship cannot be dismissed as outcasts of the rhetorical canon. . . . Embracing feelings and intuitions as rhetorical data enhances rhetorical criticism because it strengthens the critical capacity for revealing material and ideological injustices. The construct of a rhetorical climate helps us to expose the more easily ignored oppressions and socioculturally sanctioned silences that are suffered by children, women and people of minority status. (157)

For Gorsevski and many others, "nonviolent theory offers rhetorical scholars a window of opportunity for revitalizing rhetorical theory and criticism" (160). It suggests a clear antidote to Gearhart's widely accepted argument that hegemonic rhetoric's act of persuasion is a singular act of violence.

Rather than focusing on the logic of the argument itself, peaceful persuasion offers a different set of argumentative means from the rhetoric we all know so well. Gorsevski explains:

> Nonviolent rhetoric often operates on emotional, moral, or ethical levels of reasoning; indeed, it may, at times, exist beyond the bounds of traditional and scientific conceptions of order and logic. We may dismiss nonviolence hastily because nonviolence does not always fulfill the scientific requirement for perfect replicability, cool cynicism, or the desired degree of detachment in order to prove its success. (183)

In extending both a discourse that is uplifting and transformative in the public sphere (99) and one that takes into account the humanity of each participant, nonviolent rhetoric bypasses the "limits of individualistic orientation and enable[s] the critic to assume a more collectivist perspective" (161). Most significant, perhaps, the transactional goals of peaceful persuasion—the acknowledgment of distributed power, respect, and dignity—differ markedly from those of traditional rhetoric.

Whereas the goals (or ends) of mainstream rhetoric may be persuasion or at least the satisfaction that one has made a persuasive argument, the ends of peaceful persuasion include education: "[T]he goal is not to hurt anyone or to use self-sacrifice with abandon, but rather to *educate* people to come to terms and to negotiate with better understanding, as well as with a renewed sense of commonality and humanity" (187). Following Lamb, Gorsevski's rhetorical participants must "understand the range of power relationships available" to them, determining which of those relationships are consistent with an emphasis on "cooperation, shared leadership, and integration of the cognitive and affective"—all to the end of reaching a positive resolution (11). Sustained by hope, rhetorical feminists aim at such a goal.

In other words, by calling on the infinite energy that is plural, collaborative, cooperative, synergistic power (rather than anyone's limited singular power), by calling on the tactic of rhetorical feminism, practitioners of peaceful, nonviolent persuasion offer hope. Rhetorical feminists moor their hope on the belief that a better future is rooted in vision and dependent on our heroic and sustained actions to realize such a future.

Yet a good outcome for all is not always the case. In *Feminism and Affect at the Scene of Argument*, Barbara Tomlinson details the enduring roadblocks to a completed feminist rhetorical transaction. The major obstruction is the "trope of the angry feminist," which precedes women into the public sphere, where their feminist arguments are disabled before they ever begin, an echo of Campbell's feminist rhetoric as oxymoron. In other words, the powerful are not even considering (let alone being swayed by) feminist arguments, especially those spoken by women in the public sphere. Tomlinson writes that "one never encounters the feminist's argument for the first time because it comes already discredited," a move so normalized by the power relations in our culture that it seems "logical" and "fair" (1, 2). Not enough has changed with regard to women's place at the argument table since Campbell's 1971 essay.

Thus, Tomlinson explores ways that power and emotion infuse any scene of argument, for "rhetoric is not a neutral tool that can be wielded effectively by anyone in any context, but rather . . . an effect of power . . . [which] needs to be judged in relation to the interests that it seeks to advance, oppose, or displace" (29). Argument is always a scene of power. Tomlinson explains,

> [C]ritics use strategies authorized by their unacknowledged gendered and racialized status[14] to delegi[ti]mate arguments about structures of dominance, attempting to shut down feminist inquiry through the very strategies of textual vehemence that they purport to condemn when used by feminists. (20)

What rhetorical feminists can do, then, is analyze the scene of argument, explore its resources, constraints, contradictions, power differentials—and potential. The power (and, therefore, politicized) differentials include those resting in gendered, classed, and racialized models of argument, authorship, politeness, and emotion (42). After establishing the scene, rhetorical feminists can then work to open up new possibilities for equitable arguments in which power is distributed, collaboration is presumed, and emotions and experience are considered sources of knowledge. Rhetorical feminists must demonstrate "the covert power of prevailing rhetorics and uninterrogated language conventions as forces complicit in hiding power imbalances" (65), traditional practices that such rhetorical feminists as Anzaldúa, Daly, and Hélène Cixous have revealed—and interrogated. Such traditional language conventions include (but are not limited to) the interpretation of emotional expression as distraction rather than as legitimate rhetorical performance, a masculinist approach to the scene of argument that Tomlinson calls a "highly political act" (62).

Tomlinson shows us a way to leverage revealed power imbalances and use them as a site of contestation for feminist arguers, contestation that releases feminist agency—and many rhetorical feminists have leveraged these power imbalances by offering narrations rather than traditional, rational arguments. Tomlinson illustrates her point with the example of Cynthia K. Gillespie, an attorney for battered women who have killed their husbands. Gillespie has unpacked the power differentials in a courtroom where masculinist practices systematically nullify the judgments and testimony of women already victimized by domestic violence as well as those of the women attorneys who represent them. Gillespie actively disidentifies with those masculinist courtroom practices. Rather than argue court decisions, previous violations, reasons for her clients' fear, and possible outcomes, Gillespie strategically catalogs instances of violence into a narrative, as though she is telling a story rather than arguing a legal case. To that end, Gillespie draws on "specificity combined with repetitive excess" (67), using language as if it were neutral, as she recounts the inventory of violence that constitutes her cases:

> There were, of course, many women who had been stabbed, cut, shot, and pistol-whipped.... [The tally of weapons] included pistols, shotguns, knives, machetes, golf clubs, baseball bats, electric drills, high-heeled shoes, sticks, frying pans, electric sanders, toasters, razors, silverware, ashtrays, drinking glasses and beer mugs, bottles, burning cigarettes, hair brushes, lighter fluid and matches, candlestick holders, scissors, screwdrivers, ax handles, sledgehammers, chairs, bedrails, telephone cords, ropes, work boots, belts, door knobs, doors, boat oars, cars and trucks, fish hooks, metal chains, clothing (used to smother and choke), hot ashes, hot water, hot food, dishes, acid, bleach, vases, rocks, bricks, pool cues, box fans, books, and as one woman described her husband's typical weapons, "anything handy." (qtd. in Tomlinson 67–68)

Gillespie's inventory serves to distance Gillespie-as-rhetor from the emotional impact of the stories behind the weapons (a machete, for instance). Her cool recitation of weapons of domestic violence allows her to enter the realm of juridical argument (where women, their emotions, and their women-advocates are not valued in any story), where she can transform the scene of argument, "exploiting narrative conventions" in order to provide a more compelling narrative than the faulty legal narratives of the defense (66). This rhetorical feminist relies on the power of experience and emotion used as reason. (See Jaggar and outlaw emotions below.)

Though unpleasant, conflicts offer the potential to be productive. To that end, Tomlinson writes, "We can learn a great deal about the things that divide us and that might sporadically and strategically unite us by looking to the scene of argument and seeing how agency emerges there in the context of what we must contest" (199). Tomlinson encourages us to analyze carefully, exposing and critiquing the moving parts of the argument that signal positions of unequal power. Such feminist rhetorical analysis stimulates hope (in spite of the evidence) by generating a rhetorical feminism that creates a "more just, decent, and honorable world" (195).

Rhetorical Feminism at the Scene of Delivery

So far in this chapter, I have focused mainly on theories rooted in invention, theories that help us think differently about how to find things out and analyze them. Because all the rhetorical canons (invention, arrangement, style, memory, and delivery) culminate in delivery, delivery, too, offers feminist rhetoricians fresh and generative ways to invigorate our field.

From the second century BCE onward, rhetoric has been disciplined by concepts of delivery, with Cato the Elder's concept of the "good man speaking well" circulating as the means to fuse eloquence and virtue (qtd. in Quintilian 12.1.1). Aristotle describes delivery as "a matter of the right management of the voice to express the various emotions" yet laments the necessity of paying "attention to the subject of delivery," when the ideal would be "fight[ing] our case with no help beyond the bare facts: nothing ... should matter except the proof of these facts" (*Rhetoric* III.1). But, indeed, everything else matters, especially delivery, as it is the combination and culmination of all five canons. When asked to list the three most important components of rhetoric, Demosthenes is said to have replied, "Delivery, delivery, delivery" (qtd. in Quintilian 11.3.2).

In speaking, delivery has been reduced to Aristotle's volume of sound, modulation of pitch, and rhythm (*Rhetoric* III.1), which Cicero calls the "language of the body" (*Oratore* 17.55). And in writing, it has been reduced to format, genre, documentation, citation, and layout. Of course, to claim authority and rhetorical agency, many feminists adhere to the stylistic conventions of delivery that "devalue personal experience in favor of

THEORIES

'objective' facts, 'rational' logic, and established authorities" (Ede, Glenn, and Lunsford 423).

Feminist Resistance to Traditions of Delivery

But feminist theorists have been loosening the foundations of rhetorical delivery—speaking and writing—for decades, specifically in the ways traditional criteria for a successful delivery have elided women. Perhaps the French feminists are best known for disrupting traditional rhetorical delivery in the 1970s and 1980s with their radical concept of *écriture feminine* (writing the woman's body).[15] Feminist theorists are also reclaiming forms of delivery that mainstream rhetorical theorists have dismissed: oral histories, diaries and journals, schoolwork, course curricula, fashion guides, scientific papers, architectural plans, committee minutes, silence and listening.[16] These scholars are resisting the traditional, masculinist criteria for delivery as well as the steady focus on *public* address, a realm historically denied to women. Ever since American suffragists violated convention by establishing themselves as public, political feminist rhetorical activists, US women have regularly (but not as regularly as men) inhabited the public sphere of rhetoric, where they deliver their spoken and written messages, often fusing their own unique style with their delivery. Sojourner Truth's appearance at the 1851 Woman's Rights Convention serves as a case in point. Truth is one of a long line of rhetorical women who have renegotiated the rules of delivery, with Hillary Rodham Clinton the most recent and widely known, rebuked as she so often is for not smiling enough, for not having the so-called natural warmth and platform congeniality of former presidents Clinton or Obama, and for not having the ability to "connect" that President Trump allegedly has.

But as feminists have proved, public speaking and writing are not the only rhetorical venues available to women, not the only delivery systems necessary for rhetorical success—despite the Western emphasis on speech as a gift from the gods. If speech is the singular defining characteristic of humans—is what makes us human—then women's effacement from the public sphere of speaking complicates the enthymematic conclusion. After all, the authorization of speech as the medium of culture and power was determined millennia ago by powerful, public, and often political men.

Reacting to a world that "operates by the standards set up by men," Radha S. Hedge investigates the link between women's agency and rhetorical delivery: "Theoretical [masculinist] frames that assume an individual's complete control over action [are] highly problematic," especially "when representing women's experiences" (310). People never have complete control of their agency, and, for women, the situation is often more complicated. In other words, public speaking and writing are not always feasible options for women because their agency is "subject to curtailment through the control of discursive practices that reinscribe and reproduce [their] positions of subordination" (310). To explain her assertion, Hedge invokes actor-network theory, reminding her readers that "agency is not the possession of any one individual, human or otherwise, but instead is located within a vast and varied network of humans, objects, and discourses that constantly evolves in response to changing linkages among disparate elements" (19). Willingness is one part of agency, to be sure, but capacity within a specific context is every bit as important. Agency is embodied and kairic, dependent upon both the rhetor's identity and the context (the material conditions, tradition, and audience) within which the rhetor acts, reacts, and interacts.

Some contemporary rhetorical feminists are analyzing the relationship between agency and rhetorical delivery, working specifically to represent perspectives and positions of underrepresented groups: choosing silence, being silenced, and listening actively. Resistance is often expressed in the agency of women, whose silence is one indication of their "quiet determination to contest male domination" and "intrusions in the private spheres of their everyday lives" (Hedge 313). Silence serves as a tool of resistance, as empowered action, as agency. Yet because the positive features of silence and listening have rarely been foregrounded as rhetorical arts vital to our communicative effectiveness (let alone our agency), these rhetorical positions and perspectives have been regarded as natural positions of subordination (or so our cultural logics have convinced us), inhabited by the marginalized, the weak, the uneducated, and, of course, women.

Silence and Listening as Rhetorical Delivery

In their exploration of those spheres inhabited by the subaltern, rhetorical feminists who use and respect alternative delivery systems, especially those long considered feminine, have begun to scrutinize silence and listening as authentic sites of rhetorical delivery and as possible tactics of persuasion. Based on her work with battered women in South India, Hedge points to speech and silence as sites of rhetorical delivery where power differentials are both constructed and accepted, calling silencing "an instrument to force women to accept and enact the patriarchal order" and silence as resonating with much more meaning than "powerlessness and passivity. It can also be courage and quiet determination, a form of resistance" (313). Though gendered passive and feminine, silence and listening carry potential, as Marsha Houston and Cheris Kramarae make clear; they also complicate the delivery of silence as much more than submission. To wit, silence can also indicate rhetorical agency and invention, a place to contemplate one's positionality. In addition, of course, "[b]reaking out of silence means more than being empowered to speak or to write, it also means controlling the form as well as the content of one's own communication, the power to develop and share one's own unique voice" (Houston and Kramarae 389).

In *Unspoken: A Rhetoric of Silence*, I, too, investigate the rhetorical delivery of silence and silencing, parsing the gendered power differentials in play in each site, with the choice of remaining silent always a more powerful (or masculine) rhetorical position than that of being silenced (a feminine, or subordinate, position). In these ways, silence *as a rhetoric* is a

> constellation of symbolic strategies that (like spoken language) serves many functions. This is not to say that silence is always strategic, empowering, or patently engaging. Not all silence is particularly potent. However, silence is too often read as simple passivity in situations where it has actually taken on an expressive power. Employed as a tactical strategy or inhabited in deference to authority, silence resonates loudly along corridors of purposeful language use. Whether choice or im/position, silence can reveal positive or negative abilities, fulfilling or withholding traits, harmony or disharmony, success or failure. Silence can deploy power; it can defer to power. It all depends. (xi)

Yes, it all depends—just like the use of the public, spoken language.

Krista Ratcliffe has taken up the delivery of rhetorical listening, imagining listening as a productive pathway to rhetorical invention; as such, it is a conscious performance that has four functions: (a) it promotes *an understanding of self and other,* serving as it does as one means of rhetorical negotiation; (b) it proceeds *from within an accountability logic,* taking for granted that "all people necessarily have a stake in each other's quality of life"; (c) it locates *identifications across commonalities and differences,* inviting us to consciously "locate our identifications in places of commonalities *and* differences"; and (d) it analyzes *claims as well as the cultural logics within which claims function,* inviting listeners to "acknowledge both claims and cultural logics" (*Rhetorical* 27, 31, 32, 33).

For Ratcliffe and me, rhetorical silence and listening resound with much more meaning than the most-often-presumed passivity, obedience, agreement, or boredom. Both methods of rhetorical delivery can be active sites of rhetorical invention as well, integral components of rhetorical persuasion, understanding, invitation, or deliberation—all features of rhetorical feminism. These means of rhetorical delivery and invention also lend themselves to collaboration, mediation, pedagogy, cross-cultural recognition, and other ways to connect with ourselves and others, as our work *Silence and Listening as Rhetorical Arts* demonstrates.

Written from the viewpoint of various subaltern groups (such as minorities, political federations, non/native speakers of English, hurricane survivors, and systematically ignored historical and/or rhetorical women), the nearly twenty essays in *Silence and Listening as Rhetorical Arts* extend and complicate both Ratcliffe's and my own scholarly claims. The essays illuminate the ways silence and listening are as vital to rhetoric as the traditionally emphasized arts of reading, writing, and speaking. They analyze the ways contextualized silence and listening represent the cultural stances and power of both dominant and marginalized groups. Furthermore, these essays offer us multiple ways to enhance our teaching, negotiations, deliberations, and coalitions, whether in dyadic or group settings. If rhetoric is the art of finding things out and getting them across, then these essays illustrate the many ways that both silence and listening function as rhetorical arts, despite the fact that they have traditionally gone unvalued if not ignored or dismissed altogether.

The implications of silence and listening for traditional rhetorical theory are substantive, as these two arts represent a major feminist challenge to the presumption that persuasion is rhetoric's *sole* transactional goal. In addition, research into silence and listening opens up other sites of rhetorical delivery—and rhetorical invention—that elide that goal, sites such as contemplation (even beyond the strategic contemplation of Gesa Kirsch and Jacqueline Jones Royster), reflection, meditation, negotiation, empathy, emotion, and inquiry. Often gendered as power differentials, these sites of delivery and invention nonetheless provide the spaciousness necessary for the rhetor to acknowledge her own embodied experiences and perspectives as well as those of the audience—all within a specific context and moment. In these ways, "listening," Lisbeth Lipari tells us, "entails the recognition of another self, the startling presence of another being, a not-self," and, as such, can ethically enact a "recognition of an unknown other to whom we are bound and about whom we feel care and concern" (176).

As tactics of rhetorical feminism, silence and listening can make the space necessary for rhetors and audience members alike to question and challenge the limits of a traditional delivery and invention: they can begin to see differently, to notice the previously unseen, to connect through dialogue, conversation, and mutual dialectic. In the process, the participants in such a rhetorical exchange transform their blind spots, their "trained incapacities," into the virtue of an enlightened "perspective by incongruity," enriching and enlarging the rhetorical transaction (Veblen; Burke, *Permanence* 7).

Rhetorical Feminism and the Feminine

Feminist Rhetorical Responses to Ethos

Aristotle defines *ethos* as the "personal goodness revealed by the speaker" —as the *power* of the speaker's character—which "may almost be called the most effective means of persuasion he possesses" (*Rhetoric* I.2.12).[17] Contemporary rhetoricians think of ethos as the rhetor's ability to demonstrate goodwill, good sense, and good moral character, as though ethos is the sole province and production of the rhetor. However, ethos requires an audience, for it is established or created only in the relationship between the rhetor and the audience, the community. In other words, ethos does not reside in individual rhetors but in the ways they reflect the characteristics and qualities that are valued by their audience, culture, or community.

Complicating the concept of ethos further is Ratcliffe's feminist analysis, which concludes that ethos has, for the most part, been "linked to a . . . rugged white male individualist" (*Rhetorical* 124), a description that erases women, as Ratcliffe explains:

> The sight of women or the sound of feminists behind the bar or in the pulpit has almost always evoked resistance before they could ever utter a word, or The Word. . . . So women and feminists have traditionally had to argue for their right to speak or write in a public forum about private and public concerns. (*Anglo-American Challenges* 20)

Women often anticipate that they will be disregarded (if not disdained) by the very group or culture whose listening they seek. After all, "misogyny is still an accepted means for discrediting and attempting to silence women's speech" (Daniell and Guglielmo 89). So what are the options for women rhetors who want to establish a favorable ethos?

It is just this conundrum that the editors of *Rethinking Ethos: A Feminist Ecological Approach to Rhetoric* address. Throughout their collection, Kathleen J. Ryan, Nancy Myers, and Rebecca Jones work to reengage the relationship among a woman rhetor's ethos, her agency, the audience or community, and the ecology of her rhetorical situation. They describe the possible ways women can successfully establish a purposeful, even successful, ethos:

> Women can seek agency individually and collectively to *interrupt* dominant representations of women's ethos, to *advocate* for themselves and others in transformative ways, and to *relate* to others, both powerful and powerless. These three terms, *interrupt, advocate,* and *relate,* offer broad descriptive categories for the kinds of ethē [pl. of ethos] women adopt and the rhetorical strategies they employ, often in resistance to more static constructions of ethos privileged by normalizing expectations. (3)

Interrupting, advocating, and relating are all ways for women rhetors to shift the expectation from the individualistic ethos that is validated by the community status quo to an agential ethos that works for the betterment of the community. After all, the editors assure us, "ethos is neither solitary or fixed. Rather, ethos is negotiated and renegotiated, embodied and communal, co-constructed and thoroughly implicated in shifting power dynamics" (11).

In this collection, all the contributors emphasize the dual importance of location (rhetorical situation) and relation (the counterpublic sphere of subordinate status): "[W]omen rhetors take this understanding of [their] subordinate status, relative to knowledge of the entire communicative landscape, and use it to craft a viable *ethos* for participation in a dominant public" (4). With these purposeful moves, the editors unveil their concept of a feminist ecological approach to rhetoric that focuses on ethos, how it is established by the woman rhetor, how it is perceived by her audience, and what the consequences are thereof—and they do so by using tactics of rhetorical feminism.

Rhetorical Feminism and Feminine Style(s)

When Bonnie J. Dow and Mari Boor Tonn write about "feminine style," a rhetorical theory they credit to Campbell, they show how a disidentifying feminine rhetorical delivery can flip hierarchy and persuasion on their masculinist heads. These scholars demonstrate new goals for the rhetorical transaction, goals derived from an orientation used in "deliberating about and forming judgments toward practical affairs" (300n1). Using the example of former Texas governor Ann Richards, rhetor par excellence, Dow and Tonn explain how a rhetor's feminine style promotes audience empowerment at the same time that it "critiques traditional grounds for political judgment," contributes to the "feminist counter-public sphere," and "enhances our understanding of potential resistance to the implicit discourses of power that shape our culture" (286–87).

My own work on Richards focuses on what is now her best-known speech, the 1988 keynote address to the National Democratic Convention. Richards immediately established a connection with her physical and television audience (many of whom would be her Spanish-speaking Texas constituents) by speaking in the vernacular: "Good evening, ladies and gentlemen. *Buenos noches, mis amigos.*" From that moment forward, Richards carefully avoided elitism, agonism, and paternalism, enacting instead a fierce "maternalism" that was the trademark of all her speeches, as was her use of homely examples and her straightforward common sense that lent to an easy accessibility. Her favorite, oft-used line was, "Tell it so my mama in Waco can understand it."

At every speaking opportunity, she testified to the benefits of inclusion, cooperation, and connection, reaching out to women worried about their families, grandmothers yearning for a better life for their generations, and feminists who joined Richards in hoping that her own granddaughter Lily may never believe that "there was a time when blacks could not drink from public water fountains, when Hispanic children were punished for speaking Spanish in the public schools, and women couldn't vote" (Richards). Richards's feminine style, her rhetorical feminism, then, worked to bolster her ethos, just as it validated the emotions and knowledge that came from direct experience (as Anzaldúa's writings so beautifully demonstrate as well).

Following Campbell's definition of a feminist rhetoric, then, Dow and Tonn describe feminine style as "discourse that displays a personal tone, uses personal experience, anecdotes and examples as evidence, exhibits inductive structure, emphasizes audience participation, and encourages identification between speaker and audience" (287). Their theoretical point is well taken: because the feminine style has for too long been relegated to the private sphere of concreteness, participation, cooperation, and relationship maintenance, mainstream rhetorical scholars have ignored the power, efficacy, and significance of so-called feminine style. Mainstream scholars have relied, instead, on the conventional rhetorical theories at play in the public sphere, theories of abstraction, hierarchy, domination, and problem solving (288). But Richards's public-sphere rhetorical performances serve to showcase the empowering positive energy (and outcomes) of a feminine style that provides "an alternative political philosophy," reflects "feminine ideals of care, nurturance, and family relationships," and functions as a "critique of traditional political reasoning that offers alternative grounds of political judgment" (289). These feminist theorists show us how nurturing trust in connection and relationships (the rhetor's as well as the audience's) can constitute the foundation of a successful public, though often critical, political rhetoric. Dow and Tonn conclude their essay with the reminder that a critical rhetoric strives to "understand the discursive operations of power and domination" while also investigating "positive alternatives to the discourse of power," which is exactly what theories and practices of the feminine style do so very well (299). And because style, ethos, and emotion all interanimate, they all offer an iteration of rhetorical feminism that serves as an alternative to the discourse of power.

Rhetorical Feminism and Emotion

Rhetorical feminists consider the power of emotion (pathos) to effect change in invention, style, and delivery as well as in the rhetorical appeals. For instance, when Ratcliffe explains how a woman's subordination can affect her ethos and the effectiveness of her arguments, she makes the apt connection between feminist theories of ethos and feminist theories of emotion: "That these improbable impossibilities (read 'private emotional pleas') might possess logics of their own is an unpopular notion that public opinion is not often willing to acknowledge, let alone explore" (*Anglo-American Challenges* 19). She reminds us (following Jane Tompkins) that even though Western epistemology allows "no space for the emotional," the prohibition does nothing to eradicate the emotional. Rather, such an obvious exclusion only mystifies the

> power of the emotional by hiding it in the negative and renaming it *il*logical, *ir*rational, *non*sensical, *un*true, *in*valid—all of which occupy space. As a result, emotional appeals are rendered as improbable

THEORIES

> impossibilities. Because their logic does not neatly fit the dominant logic of the masses, feminists are often labelled "mad" or "angry," accused of giving way to emotional tirades, and dismissed as having no sense of humor. Such labels and accusations deny the validity and importance of feminists' different emotional appeals. (*Anglo-American Challenges* 19–20)

For feminist rhetoricians, what counts as authentic emotional appeal (pathos) has focused only on the discourse that placates a masculinist audience, an emotional appeal that produces certain frames of mind, that elicits feelings already residing in the audience. (Tomlinson, of course, makes similar arguments about the use of emotion at the scene of argument.)

Aristotle tells us that "[t]he Emotions are all those feelings that so change men as to affect their judgements," thereby linking emotion to change, action, and doing (*Rhetoric* II.1.20). And he also advises that since "[o]ur judgments when we are pleased and friendly are not the same as when we are pained and hostile," rhetors should strive to provoke such positive feelings as "pleasure and happiness, friendliness and calm" in our audience (*Rhetoric* I.2.15, II.1.32). Mainstream rhetoricians, however, remain skeptical of emotions, deriding and dismissing them as illogical, unreasonable.[18] One roadblock to accepting the power, agency, and validity of all emotions is that women's and feminists' emotions do not always elicit the familiar or positive feelings that Aristotle's audience would have them do. Tomlinson's scholarship on the "trope of the angry feminist" makes crystal clear the disconnect between feminists' emotions and the pleasure of Aristotle's audience. Ignoring, discounting, and dismissing the emotional tenor of feminist (or women's) arguments serves as yet another instantiation of masculinist power and privilege. (See Jaggar below.)

The ancients taught us that reason (logos) was superior, emotion (pathos) inferior. Plato's charioteer used reason to keep the horses of rationality and emotion under control as they proceeded toward enlightenment (*Phaedrus* 246–254e). Aristotle's humans are distinguished by their ability to reason, for "rational desires are those which we are induced to have" (*Rhetoric* I.11.25–26). And their rational animals were, of course, men: "One quality or action is nobler than another if it is that of a naturally finer being: thus a man's will be nobler than a woman's" (I.9.17). Reason has thus been rendered masculine, public, the universal (or superior); emotion feminine, private, the individual (or inferior). Therefore, the so-called problem with women's or feminists' rhetorical use of emotion is just that: it is emotion, it is women's, it is inferior.

Mainstream rhetorical displays have always included emotion. Why else would we have a catalog of great speeches by famous men, rhetorical displays that achieved authentic pathos, that stirred the feelings of the audience (within a reasonable limit)? Yet only reason (logos) has been considered the indispensable faculty for acquiring knowledge, for persuading. Not emotion.[19] Well, *maybe* emotion, if its power is (attempted to be) harnessed by intellect, by reason, and by logos.

Drawing on precepts of rhetorical feminism, Alison M. Jaggar writes provocatively about the suppression of emotion as an epistemology, linked as it has been with "non-rational and often irrational urges that regularly [sweep] the body. . . . Emotions happen to or [are] imposed upon an individual, something she suffer[s] rather than something she [does]" ("Love" 152). Reason, on the other hand, has been linked to scientific knowledge, objectivity, empirical testability, positivism, the "paradigm of genuine knowledge": "positivism stipulated that trustworthy knowledge could be established only by methods that neutralized the values and emotions of individual scientists" (152).

Jaggar, however, helps us understand the rational underpinnings of some emotions, describing them as "cognitive techniques designed to help us to think differently about situations" (158). In general, we humans do not want to consider our emotions to be rational, deliberate—as active engagements. Rather we tend to want them to be natural, spontaneous. Otherwise, how can our emotions of anger, annoyance, or joy be genuine? Jaggar explains that emotions are actually "ways in which we engage actively and even construct the world. They have both 'mental' and 'physical' aspects, each of which conditions the other" (159). In fact, "emotions provide the experiential basis for values" and vice versa, for "emotions and evaluations . . . are logically or conceptually connected" (159). Jaggar skillfully couples emotion with reason when she explains the ways "emotion presupposes an evaluation," arguing that any evaluation implies that all who share that evaluation also share the same emotional response (160). In addition to evaluation, emotion also links with observation, which is "not simply a passive process of absorbing impressions" but is "an activity of selection and interpretation" that is influenced by emotional attitudes (160).

Like many other rhetorical feminists, Jaggar moves toward the powerful conclusion that emotions have an instrumental and intrinsic value to our judgment, our reasoning, a value for every human being, especially for those who feel marginalized. There is no objectivity, no scientific evaluation, no unmitigated reason or logic—all of these so-called positivist stances are colored by our emotional responses to the situation, regardless of how disciplined we are in trying to control, suppress, or otherwise ignore our emotions. In response, the scientific method (positivist epistemology) relies on the logic of replicability for the justification of conclusion, replicability serving as the criterion "believed capable of eliminating or cancelling out . . . emotional as well as evaluative biases on the part of individual investigators" (162). After all, few scientists have compelling motives for validating another's scientific study; they recreate the original experiment to see if it is valid. Methods and methodologies prevail, for the most part. But despite such attempts to neutralize emotional and evaluative bias, replicability cannot filter out generally accepted social or scientific values.[20] Jaggar puts her argument into historical context:

> Only hindsight allows us to identify clearly the values that shaped the science of the past and thus to reveal the formative influence on science of pervasive emotional attitudes, attitudes that typically went unremarked at the time because they were shared so generally. (162)

To bring home her point that all objectivity is steeped in subjectivity, in emotion, in socially constructed values, Jaggar observes that the modern Western conception of science, "which identifies knowledge with power and views it as a weapon for dominating nature, reflects the imperialism, racism, and misogyny of the societies that created it" (163).

Finally, Jaggar calls for recognition of the mutually constitutive models of reason and emotion that illuminate the human nature of scientific and logical inquiry. Such models shatter the impossible dream of dispassionate inquiry at the same time that they shatter the abiding Western, masculinist ideology of reason as dominant (for the culturally, socially, intellectually superior) and emotion as subordinate (for everyone else). These models may crack these ideologies, but I am not convinced they shatter them—not yet, anyway.

"Outlaw" emotions, which Jaggar defines as "conventionally unacceptable" emotions, are those displayed by subordinated individuals, including women, who are "unable to experience the conventionally prescribed emotions" called for by commonplace racist jokes, sexual innuendos, and dominant religious beliefs ("Love" 166). Feminist emotions—women's emotions—are often outlaw emotions, for these women simply do not respond normatively to the alleged status quo. And yet, as Jaggar writes elsewhere, such outlaw emotions, "available from the standpoint of the subordinated," offer a perspective on reality that is actually "more reliable" (*Feminist Politics*, ch. 11). But even with (or maybe because of) their reliable, finely tuned emotional responses to and their insightful evaluations of the status quo, women and feminists are regularly dismissed, ignored, and diminished for their emotional responses to a "cruelly racist, capitalist, and male-dominated society that has shaped our bodies and our minds, our perceptions, our values and emotions, our language, and our systems of knowledge" ("Love" 170).

In other words, emotion and reason are not mutually exclusive faculties of the mind; they are, instead, mutually supportive cognitive abilities that shape us as we actively and productively engage in our personal, social, and political lives. Emotions, a key feature of rhetorical feminism, cannot be discounted.[21] Nor can they be separated from reason. Emotion and reason go together.

In "Disciplining the Feminine," Carole Blair, Julie R. Brown, and Leslie A. Baxter provide a case study in using emotions as evidence (as reason) in their response to a 1992 *Communication Quarterly* report, authored by men, that evaluated and ranked "Active Prolific Female Scholars in Communication."[22] In a rhetorical feminist act of disidentification, Blair, Brown, and Baxter call out this report as a "thematic marker of masculinist ideology" (384). The initial iteration of the women's response to men's report was rejected on the grounds that their response was biased, feminist; in other words, it was emotionally charged and revealed their convictions. So the women revised and resubmitted, enacting many of the feminist (and feminine) stances that Jaggar describes: speaking from a subordinate position; experiencing the same emotions despite remarkable professional dissimilarities; using emotions to gauge evaluations and vice versa; and identifying and confronting hierarchy, dominance, and gender-normed practices and cultural norms. In other words, the women used emotion as an analytic tool. Their purpose was to reveal the cultural and professional norms underpinning the publication of such an evaluation and ranking of women scholars, a publication that revealed both their "discipline's continuing fascination with identifying the most prolific scholars" (a fascination these three women find misguided) and the very "chilly climate" that confronts women faculty in every academic discipline (387, 388).

Blair, Brown, and Baxter describe the reviews of their original response essay as "unusually explicit manifestations of the apparatuses that sustain and enable those [masculinist] ideological themes" (384). The authors are passionate (if not altogether dismayed), and they evaluate the entire discipline of communication, calling out the dominant masculinist paradigm of publishing, career trajectory, research content, competition, reasoning, and measurement as detrimental to women's role and influence in the field. The women are especially vehement with regard to the absence of rationale for this study, given its potential to harm faculty, women and men alike: "Without any clear warrant, three men have conducted surveillance on women's research records . . . and proceeded to rank order the most prolific among them," a process Blair, Brown, and Baxter equate with "the academic equivalent of a beauty pageant" (394). Given their ideologically based objections, they remind their readers that if such mainstream, hegemonic research projects as "Active Prolific Female Scholars" are allowed to prevail, if feminist responses such as theirs are silenced, then "we will return to the era (if, in fact, we ever left it) that witnessed feminist study of *any* kind declared to be outside the mainstream" (388, 402).

Their emotions are high—and their evaluations are on point. Therefore, or so these authors predict, their experience-based, emotionally tinged arguments will probably go unheard.

Laura R. Micciche explores the role of emotion in our professional rhetorical lives, linking its use (following Aristotle) with change, judgment, action, and doing. In *Doing Emotion: Rhetoric, Writing, Teaching*, Micciche focuses on emotions as "technologies for *doing*" (14; emphasis added). *Emotion* functions as her key term because "it best evokes the potential to enact and construct, name and defile, become and undo—to perform meanings and to stand as a marker for meanings that get performed. These are rhetorical activities" (14). Successfully decoupling emotion from weakness, irrationality, individuality, and intellectual chaos, Micciche explains the role emotion plays in critical thinking, invention, reasoning, evaluation, and knowledge production—the cognitive moves that other feminist scholars, such as Jaggar; Tompkins; Ratcliffe; and Blair, Brown, and Baxter, also establish for emotion. Like them, Micciche, too, argues for emotion as a socially constructed phenomenon that "binds the social body together as well as tears it apart" (14).

And like other rhetorical feminists, Micciche is also dismayed that reason continues to overshadow emotion, when both reason and emotion can serve as judicious, practical mental resources and reflections of cultural ideology—as well as discourses of both oppression and resistance. When she writes about emotion and writing program administration (WPA) work, Micciche focuses on disappointment, an evaluative emotion reasonably reached by way of comparing the status of men and women doing WPA work: men are paid more, are tenured more often, and are publishing at much higher rates than their women counterparts ("More"). Women WPAs, on the other hand, are usually counted on to collaborate and mentor more as well as to deliver much more of the emotional labor necessary for administering a successful program and employing satisfied workers, whether staff, faculty, or students. Therefore, men administrators are perceived as having status, whereas women WPAs are merely doing "women's work"—"not serious, rigorous, or intellectual" but "emotional" work that goes unvalued (441). Her disappointment in WPA work is an "outlaw emotion," to be sure, a threat to the status quo, and yet an authentic, reasonable, purposeful act of sparking change. For Micciche, "disappointment erects obstacles to the hopefulness . . . necessary to sustain teachers and learners" (454).

Indeed, rhetorical feminists rely on hope, despite knowing full well that it cannot solve all material realities or overcome all roadblocks. But hope can push us forward, and the socially constructed obstacle of disappointment can be overcome by the socially constructed pathway that is hope: "Hope is an emotional investment that we develop collaboratively; it is an act of mutuality that is nourished by our collective expectations" (Micciche, "More" 454), thus leaving Micciche facing the big question of "whether, en route to hope," we can speak candidly about "professional inequities and disappointments without being regarded as doomsayers" (454–55). Rhetorical feminists might well consider the emotion of disappointment—not as a sentiment of weakness or subordination but rather as a judgment, an action, an inquiry that leads directly to hope. Disappointment is a meditation on hope.

Feminist Responses to Feminist Rhetorical Theories

> I have seen a woman sitting
> between the stove and the stars
> her fingers singed from snuffing out the candles
> of pure theory
>
> —Adrienne Rich, "Divisions of Labor"

THEORIES

Given that most rhetorical theorists—women and men alike—are tethered to the "best" of a rhetorical tradition, the most intrepid feminist rhetorical theorists have found ways to loosen those ties in order to open up the possibilities for invigorating rhetorical theory. One way they have done so has been to turn away from a singular set of rhetorical practices and focus, instead, on human communication. The early 1980s psychological-development work of Carol Gilligan was, of course, a game changer in terms of feminist rhetorical theory in that Gilligan found that women—in contrast to men—define themselves "in a context of human relationship" and "judge themselves in terms of their ability to care" (*Different* 17). Studies that had long touted moral development as culminating in concerns with persuasion and being right, studies that were considered to be "universal" in their findings, were actually studies that had elided women and girls all along. In general, boys and men use language along the continuum of moral development to demonstrate their persuasive abilities—but not everyone does. Girls and women, Gilligan determined, are more concerned (than are men and boys, in general) with using language for connecting and caring; therefore, they use their language to those ends.[23] Most adolescent girls, she found, negotiate their relationships through an ethic of care rather than by establishing dominance and subordination, long the practices of hegemonic rhetoric. Gilligan was one of many who tilted the trajectory of rhetorical theories.

The research and practice of Mary Field Belenky, Blythe McVicker Clinchy, Nancy Rule Goldberger, and Jill Mattuck Tarule culminated in the 1986 publication of *Women's Ways of Knowing: The Development of Self, Voice, and Mind,* in which the authors constructed five basic ways that women come to know, starting with silence and listening (rhetorical arts that rhetorical feminists have developed) and culminating in constructed knowledge, which the authors define as "a position in which women view all knowledge as contextual, experience themselves as creators of knowledge, and value both subjective and objective strategies for knowing" (15). Most relevant to rhetorical theory is the authors' advice for those who want to nurture the development of women's authentic voices: "emphasize connection over separation, understanding and acceptance over assessment, and collaboration over debate"—rhetorical stances that again diverge sharply from, at the same time that they implicitly critique, hegemonic rhetorical practices (229).

As all the theory in this chapter makes clear, rhetorical feminism is thriving and making valuable inroads into rhetorical thinking, what with the development and implementation of theories that are dialogic (inviting speaking, listening, and re/consideration), transactional (aimed toward understanding, contemplation, and a rethinking of what constitutes persuasion), aware of alternative means of delivery and knowledge production (such as silence, listening, and emotion), directed to and delivered from marginalized positions, and deeply committed to hope and possibility. These fresh ways of being rhetorical and doing rhetoric are not mutually exclusive; rather, they overlap to interanimate each other, as such serving as sites of invention, arrangement, style, memory, and delivery. The following chapter extends these discussions by examining the research methods and methodologies that have led to the development and application of these theories.

FOUR: METHODS AND METHODOLOGIES

> I have written so many words
> wanting to live inside you
> to be of use to you
>
> —Adrienne Rich, "Upper Broadway"

In 1992, Patricia Bizzell declared that the feminist rhetorical project presented "the most trenchant challenges to traditional scholarly practices . . . not only in the materials scholars can study, but also, and perhaps ultimately more significantly, in the methods whereby we can study it" ("Feminist" 8). At present, feminist rhetoricians are routinely paying especial attention to the ways we conduct research—to the methods we use to gather information and the methodologies we use to analyze that information, including the information produced by vernaculars, experiences, and emotions. Doing so is allowing our field to grow and define itself in ways that reflect the critical and inclusionary goals of feminist rhetoric, yet not enough of us are aware of the specific interventions feminist rhetorical researchers are making into the masculinist project by way of methods and methodologies.

Our research methods, methodologies, and goals are continually under interrogation—and they should be, if we are to shape an ethical agenda. Feminist researchers work to transcend the myths of "objectivity" and "value-neutrality" that have, for too long, conditioned our research and yet do not ethically enhance research like ours, which is rooted in ethics rather than alleged objectivity.[1] Those masculinist myths work best "for people who believe in the possibility of achieving 'a view from nowhere' . . . through the autonomous exercise of their reason" (Code, "How" 15). Those myths, however, do not work so well for feminist researchers who conduct mostly value-laden research, in which our reason and our values are influenced by the experiential accounts of our research subjects.

Of course, all ethical researchers strive for objectivity; we all want to submit the most accurate findings possible. But absolute objectivity is impossible and claiming it irresponsible. For that reason, claiming objectivity in our research is much less important than striving for research transparency as we rhetorical feminists gather and analyze information (knowledge). Whether we locate the subjects of our research in the library, the archives, or the face-to-face interview, our goal is respectful interaction and rhetorical listening. Often the subjects of our research interact directly with us, participate in and influence our research, and recognize themselves in our findings. Rather than provide distanced, authoritative, elitist observations, or "objective" arguments, our major priority is to open new directions for ongoing inquiry. In these ways, researchers following the precepts of rhetorical feminism acknowledge the integrity and intersectionality of women's personal experiences and emotions (within masculinist, racist social structures) and concede that all human experiences (including research projects) resonate with values as well as facts.

Our understanding of the values, experiences, and knowledge of women and other Others allows us to surmount Burkean "trained incapacities" as well as the strictures of objectivity (*Permanence* 3). And to achieve those ends, much of our research reconsiders traditional, text-based research methods (books, archives, manuscripts, and e-resources) and moves beyond those more traditional methods to person-based research (naturalistic studies, ethnographies, and autoethnographies) and to Web-based research (case studies, qualitative and quantitative studies), fresh methods that foster deeper transformations, more authentic insights, and broader invitations into the field of feminist rhetorical studies.

As I write these words, three monographs in particular come to mind, studies that help rhetorical feminists see what riches lie around the corner: Wendy Sharer's *Vote and Voice: Women's Organization and Political Literacy, 1915–1930*; Charlotte Hogg's *From the Garden Club: Rural Women Writing Community*; and Vicki Tolar Burton's *Spiritual Literacy in John Wesley's Methodism: Reading, Writing, and Speaking to Believe*. In some ways, these research projects illustrate sharp departures from the traditional research route, with each of these valuable, carefully researched histories taking root not in a library, special collections archive, or graduate seminar but in a grandmother's cache of letters and journals that recounted her civic engagement and activism, rich information that had long been tucked under her bed; in the records of a small-town Nebraska library, where a grandmother contributed a wealth of information and details about her writing club; and in a seemingly useless gift from an elderly cousin, the significance of which returned in a dream.

In the preface of her impressive study, Burton explains how she became captivated with eighteenth-century Hester Ann Rogers, who held a central role in John Wesley's Methodism:

> Hester Rogers came to me as a gift. An elderly cousin heard I was doing genealogy research on my mother's line, the Rogers family of the South Carolina low country. When she came to visit, Lorraine Rogers brought me a small, leather-bound volume, published in 1837, titled *Account of the Experience of Hester Ann Rogers*. Someone had given the book to Lorraine, suggesting Hester might be kin to us. I read the first ten or twenty pages, concluded that I could not connect my family to Hester Rogers, and put the book aside.
>
> Eight years later, Hester Rogers came to me again, this time in a dream. The dream's message was so strong that it woke me up: That small leather volume is important, and I should read it. We had just moved, and all my books were still in boxes. I got up in the night and sorted through boxes until I found Hester Rogers, then I stayed up the rest of the night reading her account. (xiii)

Like Burton's, Sharer's and Hogg's studies offer just a sample of fresh methods for opening up the histories, theories, and practices of rhetoric. Each of them illustrates the inventive power of personal experience and emotional connection with regard to research projects, with personal experience and emotion constituting two knowledge-producing qualities of rhetorical feminism.

The theoretical breakthroughs discussed in the previous chapter provide the foundation for this chapter, which extends the discussion of rhetorical feminism and the ways its theories result from or generate research. Some of the most groundbreaking scholarship for feminist rhetoric has appeared since the 1980s, launching cascades of exciting work (like those just mentioned), ranging from historiographies and ethnographies to case studies and cross-cultural investigations. All the scholars whose theories were profiled in the previous section (together with far too many whose work went unmentioned) are helping to regender the study of rhetoric, to expand rhetorical theorizing, and, most certainly, to reenvision what Jacqueline Jones Royster refers to as our "disciplinary landscape," in terms of research methods, methodologies, and subjects.

In Search of Excellence

Feminist rhetorical research is alive and well, multifaceted and in motion, reaching into continuing and new branches of inquiry, places, and spaces. . . . We, feminist scholars in rhetorical studies, are constantly in motion, "working within, against, and across" methods and methodologies, "combining elements from different perspectives" and different disciplines, addressing questions about the value and purpose of the work we do, and working to reconcile our methodological differences even as we realize that some of those differences cannot be reconciled.
    —Eileen Schell and K. J. Rawson, *Rhetorica in Motion*

Individually and together, Gesa Kirsch and Jacqueline Jones Royster have, for years now, argued that feminist rhetorical studies is a convergence of interests, from a suite of feminist stances and operational paradigms to an array of research methods, methodologies, and goals, with both scholars using their own research agendas to blaze the trail (see Works Cited and Consulted). As they write in their 2010 essay, "Feminist Rhetorical Practices: In Search of Excellence,"

> [t]he idea is that feminist rhetorical scholarship is now moving far beyond the *rescue, recovery, and (re)inscription* of a diversity of women participants and on to the establishing of new watermarks of regard and worthiness in rhetorical studies more generally for the methodologies that we have been using and the types of insights that such methodologies have the capacity to yield. (642)

The authors admit that most of this scholarship continues to be conducted by women and that they do not expect to dismantle entirely rhetoric's patriarchal power base. Nevertheless, Kirsch and Royster call our disciplinary attention to the necessity of designing "research that enriches, honors, and supports the lives of those we study," research that renders those lives as "participants in discourses that must be interrogated actively, critiqued vigorously, and negotiated carefully and caringly" (643). The research methods of rhetorical feminists attempt respectful, dialogic connection rather than impartial detachment.

METHODS AND METHODOLOGIES

By 2012, when they published *Feminist Rhetorical Practices: New Horizons for Rhetoric, Composition, and Literacy Studies*, Royster and Kirsch had consolidated their arguments on research methods and methodologies into a set of four key feminist rhetorical practices: *critical imagination, strategic contemplation, social circulation,* and *globalization.* These four feminist rhetorical practices, used separately or in combination, can be employed toward the goal of recovering and recuperating women rhetoricians and rhetors. But Royster and Kirsch ask us not to rest on these laurels, for if we were to stop there, we would be placing historical women's lives mainly in service to our own lives and works (75). These four research methods and methodologies underpin the best of historical studies in rhetoric, serving as necessary cognitive tasks for analyzing evidence and artifacts, for ethical interactions with research subjects, and especially for moving our discipline forward.

Perhaps most compelling about their four tools of inquiry is their emphasis on ethical responsibility, to the discipline, of course, but even more so to the research subjects themselves:[2]

> The commitment is to learn to listen deeply to texts and images and for voices and sounds in order to better understand both what is happening and what is going on; to listen to their views and ideas instead of just our own, to their stories, rather than ours. . . .
>
> . . . If we wish to honor and do justice to those whose lives and works we study and bring their visions, voices and accomplishments into academic or knowledge-making circles, we need to be cognizant of how rhetorical practices that have not been privileged to interrogation and documentation as academic subjects are passed on, modified, and revised from one generation to the next, from one social setting to another. (147)

Royster and Kirsch give considered space to the ethical relationship between researcher and research subject and the ethics of researching an Other, of listening to and then telling, retelling, or analyzing an Other's story, experience, life.

In the following section, then, I trace out these four practices, starting with *critical imagination,* the term of engagement that underpins all the rest, which Royster describes as

> a term for a commitment to making connections and seeing possibility. . . . [It] functions as a critical skill in questioning a viewpoint,

an experience, an event ... and in remaking interpretive frameworks based on that questioning. ... The use of critical imagination does not at all negate the need to do the hard work of engaging systematically in theoretically grounded processes of discovery, analysis, and interpretation. (*Traces* 83)

In *Feminist Rhetorical Practices,* Royster and Kirsch argue for critical imagination as a tool of inquiry, one useful, of course, in the rescue, recovery, and (re)inscription of much feminist rhetorical scholarship.

The seeds of this method may have been planted in Royster's 1996 "When the First Voice You Hear Is Not Your Own," in which she emphasizes the import of critical imagination to our research, particularly when it involves cross-boundary exchange: critical imagination helps us avoid the appropriation of another person, group, or culture outside ourselves. When we employ our critical imagination, we make no claim about Other(s) without sufficient grounding, either through serious study, through highly self-aware experience, or from the voices, research, literatures, and actions of Others themselves.

Notwithstanding its use in historical recovery projects, critical imagination can also be deployed in making rhetorical studies more representative and inclusive. To do so, we need to consider how the women and Others we study navigated their lives and the questions and traditions that gave their lives meaning. "The objective," write Royster and Kirsch, "is to develop mechanisms by which listening deeply, reflexively, and multisensibly become[s] standard practice ... in rhetorical studies writ large" (20). In the conclusion of their book, they remind us of the delicacy necessary in "reaching deeply into these communities" (147). We must do so "respectfully and carefully," they remind us, for

> our obligations are not only to "create new knowledge and make an original contribution" in an academically self-centered way but instead to create relationships with those communities as they invite us into their worlds, their lives, their issues and concerns. Our obligation is to partner with them as we join our world to theirs and work with them to set in motion a different, more fully rendered sense of rhetoric as an enterprise with a future. (147)

In these ways, the concept of critical imagination forms the foundation for all rhetorical feminist inquiry: ethical and dialogic transactions moored in a deep commitment to hope and possibility. Despite my resistance to taxonomizing the theorists in chapter 3, I will loosely taxonomize some feminist researchers according to Royster and Kirsch's four (sometimes overlapping) methodological precepts. For instance, given their imaginative reconsiderations of language, the French feminists and Alison Jaggar seem to fall under the rubric of critical imagination.

The second of Royster and Kirsch's feminist rhetorical practices is *strategic contemplation*, which offers space for "rigorous" contemplation on "well-grounded scholarly work" (21)—theoretical work, such as that of Carole Blair, Julie Brown, and Leslie Baxter. Royster and Kirsch describe the effort as enacting "more conspicuously what it means to think critically and innovatively and to pursue actively a robust, intellectual agenda" (21). This second tool of inquiry works to slow down the process of research, thinking, and writing to prevent premature conclusions, "neat resolutions," or "cozy hierarchies and binaries" (22). In order to render the lives, works, and experiences of our research subjects with authenticity and respect, we must take the time to allow—even invite—"new vistas to come into view, unexpected leads to shape scholarly work, and new research questions to emerge" (22). Strategic contemplation also prompts us to acknowledge the women's work (feminist and otherwise) on which our own scholarship is built and the ethical and scholarly responsibilities our work carries into the future, with the ethos of the researcher, her ethical stance toward the subject, front and center.

The third research method (or strategy of inquiry) introduced by Royster and Kirsch is *social circulation*, which illuminates the complex interanimation of generational feminist scholarship and women's activity—past, present, and future, public *and* private (that is, social). The authors urge us to expand our consideration of rhetoric as a "cultural phenomenon," a "human enterprise," consisting of "performances" that "ebb, flow, travel, gain substance and integrity, acquire traction" (23), much like the work of bell hooks. Royster and Kirsch are interested in the ways rhetoric has gained feminist substance and traction over the years, in the ways it is employed as both an analytical tool and an energizing convergence between rhetorics and feminism. For the authors, the concept of social circulation earns its significance in three major ways: not only does it direct our attention to the (a) "importance of rendering women's rhetorical practices across space and time" as well as to the (b) "conditions, impacts, and consequences of those practices," but, in doing so, it thereby (c) casts women's rhetorical practices as "research, scholarship, and knowledge that are worthy and worthwhile" (24). In this way, social circulation tracks how women's rhetorical work moves and is picked up by others. Social circulation fulfills one of the features of rhetorical feminism, that of valuing women's daily and scholarly experience as a knowledge-producing epistemology.

Finally, Royster and Kirsch offer us the concept of *globalization,* which goes far beyond establishing connections between the rhetorical performances of ancient Greek and Roman women, those of medieval and Renaissance women, and those of more contemporary North American women, connections that have long sustained, shaped, even legitimated our work. In the twenty-first century, globalization offers feminist rhetorical scholars stances and methods for "connecting the dots" among women rhetors and feminist scholars across time, space, hemispheres, cultures, ethnicities, and modalities—offering a portal into "rhetoric and writing as age-old global enterprises" that continue to flourish (25).[3] The rescuing, recovering, and reinscribing of feminist rhetorical scholars now play in a new key, that of situating rhetoric as a "transnational, global phenomenon rather than a Western one" (25), as Trinh T. Minh-ha's and Gloria Anzaldúa's work demonstrates, writing as they do beyond a mainstream Western audience. Royster and Kirsch are confident that these four feminist rhetorical practices are changing the field itself, by shifting its values and expectations (25)—and indeed they are. These practices help us "understand more fully what is accounted for in our inquiry paradigms and what we may find to be missing; what is there now and what could be there instead" (145).

Clearly, the insights and assessments of Royster and Kirsch influence feminist rhetorical practices and may, in the process, transform masculinist rhetorical studies itself into a more representative, inclusive academic discipline. The scholarship that follows indicates how much impressive work has already taken place as well as how much research there still is to do. All this feminist research on methods and methodologies is powered by the driving force that is hope for a better, more equitable, more expansive rhetorical future, a future of rhetorical feminism.

Rhetorical Feminism at the Scene of Historiography: When Methods and Methodologies Collide

The past wasn't past. Just curled up like a prophet in the bosom of time.
—Hélène Cixous, *Coming to Writing*

METHODS AND METHODOLOGIES

Many of us working in rhetorical history accept the assertion that historical narratives are a matter of interpretation, not truth, that those narratives are primarily motivated actions to *do* something, something contributing to the growth, vitality, and strength of *a* person, *a* people, *a* culture, usually at the expense, erasure, or silencing of *another* person, *another* people, *another* culture. As Joan Cocks explains, culture seems "impelled to create out of its variegated history" a narrower past consisting of significant events, some for "emphasis and celebration," others for "revilement" and "stigmatization," and still others for neglect, dilution, deactivation, or exclusion altogether (52). Indeed, such a practice has long been the case for both historical study and history writing. While historians claim neutrality, historiographers admit that their histories are intended to *do* something, to emend and shape our perceptions.

Now, each of us wants *history* (and our *view* of that history) to contribute to the *positive* value of our daily life, so when it does not meet this requirement, historiographers go to work. After all, if we were content with the way history was being told and written, if we accepted the past as a set of determining factors that once and for all prefigure the present, or if we believed that history could tell us about a past that was really "there," then history, once gathered and written, would never fall apart. We would not need historiography.

In other words, many of us understand that rhetorical history has, as Royster teaches us,

> a deeply entrenched habit of standing in one place (that is, territories deemed Western), shaping inquiries with a particular set of interests in mind (for example, the desires and experiences of elite males), and interestingly disregarding some feature even within its own scope (for example, the desires and experiences of women or people from non-elite classes). ("Disciplinary Landscaping" 149)

Even those scholars who disagree with assertions of interpretation and motivation would surely concur that our Western traditions of rhetoric are masculinist, elitist, and focused on the public sphere. For these reasons, feminist scholars continue to speak back to these dominant scholarly perspectives and call for a more representative history—and future—of rhetorical studies, one that can accommodate rhetorical feminism. As Bonnie Dow admonishes, "If feminism turns its back on the centers of power, privilege, and individual achievement that men have monopolized [that is, on rhetoric], those men will continue to monopolize them and nothing significant will change" ("Feminism" 112). Feminist scholars must continue to intervene in rhetorical histories, especially when their interpolations invigorate our understandings of rhetoric's capacities and infinite instantiations across time and space.

When, in 1993, Thomas P. Miller predicted that the "fiction" we refer to as "the rhetorical tradition" has "just about outlasted its usefulness," he was correct (26). Many of us in rhetorical studies realize that "historical analysis is nothing other than the interpretation or even transformation of documents given and frozen into moments" (Trinh, "Difference" 10). Thus, we are becoming ever more reflective in our rhetorical histories—both in our teaching and in our research. Feminist historiographers, in particular,

> believe that carefully researched and thoughtfully critiqued materials will not only assist us in setting aside our own historically acquired prejudices in favor of a clearer understanding of the rhetoricians we study, but also permit us to consider evidence not typically considered in determining rhetorical acumen—evidence essential to a worthy reshaping of our tradition. (Mattingly, "Telling Evidence" 105)

In other words, our historiographies must do more than simply rescue, recover, and reinscribe neglected rhetors. We must reflect—on the ways that "hegemonic culture [is] powerful but vulnerable too, through the exertion it takes to attend to a past that is never complete" (Cocks 52). Rewriting rhetorical history is an endless task, one based on the discoveries and recognition of artifacts, manuscripts, and fresh understandings. Rhetorical historiography is a task to which feminist researchers are committed, so much so that feminist rewritings have become a burgeoning industry.

One of the earliest and most influential collections of essays on women's rhetorics is Karlyn Kohrs Campbell's 1989 two-volume *Man Cannot Speak for Her*, the first volume a critical survey, the second a collection of speeches and writings. Since then, countless scholars (in addition to the ones who are mentioned throughout this book) have followed in her footsteps by editing collections or producing monographs at the intersection of rhetoric and feminism.[4] Such publications are only the tip of the iceberg.

For feminist researchers, then, the obligation is to become even more reflective, immersing ourselves "in a broad range of historical texts, across genres, including but not limited to texts of speeches, to gain a clearer understanding of both the politically active women in our history and the evidence that demonstrates their facility with rhetorical matters" (Mattingly, "Telling Evidence" 105). Shirley Wilson Logan's career-long study of nineteenth-century black women rhetors did not start out with a specific methodology. Yet she always seemed to apply the rhetorical tools that best opened up a text for her in collections ranging from women's organization conference proceedings and political conventions to women's religious conventions and gatherings. As Trinh T. Minh-ha says, the more researchers like us "dig into the maze of yellowed documents and look into the non-registered facts of [our] communities, the more [we] rejoice upon discovering the buried treasures of women's unknown communities" ("Difference" 10). Yet despite the diversity, respect, and explosion of feminist historiographic research, not all projects meet with a positive reception. (See exchanges below.)

Within the expansive circle of feminist historiographers, two issues generate disagreement at the same time that they energize further research. First of all, feminist scholars themselves often disagree on the value, methods, and consequences of the rhetorical historiographic endeavor; and, second, when those disagreements become published scholarly arguments, the arguments themselves tend to draw a great deal of professional attention (from mainstream, feminist, and marginalized rhetorical historians), too often overshadowing the positive scholarly accomplishments of all the researchers involved and distracting us from even bigger issues of truth, methods, objectivity, and what we might learn from researchers in other fields (the social sciences or history, for example).

Feminist theory has already enabled researchers to "resist traditional histories and historiographic practices inside the field of rhetoric as a means to create new kinds of historical inquiry, fresh archival reading practices, and, of course, new histories" (Glenn and Enoch 333). Given controversies among researchers in the same field and across the disciplines, resistance to change in research methods and historical findings should provide rich ground for further study. Instead, such resistance too often results in public displays of suspicion, even insult (see below). Unfortunately, disagreements about purpose, theoretical stance, or outcomes among feminist rhetorical historiographers have sometimes served to emblematize the entire feminist project rather than as stopping points for all concerned to listen dialogically and rethink their positions and their agendas.

Two major controversies of this sort come to mind: one situated in communication studies, between Barbara Biesecker and Karlyn Kohrs

Campbell; the other in English studies, among Xin Lu Gale, Susan Jarratt (with Rory Ong), Hui Wu, and me. These two heated exchanges are frequently referenced, with scant attention given to their knowledge-producing power. After all, if we were all housed in a Department of Rhetorical Feminism, what methodological grounding might we agree to share? How might we reimagine academic debates and dialogues?

The Biesecker-Campbell Exchange

One of the earliest communication scholars to take women's contributions seriously, Campbell herself has contributed game-changing scholarship to the discipline. Her 1971 "Rhetoric of Women's Liberation: An Oxymoron" sparked the connection between feminists and rhetoric, but her 1989 collection of key texts and analyses of those rhetorical performances in two volumes, *Man Cannot Speak for Her,* electrified the entire scene. The collected writings and speeches in volume 2 showcase women's rhetorical performances—key speeches and texts (all previously unpublished) of early feminist reformers who played central roles in alleviating inequalities of sex, race, and class. Writing women into the history of rhetoric had just become normalized—or so scholars thought. Articles, edited collections, and monographs on the subject were lighting up the academic stage.

But Biesecker was not blinded by the lights. Although she appreciated the recovery and recuperation work necessary for writing women into the history of rhetoric, she refused to settle for what she considered the affirmative action inclusion of women based solely on their individual, public performances, those akin to the performances of the great men. Rather than including "great women speakers" along with the already canonized men speakers, Biesecker would have feminist rhetoricians challenge the definitions of "rhetoric" and "rhetor" alike:

> In short, the danger in taking an affirmative action approach to the history of Rhetoric is that while we may have managed to insert some women into the canon (and, again, this is no small thing), we will have not yet begun to challenge the underlying logic of canon formation and the uses to which it has been put that have written the rhetorical contributions of collective women into oblivion. ("Coming" 144)

Biesecker admits that although the feminist rhetorical historiographies are "landmarks," they are not "immune to ... critique" (144). Perhaps because Biesecker used the work of the much-lauded Campbell as a case in point, her essay opened the first major controversy within feminist rhetorical historiography, research methods, and methodologies.

The critique of Campbell's scholarship garnered attention, to be sure, but another equally significant contributor to the scene was the heavy influence of poststructuralism. The time was ripe for Biesecker's critique. Undermining any stable conception of the accomplished speaking subjects (those who embody "the" history of rhetoric) was Jacques Derrida's challenge to the idea of an individual identity, Michel Foucault's to subject formation, and Gayatri Spivak's to an essentialist subject. These challenges to an objective rhetorical history, to an "animated and unilinear narrative of progress," to a men-only history, and to the exceptional individual subject all coalesced to confront claims of extraordinary speakers and an objective, "grand narrative" of rhetorical history (Biesecker, "Of Historicity" 124).

Biesecker singled out Campbell's revisionist history of rhetoric, describing it as resolidifying rather than undoing "the ideology of individualism that is the condition of possibility for . . . effective rhetoric" ("Coming" 144). After all, Campbell's research method for rhetorical recovery relied on the criteria for public speaking that had long been applied to men. In contrast, Biesecker demanded that we reconsider the criteria by which we recognize and ratify anyone—man or woman—into a history of rhetoric, particularly given the fact that different women and men, "due to their various positions in the social structure, have available to them different rhetorical possibilities and, similarly, are constrained by different rhetorical limits" (157). Biesecker laid down the gauntlet, arguing for the "*radical contextualization of all rhetorical acts*" in order to "forge a new storying of our tradition that circumvents the veiled cultural supremacy operative in mainstream histories of Rhetoric" (147).

Quickly, Campbell published her response, "Biesecker Cannot Speak for Her Either," and called out the destructiveness of internecine battles, in this case, a feminist one: "Men empower women who are willing to attack other women who attempt to change the status quo" (154). Never referring to Biesecker's essay as a "critique," Campbell, instead, repeatedly calls it an "attack" on Campbell herself, her honesty, and her scholarly independence (153). And she responds to each attack with evidence of her integrity and intellectual autonomy. Campbell confesses to Biesecker's accusation of implying "that most women do not have what it takes to play the public, rhetorical game." "Guilty as charged," Campbell declares:

> Most women do not have the ability to excel in public discourse. . . . [However,] the most vicious misogynists who claimed that women were by nature incapable of rhetorical excellence *never* claimed that all men *were* capable of such excellence. . . . Hence, to include the works of rhetorically gifted women merely gives their voices equal weight with those of men. (154–55)

Campbell does not back down from the fact that individual achievement reigns in rhetoric; after all, "the rhetorical efforts of women were, with some exceptions, created by individual women, those of men, by individual men" (155). Nor does she relinquish the fact that men's individual rhetorical achievements were systematically recorded while women's simply were not. And after Biesecker's sustained critique of "individualism," Campbell finds it ironic that "we witness here the striking spectacle of an individual attacking another individual in the cause of abolition of individualism in rhetoric" (158). For Campbell, Biesecker's attack is misogynist and retrograde: "Now that some women have helped to make some of the voices of these once-silenced women heard again, Biesecker wishes to silence them once more" (158).

Both scholars make strong points, and both scholars are right in many ways. In fact, their debate can be read productively, as an example of rhetorical feminism in progress, one that showcases the strengths of each of their stances, not as an example of one-sided, overwhelming defeat of the other. A conscious enactment of rhetorical feminism might be liberating at such moments. Most compelling about Biesecker's argument is her charge that historiographers must broaden our definitions of "rhetor" and "rhetoric," which, notably, Campbell did the minute she included women. This inaugural controversy surrounding feminist rhetorical historiography illuminates the importance of conducting deep historical research and building a complex, contextualized knowledge of the subject(s) before taking flight into theory. What only now seems obvious is that their heated exchange could have opened up a generative, interactive discussion of feminist rhetorical research methods and methodologies. Both essays imply the necessary discussion, but neither essay is explicit on that necessity. Campbell's feminist historiographic scholarship has withstood the test of time, just as Biesecker's critical reminder about the mutually dependent relationship between research and theory continues to circulate through all of our scholarly projects.

METHODS AND METHODOLOGIES

The Gale-Glenn-Jarratt-Ong-Wu Exchange

The second heralded exchange with regard to feminist research methods and methodologies was that set off by Jarratt and Ong's and my own early publications about Aspasia, Socrates's teacher of rhetoric. In my 1994 "sex, lies, and manuscript: Refiguring Aspasia in the History of Rhetoric," I address Biesecker's concerns, troubling the very foundations of masculinist rhetoric by using the work of men historians and rhetoricians to argue my case and by drawing on the work of Athenaeus, Cicero, Plato, Plutarch, and Xenophon to uncover and celebrate Aspasia's rhetorical accomplishments. Jarratt and Ong's 1995 publication of "Aspasia: Rhetoric, Gender, and Colonial Ideology" centers on Aspasia's role as a Sophist, a foreigner, and a woman colonized by Athenian ideology and a colonizer herself. Xin Lu Gale vehemently objected to and was frustrated by the methodologies we three used for analyzing the information we had gathered, and she made her sharp criticism of our feminist historiography (our research methods, methodologies, and findings) known in the pages of *College English*. Gale had never identified as a rhetorician, let alone a feminist rhetorician, so her censure of our feminist historiography seemed odd, serving more as an attention-getting conflict among women than a valuable display of barely masked masculinist prejudices.

Over time, Gale's incursion has done much more than draw attention. Her condemnation of feminist historiographic methods, methodologies, and research stances provides a portal into the reasons that mainstream rhetorical theorists and historians have too often given so little credence to feminist research and findings. The further comments of Jarratt, Wu, and me not only counter the mis/understandings and assertions of Gale but help to elucidate the methods, significance, and implications of the feminist project in general and feminist rhetorical historiography in particular.

In response to the methods (traditional library and archival research) and the methodologies (postmodernism, historiography, gender studies) I used to develop my argument that Aspasia of Miletus had been a rhetorician, Gale asks,

> Should we eschew the traditional concern about validity, reliability, and adequateness of historical sources when we purposefully turn away from the traditional way of doing history? Does the postmodern view of history and of doing history necessarily entail an abandonment of the traditional concern for truth and evidence? ("Historical Studies" 366)

METHODS AND METHODOLOGIES

I respond by identifying Gale's essay as a "polemic" affirming "a set of unquestioned privileges referred to, with numbing regularity, as 'tradition' and 'truth'" ("Comment" 387). I describe Gale's approach as taking the

> reactionary criticism *du jour* that associates much postmodern thought with the end of truth and the decline of standards and reduces it into a simple binary: on the one hand, there is traditional objective historiography, and, on the other, subjective feminist fictionalization. (387)

"What is missing," I counter,

> is the recognition that postmodern historiography does not attempt to do away with the notion of truth; instead, it attempts to think of truth outside the confines of a mythical objectivity, or, at the very least, to decouple the link between "objectivity" and "truth." Ignoring historiography's imbrication with truth, power, and ethics results in a reading of Susan Jarratt, Rory Ong, and me (and presumably many others) only as adversaries, enemies of tradition, obstructionists of the Truth. (387)

I map out Gale's objections at the same time that I trace the underlying reasons for the dismissiveness of the mainstream rhetoricians: the politics of historiography (its aims, methods, and methodologies; in other words, its relationship to foundational knowledge and objective "truth").

If the writing of history is considered to be the objective writing of truth, of how things really were, then historiography can only be considered suspect. After all, historiography must work as if the "real" (how things really were) can actually be connected with discourse on the "real," a play between the object under study and the discourse performing the analysis (Certeau xxvii). Even the most traditional history writers play this game—and some of them, including Gale, do not want to admit that they are participating in anything less than the recording of objective, truthful history. So why pay any heed at all to feminist historiographies, particularly those that are not always/already canonized? Those with no unmitigated claims to the truth?

Gale describes the Jarratt and Ong essay as "depending so heavily on interpretation and speculation, with a preoccupation for their feminist goals, that it accentuates the question of the roles that interpretation and speculation play in the writing of history" ("Historical Studies" 373).

Jarratt's response, "Comment: Rhetoric and Feminism: Together Again," demonstrates her understanding, too, of Gale's concerns: "What will be the criteria for judging or verifying postmodern histories in the absence of foundational theories of knowledge?" (390). Like me, Jarratt acknowledges that disciplinary disagreements centering on "truth, evidence, and method" are crucial to the continuing development of rhetorical studies (390). And also like me, Jarratt responds to Gale's seemingly distorted reaction to a deeply contextualized argument:

> Gale finds a problem in feminist historians making both factual claims and interpretive assumptions.... Gale, using [Richard] Rorty's categories of historical and rational reconstruction, finds a contradiction between the speculative leaps required to initiate feminist history—to imagine the world differently from the way it has been handed down to us—and the factual claims needed to make those claims persuasive. (391)

Jarratt leads readers further into Gale's faulty argument by citing Rorty's actual words: "The two genres can never be *that* independent.... These two topics should be seen as moments in a continuing movement around the hermeneutic circle, a circle one has to have gone round a good many times before one can begin to do *either* sort of reconstruction" (Rorty 53n1).

Hui Wu mounts a spirited defense of Jarratt's, Ong's, and my own historiographic methods, distilling what she describes as a "debate" over the "question of whether feminism can be validated and legitimized as a credible methodology in terms of historical studies" ("Comment" 102). Harkening back to Gale's and her own shared experiences in China during the Mao Zedong regime (1949–76), Wu resolves that many women (implying Gale) have internalized the ideology of patriarchy: "Our critical thinking, trained rigorously and professionally in a patriarchal system with all sorts of male-dominated-isms, sometimes prevents us from understanding fully the goal, scope, and method of feminism" (105). Gale then responds to Jarratt, Wu, and me by reiterating her arguments against speculation, progressive political goals, and academic privilege (namely, Jarratt's and mine) and closes with an unexpected reminder that "self-perpetuation is an intrinsic feature of rhetoric and that the only way to make rhetoric accountable is through democratic debate" ("Xin Lu Gale" 107). In this latter case, she is right.

Faulty or no, many mainstream rhetoricians follow arguments such as Gale's original one, using them to dismiss feminist rhetorical scholarship, save when focusing on public conflicts among women, which Gale herself refers to as "catfights" that "undercut the importance of exchanging different views and perspectives about theory and method" ("Historical Studies" 384n6). That she would ultimately request democratic debate seems reasonable, yet such debate is rarely engaged. After all, feminist rhetorical historiography is still mostly ignored in the scholarship of mainstream rhetoricians.

Nevertheless, feminists and others whose voices have been rendered inaudible are working to expand and deepen our rhetorical histories and understandings. As Cocks reminds us, "The continued working through of its own once-lived life . . . makes hegemonic culture powerful," to be sure, but that culture is "vulnerable too" (520). And it is feminist rhetorical historiography that reveals just how vulnerable that traditional rhetorical past is; it is "never complete," can never be complete (520). "Feminism's history," Joan Wallach Scott tells us, "has exposed as instruments of patriarchal power stories that explained the exclusion of women as a fact of nature" (33). As such feminism's history gives us a "new history to counter the lie of women's passivity, as well as their erasure from the records" (33).

Rhetorical feminism offers us a productive tactic for reflecting on and generating histories as well. Scholars can start by disidentifying with hegemonic rhetorical histories, thinking creatively and strategically, engaging in dialogues with traditional and feminist scholars alike, and listening to the vernaculars, emotions, and experiences of rhetors who reside at the margins—all in an attempt to understand other points of view and research stances, all toward the goal of expanding and enriching our rhetorical histories.

In these ways, the advances feminist scholars are making offer complex, multivocal starting points for continued historical inquiry, for interventions into the history of "patriarchal power," and for the rewriting of rhetorical histories. Writing from a cross-boundary rhetorical perspective, Bo Wang describes such starting points as helping us "examine our assumptions, reconsider our priorities, and discover and develop . . . deeply reflective and reflexive practices and processes" that have transformed "the disciplinary landscape and invigorated new areas of study" ("Rethinking" 28, 30, 29). Not debate, perhaps, but a public deliberation on the methods and methodologies of feminist rhetorical historiography could provide a richly stimulating experience for novice and expert historiographers alike, to be sure.[5]

Rhetorical histories may still be mainstream—they may even be hegemonic—but they are no longer unquestioned, unwavering, complete, let alone "classic." Rather, rhetorical histories are themselves considered to be rhetorical, even if they have for too long (and ironically) been "blind" to their "own rhetoric" (LaCapra 17). According to Carole Blair, "Histories of rhetorical theory are not neutral or objective reconstructions of facts. They are themselves rhetorical iterations, saturated with the impure representations, intrinsic interestedness, and general obstreperousness of any discourse" ("Contested Histories" 417). The tensions within feminist historiography expose those histories as the rhetorical iterations they are, as Gale helps clarify. I can listen to Gale more easily than I could years ago. Her voice has helped me realize that too often, middle-class heterosexual white cis-women scholars like me (try to) speak for all rhetorical women throughout history. Fortunately, rhetorical feminism offers me and others portals for exploring other sides of rhetorical production and histories through dialogue, listening, respect, and attention to those rhetors who might, however provisionally, reside at the margins. The work of feminist rhetorical historiography is far from done; in fact, it has just begun—and it is anchored in hope.

Methods and Methodologies for Invigorating Historical Inquiry

The silences, the empty spaces, the language itself, with its excision of the female, the methods of discourse tell us as much as the content, once we learn to watch for what is left out, to listen for the unspoken, to study the patterns of established science and scholarship with an outsider's eye.
       —Adrienne Rich, "What Does a Woman Need to Know?"

Gale's provocative questions, the four feminist rhetorical principles set forth by Royster and Kirsch, and additional feminist historiographic methods and methodologies all help us rethink our research methods as well as better understand the challenges—and payoffs—of conducting archival research, one of the most profitable means for uncovering or recovering women figures in the history of rhetoric. In terms of traditional library and archival research, several monographs and collections are invigorating our practices of inquiry, our sites of exploration. Many of these books are stimulating our knowledge of how archival materials are received, prioritized, processed, cataloged, and described. Several encourage our collaboration with librarians and archivists in the preservation of historical data sources that may be threatened. These scholarly works direct us in how to read and negotiate archival materials in capacious and complex ways. (See Donahue and Moon; Gaillet, Eidson, and Gammil; Ramsey, Sharer, L'Eplattenier, and Mastrangelo; Kirsch and Rohan; Schell and Rawson; Helle; S. Miller, *Trust*; Hogg; Sharer, *Vote*; Burton.)

In brief, all these books call for recovery or gender critique at the same time that they expand the definition of library and archival research to include both public- and private-sphere texts, official and unofficial materials, material and digital accumulations—in short, whatever materials illuminate the project, from traditional library and archival holdings (including newspapers and photographs) to student essays, letters, journals, and diaries (which demand that we follow the protocol of rhetorical feminism and listen to and respect the voices, experiences, and emotions of their authors).

Vicki Tolar Burton's project, a feminist rhetorical analysis of a masculine historical figure, is rooted in her archival research, which she explains so well. I pause here to reconsider her book for several reasons having to do with her methods and methodologies. First of all, hers is a model of how one might conduct feminist research on a powerful man and the people he influenced. Second, she shows us how to let the research findings shape the thesis rather than how to conduct what I call a "thesis-chase" (entering the archives with thesis in hand and acknowledging only the materials that support that thesis). Third, Burton's is a feminist analysis of the patriarchal figure John Wesley, an analysis that appreciates his anti-sexist (but authentically Christian) moves but wisely contextualizes those moves within his eighteenth-century sociocultural constraints (rather than awarding him a twenty-first-century sensibility). And, fourth, Burton explains exactly how specific archival collections help her arrive at her historical findings, her scholarly conclusion, at every step. In other words, she explains her method(s) (how she acquires information) as well as her methodologies (the theories she uses to analyze that information).

To wit, she writes:

> Feminists are good at taking down the patriarchy, but we have not been good at looking at the complex relationships between men and women in which women gain public agency with the assistance and support of a powerful men—relationships both fraught with power differentials and brimming with opportunity.... I did not enter this

> study searching for protofeminist foremothers in early Methodism, nor am I arguing that John Wesley was a feminist. . . .
>
> Often, male leaders gain power over women by seeking to isolate women or set them against each other. Wesley, conversely, promoted friends and collaborations among talented women Methodists, connecting women who did not know each other when he thought they would be good spiritual companions. Wesley struggled to reconcile the letter of scripture concerning women's roles with the public effectiveness of spiritual women every day. (xv)

In these ways, Burton grounds her feminist historiographic project in the social and religious realities (the powers and constraints) of eighteenth-century England.

And to bolster her thesis that although Wesley was a powerful patriarch, he was often supportive of women's religious literacy, she calls up the archival work she has employed:

> Chapter 2 . . . considers diaries, journals, and deathbed accounts of ordinary Methodists that were solicited, edited, and published by John Wesley over his long lifetime. Chapter 4 . . . examines archival evidence of the literacy practices of two Methodist itinerant preachers—Samuel Bardsley, a bottle-washer from Manchester, and Samuel Bradburn, a former shoemaker who was called "The Demosthenes of Methodism."
>
> . . . Chapter 7 . . . presents . . . an analysis of the inventory taken of [Wesley's] press immediately after his death in 1791. The inventory, which I read alongside Wesley's comments and observations on reading and writing, provides a special opportunity for understanding Wesley's vision of literacy and spirituality as they applied to ordinary Methodists. (31–32)

In addition, Burton's archive-related studies offer practical advice to feminist scholars in terms of methods for reading materials and methodologies for analyzing them.

These works also guide researchers in ways to avoid appropriation of sources, anachronism (as Burton so wisely dodges), and decontextualizing (which she, and all the others in the list, also sidestep). As a conceptual action, rhetorical feminism requires that they listen to and respect the figures they are studying, the context they are entering.

Methods and Methodologies for Naturalistic Research

Even as feminist scholars are sharpening their focus on more traditional research methods, we are also interrogating the epistemological and ethical implications of naturalistic studies, ethnography, and interviews. Caroline B. Brettell led the way with *When They Read What We Write: The Politics of Ethnography*. In her edited collection, she and ten other ethnographers extend the thorny issues raised by reflexive, interpretive anthropology in order to encompass the perhaps even thornier relationship between the researcher and the informants, "who have a vested interest in the anthropological text that has been or will be produced" (3). Peter Mortensen and Gesa Kirsch's *Ethics and Representation in Qualitative Studies of Literacy* encourages researchers to establish a "mutually enriching research relationship" with the subjects of our research, with Kirsch insisting that we "open up the research agenda to subjects, listening to their stories, and allowing them to actively participate, as much as possible, in the design, development, and reporting of research" (257). Patti Lather and Chris Smithies's *Troubling the Angels: Women Living with HIV/AIDS* demonstrates the power of layering expert and personal information so that the researcher's knowledge and voice do not drown out the "stories of people willing to put their lives on public display in the hope that it will make it better for others" (xiii). In *Ethical Dilemmas in Feminist Research*, Kirsch enumerates feminist ethical principles for conducting ethnographic or naturalistic research. Royster's emphasis on ethics surfaces in her Afracentric methodological approach, a purposeful feminist triangulation of scholars, subjects, and their audiences that emphasizes the researcher's clear perception of "*who* the primary and secondary audiences are and *who*, even, the *agents* of research and scholarship include" (*Traces* 274). And Heidi A. McKee and James E. Porter explain the importance of being self-reflexive and critically conscious about "one's own position, gender, and status" and of staying "attuned to the dynamics of power in all phases of a research project" (155). They also emphasize the feminist commitment to transparency, "to making the process and constructed nature of research visible to multiple audiences" and to discussing the "dilemmas and the process instead of presenting [the research study and findings] as a fait accompli" (156). In other words, feminist researchers must remember that their subjects are human beings and as such embody membership within a community to whom the researcher has obligations and to whom the researcher must listen, someone the researcher must respect. And together, Royster and Kirsch have given us the aforementioned *Feminist Rhetorical Practices,* challenging researchers "to study those with whom we disagree, whose values we don't share, whose worldviews might be foreign to us" (76). The authors continue:

> What feminist rhetoricians have taught us is to attend to our own levels of comfort and discomfort, to withhold quick judgment, to read and reread texts and interpret artifacts within the contexts of the women's chronologies, to interrogate the extent to which our own presence, values, and attitudes shape our interpretations of historical figures and periods. They have also taught us to attend the twofold challenge of being aware, not only of what enters our field of vision—what we see and recognize—but attuned also to our blind spots in order to consider with critical intensity what may be more in shadow, muted, and not immediately obvious. (76)

For many feminist rhetorical researchers, especially those following the precepts of rhetorical feminism, the relationship between researcher and "researched" should be a dialogic one.

A number of such dialogic ethnographic projects come to mind: Heather Brook Adams's in-progress book project "Shame, Secrets, and Silences: The Rhetorical Legacy of Unwed Pregnancy in the United States, Since 1960"; Michelle Ballif, Diane Davis, and Roxanne Mountford's *Women's Ways of Making It;* Brenda Brueggemann's *Lend Me Your Ear* and *Deaf Subjects;* Lather and Smithie's *Troubling the Angels;* McKee and Porter's "Rhetorica Online"; Beverly Moss's *A Community Text Arises;* and my own *Unspoken: A Rhetoric of Silence.* I also think of Moss's ongoing ethnographic study of African American women who belong to Phenomenal Women, Inc. and come together in what they refer to as their "sista space." As Moss explains, the primary purpose of the meetings is not necessarily to develop their literacies further, yet the women often do just that, using the occasion of their meetings to develop their skills in civic action and engagement as well as cultural enrichment ("'Phenomenal Women'").

In addition to being a tantalizing study of self-sponsored community action and literacy development, Moss's ethnography offers feminist ethnographers two important lessons. First of all, her project demonstrates how a personal experience ignites her interest in the group, in much the way Hogg, Sharer, Burton, and many other researchers reveal when describing the inception of their own research projects. The point here is that all researchers must pay attention to the subjects, issues, or problems that pester them, to the point of inspiring them.

In an article that prefigures her book-length project on the subject, Moss writes,

> In June of 2009, I was sitting in a small black church in a rural town in South Carolina at the funeral of my father's last aunt, my ninety-three-year-old great-aunt Alverta, listening to one of her friends talk about how my aunt, as a young woman, had been a member of a black women's club called the "Jollys." It seemed that the Jollys got together so that they could do community service in the black community in this small town and participate in social functions. It was the first time that I had ever heard of any of the women in my family being part of such a community organization as a women's club.... I was struck by how I had just spent the past sixteen months researching other black women in a club when I had a resource, now gone, in my own family.... That moment made the literacy stories of the women of Phenomenal Women Incorporated (P.W. Inc.), the [Columbus] Ohio-based African-American women's club ... even more important to me. ("'Phenomenal Women'" 1–2)

Another impressive feature of her rhetorical feminist project is the care Moss takes, even in an article-length study, to document her research goals, detail her research methods, and account for her own involvement as a participant-observer within a noninstitutional community space where African Americans use literacy:

> I have just completed data collection for a 16-month ethnographic study of ... Phenomenal Women Incorporated.... Data collection consisted of fieldnotes at monthly meetings, club-sponsored events, and events that the group members attend as official representatives of the club. I audiotaped meetings and audio or videotaped club-related [intellectual] events.... I have also interviewed individual members and focal groups within the organization. Finally, I made copies of documents written and/or read by the group at meetings and by individual members of focal groups. I participated when possible and appropriate (and when invited) in club events; however, I remained primarily an observer-participant. (5–6)

Moss's research (which employs the tactic of rhetorical feminism) offers her the opportunity to engage in dialogues with her so-called subjects, to listen to them, to delight in their vernaculars, experiences, and emotions.

Like Moss's study, Adams's ongoing ethnography into the rhetorics of unwed motherhood carefully calibrates the balance between honoring the requirements of institutional compliance and the experiences and words of research subjects. In "Institutional 'Protections,' Assumptions of Research, and the Challenges of Compliance: Opening a Conversation Space for Feminist Scholars Working with Participants" (a forthcoming chapter that represents a part of her larger project), Adams speaks to the delicacy of that balance. She had just finished taping an interview with an eighty-year-old informant when Elizabeth said, "I hope you get an 'A' on your paper."

At that moment, Adams realized that in being so careful to assure Elizabeth (and all the other women in her study) that her rights as a participant included the right to "determine what part of her story to share," neither she nor Elizabeth truly understood "the scope and stakes of this project [Adams's dissertation]" or what the terms "'harm' or 'risk'" might mean to a subject who was disclosing her "semi-secret past." Adams recounts the methods she had undertaken to get her project approved by the Institutional Review Board (IRB):

> I... completed online Human "Subjects" Research training through the Collaborative Institutional Training Initiative (CITI). Subsequent document review with the compliance office would ensure that I was transferring the principles of CITI training to my study design—namely that I was ethically and fairly recruiting participants, communicating my assessment of the risks and rewards of being involved in the study, enabling them to provide informed consent to participate, and explaining how I would protect their confidentiality.

Once she received IRB approval, Adams ventured into the field, following rules and availing herself of "field-developed best practices." Yet however well she had been prepared for her research practices, she was not prepared for the personal, even emotional connection she felt with Elizabeth, particularly when she saw that Elizabeth thought of the entire procedure as a course requirement rather than as Adams's effort to "shed light on a silenced history for future audiences." Adams admits that she had, mistakenly, relied too much on the university-managed governmental regulations in establishing her collaboration with Elizabeth rather than tilting the balance in the direction of enacting rhetorical feminism, making a personal, mutually trusting, dialogic relationship between her and the women the IRB referred to as her "informants."

From her experience, Adams calls for better collaboration between researchers themselves and offices of compliance. Instituting dialogues with those offices would provide a platform for feminist researchers to explain feminist research practices and women's ways of knowing to members of IRBs and for those same members to explain the assumptions of their institutional review. Maybe feminist researchers can even intervene in the process of review by illuminating the assumptions of their review. After all, as Kirsch reminds us, "So far, qualitative research [often naturalistic studies] has received neither the close scrutiny nor the careful guidance that IRBs regularly provide for experimental, quantitative research in the behavioral sciences" (*Ethical Dilemmas* 42).

I take the time to examine Moss's and Adams's research projects because they both serve as models for responsible yet creative naturalistic study. Like those in the list above, theirs are sensitive, ethical ethnographies, conducted in the spirit of rhetorical feminism, that honor and listen to the subjects of their research and respect the emotional and experiential contexts in which those subjects live and work. Each of the research projects mentioned here considers the agency of the subjects whose writings, speeches, and actions they study and observe, and all exemplify the evolution of feminist research methods to include ethical, dialogic ethnography throughout the process, from initial interview to final, written-up draft.

The Possibilities of Methods and Methodologies for Rhetorical Feminists

Hope calls . . . for sharp analytical skills.
    —Jacqueline Jones Royster and Gesa Kirsch, *Feminist Rhetorical Practices*

All the research projects, guides, methods, and methodologies I have recounted in this chapter are models for feminist scholars. They are not the only examples of solid research, nor do their inner workings reveal the myriad research methods and methodologies that feminist rhetoricians are employing. However, in all of this scholarship, feminist researchers are acknowledging the location of themselves in research and writing and working to connect the experiences of *someone else* to the representation of those experiences by *the researchers themselves*. As rhetorical feminists, they are taking special care to acknowledge and attend to locations and positionalities, the margins and the center.

To that end, we rhetorical feminists who are conducting research recognize our own self-interest, acknowledge how that interest might affect others, and resolve to participate in a reciprocal cross-boundary exchange, in which we talk *with* and listen *to* others, to their vernaculars, experiences, and emotions. Still, as Gayle Letherby admonishes, we must remember that the production of knowledge is a dialectic loaded in favor of the researchers themselves, no matter how hard we try to do just the opposite (9). She goes on to explain that biologically reinforced stereotypes continue to be peculiarly tenacious determinants of women's positions, especially in epistemic communities that have achieved the status of objectivity, as though gender has nothing to do with knowledge, societal performance, or cultural expectations. All the researchers in this chapter have un/consciously taken Letherby's cautions to heart, remembering the sociocultural status of women, of Others, acknowledging their role of researcher vis-à-vis the research subjects.

In the conclusion of their impressive compendium "Feminist Rhetorical Methodologies in Historic Rhetoric and Composition," Elizabeth Tasker and Frances B. Holt-Underwood assure us that

> the progress of feminist scholarship in codifying new methods, new subjects, and previously ignored sites in the study of history . . . is irrefutable. Traditionalist, postmodern, and activist research agendas; theoretical and practical methods; close readings; archival studies; case studies; cultural studies; genre studies; and comparative studies all coexist in the spectrum of feminist historical research. Pluralism thrives. Guided by the paradigms of recovery and revision, feminist methodologies are plentiful, flexible, and tailored by each researcher. (67)

Such impressive progress in feminist rhetorical research—just over the past thirty years—gives me great satisfaction and much hope.

As Royster and Kirsch remind us, "An ethics of hope and care requires a commitment to be open, flexible, welcoming, patient, introspective, and reflexive" (145)—all features of rhetorical feminism, in which feminists are not afraid to go back, rethink, revise, forge ahead, and even "withhold judgment" (146). In these ways, hope circulates widely as a trope of rhetorical feminism, a trope that takes root in feminist political displays, pedagogy, mentoring, administration, theory, and especially research, in the hope that such sites will eventually blossom with intellectual and academic respect and equality.

Forward-looking, future-oriented, yet prescriptive and recursive, hope presents scenarios for how attitudes toward women might shift and offers methods and methodologies for how such transformation could be made possible, even at the scene of crisis, disappointment, confusion, or curiosity, as much of the feminist rhetorical work in this chapter attests. Joan Haran writes that feminist theory (which would, of course, include the conceptual theory that is rhetorical feminism) is "always already utopian or hopeful, despairing it might seem in its specific manifestations, because of its production from within an imagined or interpretive community that is passionately invested in the possibility of social transformation" (95).

Like emotions (another crucial feature of rhetorical feminism), hope is socially constructed and agreed upon in that it is recognizable, understandable. And with hope comes a collaborative belief in some kind of future, some alternatives to the current situation. In "Hope, Passion, Politics," Chantal Mouffe and Ernesto Laclau reflect on hope and meaning: "Even in the ordinary realm of life there is a need to look forward to something and feel some kind of meaning in life. . . . It is very important that people think that their present condition could be better" (123). Thinking that their present situation could be better, and the future better still, is the hope of rhetorical feminist researchers.

FIVE: TEACHING

> I would   so help me   tell you if I could
> How some great teacher
> Came to my side and said:
>
> *Let's go down   into the underworld*
> —the earth already crazed
> *Let me take your hand*
>
> —Adrienne Rich, "Terza Rima"

In his 2012 State of the Union address, President Barack Obama reminded members of Congress as well as his viewing audience of our nation's educational shortcomings:

> At a time when other countries are doubling down on education, tight budgets have forced states to lay off thousands of teachers. We know a good teacher can increase the lifetime income of a classroom by over $250,000. A great teacher can offer an escape from poverty to the child who dreams beyond his circumstance. Every person in this chamber can point to a teacher who changed the trajectory of their lives. Most teachers work tirelessly, with modest pay, sometimes digging into their own pocket for school supplies—just to make a difference.
>   Teachers matter.

Many of the people who read this book are teachers (or aspiring teachers) of rhetoric, writing, speaking, or women's studies. As such, we know that teachers—and teaching—matter.

Teachers at every level work tirelessly, usually with modest pay, just to make a difference—at the same time that they are constantly pressured to invigorate their current classes (or as Obama said, "to teach with creativity and passion"), raise up their evaluations, master new technologies of every kind, and handle the paper load. Some of us even try to have personal lives. Teachers are busy, pressured. Many of us sometimes feel as though we are hanging on by a thread—just to make a difference. Yet teaching is too often perceived as "second" in the university's trinity of research, teaching, and service, "a sad reminder," offers bell hooks, "of the way teaching is seen as a duller, less valuable aspect of the academic profession" (*Teaching to Transgress* 12). Teaching matters, what with its power and responsibility that can be harnessed for creating—or thwarting—a good and just future. For rhetorical feminists, teaching is hope embodied. It is a forward-looking endeavor, one that has power to change lives—our own, our students'. To pretend otherwise is irresponsible.

Teaching matters.[1]

Rhetoric has always been a teaching tradition, the pedagogical pursuit of good speaking, good writing, and, just as often, the good (that is, ethical) human being. Quintilian was not the first to link the study of rhetoric with the development of the good man (and much later, of course, good woman). Isocrates made famous his program of rhetorical education emphasizing that same crucial connection, coupling rhetoric with eloquence, a kind of philosophical eloquence akin to "wisdom in civic affairs emphasizing moral responsibility" (Conley 17). By fusing Plato's truth-seeking philosophy with his own conception of a well-expressed, morally responsible, politically responsive rhetoric, Isocrates was able to weave together a pedagogical program of rhetoric, ethics, and civic duty, a program of hope for the future. Versions of his exclusive, aristocratic program (paideia) flourished throughout both the Greek and Roman Empires as well as during the European and English Renaissance and into the New World at Harvard, Yale, and Princeton. Obvious vestiges of the paideia remain today in nearly every writing and reading textbook. But two contemporary collections in particular have offered us clear theories, practices, and pedagogical examples of inclusionary, representative feminist rhetorical teaching: Kate Ronald and Joy Ritchie's 2006 *Teaching Rhetorica*, and Lindal Buchanan and Kathleen Ryan's 2010 *Walking and Talking Feminist Rhetorics*. In addition, several noteworthy anthologies of women's rhetorical performances have been prepared especially for classroom use: Gwendolyn Pough's 2004 *Check It While I Wreck It: Black Womanhood, Hip-Hop Culture, and the Public Sphere*; Pough, Elaine Richardson, Aisha Durham, and Rachel Raimist's 2007 *Home Girls Make*

TEACHING

Some Noise: Hip Hop Feminism Anthology; and Ritchie and Ronald's 2001 *Available Means*. Each of these collections marks the power of feminist rhetorical practices, theories, and pedagogies to liberate—even revolutionize—the classroom.

In this chapter, I return rhetoric to its roots as a teaching tradition, the pedagogical pursuit of good (that is, artful and ethical) speaking, writing, and being. To these pedagogical roots, I graft feminism and feminist pedagogy, whose flowers and fruits bear a rhetorical scent. This chapter opens with a thumbnail sketch of contemporary American education, followed by a depiction of the rhetorical feminist in the classroom. Many of these teachers, alert to the concerns of those experiencing marginalization, help students recognize and work with (and against) the power differentials that constitute mainstream cultural and rhetorical practices. Those practices include the familiar rhetorical grammar of who speaks/who can speak, who can/not listen (and what those listeners can/not do), who has power-over or power-with whom, who has/claims agency—concepts developed in (feminist) rhetorical theory. These teachers demonstrate and affirm the values of dialogue, mutual understanding, silence, and listening—all tactics of rhetorical feminism. And some—like bell hooks, Adrienne Rich, and Mina Shaughnessy—express rhetorical feminism in their teaching, as well.

Like the goals of the paideia, the collective goal of feminist teaching is to articulate a vision of rigorous scholarly preparation, high scholarly expectations, critical reflection and exchange, and ethical, civic participation aimed toward progress—all anchored in a distinctly feminist politics of hope for a more equitable future across and among differences. As such, feminist pedagogy can be the performance of rhetorical feminism: it is self-aware, purposeful, invested in dismantling hierarchy, and both cognizant and respectful of the practices of women and Others. Rhetorical feminism is harnessed in service of feminist pedagogy in its insistence on a forward-looking and hopeful stance—even when "it doesn't look good at all" and there are "no guarantees whatsoever" (C. West).

The Current State of American Education

History is becoming more and more a race between education and catastrophe.

—H. G. Wells, *Outline of History*

Yet as we settle into the twenty-first century, hope for teachers, students, and their parents seems to be at a premium, especially given the endless chant of pundits that "the sky is falling." The international ranking of US education has fluctuated from seventeenth to twenty-fourth from 2007 to 2017 alone, depending on the metric: spending per pupil, class size, or test scores.[2] Scandinavia and Asia continue to lead the world's rankings.[3] Yes, continual defunding of public education (from K through PhD) is the norm at a time when the number of lower-income students, students of color, and English language learners—those who most desperately need a good education—is on the rise. Know-it-all legislators, mostly white, mostly men, regularly vote to decrease spending at the same time they work to shape education (with No Child Left Behind morphing into the Common Core); major funding cuts translate into classrooms of thirty students, no art, no physical education, and no music—while emergency lockdown drills are standard.[4] Poverty and hunger affect at least 22 percent of our students, which, in turn, affects their learning (Chen). Teacher autonomy has been eroded by standardized, high-stakes testing. Attracting and retaining good teachers has become a national crisis, with few school systems finding ways to pay teachers what they merit, let alone to consider tenuring them.

Higher public education faces many of the same problems: consistently decreased funding, program cuts (usually aimed at the liberal arts, especially ethnic, women's, and gender studies), threats to a long-established tenure system, and the attrition of good teachers. That most college students do not earn a degree in four years is another problem; only 19 percent of students accomplish this at most public colleges or universities and only 36 percent at state flagship universities (Lewin). According to the National Center for Education, 59 percent of full-time students graduate in six years, which seems to be a more realistic measure. In addition, higher public education continues to overproduce PhDs and then send them out into a compromised pipeline, with little hope of job security.[5] (As I write this, tenured faculty represent only 17 percent of college instructors.) And in an attempt to attract research dollars, most public colleges and universities have come to rely on corporate partnerships, which tint academic culture with a dark shade of business culture.[6]

Thus, the current level of US support for education continues to dwindle politically, financially, and culturally. Many of our lawmakers attended university when doing so was affordable, when student loans were a great investment, when state and federal governments were supplementing the costs. Ironically, many of those aforementioned legislators who themselves benefited from government support are now systematically cutting off such opportunities for today's students.[7] This generation of richly diverse students is not only paying high tuitions but is also pursued relentlessly by predatory lending agencies and, as a result, is carrying staggering student loan debt.[8] Given the sharp decrease in public funding and prohibitive tuition costs, higher education has reverted back to being a private investment rather than a public good—a study in inequality and restricted access, no longer emblematic of democracy, with the value of a college degree shifting from a public good to an individual (or private) one. Thus, students who attend public colleges and universities have come to accept this disincentivizing (if not punitive) financial structure, along with a system of mostly well-educated, pedagogically effective adjunct faculty.

The overall financial picture seems even more dire at many historically black colleges and universities (HBCUs).[9] The loss of revenue from declining enrollments, endowments, government support, alumni giving, and real-estate assets has led to the closing of eleven HBCUs in the past twenty years. No amount of cost cutting, restructuring, or tuition raising can offset these revenue losses.[10] And yet HBCUs, especially the flagships (Howard, Morehouse, and Spelman), remain committed to growing their endowments, looking beyond the African American community and into the broader world for students, and moving—with a sense of purpose and hope—into the future.

Despite these real setbacks in American education, classroom teachers remain the best hope for the future of our democracy. In fact, the *only* way to raise our education standards is to hire, retain, and professionally develop teachers from among our top graduates. Any government that wants to attract the best and brightest to teaching must consider ways to raise their pay and status. (Status never rises without a corresponding pay raise.) We Americans know that having a good teacher is linked to higher income as well as to a range of other social results. Yet we continue to place many demands on our schools and teachers, expecting them to produce well-prepared students who are workplace-ready: knowledgeable, innovative researchers and effective communicators, ethical critical thinkers, problem solvers, and collaborators (especially across differences). Nevertheless, for the most part, we neither fund our schools nor support our teachers.

Somehow, even in the midst of declining funding, escalating critiques of and controls on teachers, and the low societal status of teachers themselves, Americans all know that teaching really matters—even when both good teaching and bad are taken for granted, when the material conditions of teaching are rich or grim, even when teachers themselves are frustrated, nearly hopeless. In many of her works, bell hooks evokes the positive influence of those teachers who took her seriously and pressed her to learn:

> I have sought teachers in all areas of my life who would challenge me beyond what I might select for myself, and in and through that challenge allow me a space of radical openness where I am truly free to choose—able to learn and grow without limits. (*Teaching to Transgress* 207)

Yet in colleges and universities, as I mentioned above, excellent teaching is too often seen as mere icing on the cake of institutional maintenance, with scholarly research (most of all) and large-scale administration deemed more substantive.

Even worse, effective teachers are sometimes considered suspect, receiving neither the respect nor the support that their engaged pedagogy might well deserve, as though "education is neutral, . . . enabl[ing] us to treat everyone equally, dispassionately" (hooks, *Teaching to Transgress* 198). Ethicist Nancy Tuana, however, reminds us that we should—and generally do—respond more responsibly to those for whom we care the most.

Regardless of the pedagogical context, "It is imperative that we maintain hope even when the harshness of reality may suggest the opposite" (Freire, *Heart* 106). Rhetorical feminism compels us to maintain hope. Maintaining hope is not the same as wishful thinking or mindless optimism. Rather, hope is *will*ful thinking combined with willful action, for "to take on hope," as Paula Mathieu writes, "is to take on risk and responsibility while maintaining a dogged optimism" (17). For Cornel West, hope is a nonrational optimism, a leap of faith *beyond* the evidence.

Hope, the Classroom Teacher

In "What Spurs Students to Stay in College and Learn?," journalist Dan Berrett mines the findings of Patrick Terenzini and Ernest Pascarella, who have established the specific ways in which college affects students. In two separate studies, Terenzini and Pascarella confirm what many of us already suspect: the strongest predictor of student retention and student learning is good teaching. Terenzini and Pascarella define good teaching according to a six-dimension scale, including skill, rapport, structure, difficulty, interaction, and feedback (qtd. in Berrett, par. 4). Of those six dimensions, two stand out as most valuable: the teacher's skill, which is demonstrated by the teacher's "good command of subject matter" and ability to "give clear explanations," and the structure of the course itself, how well the teacher plans and organizes the course and uses class time. Not the latest technology, not even test scores, it is the rhetorical feminist teacher—and her course; her acknowledgment of and respect for students' vernaculars, experiences, and emotions; her hope for the future—who keeps students in college and keeps them learning.[11]

The Effective Feminist Teacher

Effective feminist teachers (regardless of gender), then, are supportive, inviting, and yet demanding (even the least-prepared students will do better than most people, including themselves, ever expected if we put challenging materials in front of them instead of simplified stuff). They encourage students to engage, and they provide feedback in order to keep students on the right track, the track to self-respect, intellectual curiosity, financial stability, and continued hope. These teachers couple hope with the fierce struggle necessary for transforming that hope into concrete reality (Freire, *Hope* 3). Yes, other pedagogies seek similar ends, but teaching embedded in rhetorical feminism distinguishes itself by "its investment in a view of contemporary society as sexist and patriarchal, and of the complicity of reading, writing, and teaching in those conditions" (Jarratt, "Feminist Pedagogy" 116). Such teaching is cognizant of hegemonic discourse and pedagogical practices, especially vis-à-vis the knowledge and languages students bring to class. The pedagogy A. Abby Knoblauch describes is imbued by rhetorical feminism, what with its focus on intersectionality, emphasis on the connections between the personal and the political, recognition of and challenges to unequal power relations, attention to "overlooked discursive and epistemological practices" (that is, the vernaculars and experiences of the marginalized), and acknowledgment of meaning-making that is "often associated with women, with the feminine, and/or with the body" (that is, silence, listening, emotion).[12]

These teachers unveil continual opportunities for hope put into the service of productive struggle, with teachers and their students working through the process of transformation together. As Suzanne Clark and

Lisa Ede write, such struggle can manifest itself as resistance, which "opens up possibilities for learning for teachers and theorists, as well as for students" (284). "Without hope," Paulo Freire tells us, "there is little we can do" (*Hope* 3). He continues: "My hope is necessary, but it is not enough. Alone, it does not win. But without it, my struggle will be weak and wobbly" (2).

Holding on to hope is not always easy, not even for a rhetorical feminist.

Positionality (and Intersectionality)

To the end of neutralizing various forms of oppression, feminist pedagogues work to transform the world, awarding central status to the role of "positionality," Linda Martín Alcoff's concept of accounting for gender, race, class, ability, sexuality, language, religion, or other features of our identity that mark relational positions rather than essential qualities (markers that provisionally call up the center—and the margins). As I have said throughout, our positionality both acknowledges and illuminates our personal experience and language, colors our perception and production of knowledge, works to keep us in position, and plays a central role in our rhetorical transactions. Lorraine Code explains positionality as always relative within an ever-shifting context that includes others, economic conditions, cultural and political institutions, and ideologies (hence the margins and a center). And then there is masculinity. A woman's positionality is, in addition, always defined *in relation* to that "single undisputed norm" (*What* 180). In these ways, positionality influences personal experiences, which in turn serve as critical lenses through which rhetorical transactions (classroom understandings, discussions, and the construction of knowledge) and personal relationships are understood and refracted in the feminist classroom.[13]

Naturally, intersectionality comes into play as well, always complicating (and sometimes enriching) positionality by revealing the multiplicity of positions that coexist in any classroom. Feminists have legitimized personal experience, to be sure, but they also acknowledge the limits of that experience, a stance rhetorical feminism expands. To wit, white people simply do not experience the world the way people of color do (and vice versa), so white people must expand their "book" and experiential knowledge in other ways. Nor do men and women experience the world in the same way, providing men an opportunity to learn more about women's lives and experiences. These cross-cultural issues are crucial to the workings of any classroom. The following pedagogical examples demonstrate the power of positionality and the insights of intersectionality.

Rhetorical feminists are keenly aware of positionality—their own as well as their students'—and the way positionality plays out as the power dynamics of the classroom. No matter what obstacles or advantages her positionality might include, each teacher recognizes, discusses, and works through them through pedagogy, curriculum, and assignment design. She may (or may not) be fully aware of her students' position, of course, but she is keenly aware of her own—her position within her institution, her position vis-à-vis her students, her position particularly if she is Othered in any way. Her body, her identity, her political stance—and peculiarization of her embodiment—affect who she is, how she relates to others, how they relate to her. Her body c/overtly implies the great diversity in experiential epistemologies and yet unreliably marks itself as a conclusive representation of that epistemology (in what way/s her body presents). Thus, the teacher's body often and instantly calls attention to what too many perceive as an unsettling mind-body split (as in the case of the pregnant teacher or the gifted teacher of color) much more often, in fact, than her body offers that idealized fusion of the mind and body (of power *and* enfranchisement) so often fictionalized by Professor Keating, Mr. Holland, and Dumbledore.

In "Women's Bodies in the College Writing Classroom," Jill Eichhorn recounts her history of wearing clothing that minimized her womanly shape, "dissociating" her "feminist voice" from her "female body"—that is, until her second trimester of pregnancy made doing so impossible: "Less and less disguisable, I embodied difference from dominant ideology" (310). Eventually, she came to embrace her pregnant body as a symbolic, concrete sign of resistance within "public space, space that has been organized and defined as male" (310).

In writing about intersections of class, gender, region, and race, Beverly Moss wonders if

> my white colleagues, especially the men, are questioned as many times as I am about whether I have a Ph.D., or whether their authority is challenged by their students as much as mine is, or if their students seem as surprised to see them walk into the classroom on the first day as many of mine are when I walk in. ("Intersections" 159)

And in "'When and Where I Enter': Race, Gender, and Composition Studies," Shirley Wilson Logan writes about the effect her black body has on a class of mostly white writers: "Black women are especially challenged to teach communication skills in settings where they must often first overcome resistance to their very presence.... When... designing our courses and assignments, we [must] pay attention to the interaction among teacher, student, and subject matter" (56).

The power dynamics play out in many ways and become readily apparent when students resist the feminist teacher's authority, her feminist pedagogy, her feminism—perhaps on the basis of how her body resonates for them. Just because the feminist teacher pays respect to the marginalized does not automatically mean her students will give her the same respect. Just because she gives credence to the vernacular, to personal experience, to emotion, does not mean her students will reciprocate. Yet even in the face of these challenges, feminist teachers still claim their authority, their expertise, their passion, and their position—another principle of feminist pedagogy, one bell hooks especially supports:

> We must acknowledge that our role as teacher is a position of power over others. We can use that power in ways that diminish or in ways that enrich and it is this choice that should distinguish feminist pedagogy from ways of teaching that reinforce domination. (*Talking Back* 52)

Critical Engagement

Feminist pedagogy emphasizes engagement over mastery, with engagement toward mastery the goal. Charlotte Bunch offers a four-step pedagogical method of critical engagement for achieving these goals: describing what exists, analyzing why that reality exists, determining what should exist, and hypothesizing how to change what *is* to what *should* be (251–53). In these four ways, Bunch and her students move from a self-aware analysis of what is, particularly in terms of power relations, to a purposeful, hopeful plan for realizing what ought to be, what can be.

Moss emphasizes engagement *toward* mastery (her students' as well as her own) by articulating the ways her background "provides a foundation for [her] to see the diversity within seemingly homogenous classes" ("Intersections" 163):

> I do not ask my students to leave their pasts behind, to erase racial, class, ethnic, and gender markers ... [that] may be sustaining, supporting, enriching many of them. Equally important, however, I do not ask them to wear the banners for their race, class, ethnic group, or gender. (163)

TEACHING

And she works out a plan for them:

> My path into the academy also provides me with a perspective from which to question long held racist, sexist, and classist assumptions and practices that have been perpetuated by the academy. I question those practices through assignments that ask students, and consequently the academy, to expand their definition of what counts as literacy, what counts as text, what counts as scholarship—ultimately, what counts as valuable. (163)

Self-identified "relatively out, but not terribly vocal gay faculty member" and feminist writing center director Harry Denny describes the rhetorical value of such critical engagements to his work, writing about the intervention necessary when a student writer brings a homophobic text to the peer tutor. The peer tutor is stunned, offended by the rabidly homophobic text, and turns to Denny. "Our jobs," writes Denny,

> are to mentor and collaboratively learn; yet common decency, learning climate, and workplace environment dictate safety, not just against physical violence, but also the harm that can result in verbal abuse. Would we require an African American tutor to mentor a white supremacist, or a Jew to help an anti-Semitic skinhead? Why would sexuality be any different? . . . I'm under an obligation to complicate and make possible a whole range of understanding, not to let any particular ideology go unchecked or position take on a naturalized status. . . . One valuable way to make learning resonate is to enable students to connect their own lives (and our own) to their subject matter and to foster the sorts of critical thinking and literacies that assume their perspectives aren't totalizing. To have students understand the moral and intellectual merit of our partial perspectives is one of the best and lasting gifts we can provide. (106)

Nancy Schniedewind outlines a set of feminist pedagogical precepts that complement those of Bunch: building a trusting learning community, sharing leadership within the classroom, cooperating, integrating affective learning (about self, others, emotions), and acting in the community (outreach and activism) (262–70). Her precepts are predicated on the twofold belief that individual involvement (engagement) is worthwhile and that public-sphere activism is never in vain, not even for women and Others whose full participation in society has been restricted when not denied altogether.[14] "For those of us who teach writing," explains writing center specialist Meg Woolbright,

> the conflicts that result at the boundary between feminist rhetoric and pedagogy and the patriarchal values of the academy are manifested in our conversations with student writers. These conversations are dynamic, ... fraught with uncertainty and ambiguity. (17)

As such, these interactions reveal our "hidden curriculum"—our feminism, our feminist practices—which Woolbright believes characterizes "peer tutoring at its best" (18). The best of peer tutoring, then, involves "understanding as power" (17), "negotiating uses of power" (17), cooperation, interaction, respect for students' own experience, and the construction of knowledge (18).

But feminist pedagogy is more than a set of guidelines or precepts: it is a political standpoint, a stance of informing and reforming ways of acting in and on the world, a positionality that rhetorical feminism helps illuminate. Helping students delineate their positionality and embrace hope are necessary first steps for co-creating conditions and co-constructing knowledge for those students who want to change their worlds—and do the work to achieve just that. Indeed, a major goal of rhetorical feminists is to work with students in shaping a world that is more humane for everyone—regardless of their positionality, particularly for the marginalized, and especially for women.

Agency, Authority, and Action

In addition to acknowledging their positionality and claiming their own authority (within those relations that constitute positionality), effective teachers ask the same of their students, with the full expectation that the students will *claim* (rather than merely *receive*) their own educations, their agency, just as legendary feminist poet and teacher Adrienne Rich tells the women of Douglas College:

> If university education means anything beyond the processing of human beings into expected roles, through credit hours, tests, and grades ... , it implies an ethical and intellectual contract between teacher and student. This contract must remain intuitive, dynamic, unwritten; but we must turn to it again and again if learning is to be reclaimed from the depersonalizing and cheapening pressures of the present-day academic scene.

TEACHING

> The first thing I want to say to you... is that you cannot afford to think of being here to *receive* an education; you will do much better to think of yourselves as being here to *claim* one. ("Claiming" 231)

Those effective teachers have hope, agency, and authority. Freire admits, "I am hopeful, not out of mere stubbornness, but out of an existential, concrete imperative" (*Hope* 2). His imperative of hope grows out of a deep satisfaction with his own earned authority and embraced agency.

Rhetorical feminists consciously employ hope, looking critically (along with their students) at their present condition, assessing what is missing, and then longing for and working toward a not-yet reality, a future anticipated (Mathieu 19). As Woolbright tells us, students need more than our feminist pedagogical encouragement. They need for us to help them name the "political circumstances in which we write and talk" so we can

> create a space in which we talk openly about the conflicts between feminism and the patriarchy. We can consider how and why different rhetorics and pedagogies come to be privileged and the implications for this privileging for how we both construct ourselves and are constructed by the institutions in which we work. With this naming, our students can be given the power and the responsibility to negotiate between feminism and the patriarchy, between writing vibrantly, sensuously, in their own voices and writing the tightly argued prose of the academy. (28)

Hope requires imagination as well as risk—and action. This is not to say that working for change is easy (despite the buoy of hope) or that students readily agree to engage in the process. Rather, it is to say that hope, struggle, and change are the troika of feminist rhetorical pedagogy, for students and teachers alike. Rhetorical feminist pedagogy signifies action, agency—it does something. After all, and as I have said before, the point of any rhetorical transaction is to *do* something.

Feminist *Rhetorical* Pedagogy

Until recently (the last forty years or so), American education was thought to be one-size-fits-all, projecting the illusion that it spoke to everyone. (See Rich, "Claiming.") We now know that it is true: American education speaks to everyone—just so long as they are privileged by gender, race, socioeconomic class, ability, heteronormativity, and cultural-ethnic background. In other words, we now know that American education has always obscured the needs, experiences, perspectives, and expectations of Others. (See Rich, "Compulsory Heterosexuality.") For these reasons, feminist teachers bring historical and political knowledge of the feminist movement, sexism, and racism (and all the concomitant analyses) into the classroom, working in dialogic ways in order to encourage their students to inhabit their own agency and to share their knowledge, experiences, and insights through language. As Susan Jarratt tells us, "Feminist [rhetorical] pedagogy is not about forcing all the students to subscribe to a particular political position but rather engaging with students on the terrain of language in the gendered world we all currently inhabit" ("Feminist Pedagogy" 118).

An Ethical Stance toward Difference

Classrooms are more diverse than ever, with diversity, identity, positionality, and intersectionality acknowledged and embraced by the rhetorical feminist teacher who takes an ethically orientated stance toward subject matter, teaching and learning, and students alike—as well as toward the gendered and raced realities of the world. Tina Chen translates these ideas into the pursuit of an "ethics of knowledge." The ethical component of feminist rhetorical pedagogy is not teaching *what* to believe but rather helping students develop an ethical approach for making decisions about *how* to believe, about how to make decisions that lead to belief.

In "A Symposium on Feminist Experiences in the Composition Classroom," Jill Eichhorn, Sara Farris, Karen Hayes, Adriana Hernández, Susan J. Jarratt, Karen Power-Stubbs, and Marian M. Sciachitano all offer their reflections on their "intertwining of theory and practice" (298) and their feminist ethical stance toward the two key terms of their experiences: "difference and authority" (298). In her introduction to the symposium, Sciachitano reminds us that "taking up a feminist politics of location in the classroom . . . means taking differences seriously" (299). And in each of their accounts, the women rely on their individual (and shared) system of ethics to approach these key issues. This is not to say that the ethical decision is the only (right) decision, but it is a considered one. The ethical action and way of being is, according to Aristotle, the greatest good: "By human virtue, we mean that of the soul, not that of the body; and the happiness we speak of is an activity of the soul" (*Nicomachean Ethics* 1102a).

And keeping an ethical orientation in mind when attending issues of difference is paramount in the rhetorical feminist classroom, for "constant critique" anchors its pedagogy, as the teacher and the students produce knowledge together.[15] It is this diversity, this attention to diversity (or to division) that calls for a rhetorical intervention, for whenever identification and division are put "ambiguously together, you have the characteristic invitation to rhetoric" (Burke, *Rhetoric of Motives* 25).

In Karen Hayes's symposium teaching experiment, "Al" became one of the "most outspoken first-year students," his loud and proud prejudices foregrounding difference in the classroom. In response, Hayes tapped her authority. She issued ethically based, powerful critiques of his assertions that "gays . . . brought us AIDS," "men deserve to be paid more than women," and "Moslems [sic] enjoy killing Jews" (303). "Al was so outrageous that I could and did flatly state that I disagreed with and was actually offended by his remarks. I believe that other students, especially females, were empowered by my stance and began to assert themselves as well" (303). Hayes's rhetoric helped mend the division between Al and the rest of the class, for "Al's presence . . . [made] it possible for issues to arise and be addressed that normally are subsumed in consensus" (303). Al's assertions created deep divisions within the classroom, a Burkean invitation to Hayes's tactical, rhetorical response, a response that helped mend that division. Her response promoted invitation for others to speak, a scene for listening, and a dialogue on hard topics.

In these ways, rhetoric can be employed for discerning the realities and ethical components of those pedagogical situations. It can also be used for developing ethical reasoning skills and maintaining ethical human transactions, transactions that engage the complexity of alterity. That alterity becomes the theoretical subject of the classroom—regardless of the subject under investigation—because difference inhabits every history, every theory, every praxis, every story, every day.

Difference in a rhetorical feminist classroom serves as an invitation to teacher and students alike to consciously see themselves as positioned subjects—and actors—in terms of their race, class, sexual orientation, cultural-ethnic background, and gender. Their positionality and accorded measure of authority hold transformative potential: they can contribute to the evolution of knowledge inside the classroom and take responsibility for political activism outside—or they can choose not to, as in the case of Sara Farris, who writes about the ways her men students challenged her "overtly feminist teaching strategies" and her own difficulties in articulating the liberatory possibilities for her women and men students alike: "'What's in it for me?' is the question asked by every student of every class, and rightly so" (307).

Awarding-winning feminist teacher of rhetoric Nan Johnson strategically leverages positionality and argument culture to stimulate ideas of social change in her classroom. Rather than foregrounding her politics, Johnson orchestrates the emergence of such concepts as justice, prejudice, and equality by leading her students in tracking "the appearance and progression of a social-change issue," an issue that the students introduce. Using a "rhetorical model of social change" (which she developed), the class follows an issue through at least three distinct stages: articulation and definition of an issue, debate, and institutionalization/cultural inscription of the sociocultural consensus. Often these three stages lead to a fourth stage of cultural upheaval. Whether that fourth stage starts immediately or decades later, it can lead to what Johnson labels a "backwave," starting the entire process again. Whether she and her students are discussing environmental issues (they start with Rachel Carson's *Silent Spring*), reproductive rights, or a presidential-election concern, the entire class focuses on the *process* of defining, debating, and enacting an issue rather than on whether an issue is "right" or "wrong," fair or not, ethical or not. In this way, Johnson helps students focus on the evolution of social change and the sociocultural forces that bring such change into being, for however long. Her pedagogy offers a process for students to think critically, carefully, and together—with time to pause and reflect on issues. Johnson does not have to state her own opinion (let alone persuade students) to guide her students to their recognition of inequalities and injustices. She taps the resource that is rhetorical feminism—a clear understanding of marginalization, a promotion of dialogue and mutual understanding, for instance—in the process of helping students track the power of sociocultural forces and come to their own conclusions.

A classroom like Johnson's provides the perfect venue for enacting the pedagogical tactics of rhetorical feminism, features that John Duffy heralds in "Post-truth and First-Year Writing." Duffy calls "mutual honesty" the foundation of any productive classroom interactions, whether between peers or between students and their teacher. Duffy draws on the strengths of rhetorical feminism to teach his students how "basic honesty" and mutual trust can enable them to research a topic by reading information they agree with as well as information with which they do not.

The aim is not to be persuaded by the unwelcome opinion but to listen to it, to understand it. Honesty and trust also enable students to engage in generative in-class dialogues about their own positions (arguments) and those of others—all their ideas judged for their "scrutiny, criticism, and [even] rejection." But perhaps most important, Duffy's rhetorical feminism lights the classroom scene with the hope that student writing can be used for "inquiry, exploration," and, yes, for "reconciliation."

As these examples illustrate, rhetorical feminism in the classroom is concerned with overcoming oppressions, opening up liberatory possibilities, recognizing and establishing equity, and affording students the space and time to listen to one another, engage in dialogue, and contemplate issues as they form their opinions on those issues. It also recognizes the ways knowledge claims exist within an already-in-place knowledge-validating process and how the concept of objectivity can be equated with the views of those already in power, as well as the effect so-called objectivity has on women and Others. Feminist pedagogies are predicated on the belief that knowledge claims created outside of that already-in-place process (feminist, critical-race, queer, or class-conscious claims, for instance) rarely acquire status as bona fide knowledge.

As I have argued throughout this book, mainstream culture is hardly inclusive. Therefore, voice, identity, knowledge, and authority are achieved only by understanding one's own situation vis-à-vis others, that is, by recognizing the importance of positional knowing. An awareness of one's own and one's students' positionality allows teachers to better teach and care for their students. Rhetorical feminist teachers embrace educational values that respect personal experience and encourage active engagement and collaboration, values that are imaginative, often liberatory, and can diminish the assertiveness, competiveness, and hierarchy that have long held rein in the academy.

The Feminist Pedagogy of Adrienne Rich

One such teacher is Rich herself, who, in 1968, began teaching writing in the SEEK (Search for Education, Elevation, and Knowledge) program at the City College of New York in Harlem, an access program attracting mostly black, Puerto Rican, and other previously excluded students. As Krista Ratcliffe reminds us, Rich's work is as relevant to rhetorical studies as is Aristotle's, speaking as it does "with clarity, with dignity, with ethics, and wisdom" ("Coming Out" 32). And Rich's work serves as an example of rhetorical feminist teaching at a classroom site of hope. Rich writes, "In order to live in the city, I need to ally myself, in some concrete, practical, if limited way, with the possibilities" ("Teaching Language" 55). The SEEK program offered her an opportunity to create possibility. In "Teaching Language in Open Admissions," Rich discusses her being interviewed for a teaching job and hired as a poet-teacher, along with such writers as Toni Cade Bambara, Paul Blackburn, Robert Cumming, David Henderson, and June Jordan, and describes the students as

> black and Puerto Rican freshmen entering from substandard ghetto high schools, where the prevailing assumption had been that they were of inferior intelligence. . . . Many dropped out (a lower percentage than the national dropout rate, however); many stuck it out through several semesters of remedial English, math, reading, to enter the mainstream of college. (55)

According to Rich, nearly 40 percent of these students graduated from college and 10 percent of them went on to graduate school, defying societal expectations. And she describes herself as an inexperienced teacher of basic writing who was "working on new frontiers, trying new methods" (55).

In their profile of Rich's gratifying SEEK experiences, Iemanjá Brown and her vast network of colleagues report on the many ways SEEK students and teachers stimulated and learned from one another, a pedagogical tactic of rhetorical feminism that puts students—their intellectual and political interests, personal experiences, and vernaculars—front and center in the writing classroom. Rich describes her eye-opening experiences as mutually informing for students and teachers alike:

> Most of us felt that students learn to write by discovering the validity and variety of their own experiences; and in the late 1960s, as the black classics began to flood the bookstores, we drew on the black novelists, poets, and polemicists as the natural path to this discovery for SEEK students. . . . For many white teachers, the black writers were a relatively new discovery. . . . In this discovery of a previously submerged culture we were learning from and with our students as rarely happens in the university, though it is happening anew in women's studies. ("Teaching" 57)

At the time, Rich was working to answer the question, "How does one teach order, coherence, the structure of ideas while respecting the student's experience of his or her thinking and perceiving?" (57), giving credence to the feminist pedagogical stance toward identities and positionalities.

Thus, fifty years ago, Rich and her colleagues were practicing feminist rhetorical pedagogy, infused with the hope that underpins rhetorical feminism, in a framework of education intended to be intellectually reciprocal, liberating, and socially just. A basic tenet of their pedagogy was bringing voices into the classroom that had long been silenced or marginalized, voices the students had not heard before:

> We were not merely exploring a literature and a history which had gone virtually unmentioned in our white educations . . . ; we were not merely having to confront in talk with our students and in their writings, as well as the books we read, the bitter reality of Western racism. ("Teaching" 57)

Rich is careful about sounding "pious and patronizing" in her assessment of her early teaching experiences. After all, a commitment to serving the needs of students is not without its pitfalls (a do-gooder feeling being one of them).

Nonetheless, Rich holds her ground when she asserts, "The fact remains that our white liberal assumptions *were* shaken, our vision of both the city and the university changed, our relationship to language itself made both deeper and more painful" ("Teaching" 57). An effective teacher, Rich changed along with her students, just as most of us change when we read (and then teach) a nearly forgotten text for the first time (think the anti-lynching campaign of Ida B. Wells, for example). She was herself learning from and with her students about what she refers to as a "previously submerged culture": "We found ourselves reading almost any piece of Western literature through our students' eyes, imagining how this voice, these assumptions would sound to us if we were they" (57). Trying to read from their positionality, Rich seems determined to harness her students' intellectual curiosity, earned knowledge, positionality, standpoint, and ways of knowing at the same time that she engaged her own.

Like contemporary feminist teachers Staci Perryman-Clark, Haivan Hoang, and Iris Ruiz, whose pedagogical scholarship focuses on the classroom power of Afrocentric Ebonics, Asian American student rhetoric, and Chicano/a culture and language, respectively, Rich knew well that knowledge and purposeful rhetoric are produced by all groups in society, including students, notwithstanding their sexuality, gender, sociocultural or socioeconomic status, or cultural-ethnic identity. Knowledge has never been the sole province of academic disciplines, experts, or teachers, let alone that of privileged white men. Rich taught for social change, acknowledged and negotiated differences, and spoke out against traditions that continue to be oppressive, including hegemonic language conventions and rhetorical traditions. She seems to have believed feminist pedagogy to be prescriptive as well as futuristic, guided by a vision—a rhetorical feminist hope—of what education could actually be, could actually achieve, if diversity and intersectionalities of all kinds could circulate freely. Such a hope was guided by the promise that is a rhetorical education.

Feminist Pedagogies at Work

In her now landmark 1988 essay, "Composing as a Woman," Elizabeth Flynn writes that "for the most part . . . the fields of feminist studies and composition studies have not engaged each other in a serious or systematic way" (425). Flynn's argument modeled the way to do just that. Hence, in the past thirty years, compositionists of all types have been aligning their pedagogical goals with feminist principles. Thoughtful practice, a theory of teaching grounded in positionality (the instructor's as well as the students'), talk of agency and process, a reevaluation of how knowledge is constructed and delivered, and a sense of hope and possibility are all concepts that have taken root in the composition classroom.

Patricia A. Sullivan addresses Flynn's concern that feminist principles were missing from the composition classroom, offering her stance that composition has always been a kind of feminist endeavor, but a field developing in parallel—not in concert—with feminism. "Composition itself was marginalized, and composition scholars had to constitute the discipline as a viable field of inquiry" before it could be critiqued (38). Sullivan continues by reminding us that "women have been present and influential from the start . . . articulating questions and issues for research, crafting new pedagogies, and overseeing program design and administration" (38). In these ways, composition has long served as a site of feminist inquiry and program building, then, but not until recently as a site of feminist critique. Composition studies has challenged many of the same academic traditions that Rich and her colleagues challenged in the early SEEK program, particularly the masculinist conventions of academic rhetoric (which Sullivan recounts as the dominant genre of thesis-proof-argument), the teacher as font of knowledge and power (with students as receptacles of that knowledge and power), and the teacher as diagnostician and evaluator of those students.

Mutual Learning

Like the teachers in the SEEK program, feminist compositionists enact the belief that, just as women and all other nondominant groups have much to gain by their academic involvement, academia itself has a great deal to learn from those same students. Writing center interactions offer a prime site of mutual learning. Catherine G. Latterell writes about the synergy unleashed when she "decenters" "student centeredness" (long a feature of peer tutoring). Months of enacting traditional writing center practices (the allegedly liberating and agency-producing questioning) only shored up her own power, agency, and authority rather than that of her struggling tutee, Carlos. So Latterell returned to feminist pedagogy, rearticulating the notion of authority, so that Carlos understood it as "varied, temporary, and mutually dependent on the other" (118). By doing so, Latterell opened up an authentic conversation with Carlos about how "roles are defined" and negotiated, how they can take turns having authority, and, perhaps most important, how the "ever-present influence" of Carlos's writing instructor was influencing their interactions and his development as a writer (118).

Feminist teachers respect and foster the students' growing awareness of agency, both the personal agency necessary to make smart personal choices and the collective agency necessary for shaping social processes and their community. In addition, feminist teachers also foster students' willingness to engage in and respect their own process of self-actualizing rhetorical growth.

Such self-awareness in the possibilities of agency happens, Kathleen Weiler reminds us, when feminist composition teachers "expand the limits of discourse by directly addressing the forces that shape their students' lives ... attempt[ing] to legitimize their students' voices by acknowledging their students' own experiences and by calling for these students' own narratives" (*Women* 131). Students in courses taught by rhetorical feminists (and in writing centers with rhetorical feminist tutors) learn to locate their personal experiences and reactions within the historical and social contexts that fostered (un/intentionally) their exclusion in the first place. Such a site helps them better position themselves in discussions of differences and personal interests, talking and writing about these issues in a public voice—claiming their agency, so to speak. Consequently, rather than grammar exercises, syntax studies, or the writings of great men, the content of such a composition course would be the growth of the writer, the process of rhetorical discovery, and the development of that public voice through writing, reading, listening, and revision that motivates students to recognize and employ the full range of their rhetorical proficiencies (Jung 7).

Weiler goes on to explain that teachers present themselves, too, as "gendered subjects with a personal perspective" (*Women* 131), using personal anecdotes to contextualize their own experiential knowledge and agency. Their goal is to ensure that all of their students have opportunities to draft, revise, write, and speak themselves forward in the structure (created mostly by white men) that is academia as well as in the world at large. Thus, in valuing and leveraging students' experiential, vernacular, and emotional knowledge, the feminist rhetorical teacher also helps students foster their own rhetorical agency, that "ability to act to shape one's own life, to resist victimization, and to improve the communities and societies in which we live"—rhetorical feminism at its classroom best (Briskin 59).

The Possibilities of Discourse

In addition to respect for students' positionality, intersectionality, and agency in the composition classroom, the rhetorical feminist in the classroom expands the possibilities of discourse itself, broadening genres of speaking and writing far beyond the predominant masculinist convention of the thesis-proof-argument. As Jarratt reminds us,

> This critique of academic discourse has led a number of feminists to suggest that argument is a particularly masculine genre and as such either is agonistic, even violent, and thus shouldn't be used by feminists, or, because it is based in a masculine tradition of logic and linear reasoning, does not allow for the expression of women's experiences and ways of making sense of the world. ("Feminist Pedagogy" 122)

The genre of argument itself has been critiqued by feminists—rejected whole cloth by some—following Sally Miller Gearhart's oft-repeated dictum "Any intent to persuade is an act of violence" ("Womanization" 201). Sonja K. Foss and Cindy L. Griffin's theory of invitational rhetoric also offers an alternative to the persuasion model, one that is grounded in the feminist principles of equality, immanent value, and self-determination, values that beautifully align with those of feminist rhetorical pedagogy.

In addition to using feminist approaches to argument, feminist rhetorical pedagogues employ composition's process(es) and post-process movements, with their emphasis on teaching and learning as recursive processes. Composition has made a dramatic paradigm shift from an emphasis on final product, with its top-down teaching and prescriptivism, to a focus on process itself, with teacher-as-guide for students' risk-taking, imagining, drafting, editing, and revising all working in the service of exercising agency and developing rhetorical power across the genres.

In expanding the genres and styles of writing in the composition classroom, feminist rhetorical teachers encourage students to develop their research abilities and public writing and speaking skills. These students are, as Plato's Protagoras would have them, gaining "prudence in affairs private as well as public" (line 318). Not only are they preparing to address the ills of their world (through careful research, rhetorical power, and various outreach and service-learning opportunities), but they are also learning to rely on their personal experiences as sources of knowledge, so much so that they develop the confidence to use the word "I" (claiming that knowledge) and write in a personal style. In "Taking Sides," Nancy Welch describes her goal in developing rhetorically nimble students who have "a full range of rhetorical practices" (157). To that end, she encourages and prepares students to advocate for positions, for themselves and as part of a coalition, helping us rethink the value of argument to a feminist stance. As these students compose and revise through a broad range of composing styles and genres, then, they acquire the ability to pay close attention to words and their effects, attune themselves to the social contexts for their writing and speaking, and see for themselves that language has power, that rhetoric can actually do something. These students could—and do—become "responsible language user[s]" who understand the ways "language inscribes difference" (Jarratt, "Teaching" 317).

In her first-year writing course, for example, Jarratt joined her students in the "process of cultural critique and production, an engagement reflected in their evaluations: 'I'm addicted to this analysis stuff!'" ("Teaching" 318). Jarratt writes that very few of her students were ready to "sign up as feminists" (which was never her goal, anyway), but "most of them were ready to describe themselves as language users engaged in a socially located and responsible practice of analysis and production" (318). Jarratt's argument is that "socially oriented and personally satisfying composition teaching can happen across and within different kinds of differences" (318). Thus, her students claim their authority—and their rhetorical power.

But, as Paula Mathieu writes, "Claiming that power through acts of . . . writing is insufficient [in and of itself]. It is an act of hope" (54). In anchoring writing in the feminist rhetorical classroom, Mathieu helps us acknowledge the power that is writing and the potential for realizing power that all people, powerful and disenfranchised alike, already possess. Yes, the subaltern can speak—and write. Working dialogically with their instructor, these students learn to articulate the barriers to authentic change, which include their access to a listening audience, to an appropriate venue, to nondiscriminatory policies and beliefs, at the same time that they share their knowledge, experience, plans, and hope through language. This emphasis on process reveals a feminist goal of extending what composition instructors can teach their students beyond expanding their mastery of various genres and styles. Yet, the emphasis on process, what with its crucial reliance on teacher-student interaction, also reveals what those teachers—what academia itself—can learn from students, particularly those from well-represented yet unprivileged groups of people who, like their mainstream counterparts, are also potential resources, sources of embodied knowledge, and beacons of hope.

Whether labeled as such or not, not all of our students will come to us prepared in all the ways that make our teaching—or their learning—easy. Even Gloria Anzaldúa's teacher scolded her to speak "American" or "go back to Mexico" ("How" 75). Still, they come with all the knowledge and life experience (from the inspiring to the tragic) that their eighteen, twenty-five, or forty-eight years have earned them. And we can make clear to them that their experiences are valid locations of knowledge production. Regardless of the diversity of their backgrounds and identities (their intersectional positions), they all come to us with the same (however suppressed) hope we have long held for our own better-educated selves: that education—that our teaching—will change their lives. Even those students from the most impoverished backgrounds come to us with one hope, one dream in mind: that their lives might be better than their parents', that the lives of their own children might be better than theirs so far have been.[16]

To be sure, diversity, finances, and testing efforts (writ national, statewide, and local) pose serious challenges for our hopeful selves. And it is unfortunate that I can so easily enumerate additional constraints to the connections that count, constraints such as the devaluation of a college degree; the lure of the semiskilled workplace; the seduction of parties and bars; the limited resources families have for an ever more costly education; the overt restrictions and hidden injuries of class bias, racism, ableism, and heterosexism in the classroom; and the constant threat of school shootings. Still, we carry our hope back into the classroom each term.

    I could go on to detail these difficulties, but who wants to think that we live in a world where the ethical fenders are about to fall off the wheels? After all, despite those challenges, there is still hope—or as poet Kathleen Raine says, "hope for hope." If that were not the case, none of us would be considering ways our feminist teaching might translate abstractions about a better life into actions that make that life a reality. After all, teaching is not *only* about our own intellectual achievements or *only* about our students' lack thereof. It is not about our honors or status. Nor is it really about grades, schedules, or syllabi. Rather, teaching is about our movement between worlds, arms out, changing students' lives at the same time that they change ours, making the connections that count.

    In these ways, feminist pedagogies are both radical and prescriptive (as well as normative within a feminist cultural logic) in that they demand that we work to change the status quo through daily practices that prepare students to claim their education (just as Rich would have them) and develop their rhetorical agency so as to make a difference in their lives, their worlds. That is the true payoff—and the realized hope of rhetorical feminism.

SIX: MENTORING

> If not this then what
> would fuse a connection
>
> —Adrienne Rich, "Memory"

> *Lifting as We Climb*
>
> —motto of the National Association of Colored Women's Clubs, established 1896

Rhetoric has always been a mentoring tradition, aligning with pedagogy in the pursuit of artful and ethical speaking, writing, and being. And like rhetoric, mentoring has been a predominantly masculinist enterprise. Yet the mythical status of mentoring originated in Homer's *Odyssey*, where a Greek woman (well, actually a god) served as the original model of how mentoring was to be done. As the story goes, Odysseus has been gone for twenty years, having left behind his wife, Penelope (who is harassed by hordes of suitors), and his son, Telemachus (who is uncertain about his own future). Intervening, Athena (daughter of Metis, goddess of wisdom) transforms herself into Mentor, Odysseus's most trusted friend, appears before Telemachus, and advises him to challenge his mother's many suitors and to set out on a quest for his long-missing father. Athena-as-Mentor instructs Telemachus as to where to go, whom to meet, and how to speak and behave—and she ensures the outcome: "She spoke in prayer, though she herself was bringing it all to fulfillment!" (3.55).

This age-old master-apprentice model worked successfully for millennia, especially for aristocratic men—despite the fact that it is a woman, Athena-as-Mentor, who imparts wisdom, shares knowledge, and controls the outcome (as only gods can do). Still, the first beneficiary of that mentoring relationship was a young man, conjuring the long tradition of a relationship between men only, one of whom functions as a paternalistic figure.[1]

Such was long the tradition in academia. "When men were the only models we had," writes feminist critic Carolyn Heilbrun, "only [white] men could exemplify the ideal life of a thinker, a writer, a public figure, an academic" (1). Such was the life this powerful academic eventually enjoyed, no thanks to the dismissive, masculinist mentoring she received during the 1940s, 1950s, and 1960s. Had Heilbrun come on the scene later, when the feminist movement lit the way for women to enter and transform the university, when the teaching and mentoring of women became a concern, an academic career would have been more easily accessible to her.[2] Over time, some mentoring practices have proved to be more fruitful than others, particularly those with a feminist slant, as Michelle Eble and Lynée Gaillet's *Stories of Mentoring* makes so clear.

Always in the service of feminism, the tactic of rhetorical feminism continues to offer specific ways to enhance feminist mentoring. First of all, by purposefully disidentifying with (diverging from) masculinist models of mentoring, feminist mentors demonstrate their commitment to the equality of women and other underrepresented groups and to reciprocity of engagement (on part of the mentor and mentee). Second, mentors and mentees alike who are working within a spirit of rhetorical feminism recognize full well that the mentor (usually and provisionally) resides in the center, the mentee in the margins. The goal for both of them is to establish supportive ways for the mentee to make her way to the center. No matter how trusting or deep the friendship between them, there are no illusions: they both share this same goal. And in this spirit, they share an informed awareness of their positionality and intersectionality.

Third, mentors who engage in the conceptual theory of rhetorical feminism are, of course, fluent in the use of rhetorical concepts, practices, and deliveries, especially of the power of dialogue, silence, and listening to enhance any rhetorical transaction. These mentors mindfully expand their rhetorical portfolio with an alertness and respect for the vernaculars, emotions, and experiences that tint the relationship, for doing so is the basis for a mutually trusting relationship (the establishment of ethos); they also serve as epistemic resources. How else might mentors and mentees speak freely and openly with each other, if not in their vernacular? What better way to make an authentic emotional connection (pathos) with the other than to reveal one's emotions and know they will be respected? And how better for one of them to reason (logos) than by drawing on experience? Maybe it is experience that is the key to a successful mentoring relationship: the mentor has the experience—has been through the process the mentee is currently experiencing. The mentor now embodies the experience that the mentee seeks to achieve. And if the mentor subscribes to rhetorical feminism, she can more easily identify with the mentee and her experiences as she moves from the margins to the center.

Of course, such a rhetorical feminist relationship between mentor and mentee is a shared commitment to hope. Perhaps most important in this relationship—and a true divergence from the Athena model—is that the best mentor does not play god.

This chapter provides an overview of mentoring models and practices, alluding to the traditional hierarchical mentoring models between men but focusing on more contemporary feminist models, including those that are supported by the conceptual theory of rhetorical feminism. Indeed, rhetorical feminism readily supports mutual mentoring that is rooted in ancient values of ethics, eloquence, and eudaemonia (the greatest good for human flourishing), with mentors traveling alongside mentees through stages of becoming, being, and belonging.

Feminist Mentoring and the Politics of Becoming

Unlike the traditional top-down mentoring model between like-minded men of different ages and ranks that Heilbrun limns so well, feminist mentoring in academia strives toward greater nimbleness, variety, and interaction. It calls for collaboration, reciprocity, and connection. Aimee Carrillo Rowe tells us, "Power is transmitted through our affective ties. Who we love, the communities that we live in, who we expend our emotional energies building ties with—these connections are all functions of power" (16). Rowe helps us appreciate the primary goal of feminist mentoring: a sense of relationship, a concept she describes as a "politics of relation" (15). Rhetorical feminism works in service to this feminist goal, guiding us to consider the location, positionality, and intersectionality of ourselves and others, particularly vis-à-vis one another. All of us long to relate to others. Adrienne Rich's "politics of location" is a good starting point for making these connections, a starting point for relationships and for moving forward—with the hope and possibility that ground rhetorical feminism.

The Politics of Location

Rich defines "recognizing our location" as an occasion for "having to name the ground we're coming from, the conditions we have taken for granted" ("Notes" 219). Rowe's politics of relation, on the other hand, "gestures toward deep reflection about the selves we are creating as function of where we place our bodies, and with whom we build our affective ties" (16). We are, all of us, always longing for connection, for coalition. And what does feminist mentoring consist of but a connection: mentor to mentee, mentee to mentor, mentee to mentee? What better way to be interpellated within webs of power and agency, hailed by those with whom you long to connect?

Rich's politics of location centers on understanding the self, on the importance of understanding the ways we interact with others. Rowe's politics of relation moves us toward others "to whom we feel accountable" (18). Determining one's location is a good starting point for the consideration of mentoring—but just so long as one also determines the relations and relationships that have made such a location possible, whether that location is privileged, subaltern, in the center or in the margins, or somewhere in between, as the feminist theories of intersectionality and positionality demonstrate so well. Mentors, mentees, colleagues, and friends all make those locations possible—the belonging, becoming, and being.

In this way, feminist mentoring mobilizes interaction and coalition in all directions, with all kinds of people who help signal our location. Whereas the traditional relationship between mentor and mentee is firmly hierarchical (after all, the mentor is already a member of the world the mentee aspires to), feminist mentoring in academia yields a more malleable structure, inviting commitments among people up and down the ladder, those sharing the same rung, those alike and different—people all committed to personal growth and development. Mentors and mentees learn from one another; cooperate without domination or submission (or at least take turns doing so); respect and work with differing strengths, perceptions, and vulnerabilities; and stimulate the formulation of new ways of working together. After all, when people seek mutual support and advice, the need to maintain a power differential is diminished (though it would be naive to say that it disappears). A genuine peer can give a sense of possibility the way a mentor may not.

The Politics of Feminist Mentoring

This is not to say that the feminist mentor skirts the responsibilities or ignores the power relations that have traditionally made mentoring so useful to men. Indeed, the mentor consciously socializes the mentee into the aspired-for culture. With the influence of rhetorical feminism, though, both the mentor and mentee make explicit what is implicitly known by some but not others and never assume any tacit understanding of academia's traditionally white middle-class workings, which can nullify a vernacular, a personal experience, an emotion. The mentor and mentee together cultivate a frank, open, trusting relationship. As Joan Kelly has taught us, the double vision of feminist theory—critique of the present and creativity for the future—has sparked new feminist mentoring practices that disrupt the unidirectional flow of power and information that constitutes traditional hierarchical mentoring. Instead, feminist mentoring practices stipulate mutuality—a reciprocity in engagement, information sharing, and responsibility for the success of the partnership. As such, these practices are infused with the tactics of rhetorical feminism: hope, dialogue, attention to the margins (experiences, emotions, vernaculars, and so on) as well as to the center.

Feminist mentoring has progressed in the direction of mutual mentoring for a number of reasons. Barriers still stand in the way of women's "access to mentoring" (Rheineck and Roland 82), not the least of which is the gender stereotyping that too often limits what women and members of other subaltern groups can be expected to achieve in the first place. Women are also disadvantaged by the scarcity of potential mentors, by lack of access to information networks, and by the hazards of exploitative relationships (whether with a man or with a woman mentor). Furthermore, even in the twenty-first century, women's mentoring experiences are often disrupted by family responsibilities as well as by tokenism in fields dominated by men. Men still occupy the majority of higher-level positions, and those men still prefer to mentor younger versions of themselves, men,[3] who themselves tend to avoid women mentors anyway (Chandler 85). Finally, rather than waiting to be chosen by a mentor, striving to perform like the mentor, looking only upward toward the mentor, many women want a mutually nourishing relationship with their mentor, one that helps both mentor and mentee develop both professionally and personally. Of course, not every feminist wants or gives the same kind of mentoring—not all the time, anyway.

Both research studies and testimonies from personal experience indicate that having a mentor is important to career advancement and job satisfaction.[4] In fact, having a good mentor who will nurture a professional connection is just as important as job title or salary; lacking such a mentor usually hinders professional progress and fulfillment. In "*Doing Gender: (En)Gendering Academic Mentoring*," Gary Olson and Evelyn Ashton-Jones write that "doctoral students who had experienced a close working relationship with a faculty member had a fuller education than their counterparts who had not" (119). The most helpful qualities of a productive relationship undoubtedly include having someone trustworthy to confide in, share information with, and join in taking risks. Mutual protection and friendships are also crucial.

That said, feminist mentoring is not about the whole-cloth rejection of traditional models of hierarchical, one-way mentoring, let alone a rejection of men. Rather, it is fluid and flexible, according to the needs of both the mentor and the mentee. As Audre Lorde teaches us, "It is the work of feminism to make connections, to heal unnecessary divisions," and to "pay attention to the voices we have been taught to distrust, [to] articulate what they teach us, and [to] act upon what we know" (qtd. in Bereano 8, 11). We need all people, all models of mentoring in order to develop and sustain our nimbleness so that we may purposefully employ whichever mentoring model works best for each person at each time.

The Powers and Politics of Mutual Mentoring

Despite the kaleidoscopic variations on successful mentoring, the most sustainable mentoring relationships tend to be mutual—that is, mentoring relationships in which both mentor and mentee benefit from their ongoing collaboration on teaching, grants, publications, professional networking, service, and job placement.[5] These professional benefits enhance the competence and self-esteem of mentor and mentee alike. The reciprocal nature of the mentoring process is that it is shared, reflective, and democratic, rendering it a cultural and activist practice. Naturally, these mentoring relationships often lead to trusting relationships that guide participants through life's trajectory, through challenges, disappointments, and opportunities, whether they are between faculty and students or between students (as Beth Godbee and Julia Novotny explain so well).

If the mentors are accessible and helpful, then the interactions are usually mutually comfortable and professionally productive. Although people who are more alike are thought to interact most comfortably, such pairings often lose the potential for discovery that is available to pairs who, by their very nature, challenge each other. Furthermore, powerful pairings between dissimilar people more easily accommodate white women, people of color, and Others who might otherwise be limited in mentoring opportunities.

Of course, not every mutual mentoring situation ensures success, especially when women expect to be mentored by other women, people of color by other people of color, and so on. Too many departments still lack gender, racial, and sexual diversity, and more still decouple power and authority from women, people of color, and Others. In such cases, Christy Chandler encourages those seeking mentors to "form networks to help socialize each other and prepare each other for the realities they will face" (87), for finding a good mentor can be "just as important as title or salary" (Eagly and Carli 174). "It is imperative," Chandler continues, "that women of color [especially] create ways to overcome feelings of isolation and that they cease to be the sole representatives of their ethnic group" (95). Besides, the women and people of color who regularly mentor are often overcommitted and relentlessly pursued to take on this role, sometimes to the detriment of their own professional pursuits. Thirty years ago, Sandra Harding admonished that such work done by women—and, I must add, by people of color—is too often devalued. Furthermore, she explains, these groups of people are often excluded "from men's informational networks," and obstacles are "put in the path of women's attempts to find safe and reliable mentors (and later be perceived as such mentors themselves).... [T]hese and other informal discriminatory tactics give us increased appreciation for those women who have managed to persist" (29).

Mutual mentoring helps address some of the issues Harding enumerates. Such mutually beneficial collaborations across differences often generate a power that, according to Hannah Arendt, can "energize, enabling competence, and thus reducing hierarchy" (*Human Condition* 198). To support her assertion, she invokes the powerful rhetorical practices within the Greek polis that produced not so much a physical boundary but rather an organization more influenced by people "acting and speaking together" than by actually living together (198).

Taking Mentees Seriously: Being

Rhetorical feminism fuses the value of dialogue and listening with speaking and acting together. To that end, feminist mentors take mentees seriously by legitimizing their experiences, location, and vernaculars. They also rethink their own epistemic privilege—a mentoring act that harnesses our own expectations with our mentees' hopes. Taking mentees seriously is a purposeful act, one Nedra Reynolds might describe as a "feminist interruption," for it draws attention to "women's identities as marginalized" human beings, marginalized academics and professionals—a purposeful stance that illuminates the "ideological workings of discursive exclusion" (60). For Michelle Ballif, Diane Davis, and Roxanne Mountford, such a mentoring stance is a positive intervention, a *critical affirmation* of our mentees (931), especially those who may be different from ourselves and have different cultural histories and legacies in terms of positionality, sexuality, or identity. All of them, however, want to move from the margins to the center, where mentors reside. Staying aware of stances and locations is a precept of rhetorical feminism.

One way to take mentees seriously is to listen to them, talk with them, share struggles with them, work and act with them, and engage in hope. Mentees' stories of effective mentoring acknowledge mentoring's many guises and practices—and its various gifts to recipients. For that reason, the personal accounts of effective mentoring that I have received from colleagues all over the country occasionally appear throughout this chapter.[6] For example, one already successful associate professor admits that her feminist mentor's abiding belief in her ability to get a PhD allowed her to throw off her own doubts (Anonymous 3). She had shared her emotional experiences of self-doubt with her mentor, only to have her adviser disclose her own academic and personal struggles. Although the disclosure had saddened the mentee at the time, it brought the strength to continue: "I don't feel like my struggles are a sign of my weakness. If [my adviser] struggled, then it is okay to admit that I struggle, too" (Anonymous 3). Sharing and respecting the knowledge that is personal experience can strengthen the mentoring relationship. A young writing program administrator writes that feminist mentoring means both encouraging and holding work to "high standards," standards that create "pathways for scholars who are not sure they 'belong' or that they [can] really contribute to the field" (Anonymous 4). For her, meeting those high standards was proof that she was making her way from the margins toward the center. A graduate student writes that a "feminist mentor takes her or his mentee seriously as a fellow thinker and meaning-maker, even when a power differential between mentor and mentee undeniably exists" (Anonymous 8). Taking mentees seriously, admitting experience as reasoning, and relying on the bedrock of hope are instantiations of rhetorical feminism put into the service of mentoring, a way to mentor that is crucial to the academic survival (the "being") of many students and young faculty, especially those who represent historically underrepresented groups.

Taking mentees seriously is a kind of activism that can manifest itself in intervention into traditional, too often unacknowledged, privilege. For faculty, such intervention is sometimes necessary in cases of race-, gender-, sexuality-, or ability-based prejudice that arises when they are considering graduate program applications, responding to comprehensive exams, evaluating teaching, or considering a promotion case. Other times, such interventions into the life of mentees themselves are necessary for their overall support. Geneva Smitherman, an activist-mentor if there ever were one, outlines the ideals and realities (lest someone should think of it as easy) of taking mentees seriously:

> Ideally, mentoring should address the intellectual, social, developmental, and other needs of the mentee—helping the whole person to the extent possible.... The mentor sets standards of achievement and excellence for mentees as well as motivates them to stay on task so they can complete the journey. On occasion, this might mean nagging and butt-kickin (especially when/if the mentee starts half-steppin—which is normal, but it has to be overcome). Finally, mentoring is a kind of nurturing whereby the mentor helps/motivates the mentee to construct a vision of possibilities beyond the present moment. (qtd. in Okawa 512)

Jessica Enoch, too, reminds us of the ways our mentoring can inspire possibilities for social change. When we help students recognize the hope that is rhetorical agency, when we build on their "cultural and linguistic backgrounds," we assist them in becoming "politicized participants in a world they contribute to and create" (*Refiguring* 179).

Mentoring for realizing potential and possibility is what "taking women students seriously" (and urging them to take themselves seriously) is all about, especially in a world still mostly "organized by and for men" (Rich, "Taking" 238). It is within such a patriarchal framework that taking mentees seriously and caring about them becomes a feminist ethic[7]—and an especially valuable one for those who remember feeling "so protected by" the feminist ethic of care in graduate school and later find it "shocking to encounter non-feminist spaces in academia" (Anonymous 3).

Rich asks us to consider specifically feminist issues: "How does a woman gain a sense of *self* in a system . . . which devalues work done by women, denies the importance and uniqueness of female experience, and is physically violent toward women?" ("Taking" 239). Rich starts with the kind of mutual mentoring[8] essential to feminist mentoring, the mentoring of teachers themselves:

> In teaching women, we have two choices: to lend our weight to the forces that indoctrinate women to passivity, self-deprecation, and a sense of powerlessness, in which case the issue of "taking women students seriously" is a moot one; or to consider what we have to work against, as well as with, in ourselves, in our students, in the content of the curriculum, in the structure of the institution, in the society at large. And this means . . . believing in the value and significance of women's experience, traditions, perceptions. Thinking of ourselves seriously, not as one of the boys, not as neuters, or androgynes, but *women*. (240)

Rich's mentor serves as an "enlightened witness," a term coined by psychoanalyst Alice Miller to describe the person who stands with another to offer him or her a different model of interaction, in this case, a nonhierarchical model. Rhetorical feminism offers just such a model, one committed to hope, respectful of vernacular and personal experience, dialogic and transactional, trusting, mutually supportive, and filled with occasions of emotion, listening, and silence. As such, rhetorical feminist mentors stand as ethical, enlightened witnesses for their students, their colleagues, and themselves. They take their mentees seriously—and over the arc of their career.

Feminist mentors establish personal, intellectual relationships with their mentees, all the while demanding and pushing for excellence. Like the above example of the mentor's own struggles demonstrates, mentors consciously abandon the role of "unassailable expert" in a relationship in which "help, power, and resources tend to flow in one direction" (McGuire and Reger 56). Instead, feminist mentors strive to be enlightened others, problem posers, and learning supporters, distinguishing their mentoring practices from those of the traditional model between expert and protégé, between the expert who knows what is best and insists that the protégé do what is "best."[9]

Mentoring "Everything Else"

Although not always successful, mentors following the precepts of rhetorical feminism know they must disidentify with the tradition so prevalent in academe of producing clones of themselves in the mentoring process (see Chandler). Instead, they must listen to their mentees and find out who their mentees actually are (their experiences, their vernaculars), what kinds of academics they want to be (or do not want to be), what kind of institution they want to work in, and what kind of work-life balance they imagine for themselves, all the while emphasizing the mentees' intellectual and social development and their emotional well-being (all essential elements of "everything else"). For instance, feminist mentors do not always encourage their students to pursue only the most prestigious positions available, which is otherwise easy to do in rhetorical studies, when faculty and students alike discuss the year's "best" jobs. Instead, these mentors support mentees in identifying the positions that might make them happiest both professionally *and* personally. So rather than setting the solitary goal of building a long and impressive vita, the goal is to cultivate an enriching and satisfying life.[10]

In order to support mentees' attempts to meet their own expectations, rhetorical feminists listen carefully to the voices of their women mentees, who were taught early on that "tones of confidence, challenge, anger, or assertiveness . . . are strident and unfeminine" (Rich, "Taking" 243). In addition, they encourage their mentees to tap their emerging confidence so that they, too, can enjoy the kind of intellectual privilege that others take for granted.

When prompted to respond on the mentoring she had received, that aforementioned writing program administrator reminded me that her adviser had "commented on the connections between scholarly confidence and privilege," a move she now sees as feminist. Her adviser had talked about how these connections play out in class discussions, writing, and the talk of new projects. The brilliant young woman continues,

> I realize now how helpful it was that [my adviser] did this! I needed the scholarly confidence that I saw in some male grad students to be named and questioned. Why didn't *they* worry that they would actually get a PhD, that they had something to say, that their research agenda was worth it? Identifying this as part of a larger pattern of privilege connected to subject position and the social forces that shape one's expectations on one's self helped me to see it. (Anonymous 4)

Another graduate student reports that her adviser helped her to remember that her own health and marriage should be priorities (Anonymous 3), while an assistant professor and writing program administrator was reminded to connect what she was learning from feminist mentoring and theory with her everyday experiences. To clarify a point, she recalls the occasion on which her adviser introduced her to the term "affective labor":

> I was telling some stories about my (then) mother-in-law, I think in admiration, and the things she (but none of the men, including my then husband) did to make memories and keep different parts of the family connected. [My adviser] noted that women often do all the affective labor in families.
>
> It blew my mind that there was a name for it! (Anonymous 4)

One has only to pick up the latest *Chronicle of Higher Education* or *Time* magazine to read again about the heavy burden of affective labor (service, mentoring, even housework) that women (are expected to) take on in the workplace and in the home. Indeed, there *is* a name for it. Still, mentors can help mentees (and vice versa) recognize the difference between the affective labor that is an investment holding potential realization and the affective labor that is not a good use of time or energy (see below).

"Cultural Prodding"

Rhetorical feminists speak to personal, individual, experiential concerns as well as explicate academic culture for their mentees, realizing that the traditional privilege of the academy is not always inclusive of them. They give their mentees the kinds of "cultural prodding" that women and Others who have been traditionally marginalized so often need (and that the traditionally educated have so long received, almost by osmosis). Such cultural prodding constitutes yet another element of "everything else." Perhaps the most obvious move rhetorical feminists make is to help clarify and explain the moving parts of graduate school and the profession, thereby socializing their mentees into academic culture, which may (for all sorts of legitimate reasons) seem alien to them. Progress through academia (especially through graduate school and the tenure process) assumes a white middle-class knowledge, implicitly known by enfranchised students (and professors), that must often be made explicit to all the Others. The rhetorical feminist ensures that the mentee knows how academic culture works and that the mentee's culture, experience, voice, and language hold value everywhere, even and especially in academia.

Rhetorical feminists guide mentees as they develop at the same time that they endeavor to couple each mentee's individual passion with abiding disciplinary questions, so that the field always seems to be ready for their work—just as they are ready for the field. But even the best of mentors is not always effective in doing this, as the following example illustrates. A former mentee submitted extraordinarily strong comprehensive exams yet refers to the comps themselves as "horrible," a surprising statement given her impressive performance on them. Despite not feeling as though she did well on the exams, she nevertheless appreciated her committee's *approach* to the exams:

> [The exams] didn't feel like a test of whether or not I had read something the right way and memorized it. Instead, the questions were more interested in how my ideas were developing as I read. I appreciated that everyone took into account my goals and interests in crafting questions. At the end of it, that made the process feel more useful. I don't think that this is always the case, but I'm glad it was for me. (Anonymous 5)

For her, the pre-prospectus meeting was even better: "That conversation was very generative for me, and it helped me feel confident that everyone on the committee was on board with the project" (Anonymous 5). The mentee benefited from the dialogue, from being invited (expected even) to move from what could be considered the marginal status of a graduate student to reside in the center, where faculty discuss issues, respond to critical questions, and make plans for the future.

Still, all of her personal goals were not met in graduate school. As she finished her PhD, she lamented that she did not have more publications, admitting that "some of this is on me." Nevertheless, she wishes that her adviser had pushed her to "send things out earlier, to learn to balance publishing along with all the other parts of being an academic, [for doing so] would have helped [her] see publishing as just part of the job instead of something much scarier" (Anonymous 5). Indeed, this dissertation-fellowship awardee and now assistant professor illustrates a situation in which the mentor helped her calibrate her research project to the expectations of ongoing disciplinary conversations but missed the opportunity to cultivate the student's unspoken desire to enter the sphere of academic publishing "just to normalize that as part of academic life and to take some of the edge off" (Anonymous 5). The mentee laments that she has not sent more things out, despite academic publishing's time-consuming rhythm of submission, revision, resubmission, and sometimes rejection. Perhaps the mentor laments, too, that she had not pushed publication and that the mentee had not spoken up—or that the mentor had listened more closely for what was left unspoken.

Cultural Capacity Building

Listening to the voices of these young scholars transports me back to my own graduate school experience, where I along with my feminist cohort received much-needed cultural prodding. Like the graduate student above, I am sure I did not receive all the mentoring I wanted at the time; however, what I received has continued to sustain me throughout my career and keep me ever-vigilant to the lessons Andrea Lunsford taught me and to the mentoring role she modeled.

Whether she was planning new courses, preparing for class, meeting with students, mapping out a workshop, discussing departmental politics with colleagues, or handling sticky departmental, personal, and professional matters, she did so with high expectations, a laser-like focus, and seemingly endless generosity. But it was the even harder-to-learn lessons that impressed me the most, from her insights into when to hold her tongue, when to listen noncommittally, when to negotiate hard, when to push, and when to concede—all instances of her rhetorical stance. Those of us who worked closely with her were lucky to be able to discuss the internecine struggles that surfaced in such a department—some of that "everything else" that most of us in rhetoric and writing studies experience, no matter how green or well established we are.

The memory of my own experience as a mentee came to me when I received the following email:

> In retrospect, I suppose it would have been helpful for me to hear a bit more from you (and other P[enn] S[tate] U[niversity] faculty at the time) about department politics. I don't mean more about the specifics of the politics at PSU, but rather more about some of the common political issues that arise within English departments, particularly along the CompRhet/Lit "boundary." Knowing more about these typical areas of tension in English departments and knowing of some strategies for navigating/responding to them . . . might have saved me some stress and emotional turmoil during my first few years on the job. (Anonymous 1)

As I read this, I wonder if I was (we were) shielding this now professor from problematic interactions and departmental politics that seemed transitory, distracting, limited to the bad behavior of one (ultimately) ineffective person, or just silly. If it were a threatening problem, I surely would have coalesced with others to address or resolve it.[11] And had the student asked me about it, I would have responded frankly. More likely, I was not drawn into what I considered to be a short-lived fray and did not want her to be distracted by it, either. Or maybe I was deliberately taking a rhetorical stance of silence and listening that I wanted her to emulate. I do not remember exactly. I do, however, know that an ethical feminist mentor prods, prompts, and, most of all, models issues of professional response, trajectory, capacity building, and much of everything else that falls under Rich's demands for excellence.

Mentoring and the Ethics of Belonging

Expectations and the Ancients

With feminist mentoring comes the pursuit of the good, the artful and ethical way of being, an age-old goal. Mentoring is more than supporting those striving for professional success; it is supporting the striving necessary to be better in every way. After all, mentoring in rhetoric has long been about developing the good person who speaks well, Cato the Elder's *vir bonus, dicendi peritus* (Quintilian 12.1.1). Why mentor or be mentored if one is not improving as a human being, as one who uses rhetoric to participate responsibly and ethically in both civic and private life? Although the idea of mentoring and mutual mentoring has been foregrounded by late twentieth- and twenty-first-century feminists, mentoring for ethics, justice, virtue, and eloquence goes back to the ancients.

Homer worked toward this ideal, as the relationship between Athena/Mentor and Telemachus makes so clear. Just as Athena mentored Telemachus toward the good, Sappho mentored aristocratic women in her sociopolitical sphere toward excellence—or so strong circumstantial evidence leads us to believe. Writing some two hundred years after the works of Homer were first recorded, Sappho composed lyric poetry that recorded the ways she guided different groups of aristocratic women during different stages of their lives.

Sappho's was a time of political unrest, with Greek city-states experiencing a turbulent transition from aristocratic to democratic rule. The aristocracy of Lesbos was in power and in crisis, yet Lesbos served as the destination of young women from all parts of Ionia who willingly lived separately from men to be educated within an all-woman fellowship in order to develop a fresh political and social consciousness. Sappho's is a world of aristocratic women—and her own status in the aristocracy authorizes her great influence on these young women as she presses them to appreciate their beauty and wealth yet realize ethical excellence (eudaemonia) as the highest form of happiness:

> Beauty endures only for as long as it can be seen;
> goodness, beautiful today, will remain tomorrow. (*Sappho*, Frag. 119)

> Wealth without virtue is
>   a harmful companion;
> but a mixture of both,
>   the happiest friendship. (Frag. 120)

As an accomplished poet and mentor-guide for women, Sappho seems to have celebrated the aristocratic woman at each important stage of her life, using poetry, singing, dancing, and music to accompany women through rites of passage. Sappho was prescient when she recorded the infinite influence of her mentoring:

> I tell you;
>   in time to come,
> someone will remember us. (Frag. 6)

Women's Worth and Eudaemonia

Perhaps no rhetorician has offered more guidance to the field than Aristotle, though his ideas on mentoring were never specifically directed toward women. After all, aristocratic Athenian-born women were citizen-class yet not citizens, and Aristotle spoke to the expectations of a men-only body of citizens. He conceded that a woman could be wise: "Everyone honours the wise. . . . [T]he Mytilenaeans [honour] Sappho, though she was a woman" (*Rhetoric* 2.23.1389b). Still, Sappho could be a fluke; after all, Aristotle notes, "between the sexes, the male is by nature superior and the female inferior, the male ruler and the female subject" (*Politics* 1.2.12), and "one quality or action is nobler than another if it is that of a naturally finer being: thus a man's will be nobler than a woman's" (*Rhetoric* 1.9.15).

Of course, Aristotle's accounts of women, buttressed by the defective scientific understanding of reproduction and biological processes, work to belie women's participation in the making and perpetuation of culture. Nevertheless, in his *Nicomachean Ethics,* Aristotle found a way to address the concerns of women, going so far as to guide citizens (all men) on their relations with their wives (citizen-class women).

For Aristotle, the ultimate end in life, both political and personal, is eudaemonia, usually translated as "the supreme human good" or "happiness." More precisely, though, eudaemonia is the well-being that comes from a lifetime of right habits and wise choices rooted in reason, virtue, justice, and the pursuit of happiness—all virtues that the mentor strives to develop in the mentee.

For millennia, Aristotle's *Nicomachean Ethics* has guided men and some women as they develop in moral virtue and action, all within a context of the supreme good (eudaemonia), in which justice plays a crucial role. Just as happiness is the supreme good, justice is the "sovereign virtue" and the "only virtue that is regarded as someone else's good, because it secures advantage for another person" (V.i). For Aristotle, then, happiness plays out in the successful, generous mentoring of someone else, to the advantage of the mentee, not to that of the mentor.

Throughout the *Nicomachean Ethics* and the *Politics* (VIII.x–xii; 1.5.5, 7.57), Aristotle gives equal weight to women's and men's happiness, commenting in the *Rhetoric* that "communities and individuals should lack none" of the qualities for happiness, not in their women nor in their men (1.5.1361). Aristotle's notice of women's worth, virtue, and happiness helps contextualize the mentoring offered by fifth-century BCE Aspasia of Miletus.

Arriving in Athens brilliantly educated by means that have never been fully explained, Aspasia is best known for her enduring relationship with Pericles, yet she has also earned recognition for her contributions to rhetoric—as a teacher, logographer, and rhetorician. Because of her status as a foreigner, a freeborn, well-connected intellectual not subject to Athenian strictures for women, Aspasia could use her rhetorical prowess to conduct proto-feminist mentoring for women and men alike. She could mentor—and she did, offering guidance in the achievement of virtue, justice, and happiness while simultaneously embodying a breach of fixed social protocols that circumscribed citizen-class Athenian women.

Both Plutarch[12] and Xenophon[13] write about her, but it is Cicero who showcases Aspasia's mastery in mentoring Xenophon and his unnamed wife on achieving happiness:

"Please tell me, madam, if your neighbor had a better gold ornament than you have, would you prefer that one or your own?" "That one," she replied. "Now, if she had dresses and other feminine finery more expensive than you have, would you prefer yours or hers?" "Hers, of course," she replied. "Well, now, if she had a better husband than you have, would you prefer your husband or hers?" At this the woman blushed. But Aspasia then began to speak to Xenophon. "I wish you would tell me, Xenophon," she said, "if your neighbor had a better horse than yours, would you prefer your horse or his?" "His," was the answer. "And if he had a better farm than you have, which farm would you prefer to have?" "The better farm, naturally," he said. "Now if he had a better wife than you have, would you prefer yours or his?" And at this Xenophon, too, himself was silent. Then Aspasia: "Since both of you have failed to tell me the only thing I wished to hear, I myself will tell you what you both are thinking. That is you, madam, wish to have the best husband, and you, Xenophon, desire above all things to have the finest wife. Therefore, unless you can contrive that there be no better man or finer woman on earth you will certainly always be in dire want of what you consider best, namely, that you be the husband of the very best of wives, and that she be wedded to the very best of men." (*De Inventione* 1.31.51–53)

Cicero's Aspasia is mentoring for virtue, justice, and happiness. Whether these aforementioned instances of her mentoring are historically accurate is not as critical as the fact that these age-old accounts of Aspasia's rhetorical renown and mentoring have survived, circulating as powerful examples of ethical beliefs and appropriate practices that align with the good.

These ancient sentiments about the significance of fusing rhetoric and ethics, about mentoring for such a melding, hold true today, especially for feminist rhetoricians who are advocating for intellectual-scholarly significance, civic responsibility, women's rights of every kind, and equal opportunity in all realms of life. Much of that ethical-rhetorical work takes place in the feminist office and classroom.

Sustaining the High Standards of an Ethical and Intellectual Contract

From ancient times to the present, the ethical mentor has kept high standards and has refused to accept a mentee's "preconceived sense of her limitations" (Rich, "Taking" 244). Like Athena, Sappho, and Aspasia, Rich's mentor is "hard to please" and yet "supportive of risk-taking, because self-respect often comes only when exacting standards have been met" ("Taking" 244). One professor writes to extend these precepts:

> Feminist mentoring means taking the writing of your juniors (graduate students, younger faculty, new people, etc.) seriously and responding to make a piece the best it can be. It means being encouraging *and* holding the work to high standards, both of which are essential to creating pathways for scholars who are not sure that they "belong" or that they could really contribute to the field.
>
> I knew that I needed this in graduate school, but only after experiencing it with [my adviser's] feedback (on draft essays or in meetings). Working with [my adviser] was the first time I had the experience of picking up an essay covered in notes, arrows, and circles! I learned that didn't mean the piece was a total wreck/loss, but, rather, that there was work to do to make it really strong, which [my adviser] could see easily, but I couldn't yet. (Anonymous 4)

Being advised and edited because your mentor thinks you have what it takes is so markedly different from being corrected because your mentor does not think you have much at all.

Like Sappho, Rich focuses on women mentors and their women students. Such woman-to-woman, feminist mentoring pays mutual benefits and pays forward, spreading like a rhizome among feminists (among teachers and their students, among colleagues, among peers at every stage of professionalism). Such rhizomic feminist mentoring relationships are frequently more enduringly powerful than the dyadic model, as most mentees who receive this kind of mentoring generously pass it on.[14]

Taking women students and high expectations seriously means insisting that students stake a claim in their own educations (which may just be another version of Smitherman's "butt-kickin"). For Rich, such an education "implies an ethical and intellectual contract between teacher and student..., intuitive, dynamic, [and] unwritten," which she describes as a "pledge of mutual seriousness about women" ("Claiming" 231). This contract involves mentoring with regard to the hard work needed: "Clear thinking, active discussion, and excellent writing all require *hard work*" (235). It also includes students demanding that we take them seriously just as they take themselves seriously; otherwise, all concerned resign themselves to "low expectations," with students given only "half a chance to become more thoughtful, expressive human beings" (235). In other words, feminist mentoring aligns with feminist rhetorical teaching in that it encompasses strong preparation and high expectations. The respect, mutuality, and care entailed never equate with any measure of coddling. Just the opposite.

Rich tells young women that claiming an education is behaving "as the rightful owner" of an education, as someone who is "acting" rather than being "acted-upon" ("Claiming" 231). Such is the "experience of *taking responsibility toward* yourselves" (233); such is the experience of

> refusing to let others do your thinking, talking, and naming for you; it means learning to respect and use your own brains and instincts; hence, grappling with hard work.... It means that we insist on a life of meaningful work, insist that work be as meaningful as love and friendship in our lives.... Once we begin to feel committed to our lives, responsible to ourselves, we can never again be satisfied with the old, passive way. (233–34).

The contract Rich describes inspires mentors and mentees alike to recognize their own and one another's value and intellectual capacities and to share responsibility for realizing their potentials as valuable, ethical human beings. These mentors and mentees will extend such mentoring rhizomically—in other words, to *be* rhetorically feminist in the world as mentors, mentees, and vice versa. Ideally, traditional mentoring would work toward the same goals, but that hierarchical, nonreciprocal dyad too often thwarts such feminist mentoring precepts as reciprocity, mutuality, flexibility, power *with,* and propagation.

Multiple Mentors, Time, and Energy

In addition to personal and intellectual support, feminist mentoring includes multiple mentoring, professional development, and capacity building, all of which often overlap synergistically. A precocious graduate student (now an assistant professor) so beautifully explains,

> I knew I wanted to have a variety of experiences in graduate school— and number of different marketable skills. This is something [my adviser] and other mentors have certainly helped me accomplish (from taking coursework in Communication Arts and Sciences, attending

Ohio State's Digital Media and Composition Institute, and working with [yet another professor] on developing some expertise in multimodal writing, working as a research assistant, working as an assistant in the Program of Writing and Rhetoric, and incorporating archives into my teaching, etc.). (Anonymous 5)

She discusses the balance she has already achieved between being focused on her research at the same time that she continually works to develop a broad basis of experiences that enable her capacious nimbleness:

One of the things that I appreciate most about how I have been mentored is that I have been able to—and encouraged to—cultivate that broader base. I think that will make me competitive on the market, but it also helped me learn to juggle different kinds of academic work at the same time (and I hope that learning to do that will make the transition into a job a little easier). But I think it's important that I never felt pushed into something that I didn't want to do or didn't want to learn more about. Instead, it's more like I was convinced of the value of having these different kinds of experiences, and [my adviser] and other faculty members helped me pursue the experiences I was most interested in. (Anonymous 5)

All mentoring should empower capacity building, to be sure, but feminist rhetorical mentoring works to align the mentor's judgments with the mentee's own interests, thereby supporting the mentee's sense of being in the discipline.

Mentors discuss graduate seminar options with their students (whether the students are her advisees or not), helping them understand which courses will best prepare them for the kind of work they want to do, what additional, usually specialized, academic and *non*academic mentors they should seek out, how they can best become who they want to be.[15] If we continue to broaden our traditional conceptions of mentor, mentee, and the relationship between them, as Alexis Pauline Gumbs would have us do, then we can tap the resources of "living ancestral mentors" and "badass mentors" alike. After all, as Paula Moya tells us, "Unless we have access to alternative perspectives . . . we risk being arrested in the process of our intellectual and moral growth" (131).

Rhetorical feminists also spend time with students building reading lists for exams, arranging exam committees, thinking strategically toward the dissertation project, coordinating dissertation writing groups, and encouraging students to submit their dissertations for prizes and awards, all ways that help them dwell, *be* in the profession, and ways that support their journey from the margins to the center. The transactional goal in these discussions is mutual understanding, mutual support, mutual being—not the persuasion of one person by another. Most often, students leave such meetings with a better understanding of the possibilities and the stakes, which is not the same as being pressured to do things the mentor's way. And all of these occasions for mentoring take time, one part of affective labor.

Affective Labor as Investment

Gail Okawa provides one of the richest analyses of how mentoring time "works." Rather than seeing it as a drain on the professor and pressure on the mentee, she explains the relationship in this way:

> When mentors make themselves highly accessible and available to their mentees, this accessibility translates, from the mentee's view, into presences—in person or on the phone or on email: contact time. Mentees see time taken as a gift given, while the mentors instead see it as a vehicle, a means to an end. (527)

For these reasons, mentees sometimes feel as though they should not "bother" their mentor, yet the mentor considers such affective labor an investment in the student, one with a rich payoff. After all, the feminist mentor wants nothing more than for her mentee to join the profession as an equal partner.

It comes as no surprise, then, that one woman wrote that she wished her mentor had more time to talk about and mentor her research, admitting that she's now aware that

> being an excellent feminist mentor can easily increase one's visible and invisible workload. That's the rub, right? You might give more— in part because you're trying to change things and empower/educate people—but then you have less time. (Anonymous 4)

So whether it is investing time in mentees' dissertation progress or helping them nail the genre of the proposal, walking them through their grant applications, organizing reading groups, arranging mock job interviews and audiences for rehearsing job talks, writing all the letters of recommendation that accompany mentees' various endeavors, or listening to their considerable worries, all of this work—guiding mentees as they move from the margins to the center—takes energy and time. If they are not careful, effective mentors can earn themselves an ever-growing cohort of mentees all the while losing track of their own limited supplies of time and energy. At the same time, though, multiple mentees tend to worry about tapping that time and energy and hesitate to "bother" their mentor. In these cases, it is the mentor's responsibility to accept only the number of mentees she can effectively mentor, to provide ample mutual mentoring opportunities for them (reading groups, dissertation writing groups, and the like), and to invite her mentees to meet with her, assuring each of them that she does, indeed, have time and energy for each individual. Of course, it is also incumbent on each mentee to gauge her access to her mentor and make decisions accordingly. Being ever alert to positionality and location are essential for sustaining the mentor-mentee relationship.

As Roxanne Mountford and I explain in "Networked Mentoring," the good mentoring crucial for taking mentees seriously does, indeed, take energy and time, especially for those sought-after mentors who are also stretched thin by their commitments to the other facets of academia in which they excel: their dedicated teaching, their rich and complex research agendas, their speaking schedules, and their administrative and committee duties. Good mentors are very much in demand—as they should be, as they want to be.[16] After all, mentoring remains "an essential component in assisting the development of a professional identity" (Rheineck and Roland 80) and "the heart of graduate education" (Kelly and Schweitzer 130). In fact, many graduate recipients report that "their relationship with faculty [was] the most important aspect in their completion and satisfaction with graduate school" (Kelly and Schweitzer 13). And mentors are associated with the significantly enhanced career success of students who have had a high level of interaction with their mentors. Yes, good mentoring is crucial, is often required, and takes time—yet despite the profound impact of good mentoring, it is often invisible, too often going unnoticed, unrewarded.

Rarely recognized in annual reviews or in professional spheres, feminist mentoring is crucial for the overall development and support of graduate students and their teachers alike.[17] Unfortunately, mentoring's cultural currency most often converts into "service," which Mountford and I argue remains the least valued category in the holy trinity of academia (research, teaching, and service). Given its third-place position, the work of mentoring too often falls to those who are willing to make the time, and too often to women (especially women of color), who constitute the minority of tenured positions (181). And yet, despite its weaknesses, despite the fallibility of every mentor and every mentee, feminist mentoring remains one of the very best ways for taking women seriously.

Rhetorical Feminism, Mentoring, and This Thing Called Hope

Like the feminist movement itself, rhetorical feminist mentoring is inherently hopeful. After all, as Rich forewarned, "The question is no longer whether women (or nonwhites) are intellectually and 'by nature' equipped for higher education, but whether this male-created, male-dominated structure is really capable of serving the humanism and freedom it professes" ("Toward" 133). In response to Rich's doubts, feminist rhetorical mentoring serves as an act of faith in the conditions of possibility, a leap of generosity toward a present that can be reshaped for the future. Only hope can power such an expectation.

To that end, rhetorical feminist mentoring works to empower those involved in a practice of reciprocity, offering experience and expertise as well as creative insights and fresh directions for ethically rewriting our research, teaching, speaking, writing, and collaborations. The emphasis is on action, on mutuality, for rhetorical feminist mentoring cannot be reduced only to the mentor's telling and the mentee's listening. The potential of each singular act is immeasurable, with each act a revision of our older rhetorical-feminist selves and a provision for better preparing the next generation of rhetorically empowered scholars, teachers, and citizens.

Some rhetorical feminist mentoring relationships enact a number of opportunities: collaboration on joint research and publication projects or conference presentations, nominating the mentee for various awards, introducing the mentee to leaders in the field, and encouraging relationships with multiple mentors or networks of mentors. The professionalism that rhetorical feminist mentoring enacts also includes focusing on specific course development in rhetoric, writing studies, or communication; on developing conference presentations for the Conference on College Composition and Communication, the Rhetoric Society of America, the Coalition of Feminist Scholars in the History of Rhetoric and Composition,[18] and other such conferences; and on supporting mentees (and vice versa) as they participate in professional organizations, settle into their first (or second) jobs, and publish in various professional venues. In real terms, then, our "discipline" is made up of relationships among individuals who dwell together for a time and then go forth to do work inspired, in part, by their mentors, colleagues, and friends.

In "Mentoring Lessons," Shirley Nelson Garner describes the workings of such a mutual mentoring process as a kind of agreement

> to listen to each other, to take each other seriously, to treat each other with respect, to trust each other until there is reason not to, to speak about our differences and disagreements, rather than to hide them in silence, and to honor the inherent limits in this professional [and personal] relationship. (12)

But mentoring lessons can also be concrete, pragmatic, as simple as "Watch people, and watch especially the ways they talk to and about people," or "Locate good role models—and bad—and know the difference, especially if the good and bad inhabit the same body," or "Locate two or three mentors, which may not be the same as role models, for no one person can possibly meet all your needs." They might also include such homely reminders as "Rely on trusted friends from graduate school, whether they are former graduate students, former professors, or administrators." Such mentoring advice can travel up, down, and laterally.

After all, the rhetorical feminist model of mentoring is in and of itself a generative model of ever-expansive teaching and mutually nourishing professionalism that can be shared, passed around, and passed on. Rhetorical feminist mentoring acknowledges that we academics "embody" the discipline for the next generation of scholars, and it passes along and around a legacy of values, theories, habits, and assumptions that, especially when transformed, keep the discipline rolling.

Just as Virgil led Dante into the underworld, through Hell, Purgatory, and Heaven, so will we do for others. Feminist rhetorical mentors expect that we will reciprocate, pay it forward, and keep strict hierarchy at bay at the same time that we forge trusting relationships while recognizing power differentials. Most important, such mentors expect each of us to be ready to take someone else's outreached hand and accompany that person into the underworld whenever the earth—or the profession—seems crazed. That is how some great mentor has come along for us. That is how some great mentor wants each of us to move forward and change the world. That is the hope of rhetorical feminism.

SEVEN: (WRITING PROGRAM) ADMINISTRATION

The relationship of the individual to a community . . .
will always be the richest and most complex of questions. . . .
What do we know when we know your story?
—Adrienne Rich, "Arts of the Possible"

Adrienne Rich first appeared on my radar when I discovered that she had taught alongside Mina P. Shaughnessy, one of the most influential writing program administrators (WPAs) our field has known.[1] Rich, along with many other activist women, worked with Shaughnessy to launch a basic writing program at the City College of New York. As a response to open admissions, these women collaborated with one another, reached out and listened to smart students who had neither the grades nor money to attend college otherwise, and changed the face of higher education at a time (late 1960s, early 1970s) when the civil rights movement in America successfully effected positive change. Like the best of rhetors, the best of feminists, the best of administrators, these women made their rhetoric—their words, silences, pedagogy, and actions—*do* something. They helped transform a college education from futility to possibility.

As a collective force, these women represent the many ways to move the feminist rhetorical project into the twenty-first century, carrying forward its initial goals of recovering women historical figures at the same time that it seeks out social justice for both women and men, just as Shaughnessy had done with her basic writing program. Those possibilities for transforming the status quo into social change are realized by feminist rhetors, writers, teachers, and administrators, many of whom employ the tactic of rhetorical feminism to deliberately disidentify with traditional rhetorical practices. In their own individual ways, they strive to embody the practices of rhetorical feminism by engaging in authentic dialogue, respectful deliberation, and productive collaboration and by imagining possibilities for more fruitful rhetorical engagements. Rhetorical feminists also tap such feminist rhetorical theories as invitation (Foss and Griffin, "Beyond Persuasion"), rhetorical listening (Lipari; Ratcliffe, *Rhetorical*), and productive silence (Glenn, *Unspoken*).

In this chapter, I speak specifically to the powers of feminism and rhetoric at the site of writing program administration (also abbreviated WPA). I open by plotting women's settlements on the WPA landscape before closing in on my own location at Penn State University as a case study. Inevitably, my own "notes toward a politics of location" (to use Rich's phrasing) will contrast with those of other feminist administrators; nevertheless, my own location will resonate with challenges, interactions, and histories familiar to many. Therefore, I briefly mark the history of a university-wide writing program, illustrating its current iteration and charting its probable future, a trajectory that may also be familiar to others. All along this historical trajectory, I insert scenes of specific feminist and rhetorical contributions to administrative, curricular, and pedagogical decisions. Finally, I reflect on the powers and limits—the rewards and frustrations—of writing program administration inflected with rhetorical feminism.

Across the Nation

Listen to the women's voices. Listen to the silences, the unasked questions, the blanks. Listen to the small, soft voices, often courageously trying to speak up.
—Adrienne Rich, "Taking Women Students Seriously"

For most of the history of writing programs, women have held fewer administrative positions than men, serving, instead, as instructors who had limited input into or made substantive but unrecorded contributions to the philosophy and curricula of writing programs. Still, we have only to consider the powerful WPA work of Shaughnessy to remind ourselves that women like her (many of whom I mention in this chapter) have long shaped writing programs as well as the discipline (writing studies) itself. Shaughnessy did not identify as feminist, but since her time (1970s), many women WPAs have—and do. In their 1998 "Feminist Writing Program Administration: Resisting the Bureaucrat Within," Amy Goodburn and Carrie Shively Leverenz ask, "What does it mean for feminism to inform a site of composition studies that remains surprisingly undertheorized: that of writing program administration?" (276). So in writing, I join the cohort of feminist WPAs who relate their experiences within the context of their own location to the end of offering my rhetorical feminist voice. A good many of these eloquent and truth-telling administrators are beleaguered, if not powerless, overseeing as they do a cadre of equally overworked, often underappreciated writing instructors, most of them women.

Some feminist WPA scholars have described the situation in bleak terms. Early on, in her 1991 "Women's Work," Sue Ellen Holbrook argued that the professionalization of composition (1870–1930) was actually a "feminization" of composition:

> [I]n the status hierarchy within English[,] teaching was inferior to research. . . . ; work with undergraduates, especially freshmen, was inferior to work with graduate students; and composition . . . was inferior to the scholarly, scientific conception of literature. Hence, in the new university, composition teaching began positioned in the lower status, and there it has remained . . . as appropriate work for paraprofessionals—and for women. (207)

And longtime WPA, scholar, and teacher Susan Miller described much the same. In her 1991 *Textual Carnivals,* Miller interrogates the status of composition in the university, describing the field itself as "the sad women in the basement." In her chapter by that same name, she taps the assessments of compositionists themselves to rank their field in relation to literary studies, critical theory, and rhetoric; to position their academic ranks (fixed-term or tenure-accruing) and expectations of promotion; and to locate compositionists in the larger public sphere, what with its surplus of PhDs in English studies writ broadly. Pulling from Peter Stallybrass and Allon White, Miller describes the compositionist as "an underground self with the upper hand" (Stallybrass and White 4), someone whose identity is contradictory (someone living in the academic basement yet rousing public authority). She continues,

> It is an employment that in the majority of its individual cases is both demeaned by its continuing ad hoc relation to status, security, and financial rewards, yet given overwhelming authority by students, institutions, and the public, who expect even the most inexperienced composition teacher to criticize and "correct" them in settings entirely removed from the academy. The perduring image of

> the composition teacher is of a figure at once powerless and sharply authoritarian. (*Textual Carnivals* 139)

As Eileen Schell explains in *Gypsy Academics and Mother-Teachers*, composition's embrace of feminism, what with its values of "nurturance, supportiveness, interdependence, and nondominance," works mostly to normalize writing instruction as "women's work"—neither serious, rigorous, nor intellectual (76). Of course, being coded feminine in the workplace is rarely good; it is being relegated to the basement, the subaltern, the margins.[2] For these reasons, the tactics of rhetorical feminism include celebrating the feminine, the margins, while actively working against such a code.

In 1996, Theresa Enos expanded Susan Miller's work in her *Gender Roles and Faculty Lives in Rhetoric and Composition*, explaining that the administrative work in writing programs stretches beyond directing the program itself. Such administrative duties include serving as a director or coordinator[3] of a specific writing course (first-year writing, business writing, and so on); of the writing center; or of various programs, including ESL, peer tutoring, TA training, computers and composition, English education, summer session, assessment, and so on. Notwithstanding the fact that many rhetoric and writing specialists are involved in the full range of departmental administration (from supervising peer tutoring to serving as department chair), the women in this administrative cohort report that they are "paid less and work harder" than their counterparts who are men or who are in literature (72). Despite contending that "composition and rhetoric is a more accessible, amiable, self-reflective, and self-aware community than literary studies," these women WPAs "still worry about the apparent dominance of men in this very woman-full profession— gatekeeping in the journals, valorization of empirical research, combative panel and presentation style, back-corridor deals" (72).

Given that the term *research* is considered to be "masculine," as are the terms *rhetoric*, *theory*, and *graduate seminar*, and that the terms *teaching* and *mentoring* are considered to be "feminine," along with such terms as *composition*, *undergraduate curriculum*, and *service*, it should come as no surprise that Enos uses the phrase "female ghettos" when describing most writing programs, where from 60 percent to 90 percent of the undergraduate instruction is performed by women, whether in tenure-track, adjunct, or fixed-term positions (78). Thus, the gendered politics of writing instruction and WPA work continue to inflect the academic scene.[4]

(WRITING PROGRAM) ADMINISTRATION

In "Gender Differences in Writing Program Administration," WPA Sally Barr-Ebest invokes feminism's legendary slogan "The personal is political" and writes about the problems facing women WPAs, including their status as rhetoric and composition specialists (which makes it harder for them to relate to the rest of the English department and find mentors), their lack of knowledge about "male social networks that inform administrative decisions," and their devotion of markedly more time to administrative responsibilities than that given by their men counterparts (57). Barr-Ebest's 1995 study reveals four reasons that women WPAs experience disempowerment in terms of respect, salary, and promotion, all of which she lays at the feet of deans and department chairs who (a) cannot distinguish between service and administration; (b) remain uninformed about the complexities of writing program administration; (c) do not accommodate WPA responsibilities within tenure and promotion guidelines; and (d) are influenced by unconscious sexism and socialization (63). In fact, her respondents (men and women) provide her a list of gendered problems in WPA work that can be summarized as "women take responsibility, men take authority" (66). In far too many instances, not much has changed. Some of the problems include "Women work harder for fewer rewards... and their personal lives are more difficult" and "Women are used for the hard, time-consuming work but not rewarded with power" (66).

Lynn Z. Bloom wryly sums up the gendered problems in WPA work in "I Want a Writing Director" (modeled on Judy Syfers's celebrated feminist declaration "I Want a Wife"):

> I want a Writing Director who will want to remain a Writing Director for the rest of her days, and who will find fulfillment in this most ennobling, if humbling, of tasks. Once I have shown her the ropes I will expect her to handle everything; we will indeed be a team, but I will be the titular head, the silent partner. (177)[5]

Bloom continues in the vein of Syfers by ending with, "My God, who *wouldn't* want a Writing Director?" (178).

Drawing upon the most influential WPA-related research from the past twenty years, Jonikka Charlton and Shirley K Rose extend the exploration into the value of a writing program administrator by charting "Twenty More Years in the WPA's Progress."[6] By 2009, the authors had observed some measure of improvement in the status of WPAs in general and of women WPAs in particular, as well as in the future of WPA work itself

(138). Nevertheless, Charlton and Rose reject the idea that the Council of Writing Program Administrators has "somehow arrived at our Celestial City" (115). The authors credit such improvements to the "professionalization of our field," resulting in the recognition of WPA work as scholarly; worthy of graduate seminars, theses, and dissertation research; and requiring a PhD in the field (138, 136). They regard women's increased participation in the professional organization as a consequence of the overall feminization of our discipline, including the ever-growing number of women PhD students who specialize in rhetoric and writing (119, 123).

Likewise, in *Performing Feminism and Administration in Rhetoric and Composition Studies,* coeditors Krista Ratcliffe and Rebecca Rickly remind us that, as we settle into the twenty-first century, feminism has made fewer inroads into WPA work than earlier writers such as Holbrook and Susan Miller might have hoped. Since the 1980s, the material conditions of the work simply have not changed much. Whether men or women, feminist or not, all WPAs continue to work within an academic-administrative-organizational hierarchy with mandates for reporting (and being reported to), delivering and receiving information, and getting things done, making our rhetoric *do* something. After all, Rich reminds us, "The university is above all a hierarchy," one "built on exploitation" ("Toward" 136, 145). The nearly universal university-wide requirement that is first-year writing affects everything—from the bursar's and admissions offices to academic advising, writing program staffing, and adjunct hiring.

Even though the contributors to the Ratcliffe and Rickly collection invoke feminist practices of caring or nurturing, collaboration, active mentoring, interruption, attention to gender issues and process, and distributed responsibility, these practices are all submerged in the quotidian pressures of getting things done in what the editors refer to as the "administrative trenches" (213). In other words, no matter how feminist the administrator, she still has to meet the demands of a masculinist academy. Little wonder, then, that Nan Johnson would raise the question of the "troubled intersections of feminist principles and administrative practices" (qtd. in Ratcliffe and Rickly 213), especially since, as Rich reminds us, "style and content are inseparable" ("Toward" 143).

Johnson's point is a crucial one: what difference do feminist principles actually make within such an academic administrative arrangement? Many of the essential ideal qualities of a feminist WPA are impossible to employ when taking a position, whether the WPA is experienced or not, tenured or not. Each administrative position is contained by and contains its own scene. No one can enter being fully prepared; there is always on-the-job training as one learns the ins and outs, the backstories and the histories, of any scene.

Susan H. McLeod describes the situational constraints on WPA decision-making and positioning as a "mesosystem" of relations and general climate, circumstances in which the WPA has little or no control, regardless of individual salary, power, or responsibilities (119). In other words, despite any feminist performance of writing program administration, every iteration of feminist principles is imbricated with the material conditions of a mesosystem. As Kathleen Blake Yancey puts it so succinctly, "We all work in a context" (153). We each invoke and embody our feminist principles within our own location.

Location, Location, Location

I have been working to change the way I speak and write, to incorporate in the manner of telling a sense of place, of not just who I am in the present but where I am coming from. . . . I refer to that personal struggle to name that location from which I come to voice—that space of theorizing.

—bell hooks, Yearning[7]

It has become de rigueur in feminist circles to announce one's standpoint, one's location, before embarking on a narrative, a theoretical analysis, or an epistemological exploration. From Patricia Hill Collins and Sandra Harding to Nancy Hartsock and Adrienne Rich, scholars discuss the significance of location to epistemological consciousness as well as to one's understanding (or lack thereof) of power relations, a basic tenet of rhetorical feminism. All of these women write to the ways sex, phenotype, socioeconomic status, level of education, or religion (among the many intersectional markers of identity and positionality) form the material locations of us all.

I am called on to do the same as I describe my status vis-à-vis the well-established, rhetorically based writing program of Penn State. An older heterosexual white woman, tenured professor of English, rhetorically trained at one Big Ten university and fully employed at another Big Ten university, I spent fifteen years at Penn State (preceded by eight years at Oregon State University) before I agreed to administer its huge writing program.[8] Unlike so many other WPAs, I did not have WPA work as part of my graduate training or my professional identity, but I did have a choice of taking on the administrative position.

By 2012, I felt comfortable identifying myself as a professionally established scholar, writer, teacher, mentor, and leader. And, of course, I was older. By that time, I knew I could tap my broad administrative and leadership experience, having held presidencies and served on the executive committees of numerous professional organizations, directed several programs, established two university centers, taught a wide range of courses, and worked through the inevitable progression of thorny issues that accompany anyone's personal and professional life. I was established when I agreed to take on a big administrative commitment—and not a commitment predicated on serving as caretaker for a predecessor's agenda (as is the situation in so many places); rather, I could build upon, extend, or otherwise rethink the rich contributions of my predecessors, most of whom were men. At least this is how I perceived my location then—and how I perceive it now. My account of writing program administration—imbued with rhetorical feminism—bears the ideological weight of my own body, standpoint, location, mesosystem. I cannot reduce that weight, but I can acknowledge it.

Writing Program Administration at Penn State

The questions that we have to ask and answer about that [academic] process during this moment of transition are . . . do we wish to join that procession, or don't we? On what terms shall we join that procession? Above all, where is it leading us, the procession of educated men?
—Virginia Woolf, *Three Guineas*

What is now called "the director of the Program in Writing and Rhetoric" (PWR) is arguably one of the biggest administrative responsibilities in the Penn State English department.[9] Just the sheer number of students and instructors[10] alone complicates the responsibilities inherent in the WPA work necessary for delivering over seven hundred sections of writing and rhetoric courses each year. Additionally, the position carries with it the responsibility for two university-wide requirements, necessitating administrative contact across, up, and down organizational ladders.

Most of our writing and rhetoric standing faculty contribute to various features of the program in some way, either in terms of course coordination or design, digital outreach, new instructor preparation, committee work, or, of course, teaching. All of our senior writing and rhetoric faculty have established national reputations, and our untenured colleagues also demonstrate their commitment to PWR in important ways.[11] As such, we constitute a formidable group within our English department. And like many other large universities, we have a well-defined writing program and a large community of rhetoric and writing specialists in the Departments of English and Communication Arts and Sciences. While some thriving writing programs across the nation are anchored in writing-about-writing, process, archival research, writing-in-the-disciplines, writing-across-the-curriculum, writing-intensive, or special topics taught by actual specialists, ours remains rhetorically based. Regardless of who has run the program,[12] rhetoric has served as our common ground despite differences in our scholarly profiles and research interests.

At present the PWR director works with an associate director from the teaching faculty ranks as well as with three graduate student PWR assistants. Just as the "Portland Resolution" recommends, the PWR director has the material conditions necessary to do the job: "adequate work space, supplies, clerical support, research support, travel funds, and release time" as well as "computer" and "duplicating services" (Hult, Joliffe, Kelly, Mead, and Schuster 90).

All of us who teach writing or rhetoric within our department do so within a larger framework of Penn State's land grant mission, a mission anchored in the 1862 Morrill Land Grant Act, which transformed the traditional purpose of higher education from "classical" study to "practical" and "liberal" education.[13] Since 1855, Penn State has transformed itself from the original Farmers' High School to the Agricultural College of Pennsylvania (1862) to Pennsylvania State College (1874), with a student population of 65 (including some women), to Penn State University (1953), which now has a student enrollment of nearly 100,000 students across all twenty-four campuses, including World Campus. Most of us teach on the main campus, University Park, with a population of 46,184. Our incoming class of 2018 includes more than 9,000 students, all of whom are required to take our first-year writing course.

Toward an analysis of the ways feminism, rhetoric, and writing program administration intersect at Penn State, I will explain the organization, rhetorical foundation, and curriculum of our current program. I will end with the challenges the PWR faces and how the tactic of rhetorical feminism might contribute toward solutions.

(WRITING PROGRAM) ADMINISTRATION

The Program in Writing and Rhetoric: The Mesosystem

A feminist vision of personal power is likely to be quite different. It represents a different way of exercising power because it is based on a different notion of what power is. At base, power is seen as a limitless rather than finite quality.
—Hildy Miller, "Postmasculinist Directions in Writing Program Administration"

The PWR comprises a wide array of courses, from developmental writing[14] and various formulations of first-year writing (ranging from a one-semester, thematic honors course to a two-semester honors track in writing *and* speaking).[15] PWR courses also include upper-division writing courses in various disciplines and upper-division rhetoric courses—all rooted in rhetorical principles.[16] The pedagogical goal is to help all our students—not just the smartest, richest, or best prepared—become strong, flexible, and confident writers, capacious rhetors. They learn to write alone, draft after draft, as well as in concert with their instructors and their peers, delivering their compositions in words, images, and multimedia. In addition to being responsible for all the instructors in the PWR program, I am also attentive to the workings of our undergraduate and graduate writing centers.

Regardless of PWR course—upper- or lower-division, writing or rhetoric—all new instructors (teaching faculty and graduate students) must enroll in a semester-long, course-specific practicum led by an experienced professor. With first-year writing, the stakes seem to be even higher. It has long been the practice that all incoming lecturers and graduate students (and often new PWR faculty), regardless of teaching experience, commit to a one-week orientation, scheduled for the week before classes begin in August, as well as a yearlong practicum that meets weekly. During their first year of teaching in our first-year writing program, all of these incoming folks follow the same syllabus, with all instructors receiving an "annotated" syllabus, complete with cross-referenced resources and pedagogical apparatuses. And all new instructors use the same textbook. After a successful year of teaching, now-experienced instructors can choose a rhetorically based textbook from an approved list. (We have approved lists for all writing courses.)

Because our program provides two of the three university-wide requirements (first-year writing and an upper-division writing course in the major), we abide by the contract between the English department and our faculty senate that specifies the number of formal assignments (six) students will submit. In addition, all writing instructors must submit their syllabi and written-out assignments to the PWR office. There are no exceptions to these requirements.

In any single semester, the PWR enrolls over eight thousand resident-instruction students and eight hundred online students, most of whom are fulfilling their requirements. Given the directed self-placement of our first-year program, we usually offer only 1 or 2 sections of the noncredit-bearing developmental writing course but 136 sections of first-year writing (including 1 or 2 enhanced and 11 online versions), 8 sections of honors first-year writing, and 13 sections of the two-semester honors writing and speaking course. For students fulfilling their second, upper-division writing requirement, we offer around 135 sections of upper-division, discipline-specific writing (18 of them online). Our most populated upper-division, discipline-specific writing course is Writing in Business, perhaps the most in-demand advanced writing course in the nation—and a course that brings to the surface some of the current administrative issues (hiring, budget, online instruction) faced by nearly every WPA, issues that are the subject of the following section.

Putting Feminism to Work

Writing in Business is open to any junior or senior student who wants to use it to fulfill the second writing requirement, but our Smeal College of Business wants sections reserved for just its students, as sections quickly fill.[17] As a result of their students' frustrations in not being able to enroll and schedule when they want, Smeal administrators put pressure on me to "*do* something." This demand from the College of Business was one of the earliest challenges I faced. For the first time, I was feeling institutional pressure to do something another way. In response, and as the rhetorician I am, I tried to make my words *do* something akin to Kate Ronald's "bold vision" (Ronald, Beemer, and Shaver 160). And like Ronald's, my vision, too, was a negotiated one.

Smeal pressured me to add more sections right away, which was impossible for many reasons, most of which centered on staffing extra sections.[18] Therefore, I leveraged this exigence as means for making additional hires, specialists in business writing. Initially, I was told by the administrators in my department that we should simply use our (already overcommitted) fixed-term teaching faculty to meet this challenge. These excellent instructors carry heavy teaching loads (4/4 to 5/5) and teach at a modest pay. The issue for me was not their expertise, which is terrific. Rather, I saw this institutional pressure as an opportunity to reenvision the rank, teaching load, and salary for at least a few writing faculty. Fortunately, my framing the discussion with "courses worthy of Penn State students" (more about that phrase below) successfully raised the rank of candidates we could consider. And from there, I worked through a series of mediated negotiations with regard to hiring and salary that resulted in our hiring three visiting assistant professors of business writing, new PhDs, specializing in business and professional writing.[19] At competitive assistant professor salaries, these three new hires taught a 3/3 load during their two-year contracts, after which they were expected to move into tenure-track appointments elsewhere. Given that the backlog of Smeal students wanting to enroll in the course had not yet been alleviated, we then hired three senior teaching faculty for a three-year contract to teach business writing.[20] I am not sanguine that this current effort will resolve the course-registration problem, either, especially given that I have no influence over what times and days Smeal students will take their classes or who will pay for their business writing instruction. Still, I am delighted that my negotiations resulted in being able to hire these productive colleagues.

Not surprisingly, perhaps, my initial preference was (and still is) to hire a tenure-track professor (or two) in business writing who can help us prepare even more graduate students and teaching faculty to teach business writing and technical writing, as well as additional courses in professional communication, both residential and online. But, in my location (even as a senior faculty member), I do not control the PWR budget and cannot, therefore, move line items around to accommodate tenure-track hires, even those who I feel would enhance the program in a number of ways. I do not have control over everything (on the other hand, it could be said, I do not have the burden of controlling everything). Hiring, budgets, and online instructional demands all constitute major issues for the future of the PWR. Such are the material resources and constraints of my position.

In "Defining Moments," Yancey speaks to the importance of "taking hold of the budget" for WPAs, and especially for women WPAs (149). I think she is right for many reasons: understanding how the money "works," how budget lines can be realigned with priorities, and how to combine responsible planning with agency can all produce positive results for individual units. Yet the material conditions of Penn State's PWR do not easily lend themselves to such a model: the director of the PWR (formerly "comp coordinator") has always been a rotating position; the PWR's hiring needs have always been determined by the registrar's office; and our dean supplies the funds for our fixed-term appointments.[21] Our dean also controls the tenure lines, even after our department has voted on hiring priorities.[22] And given that we remain a comprehensive English department, the PWR's hiring needs and budget remain inextricably intertwined with those of literary studies, creative writing, critical-cultural theory, visual studies, and other emphases.[23] It is within such a context that I work to conceptualize how best to meet the demands of all our PWR courses, but especially our upper-division courses and our online curriculum. In other words, I work as part of a distributed administrative model, within which we all listen to and talk with one another; in which our transactions are meant to be informative, not persuasive; and in which we all recognize the others' locations—in short, within a context that could be described as one of rhetorical feminism. Linda Alcoff reminds us, "We must . . . interrogate the *bearing of our location and context* on what we are saying" (112), and I do. I consider my positionality (as well as my intersectionality) as I think through the daily and future demands of hiring, courses, and curriculum.

How to face those demands as a WPA employing the tactic that is rhetorical feminism is a concern I take seriously. So with Yancey's good counsel always in the back of my mind, I must balance the feminist models of WPA work put forward by Bloom, Marcia Dickson, Goodburn and Leverenz, Jeanne Gunner, Laura Micciche, Hildy Miller, Schell, and Ratcliffe and Rickly. All of these feminist scholars have critiqued the idealized centralized-power model of WPA work and have urged WPAs, instead, to develop more of a willingness to relinquish control, which I have surely done, in the process forging trusting, mutually supportive relationships within the web of administration. These feminist WPAs resist models of administrative work that centralize power in one individual (Micciche 449). In response to that traditional administrative model (which would, for good reasons, include control of the budget and hiring), both Gunner and Micciche invoke the importance of rotating the position, distributing power and responsibility, establishing productive committees, and rewarding excellence and effort. I would add to their feminist models the ability and willingness to reach out, collaborate, negotiate (use listening, silence, and dialogue), strive for mutual understanding (rather than persuasion), and work strategically—and with hope—toward a vision.

Wisely, Hildy Miller cautions that such "leadership can appear weak if receptivity is mistaken for passivity; affective responses such as laughter for lack of seriousness; and the sharing of power for looking to others for direction" (54). And she goes on to remind feminist WPAs that

> one person at the top must function as a figure to take both credit and blame. As a result, just as feminist directors must alternate feminist and masculinist personas to cope with double ideologies, we also need to design collaborative administrative structures that can be translated hierarchically. (56)

Coupled with her advice, the feminist WPA model of distributed (rather than centralized) power and responsibility forwarded by this group of women aligns better with the material conditions of my position, with my mesosystem, including the cultural and administrative structure within which I work (from Penn State "Pride" and East Coast students to the decanal and headship structures and my English department colleagues). Of course, that second feminist model (distributed power and responsibility) also seems to align with my own disposition as well as with my experience in establishing productive ways to interact with my colleagues.

Facing the Future

All women together ought to let flowers fall upon the tomb of Aphra Behn ..., for it was she who earned them the right to speak their minds.
—Virginia Woolf, A Room of One's Own

It's our future, so we'd better be there.
—Susan Gubar, Rooms of Our Own

Facing the future as director of the PWR includes establishing positive ways to guide changes in our courses, hiring, and teaching assignments within a national culture of ever-reduced budgets, ever-expanded leveraging of media, and increasingly accomplished faculty. As I already mentioned, the PWR provides two of the three university-wide requirements, writing courses that have been built on a foundation of rhetoric. Several years ago, the faculty senate launched a general education review that threw the entire campus in a panic, as the senate wanted to make change—and fast. The last review of Penn State's gen ed requirements was nearly twenty-five years ago (1995), so it did seem appropriate to review them again. Doing so would serve as a welcome opportunity to revisit the requirements as well as the substance of the required courses themselves.

But because no one in writing studies had been included in the initial discussions, because the information circulating about changing courses seemed so ridiculous and shortsighted, I intentionally did not enter the fracas. (Sometimes, I simply remain silent on a matter, a tactic of rhetorical feminism.) I did not want to participate when the faculty senate seemed so determined to make changes fast. I knew the review board would eventually come to me for my support, so I wanted to wait until they had faced other people's dismay at their ideas, until they had considered their flimsy ideas further. Fortunately for me, my entire department supported my feet-dragging plan, even one person who was on the review board. I was also fortunate in that, aside from the grumbling emails to faculty senate members I sent about the too-rushed process, no one else in English was interested in pursuing the rumored changes, either, changes (or so stories would have it) that included a "thematized and clustered" undergraduate curriculum that would begin with a seven-themes approach to first-year writing—as though a first-year writing course has no content.[24]

Eventually, I found that the best means for rousing productive, mutually empowering, purposeful dialogues about the gen ed review (and thereby slowing down the proposed changes to first-year writing) was to ask at every opportunity, "What courses can we offer that are *worthy* of Penn State students?"—and then listen to the responses. Folks were suddenly interested and engaged. That single question touched our common concerns of a quality undergraduate education. They wanted to talk as well as listen to the ideas of others, especially to those of us who know about writing (how to teach it, how students learn).

To that end, I eventually asked members of the review committee these questions: What courses will most benefit our students? How can those courses be worthy of our students? What are new, creative, newsworthy ways to rethink such courses? Fortunately, my questions—posed within a context of a faculty-wide uproar—slowed the velocity of the gen ed review at the same time that they promoted the dialogues, respectful collaborations, and considered deliberations for the development of updated criteria for our required writing and speaking courses.

We now have new criteria because, rather than depending on a faculty senate committee to remodel our writing and speaking courses, a small committee of us (all feminist rhetoricians in the College of the Liberal Arts) was able to wrest the responsibility from the faculty senate and develop a set of readily approved criteria ourselves.[25] None of the criteria has anything to do with themes.[26] After all, as Micciche and many others continue to remind us, we WPAs are the experts. All it takes to remind others of our expertise is to employ our "knowledge of the history and current status of writing instruction" in order to "devise curricula, conduct teaching-training courses and faculty development workshops, establish goals for writing programs, and determine assessment procedures" ("More" 440). Given our collective expertise in English and communication arts and sciences, then, we six feminist rhetoricians on the committee developed frameworks for the three university-wide required writing and speaking courses, criteria that meet the Council of Writing Program Administrators Outcome Statements as well as the Statement of Principles for Public Speaking as a Liberal Art.

As we move into the future, then, the following four criteria will serve as the basic foundations for Penn State's writing and speaking courses, criteria anchored in Aristotle's definition of rhetoric as "the faculty of observing in every situation the available means of persuasion" (*Rhetoric* 1.2). James Herrick's gloss of the definition, however, helps make an even stronger connection with our courses when he explains that the word "*faculty* here is *dunamis*—a capacity or even a power. *Observing* is a translation of the term *theoresai,* from which we get the word theory" (12). Thus, we expect our students to develop rhetorical capacities, specific knowledge, communication theories, and, of course, successful practices that embrace the following criteria: (a) Students will develop rhetorical knowledge; (b) students will develop capacities in critical thinking, reading, listening, and the generation of ideas; (c) students will develop proficiency in composing processes; and (d) students will develop knowledge of communication conventions.[27]

Other than the very good news that rhetoric, writing, and speech faculty from all across our campuses work well together is the maybe even better news that members of the faculty senate now realize that our writing and speaking courses actually already had content, that it was never incumbent upon them to supply content (in the guise of themes) for our courses. My colleagues and I continue to work together to envision even more possibilities for developing engaging, transdisciplinary writing, speaking, and communication courses (whether upper-division or lower-division, resident-instruction or online) that are always/already anchored in rhetorical principles. Together, we can imagine an academic future of courses that both nourish and support student writers, speakers, and composers as they draft, write, and revise the kinds of communications that they value and we all like to read and hear.

But within the English department as well, PWR faculty have been active in the development of four new undergraduate concentrations in English studies that we hope will spark higher enrollments and greater numbers of English majors. It comes as no surprise that PWR courses provide the backbone of three of the four concentrations, which are literary and cultural studies, creative writing, professional and media writing, and rhetoric and writing. As our department and the PWR move forward into the future, these are some of the curricular—and, I would add, hiring and staffing—challenges qua opportunities we face. The hope that is rhetorical feminism continues to sustain me.

Coda

We're not trapped in the present.... We do have choices. We're living through a certain point of history that needs us to live it and make it and write it.
  —Adrienne Rich, "Arts of the Possible"

The four feminist research practices (theoretical stances) that Jacqueline Jones Royster and Gesa Kirsch lay out (critical imagination, strategic contemplation, social circulation, and globalization) help feminist WPAs stretch the "boundaries of our work ... toward the development of new paradigms for how our work itself might be shaped" and deployed into the future (13–14). In terms of "critical imagination," for instance, many of us, even those of us who regularly publish in rhetoric or writing studies, still consider our administrative work to be part and parcel of "our work." After all, as Charles Schuster assures us, WPAs "must possess both administrative skills and broad-based, up-to-date knowledge of highly specialized theory and practice" (ix). We leverage our disciplinary expertise and the tactic of rhetorical feminism to work through issues such as a gen ed review as well as to collaborate with, listen to, and understand our colleagues, all the while finding ethical ways to reenvision the status quo or to transform an initially "bad" idea into a much greater good. Maybe not the "greatest good" signified by eudaemonia, but a greater good, to be sure.

When feminist WPAs leverage critical imagination, we clear a space for "strategic contemplations" that allow us to remember, even imagine, what it is that we know, who we know, how we know, and what works. Productive silence, respectful listening, and meditation (all elements of rhetorical feminism) fuel strategic contemplation, our eventual risk taking, and our movement from conflict to resolution. Whether a colleague goes "rogue" in an instructor-preparation course, a new member of the teaching faculty reveals that her repeated absences are related to her bipolar disorder, a first-year student reports that she has "nothing to learn" in class, or a harassed graduate student breaks down in our office, rhetorical feminism makes space for everyone—especially the WPA herself—to think through and toward possible solutions. Her hope sustains her.

The "social circulation" element of rhetorical feminism invites the contextualization of any event within a scene, a Burkean scene imbricated with acts, agents, agency, and purpose (margins and a center). The "politics of [our] location" comes into consideration as well as our own personal, professional, and public histories, which often serve as reliable sources of knowledge. Those of us who get purchase from feminist histories and the feminist present have only to invoke Hillary Rodham Clinton, Ruth Bader Ginsberg, Audre Lorde, Adrienne Rich, Sonia Sotomayor, Virginia Woolf, Malala Yousafzai, or any number of others to envision how strong, intelligent, purposeful women have judiciously and productively negotiated their stances, their plans for the future. Like us, they have hope for a better future. At this point in our feminist WPA practices, consideration of women's failures is every bit as important as our successes, whether we are facing the challenges of helicopter parents, aggressive students, shortsighted administrators, disrespectful colleagues—or of opportunities to evolve, build, grow, and work even smarter toward our goal. Feminist WPAs can invoke feminist legacies of action and performance to model new scenes of writing, teaching, and administering, just as the six of us did when we rewrote the criteria for Penn State's required speaking and writing courses.

The "globalization" feature of Kirsch and Royster's practices may be one of the most futuristic of their features. As waves of international students meet on our shores, enroll in our courses, and eventually move through our universities as graduate students and professors and through our communities as the professionals they came here to become, all of us can embrace the tactic of rhetorical feminism and pay especial attention to their cultures, languages, personal experiences, and ways of being—their movement from the provisional margins into the center. Their interests in our culture have prompted many of us WPAs to reciprocate such interest, to develop a WPA consciousness toward internationalization, language differences, citation practices, professional development, course selection (and development), instructional support, cultural commonplaces, writing center support—all the facets of globalization that are transforming our work.[28] No longer do these students seem "foreign" to us—they are future leaders, like the Aung San Suu Kyis, Angela Merkels, and Iron Girls of Post-Mao China (Wu, *Once Iron Girls*) of the world, who work toward positive change, toward eudaemonia. Together, all of these feminist practices provide us (masculinists, feminists, combinations, or in-betweens) new ways to map our locations, to chart our course to new places, to imagine the new places we want to inhabit. They give us hope.

Am I a perfect feminist rhetorical WPA? Not even close. Do I continue to pursue my goals as such? You bet. Do I like the work? Surprisingly, I do. Do I like preparing teachers, developing the curriculum, working with teaching faculty and graduate students, hearing out frustrated students? Yes, I do. Would I have enjoyed this work earlier in my career? Maybe not, not if doing so were not my choice and especially not if I found myself working without the support and respect that WPAs receive at my institution. Would I enjoy the work in another location, within another mesosystem, at this point in my career? Probably, but not in just any mesosystem. Am I successful? Often, but not always. For every time I am successful, I give credit to the strong WPAs who have preceded me as well as to the ones who have helped educate powerful colleagues who could otherwise be—but rarely are—recalcitrant or just horrible. And when I am not successful, I always consider how I could have employed my rhetorical skills better; I always rethink the rhetorical situation as to whether there was actually any chance for change in the first place, regardless of who introduced the change. When I fail, I try hard to convert that failure into needed information for the future. And when I consider the material conditions of my position, I am grateful to Wilma Ebbitt, who set the course for Penn State's writing program, and to my generous, too-hard-working colleagues who are always willing to talk with me about student learning, transfer, assessment, grading, assignment design, adjunct labor, textbooks, and many other issues. Men and women alike, they also advise, help, reach out, collaborate, and listen. Even though they do not identify as such, I am beginning to think that they all may be rhetorical feminists as well.

> I dwell in possibility
>
> —Emily Dickinson, #466

EIGHT: THIS THING CALLED HOPE

Hope is necessary. It's a necessary concept, and Barack didn't just talk about hope because he thought it was a nice slogan to get votes. He and I and so many believe that—what else do you have if you don't have hope? What do you give your kids if you can't give them hope?
—Michelle Obama interview, 16 December 2016

Resisting Closure: A Meditation

This final chapter is not a traditional conclusion, one that offers closure, invites impasse. Instead, I am pausing, enjoying a sense of openness that includes contradictions, incompleteness, and hope. Every time I turned to this project, I brought with me the ideas of yet another article, another book, another speaker, each of which offered one more idea for me to weave into the fabric of my book, one more way to tweak my conceptual theory (tactic) of rhetorical feminism. Hence, this project can never be complete, closure can never be final—nor should it be. The book's imperfections, then, accommodate the as-yet-unfulfilled goals of rhetorical feminism: equality, social justice, coalition across differences, inclusion, representation, and ever-developing rhetorical effectiveness. This final chapter makes clear that the blocked opportunities we inherited should not be our bequest for those who come after us. After all, we have agency—and hope. Rhetorical feminism is fully committed to hope, and creating possibilities for realizing that hope is the key.

Creating Possibilities

Feminist rhetorical studies creates possibilities, not blueprints for an imagined utopian future. Not even sixteenth-century Thomas More dared to attempt a blueprint, knowing as he did that "Utopia" was "nowhere." He took the more productive route, that of holding up for inspection the ridiculous waste and foolishness of his present. Contemporary feminist rhetoricians are doing the same, pointing out the waste of political potential and intellectual talent when qualified women—and their groundbreaking practices, plans, and scholarship—are overlooked and underestimated solely on the basis of their being. They point out the foolishness of an identity politics that does not lead to deep (self)questioning, to thoughtful answers, or to hard-but-constructive conversations. They remind us that refusing to coalesce—even temporarily—is foolish, for how else can we move forward activist projects of equality and social justice?[1] Contemporary feminist rhetoricians fully understand the importance of paying attention to the past as well as to the present moment, for "the history we tell becomes the present that we value, and the present that we tell becomes the history that we value" (Rhodes 22). The present moment foretells the goals of a feminist rhetorical future.

During the writing of these chapters, I took pride in the history our nation was drafting for itself in recognizing the humanity of each of us, the rights we have as citizens. Our present was not perfect, but it was full of hope, possibility. Bernie Sanders's 2016 presidential campaign galvanized a new generation of voters to consider the rights and responsibilities of an engaged citizenship, to consider the working poor, the middle class, and college students. By example, he invigorated the Clinton campaign, so that by the time Hillary Rodham Clinton became the Democratic nominee (however flawed), many of us felt that we might have the chance to benefit from her experience and expertise as well as from the Democrats' now-shared, forward-looking policies on education, sexuality, the environment, poverty, health care, and global relations. After the 2016 presidential campaign, however, what with my months-long optimism and those jarring election results, I cannot help but wonder if our political ideology of democracy-for-all is beginning to crumble.[2] National correspondent for the *Atlantic* James Fallowes views "Trump's election as the most grievous blow that the American idea has suffered in my lifetime." Since he has taken office as president, Donald Trump has worked to dismantle the Affordable Care Act, climate change policies (pulling out of the Paris Agreement altogether), reproductive rights, and social programs for the most vulnerable of our citizens. He has purposefully offended various presidents and prime ministers, bombed Syria and Afghanistan, and threatened North Korea, all the while maintaining cordial relations with Russian president Vladimir Putin. This gloomy moment is our political reality, one that includes Larry Nassar, Harvey Weinstein, and a shameful regularity of school shootings. Not since the Vietnam War do I remember our nation being so painfully, politically divided.

Have we Americans changed to the point that we are now fundamentally incapable of living peacefully together, collaborating, moving ourselves into a more humane future? I wonder, yet I still have hope, the Cornel West kind of hope (that I have alluded to throughout):

> Hope and optimism are different. Optimism tends to be based on the notion that there's enough evidence out there to believe things are gonna be better, much more rational, deeply secular, whereas hope looks at the evidence and says, "It doesn't look good at all. Doesn't look good at all. Gonna go beyond the evidence to create new possibilities based on visions that become contagious to allow people to engage in heroic actions always against the odds, no guarantee whatsoever." That's hope. I'm a prisoner of hope, though. Gonna die a prisoner of hope. (qtd. in A. Smith, 105–06)

Even at the present moment, when Donald Trump has taken office, when North Korea has launched yet another nuclear missile, when Trump has initiated a trade war with China, when Democrats are blocking legislation in the manner of the Republicans during the Obama years, I remain hopeful. I must.

Even in the Age of Trump

Yes, Trump brings with him all the threats and drama of his ultimately successful campaign. Yes, he brings his daily tweets (of unsubstantiated accusations, outright lies, and bombastic threats), critical of everyone and everything from President Obama and the FBI to the United Nations and the national media. And, yes, his tweets continue to receive more media coverage than the revolving door of his cabinet, of the mostly white men who sponsor policies affecting Americans on a daily basis: jobs and wages, health care, social security and retirement, immigration, same-sex marriage, taxes, gun control, student loans, natural resources (including parks and fossil fuels), climate change, women's reproductive rights, Veterans Administration care, international trade, and nuclear power.

Trump brings his history of epideictic calls for a "total and complete shutdown of Muslims entering the United States";[3] his opinions that Mexicans who come to the United States are "bringing drugs, bringing crime, they're rapists";[4] his promise that he will build "a great, great wall on our southern border, and . . . make Mexico pay for that wall";[5] his charges that "Obama is the founder of ISIS and crooked Hillary Clinton is co-founder";[6] and his assertion that the 2018 Florida high school shooting can be blamed on an FBI that is "spending too much time trying to prove the Russian collusion with the Trump campaign."[7] Such statements are part and parcel of his trademark routine of racist, sexist, xenophobic remarks—which affect all of us citizens, as does his relationship to the truth.[8]

Trump's falsehoods have become so legendary that *New York Times* columnist David Brooks calls Trump "perhaps the most dishonest person to run for high office in our lifetimes." Trump tweets that "global warming is a Chinese plot," declares that he "watched American Muslims celebrate the Twin Towers' Fall" on 9/11, claims a financial worth of $10 billion (when it is actually less than half of that, with $650 million in debt), and regularly refers to journalists as "the lowest form of life."[9] These blatant lies and insults fall in line with his hyperbolic boast that he could "stand in the middle of Fifth Avenue and shoot someone and not lose any voters."[10] David Greenberg describes the "brazenness and frequency" of Trump's "falsehoods, and their evident expedience," as what sets Trump apart.

Or maybe not.

After all, as philosopher Hannah Arendt taught us so well, "No one has ever doubted that truth and politics are on rather bad terms with each other" ("Truth" 49).

Hope and the Politics of the Present

The Trump presidency offers three major issues for us feminist rhetoricians to address: What are the effects of living in an age of politically incorrect, factually incorrect, post-truth politics? Who will benefit and who will suffer, given the seemingly heteronormative, upper-middle-class, nationalist, masculinist, white conservative (but not compassionate) Christian agenda of the Trump presidency? And what possibilities might we imagine and work to create for a more equitable future for us all?

We do not always know how to create possibilities for, let alone meet, the future. To do so, we must make ourselves familiar with the ways the politics of the present (a present that quickly bleeds into the past) plays out in our psyches. To examine our present-past is not merely to confront what has become outlived (the waste and foolishness) but to discover the potential of what is living within ourselves. In *Reinventing the Soul*,

Mari Ruti describes potential as the "entire reservoir of riches within us," which comes to us as an "acute conviction that at times stirs and perturbs the human spirit" (244). That potential is the hope that keeps us alive and keeps us working. Even as we move, on a daily basis, toward our inevitable death, most of us create possibilities, embrace hope. Philosopher Henri-Louis Bergson describes hope as our "intense pleasure," because with hope,

> the future, which we can dispose of to our liking, appears to us at the same time under a multitude of forms, equally attractive and equally possible.... The idea of the future, pregnant with an infinity of possibilities, is thus more fruitful than the future itself, and this is why we find more charm in hope than in possession, in dreams than in reality. (9–10)

At the time of this writing, I do not see future possibilities as "equally attractive and equally possible," especially given the abrupt shuffling of what was once our national project: rights, responsibilities, and opportunities within the hope that is democracy. Rebecca Solnit assures me, though, that I "possess the power to change the world to some degree [and] . . . that the world is going to change again, and uncertainty and instability thereby become grounds for hope" (23). "Hopefulness," she continues, is chancy, "for it risks disappointment and betrayal" (23).

Yet I still hope.

I hope for a tomorrow in which the voices of *all* our citizens are encouraged and heard; when the goal of democratic debate, deliberation, and dissent is a shared commitment; when feminists' political, scholarly, and social participation and influence are extensions of their social equality; and, of course, when a woman (a feminist, no less) finally does shatter the presidential glass ceiling. Then, we might—we *might*—experience a new model of rhetorical-political success.

That president will face many of the same rhetorical challenges of her predecessors (of political figures, such as Stewart, Grimké, Mott, Truth, and Clinton, as well as of rhetorical figures, such as Campbell, Dow, the Fosses, Logan, Powell, Ratcliffe, and Royster)—specifically, the challenge of being listened to and heard. She will also confront the complications of leading a nation founded on principles of equality but too often unwilling (if not unable) to recognize its own ideological, patriarchal inequalities, a nation that rarely acknowledges the rhetorical complexities of its polity in any sustained way. I can only hope that such a woman president will inspire all our citizens to set their sights on even greater possibilities for our future.

This chapter, then, asks us to meditate on hope, to keep alive a tempered hope for the future in light of our present political moment. It reminds us that we must trust that change will come and pro/actively pursue positive change in the ways feminist rhetoricians have been doing for over thirty years now. As Sara Ahmed enjoins us, "We need a feminist account . . . of redirection" (*Living* 50). The rich and complex theories of intersectionality (Crenshaw) and interest-convergence (Bell) are models of redirection, accommodating rhetorical feminists and feminist rhetoricians alike as they move their social-justice project forward and become ever more self-aware in their advocacy work (on behalf of women and Others); their purposeful coalitions; their respect for nonhegemonic rhetorical practices, stances, and deliveries; and their commitment to hope and possibility. Now, more than ever, in this new, amped-up, masculinist order, we need the powers of rhetorical feminism as we teach, mentor, administer, write, and live productively and hopefully with one another.

A Sense of Collective Hope

> Hope is the thing with feathers
> That perches in the soul,
> And sings the tune without the words,
> And never stops at all.
> . . . .
>
> —Emily Dickinson, #254

In "Arts of the Possible," Adrienne Rich reminds us that folks like us—feminists, scholars, rhetoricians, writers, and teachers—must make and write our future through the "sheer power of a collective imagining of change and a sense of collective hope" (153), the sheer power Ahmed refers to as feminism, "which fills her with hope and energy" (*Living* 1). Whether change comes in how we identify ourselves and others; how we treat and collaborate with one another; how we develop our scholarly, rhetorical, personal, and feminist lives; or how we teach, mentor, and lead—that change is rooted in and becomes (to repeat the phrase) the "history that we value" (Rhodes 22).

Over the past thirty-some years, many feminist rhetorical scholars have coalesced to establish a history we value.[11] By now, feminist rhetorical histories are their own thriving market. Although a small number of scholars were beginning to write or edit feminist rhetorical histories in the late 1980s, they did not begin to work closely or formally together until 1990, when the Coalition of Women (now, "Feminist") Scholars in the History of Rhetoric and Composition was officially established.[12] The initial, small group of scholars has grown to nearly three hundred members, who meet annually to carry out the coalition's three-part mission of fostering and encouraging scholarship and research in the history of rhetoric and composition; encouraging exploration of women's roles in the stories we tell about rhetoric and composition; and building and sustaining a network of scholars who share these interests.[13] The inauguration of an official feminist-rhetorical coalition sparked the idea of another possibility.

In 1995, Lisa Ede and I were invited by our Oregon State University department chair to organize a national conference that would bring attention to the English department at the same time that it showcased one of the department's strengths: rhetoric and feminism. Robert Schwartz saw the possibility of such a conference, staked $7,000 on it, and then left us to turn those dollars into the reality of a one-time, special-interest conference. The 1997 Feminism(s) and Rhetoric(s) Conference, "From Boundaries to Borderlands," worked to bring together feminist scholars from rhetoric and writing studies as well as from other disciplines (science, philosophy, communication, linguistics, women's studies, ethnic studies, education, and so on).

The conference was a wild success, with attendees buzzing with hope for a future conference, which Ede and I knew our financially strapped university could not sponsor again. Fortunately, during the final dinner event, Lillian Bridwell-Bowles and Lisa Albrecht announced that they would continue the conference at the University of Minnesota. From that moment on, the conference became the biennial Feminism(s) and Rhetoric(s) Conference, which is already planned through 2019, when James Madison University will host it. "FemRhets" (as the conference is often called) is now officially linked with and partially supported by the coalition, and the conference itself has grown threefold from the inaugural one we held.

In addition to realizing the possibilities of a coalition and of FemRhets, feminist rhetorical scholars have brought to fruition the possibility of sustained scholarship in the field, which gives us hope. By 1999, I had proposed a new book series to Southern Illinois University Press, Studies in Rhetorics and Feminisms, which the advisory board approved. I worked alone for two years, soon realizing that there were simply too many good manuscripts for one person to evaluate and edit, so I beseeched Shirley Wilson Logan to join me as coeditor. Studies in Rhetorics and Feminisms has so far produced nearly thirty scholarly collections and monographs, on topics ranging from feminist approaches to ethos, women's rhetorical agency, and educating the new southern woman to feminist rhetorical practices, rhetorical listening, and gender and rhetorical space.

Studies in Rhetorics and Feminisms represents just one strand of the publishing industry that is feminist rhetoric, what with several other university presses producing influential monographs and collections, many of which I have already mentioned (see Works Cited and Consulted). A few decades ago, scholars were only beginning to imagine the ways rhetoric and feminism might work together, but as we settle into the twenty-first century, this new field is thriving, a signpost to our future. The present challenge for feminist rhetoricians is to imagine continued possibilities for allying feminist rhetoric (its theories, practices, and practitioners) with mainstream rhetoric and, thereby, further developing rhetorical feminism. Thus, feminist rhetoricians have much work to do to secure our imagined possibilities as our future.

The Possibility of Integrated Rhetorical Theories and Praxis

How do I exist?

This was the silence I wanted to break in you
I had questions but you would not answer

I had answers but you could not use them
—Adrienne Rich, "Cartographies of Silence"

Throughout these chapters, I have pointed to two major problems that the feminist rhetorical project faces. First of all, the field is splintered from within (a problem and a strength), given the various standpoints and identities of its practitioners. And second, despite the marked differences among its theories, practices, and practitioners, feminist rhetorical studies is altogether marginalized from hegemonic rhetorical studies. These two problems, however, do not vitiate the power and potential of feminist rhetorical studies, which offers many possibilities (both in methods and occasions) for feminists and nonfeminists alike to work together and to coalesce, if only temporarily and despite disagreements. The possibilities are many, but determining how, exactly, to move such a project forward is the real challenge.

Divisions and Coalitions among Feminist Rhetorical Theories

Fortunately, feminist rhetorical theories and praxes are buoyed by hope. Notwithstanding the diversity among these theories and praxes, they are, as Karlyn Kohrs Campbell observes,

> [d]istinguished by the systematic inclusion of women, by an absence of language and/or perspective that degrades women or minorities, by rigorous testing of assumptions that hark back to stereotypes and social mythology, and by a concern to rectify the omissions, the degradation, and errors of the past. ("What" 4)

Feminist rhetorical theories rely on their distinctive differences from one another and their challenges to hegemonic rhetorical theories and practices. Bonnie Dow cautions feminist rhetoricians to respect their distinctions and differences, especially as we "build a theoretical 'room of our own,'" but not to distinguish their work so far as "to withdraw from the public world, traditionally rhetoric's domain, in our longing to possess a space not colonized by patriarchy" (113).

Of course, feminist rhetorical studies will always "use the intellectual resources of feminism to understand and to valorize the contributions of women to public life [and scholarly thought] . . . and to critique the ways in which these contributions have been and continue to be marginalized" (Dow 106). But speaking from the margins (as rhetorical feminism, and Gloria Anzaldúa in particular, illustrates) can indicate strength and participation both in the public sphere and within the discipline of rhetoric, regardless of how masculinist both continue to be. Only by staying connected with one another, staying publicly engaged, can feminist rhetoricians actually reshape the practices, theories, pedagogies, and histories of mainstream rhetoric. Therefore, feminist rhetoricians are rarely separatist, functioning instead in the spirit of engagement, whether such engagement is contact, conflict, comparison, or hoped-for collaboration.

Still, I wonder if hegemonic rhetoricians would notice if feminist rhetoricians separated completely. Barbara Biesecker encourages all of us rhetoricians to put into contact "the genius of Rhetoric" and the "(very different) genius of feminism," both of which "uncramp the orthodoxy of rhetorical theory and advance the theory and practice of feminism" ("Towards" 88). But despite Biesecker's encouragement, Keith Lloyd admits that "feminist perspectives on argument remain exclusively in feminist collections" (102), where most feminist perspectives on all facets of rhetoric reside when not used as token essays to indicate the comprehensiveness of an otherwise hegemonic collection. Feminist rhetorician Malea Powell addresses the issue when she writes,

> There are a lot of ways to think about [rhetorical] practices... outside the Western code. Some of "us" have ... been doing this work for a long time, already. True, as a discipline we've alienated and marginalized most of that work to such a degree that it's not welcome in our journals, is barely visible at our conventions, and is nearly non-existent in our conversations about what "we" do in common. When it does appear, it's quickly tokenized as a "special" or "alternative" discourse and quickly set off from what "really" counts. But we could change that behavior, we could change those practices, and we could change our beliefs about the breadth of what counts in our discipline. ("Stories" 402–03)

Like the best of feminist rhetoricians, Powell imagines possibilities for a more inclusive rhetorical future—that is, if we feminist rhetoricians continue our work. Still, Lloyd's acknowledgment of these challenges serves as motivation for feminist rhetorical theorists to continue their work of broadly circulating fresh perspectives, enriching what passes for tradition, and legitimizing more ways of being rhetorical and doing rhetoric.

Perhaps Lloyd, too, identifies as a feminist rhetorician, for he urges us all—mainstream and marginal alike—to set aside the rhetorical focus on winning and persuasion and to concentrate instead on a "much more fruitful space of dialogue, one that... redefines 'defensible theses' as articulations of possibility, openness, community, as well as expressions of frustration, antagonism, and group identity" (103). Lloyd's concept is akin to that offered by Suzanne Clark some twenty years ago, a "dialogic rhetoric" not based on oppositions or conquest but on collaboration and mutuality that interrupts the "rigidities of language" and opens that language to a "subject in process" ("Julia" 309, 308). Yes, possibilities exist for opening up both the rhetorical process and the subject. But then again, such ideas, "women's" ideas, "feminists'" ideas, are too rarely recognized as theories. The theoretical work men have done might earn them eponymous theories (Aristotelian, Platonic, Ciceronian, Burkean), but the same professional courtesy, let alone disciplinary recognition, has not been given to women (no Anzaldúan, Campbellean, Ratcliffean, or Roysterean, for instance). Sometimes, it seems as though feminist rhetoricians are quarantined at the border, always/already subject to separation from other feminists or from the field at large. Halted because of their identity.

The Possibilities of Intersectionality

Kimberlé Crenshaw's theory of intersectionality, however, has worked to ease the problems at passport control. Her theory (never as yet referred to as Crenshawean theory) continues to help people understand the impact of multiple oppressions. Her cogent analysis explains how oppressions overlap, become interdependent, and, thereby, create systems of discrimination and disadvantage. Crenshaw's theory illuminates the systemic reasons a woman of color regularly faces more economic and professional obstacles than her white counterpart, why a transgender person often faces incredible obstacles of every kind. The problem with Crenshaw's theory is that it does not circulate widely, nor is it easily understood or broadly applied.

Were the theory of intersectionality talked about in the media and acknowledged across the curriculum, were families, cohorts, and professionals discussing it, then multiple identities, including that of being feminist, could be leveraged for their epistemic power and recognized for the social capital they carry or lack. Such rhetorical practices and engagements would lead us deeper into the margins and yet allow us to carry that knowledge back into the mainstream. From a feminist rhetorical vantage point, a fundamental incentive for learning from Others—from people and occasions that Jacqueline Jones Royster refers to as "non-normative subjects" and "non-normative arenas"—is so we can also hear and acknowledge their experience of reality ("Disciplinary" 157). We can live the feminist life that Ahmed describes, one that "keep[s] open the question of *how* to live" (*Living* 197; emphasis added).

All of us—hegemonic and marginal rhetoricians alike—already know that existing rhetorical theories do not yet fully account for the experiences and perspectives of all the humans who embody rhetorical expertise. For this reason, feminist rhetoricians continue to develop insights and practices into so-called alternative uses of rhetoric, drawing energy most usually from both hegemonic theories and those anchored in marginal politics.[14] Like feminist rhetorics, the so-called marginal rhetorics (theories and praxes) surfacing from efforts of the queer, raced, ethnic-cultural, and disability communities are also buoyed by hope. To ignore the experiences and hopes of these Others as well as those of women is to leave all of that knowledge, experience, and rhetoric—all of that reality—unheard, unknown, unappreciated, unused. Crenshaw's theory of intersectionality helps us understand why but also motivates us to do something to remedy the situation.

Beyond the challenge and possibilities of feminist rhetoricians receiving knowledge and training from one another is the equally serious challenge of broadening the feminist rhetorical message itself, of reaching out to liberals and conservatives alike in the social, scholarly, and political spheres—without losing their base of support, without "courting" the mainstream. After all, we cannot become "the master's tools" (Lorde, "Master's Tools" 110). How might feminist rhetoricians, then, speak to issues that benefit feminists and other Others while demonstrating just how those issues are crucial to the health of the discipline, of society at large? In "Feminism Lost. Now What?," Susan Chira advises that in order to build bridges, we "define [the] issues as broadly as possible," particularly racism's interconnection with feminism. Good advice, but perhaps easier said than done. The trick is to find a way to connect feminist rhetorical issues with the concerns of mainstream rhetoric, in the way that Kenneth Burke encourages when he explains that you persuade someone insofar as you can talk that person's language, identifying your ways with his or hers, identifying your cause with that person's interests (*Motives* 56). In short, the challenge is to persuade more mainstream rhetoricians that feminist rhetoric is not merely a luxury for sometimes-condescending liberal white academics but is essential to the vitality of rhetorical studies overall.

The Possibilities of Interest-Convergence Theory

In thinking of ways to forge stronger connections, more frequent interactions between the margins and the center,[15] I earlier rehearsed the strengths of Mark Lilla's argument for transcending identity politics to think of ourselves as "Americans" and of Gayatri Spivak's powerful concept of strategic essentialism for transforming internal disagreements into temporary coalitions. Both of those ideas can be used successfully to bridge serious differences and, therefore, constitute important resources in the arsenal for doing so. In addition to these theories, Derrick Bell's principle of interest convergence proves useful. Although Bell's work focuses only on race issues, his analysis can be applied to decisions with regard to gender, ability, and other subaltern issues as well.

An originator of critical-race theory, Harvard Law professor Bell developed what he called the "interest-convergence dilemma" to describe "a deeper truth about the subordination of law to interest-group politics with a racial configuration" (35). He anchors his analysis in *Brown v. Board of Education* to say, "The interest of blacks in achieving racial equality will be accommodated only when it converges with the interests of whites" (35).[16] In other words, white people will support racial justice only when there is something in it for them, when there is a "convergence" between the interests of white people and racial justice (primary among the interests of many black people). Applying Bell's theory to the estrangement between feminist rhetorical studies and mainstream rhetoric might prove useful, if it is believed true (to paraphrase Bell) that mainstream rhetoricians will support feminist (or other marginalized) rhetoricians only when there is something in it for them, when there is a convergence between the interests of mainstream rhetoricians and scholarly equity (a primary interest of feminist rhetoricians).

Such a claim provides rhetorical scholars a strategic method for stimulating the political and social changes that accommodate the plasticity of rhetoric itself, the adaptability of rhetorical knowledge and skill to any era, geography, culture, or people. If our discipline truly wants to prepare rhetors to know everything about everything, as Cicero would have us do (*De Oratore* I.vi.20), then would not knowledge of the experiences, truths, and values of *all* people practicing rhetoric be in the self-interest of us all, mainstream and marginal alike? Would not our discipline earn its place as the centerpiece of any education anywhere? Would making such a move, then, provide rhetorical studies with twenty-first-century intellectual legitimacy, social currency it so longs for?

And yet, at this point, I am rethinking a bit, wondering if easing a convergence between mainstream and marginal interests is always the best move. After all, much of the energy of marginal rhetorics comes from the struggle of being marginal, from speaking and listening to comrades within the margin, to establishing the marginal as a force in its own right. The legitimacy of marginalized rhetorics might be threatened if its rhetoricians and practitioners appear to be awaiting approval from or cooptation by the mainstream. Interest-convergence theory also paints subaltern subjects as passive, awaiting gestures of invitation, inclusion, and change from the mainstream, rather than as active agents in change beneficial to their own interests. And the theory implies a sense of despair about the future of authentic change: can there really be no change without advancing the interests of the powerful? Little wonder that Bell himself described his theory as a "dilemma."

Nevertheless and regardless of its shortcomings, Bell's interest-convergence theory offers feminist rhetoricians insightful analysis (explanatory power on why the power dynamics are changing or not) as well as a valuable theory for how best to create incentives that could ultimately serve as significant correctives. How we wish to employ such analysis or apply such theory will always be up to us.

As we all know well, rhetoric remains a site of contest, difference, and acknowledgment, and all humans—mainstream and marginalized alike—can meet at the site, even on different terms and with different values at different times. Rhetoric and feminism together offer all humans politicized space for discussing values and effective communication (especially across differences); processes for inquiring, conceptualizing, organizing, reasoning, and delivering information; and opportunities for self-empowerment, agency, and political action. Both rhetoric and feminism have the potential for transformation at their very core, possibilities for transforming the discipline and the disciples. The possibilities of struggling together toward something more beautiful, more humane, fill me with hope. Rhetoricians have been working singularly and together for millennia, while feminist rhetoricians have been working (across their differences) for only the past century or so. The possibilities for future work, for working together toward inclusive rhetorical theories, are limitless. Rhetorical feminism offers us the hope to do just that.

The Possibilities for Future Feminist Rhetorical Work

Hope sparkles like water in the clean carafe.
—Adrienne Rich, "Letters: March 1969"

Researching and writing this book has given me ample opportunity to meditate on our discipline, on my time spent in the field, and on age (my own aging, to be precise). At this point in my career, I had envisioned living in a country that had made huge strides in gender and racial equality; I had imagined myself as knowing much more than I do and of knowing how to teach, mentor, and research with much more confidence than I have. The older I get, the less surprised I am at the fallibilities of our discipline and of my workings within that discipline. On the other hand, it is exciting to consider just how much more scholarly and political work there is to do in rhetoric, how very much more I still need—and want—to learn.

Aging and academia go hand in hand, as the ideology of Western cultural ageism calls for men to gain power and influence as they age (up to a certain point), while aging women gradually lose their professional, financial, and social power. For women, even more than for men, then, aging is a narrative of decline and erasure. Whether sparked by a significant birthday, retirement, a health issue, or cultural expectations, the mechanism is set into motion. Accompanying that alleged gradual decline is a very real fading away, an aging woman's invisibility to those around her. Thus, ageism is rightly a feminist issue, one exacerbated by a lifetime of sexism (among other isms). Ageism is also a scholarly issue, one that must be considered alongside other isms.

Weird as it now seems, old age used to be far away—that is, until a professional meeting a few years back, when, during an extraordinary conversation with a younger feminist rhetorician, I felt the sting of professional ageism for the first time. She came to talk with me about a professional matter and came just short—on the precipice, in fact—of asking me when I was moving aside so that she could step into my place. It was an odd experience, to be sure, made more bizarre by her painfully self-conscious apology a week or so later, which I immediately accepted. She was embarrassed, and so was I. After all, she had not meant what she said to sound the way it did. And I—who pride myself on being "present"—had not had the presence of mind to assure my younger colleague that no matter how much I enjoy my work, I will inevitably move aside. Nor did I think to assure her that there is plenty of work for all of us rhetoricians (feminist or not) to do, or of how much I admire her impressive research agenda and scholarly productivity. She obviously felt that she had failed in that moment. I failed, too.

Yet ours proved to be a generative failure for me: once I realized what we had both experienced (a transaction of ageism), I identified a problem that I wanted to address in this book. I originally planned to test the connections between the feminist rhetorical objectives of representation and inclusion and the singular premise that identities are epistemic resources. After all, any identity is created in the presence of complex others (as I've said before) largely through speech and action, but also through skin. Given that our skin literally embodies our chronological identity, age should be examined for its knowledge-producing potential. Indeed, the knowledge I have gained over the years is evidenced throughout this book, and my knowledge about what I still need to learn (as well as what I think our discipline needs to consider further) in terms of teaching, mentoring, and research appears in this concluding chapter. I reflect upon a number of pressing concerns for our future work.

First of all, we need to further contemplate our teaching. In our undergraduate and graduate courses, we may want to reevaluate what and how we are teaching toward disciplinary expertise and what "disciplinary expertise" might mean to our twenty-first-century students. Most of us teach academic speaking and writing as well as rhetoric courses that are often centered on "the" rhetorical tradition, but some of us are offering our students less-familiar rhetorical traditions as well. Many of us—especially younger scholar-teachers—are creating new opportunities for students to claim agency in the classroom. These teachers are rethinking the classroom as a place to learn rhetorical histories, conduct history, and grapple with the complexities of historiography that feminist rhetoricians have come to know so well. Joyce Rain Anderson, Jessica Enoch, Lynée Gaillet, Jane Greer, Wendy Hayden, Jordynn Jack, Pamela VanHaitsma, and Elaine Richardson represent the growing numbers of feminist rhetorical teachers who are turning the undergraduate classroom into an opportunity for students to visit university archives, community archives (including the resource that is human beings), and private archives; to conduct recovery work; to interrogate the archive's power and inherent rhetoricity; to apply and resist long-established research methods and methodologies; and to write often-marginalized and unknown figures into the rhetorical record. This work gives me hope that our feminist rhetorical practices will transform these student researchers, enrich our histories, and attract the attention of our local communities.[17]

In our courses, we may also be redefining what counts as persuasive rhetorical display, giving recognition to the roles silence, listening, the visual, the aural, the electronic, and the embodied always play out in any rhetorical situation. We have even rounded the sharp corners of argument, working to change its transactional goal from that of winner-take-all persuasion to one of sharing understanding, attended by invitation, productive reception, and collaboration. All such projects force us to ask ourselves how we teach, how we ask students to write, what definitions and visions for participation we put before them, and how we assess them.

And we have also found ourselves cutting under-the-table deals with students in order to accommodate their schedules, errors, pressures, and, yes, immaturity—after all, what do we have to lose? We are taking our students seriously, helping them claim their educations. Yet the gap between the hope for teaching and learning and the material conditions that encompass our teaching lives (and our students' learning lives) is too often alarmingly vast. These contrasts present some of the biggest challenges to our teaching. Most everyone agrees that education is the key to better jobs, higher incomes, and greater growth of all kinds, with many concurring that nothing is more important than education. Yet the challenges of diversity and disparity are writ large on our students, what with mandated testing, staggeringly insufficient financial support, the reliance on adjunct labor, and the constant specter of neighborhood, home, and school-related abuse and violence. Such challenges continually vitiate the teaching life, education, and hope itself. We find ourselves paying especial attention to our students' mental health, regardless of how much we love our teaching. As Frankie Condon reminds us, "More than our disciplines, more than the subjects we teach, more than the assignments we give, the humanity of our students and the quality of humaneness with which we treat our students is at the heart of teaching and learning" (par. 2). Thus, we must stick with our goal, that of inviting *all* students, regardless of their perceived/proclaimed identity, into the world of rhetoric, where human agency is best developed. Ours is an inclusionary rhetorical world, one sustained by the pedagogies and practices of scholars like Condon and Vershawn Ashanti Young; Asao Inoue; Inoue and Mya Poe; Poe, Inoue, and Norbert Elliot; and Stacy Waite.

Second, given that rhetoric has always been a teaching-mentoring tradition, we feminist rhetoricians need to continue to enrich the teacher-mentor relationship. As I discuss earlier, the teacher-mentor role has long indicated a master-apprentice model. The feminist intervention into the teacher-mentor role frames a humane model of high scholarly expectations, rigorous academic preparation, and open communication. The responsibility for such communication is shared, resting in both the teacher-mentor and the student-mentee, for how else will each of them understand the resources and constraints of the other's life?

To be long-lasting, the teacher-student/mentor-mentee relationship must be tempered by the honesty and hope that results from mutual respect, flexibility, and open dialogue. Andrea Lunsford describes such a relationship as "one in which graduate students [are] our partners in exploring major issues, in constructing new knowledge, and in sharing the wealth of our experiences, our learning, and our teaching" (*Writing* 69). The mentoring stories in Michelle Eble and Lynée Gaillet's collection illustrate the multiple ways successful feminist rhetorical mentoring can look—and feel—within the marked iterations of a friendship, a shared future.

Third, many of us feminist rhetoricians need to rethink our own research agendas and scholarly stance as we widen our understanding of who and what can be defined as rhetorical and as we appreciate more fully the vast range of methods, methodologies, and epistemologies currently in circulation. In terms of our research we are making the most exciting personal and disciplinary strides, because, in the process, we are continuing to learn from the brave and insightful research of our own cohort and especially from the younger generation of scholars. In fact, Lunsford pushes a new relationship to research in terms of how we are preparing graduate students, nudging our discipline to consider collaborating with them on "large-scale research projects" as well as encouraging them to take on other kinds of exciting and maybe even scary collaborative endeavors, the kinds of research that "will present a great challenge to our imaginations and organizational abilities." Scholars are successfully connecting their scholarship and pedagogy. For instance, Gwendolyn Pough and Elaine Richardson, as well as Brian Stone and Shawanda Stewart, have developed hip-hop language pedagogies; Richardson and Wendy Hesford have applied their work on human trafficking (and other abuses of women); Enoch, Kimberly Hensley Owens, and Lindal Buchanan have connected their study of the private sphere to their teaching; and others still are helping their students understand the connections between the body and rhetoric (Jean Bessette, Debra Hawhee, Sarah Hallenbeck, Carolyn Skinner). These scholarly-pedagogical-research projects exemplify the wake we are making together through the twenty-first century, as we ride feminism's third and fourth waves (see Adichie; Ahmed, *Feminist Attachments* and *Living*; Bates; Baumgardner and Richards; Dicker and Piepmeier; Gilley; Gillis, Howie, and Munford; Jensen; Walker, "Becoming" and *To Be Real*; and L. West).

The Hope of Reimagining

The moment of hope is when the "not yet" impresses upon us in the present, such that we must act, politically, to make it our future.
—Sara Ahmed, *Feminist Attachments*

Notwithstanding the progress women have made all around the world, biologically reinforced stereotypes continue to diminish the accomplishments of women, no matter how progressive any nation or any culture might seem. We Westerners are only a bit surprised at Turkish president Recep Tayyip Erdoğan's position that "[a] woman who rejects motherhood, who refrains from being around the house, however successful her working life is, is deficient, is incomplete." But when a Brit—and a woman at that—allegedly says the same, we are nonplussed. In the summer of 2016, the British press ran with the story that then Tory leadership candidate Andrea Leadsom claimed to be a better candidate than her childless rival Theresa May, wrongly quoting Leadsom as saying, "I feel that being a mum means you have a real stake in the future of our country, a tangible stake." Leadsom was furious that her mis/quoted sentiments were applauded by many Brits. Unfortunately, it came as no surprise at all that our own 2016 Republican presidential candidate Donald Trump was recorded bragging about his own disrespect for women: "When you're a star, they let you do it. You can do anything . . . grab them by the pussy. You can do anything."[18] Nevertheless, all over the world, women—childless and childbearing alike—continue to fight for the right to be recognized as full human beings, as active agents capable of making change and staying the course, as the "Me Too" and "Time's Up" movements are making so very clear. Strong, successful women leaders such as Germany's Angela Merkel, France's Christine Lagarde, Sweden's Margot Wallström, and the United States' Hillary Rodham Clinton, Elizabeth Warren, and Ruth Bader Ginsberg continue to bear strong criticisms as they lead the charge.

In a recent *Guardian* essay, Catherine Bennett outlines all the reasons 2016 was one of the "worst, most retrograde [years], in women's history." Invoking Madeleine Albright's "special place in hell" for women who do not help each other, Bennett wants to ensure a spot for "all the US voters who surrendered hard-fought progress in female self-determination for leadership by two apprentice patriarchs, the pussy-grabber and Mike Pence." In contrast, Zadie Smith uses the occasion of her 2016 Welt

Literature Prize to outline the progress that women and people of color (like her) have made, contrasting that progress to darker days ahead and speaking of her despair—and optimism—in facing the future:

> Things have changed, but history is not erased by change, and the examples of the past still hold out new possibilities for all of us, opportunities to remake, for a new generation, the conditions from which we ourselves have benefited. . . . [P]rogress is never permanent, will always be threatened, must be redoubled, restated, and *reimagined* if it is to survive. I don't claim that it's easy. I do not have the answers. I am by nature not a political person and these are the darkest political times I have ever known. . . .
>
> . . . If novelists know anything it's that individual citizens are internally plural: they have within them the full range of behavioral possibilities. They are like complex musical scores from which certain melodies can be teased out and others ignored or suppressed, depending, at least in part, on who is doing the conducting. At this moment, all over the world—and most recently in America—the conductors standing in front of this human orchestra have only the meanest and most banal melodies in mind. . . . But there is no place on earth where they have not been played at one time or another. Those of us who remember, too, a finer music must try now to play it, and encourage others, if we can, to sing along.

I am hopeful, but I am not naive. I am a rhetorical feminist.

When rhetoric and feminism become allies in contention with the forces troubling us all, our shared goal is to articulate a vision of hope and expectation. Toward such a future, we can support our friends, colleagues, and students as they come to voice; feel empowered in critical discussions; and write, speak, and teach the words that reshape (and repair) the world and pave our future. Of course, our imagination of the future will always be richer than any actualized time to come. But to have such hope is to envision a future that requires not only imagination but action (Mathieu 19). And that is the work that we feminist rhetoricians do so well. We are all working toward the goals of rhetorical feminism and this thing called hope.

NOTES

WORKS CITED AND CONSULTED

INDEX

NOTES

Preface

1. Feminist rhetorical perspectives and those by people of color (including those in whiteness studies; see Kennedy, Middleton, and Ratcliffe) are most often segregated in collections or syllabi of mainstream rhetoric, serving mostly as subjective counterpoints to objective (masculinist) rhetorical history and theory. Django Paris calls for a simple audit to help us see whose work, whose lives, and whose art are valued enough to be studied and engaged. Such an audit provides an intersectional view of how race, sexuality, cultural-ethnic groups, gender, class, sexuality, and disability are represented.

Introduction: Rhetorical Feminism—Definitions, Terms, Parameters

1. See Enoch's *Refiguring Rhetorical Education*, Logan's entire body of work, Lunsford's *Reclaiming Rhetorica*, Lunsford and Ede's "Crimes of Writing and Reading," Powell's "Princess Sarah, the Civilized Indian," Royster's *Southern Horrors and Other Writings*, and my own *Rhetoric Retold*.
2. In some ways, rhetorical feminism operates akin to Ratcliffe's theory of rhetorical listening.
3. Whether I refer to traditional rhetoric as "mainstream," "masculinist," or "hegemonic," I recognize it as a vitally important discipline that continues to sustain and withstand our feminist rhetorical interventions.
4. My hope is that other scholars will contribute to a further clarification and greater circulation of rhetorical feminism.

1. Activism

1. See the introduction for definitions, distinctive features, and explanations of the following terms: feminist rhetoric, rhetorical feminism, Others, the subaltern, and the marginalized.
2. The public sphere is where rhetoric and politics overlap and where the unremitting focus on persuasion, dominance, and winner-take-all competition has long discouraged, even blocked, women and other marginalized groups from rhetorical-political histories, treatises, practices, and leadership positions. Instead, these groups have been delegated to the private sphere, to the margins of history, politics, and leadership.

3. Of course, Native American, Chicana, and Asian American women contributed to the struggle for women's suffrage, as did some free black men. I focus on the tradition of African American and white women because their shared history is the most familiar for the compressed history I am providing.
4. Even in 2016, US men regularly earned at least 20 percent more than women for doing the same jobs. In 2017, President Trump revoked the 2009 Lilly Ledbetter Equal Pay Act. Women are underrepresented in government, executive suites, the news media, the sciences, and the tech sector.
5. For many Americans (the majority, in fact), Clinton's loss was a loss for feminism and for the advances feminists (and others) have made: from public educational opportunities and reproductive rights to equal pay and government-funded child-care programs—all of which are threatened under the Trump administration. This is not to say that Clinton was not a flawed candidate.
6. Worldwide the figures are not all that impressive, either. In 2017, there are twenty-some women world leaders, but the pool of national leadership possibilities is nearly two hundred.
7. Democratic candidate Clinton was regularly referred to as a "bitch"; threatened with impeachment and incarceration; and harassed by politicians, the media, and citizens for everything from the decades-old Whitewater scandal and her husband's infidelities to the Benghazi raid and her email server. Despite winning the popular vote by nearly three million votes, she was not elected president of the United States in 2016.
8. When, in 1776, the Continental Congress declared independence from Britain and established the nation of the United States, property owners (all of them men, nearly all of them white) composed the category of "men" who were created equal and who assumed voting rights as perquisites to citizenship. Nearly all the rest of the people—free or slave, man or woman, citizen-class or not—remained unequal to those white property-owning men in every way.
9. The first group to take up the cause of suffrage were land-owning immigrant men who had become naturalized citizens, followed by non-property-owning men.
10. Though always inferior to that of a white man, a white woman's legal status fluctuated, depending on the state in which she resided. If a white woman's husband died without a will, her inheritance was restricted to one-third of his estate. If she rightfully inherited the estate (and lived in Maryland), she had to remarry within seven years or forfeit her inheritance. In New York,

> [a] widow could inherit only a Bible, pictures, books, and the like under $50 in value, the spinning wheel, stove, loom, 10 sheep, two pigs and their pork. Along with clothes, bedding and so forth, she also received "one table, six chairs, six knives and forks, six tea cups and saucers, one sugar dish, one milk-pot and six spoons. . . . [G]irls were regularly excluded from their fathers' wills." (Frost-Knappman and Cullen-DuPont 2)

11. In the Declaration of Sentiments, these white women outlined the specific rights denied to them and the specific actions white men (citizens) had taken to deny women those liberties and rights.

12. In 1888, Douglass relented and spoke to the International Council of Women in Washington, DC: "Men have very little business here as speakers . . . ; and if they come here at all they should take back benches and wrap themselves in silence" (*Woman's Journal*).
13. Stanton, Mott, and Gage all had personal relationships with members of the Iroquois Confederacy and knew full well that "unlike the European American women of the nineteenth century, Iroquois women had tremendous political authority" (Nordell).
14. Women in a number of other countries had already achieved just that: New Zealand (1893), Australia (1901), Finland (1906), Norway (1913), Denmark (1915), Iceland (1915), Russia (1917), Austria (1918), Poland (1918), England (1918), Ireland (1918), Scotland (1918), Wales (1918), Germany (1919), Luxembourg (1919), and the Netherlands (1919).
15. At the 1848 convention, no black women were invited. When Sojourner Truth attended the 1851 convention, the white women in attendance complained about her appearance for fear that Truth's testimony would distract the audience from a focus on (white) women's rights to a consideration of abolition as well. Fortunately, Truth's testimony about working in the fields like a man turned on its head the accusation that all women were too weak to carry the burden of voting. She was a woman.
16. Eventually, the sisters had to leave the relatively liberal Quaker church, which did not condone the extent of their very public feminist rhetorical activism.
17. Sojourner Truth embodied this expanded definition at the 1851 Woman's Rights Convention in Akron, Ohio.
18. The 1837 "Pastoral Letter of the General Association of Massachusetts to the Congregational Churches under Their Care" cautions churches about the dangers of outspoken, public women. When a woman "assumes the place and tone of man as a public reformer . . . her character becomes unnatural" (Stanton 1: 81).
19. Dana extolled such fictional (and tragic) characters as Shakespeare's Desdemona, Juliet, and Ophelia, women whose tenderness, innocence, and domesticity the American woman should strive to replicate.
20. All biblical citations are taken from the Revised Standard Version.
21. Such scriptural citations served as enthymemes, logical shortcuts that smoothly aligned with the Christian values of her ever-more-receptive audience. Her juxtaposition of purposeful biblical women and public activism offered an occasion for Burkean "perspective by incongruity" (*Permanence* 112), a chance to "see around the corner of everyday usage" (*Philosophy* 400) and be wrenched out of "customary habits of perception" (Selzer 104, 162). If Mott's audience could be inveigled to inhabit such a perspective, even temporarily, they would be able to recognize their own "trained incapacities," their habitual patterns of thinking and doing.

    As Mott instructs her audience, "If these scriptures were read intelligently, we should not so learn Christ as to exclude any from a position, where they might exert an influence for good to their fellow beings" (321). After all, Jesus included women into his ministry and demonstrated ethical sensitivity to the plight of women, for example, the "fallen woman"

who would be stoned. In other words, Mott disidentifies with traditional readings of the Bible that influenced contemporary sociocultural values.
22. Because petitions were described as "prayers," churchwomen wisely shaped their political expression as such, which would therefore be heard by an audience.
23. Following her influential address (which was soon after circulated as a pamphlet), Mott resumed the lecture circuit to speak to issues of peace, justice, and equality for each and every person (man and woman, free and slave alike).
24. Shirley Wilson Logan's *Liberating Language* and Jacqueline Jones Royster's *Traces of a Stream* both illuminate this movement.
25. Established in 1896, the National Association of Colored Women's Clubs represented the joining of the National Federation of Afro-American women, the Women's Era Clubs of Boston, and the Colored Women's League of Washington, DC. Josephine St. Pierre led the merger.
26. Her talk was later referred to by the title "Ain't I a Woman," though the title itself reads "Ar'n't I a Woman" (qtd. in Logan, *With Pen* 24–25).
27. The cause of women's suffrage was also referred to as woman suffrage or women's right to vote.
28. Free black women participated in the American Equal Rights Association (which supported the enfranchisement of black men), the National Woman Suffrage Association, the American Woman Suffrage Association, the National Baptist Woman's Conference, and the Alpha Suffrage Club of Chicago (founded by Ida B. Wells). Many of the clubs affiliated to form the National Association of Colored Women, which included suffrage as one plank of its platform.
29. Men formed the largest group of those combating suffrage, on the grounds of "women's unsuitability for citizenship duties" (Palczewski, "Male Madonna" 375). Catherine Helen Palczewski explains: according to arguments opposing women's suffrage, women lacked the physical power necessary to enforce the vote, and the public realm was unsuited to proper women (375). Even some well-organized white women believed that "woman suffrage was a misguided and unnecessary reform," for "women of good character [in other words, citizen-class women] would be better able to influence public policy by means other than the vote" (375). Catharine Beecher, half-sister of abolitionist Harriet Beecher Stowe, believed that women could have greater impact as teachers and educated homemakers. And during a slightly later period, political activist Emma Goldman expressed the belief that woman suffrage would conform to an already corrupt government system.
30. The American Equal Rights Association grew out of the 1866 Eleventh National Woman's Rights Convention in New York.
31. However, she had earlier written to William Still, author of *The Underground Railroad*, that "between the white people and the colored there is a community of interests, and the sooner they find it out, the better it will be for both parties" (qtd. in Still 770).
32. By 1893, Harper had come to believe in suffrage for only the educated and the moral: "I don't believe in unrestricted and universal suffrage for either men or women. I believe in moral and education tests.... Great evils stare us in the face that need to be throttled by the combined power of an upright

manhood and an enlightened womanhood" ("Women's Political Future," qtd. in Logan, *With Pen* 45).

33. Their limited access to various committee and caucus leadership positions denies women any substantial power to shape public policy (Swers 133). And their minuscule representation on "prestigious committees with broad legislative jurisdictions, such as Ways and Means, Appropriations, and Energy and Commerce," diminishes "their ability to bring gender-related concerns and their unique experience to the policy-making table" (133).

34. Ranked second on the 2016 Forbes list of the world's most powerful women (after Angela Merkel, chancellor of Germany) and first on the list of the most powerful women in the United States ("World's 100 Most Powerful Women"), Clinton was lauded by President Obama as "one of the finest secretaries of State we've had" (@POTUS, 1 Feb. 2016).

35. As senator from New York, Clinton used the same strategy to build relationships quietly with senators from both parties at the same time that she served on a number of important Senate committees, including the Committee on the Budget; Armed Services; Environmental and Public Works; and Health, Education, Labor, and Pensions.

36. When she withdrew from that race, she assured her supporters of her steady hope in the American democratic system, her voice breaking with emotion: "Although we weren't able to shatter that highest, hardest glass ceiling this time, thanks to you, it's got about 18 million cracks in it and the light is shining through like never before, filling us with the hope and the sure knowledge that the path will be a little easier next time" (qtd. in "Women in Politics").

37. Ironically, the majority of white women voters—53 percent—cast their ballots for Trump, whereas 94 percent of black women voters went to Clinton.

38. Berit von der Lippe offers one of the clearest analyses of Clinton's hawkish stance.

39. Susan Bordo blames sexism for Clinton's defeat as Clinton has long been a "living Rorschach test of people's nightmare images of women's power. It's no surprise that as she came closer and closer and closer to the most powerful position in the world, the misogyny directed toward her became increasingly vicious" (27).

40. Argentina, Australia, the Bahamas, Bangladesh, Barbados, Brazil, Central African Republic, Chile, Croatia, Estonia, Germany, Grenada, Iceland, Indonesia, Jamaica, Kosovo, Latvia, Liberia, Lithuania, Malta, Marshall Islands, Mauritius, Myanmar, Namibia, Nepal, New Zealand, Norway, Poland, Romania, Serbia, Singapore, South Korea, Switzerland, Taiwan, Thailand, Trinidad and Tobago, and the United Kingdom represent countries that have elected women leaders to forge public policy.

41. Since 1988, this movement has spread across the globe, with large groups in the United Kingdom, the United States, Europe, South America, Australia, New Zealand, Canada, Bahrain, Egypt, India, Japan, Mexico, and Turkey.

42. Just consider the 2012 fatal gang rape in New Delhi, India, the 2012 shooting of Malala Yousafzai (by Taliban militants) for advocating for girls' education, and the 2014 kidnapping of two hundred Nigerian schoolgirls by Boko Haram.

2. Identities

1. At the end of the 2016 presidential campaign, the unsuccessful Democrats were scolded for spending too much energy celebrating America's identities rather than a sense of shared "American-ness." *New York Times* writer Mark Lilla warns, "This fixation on diversity . . . has produced a generation of liberals and progressives narcissistically unaware of conditions outside their self-defined group, and indifferent to the task of reaching out to the Americans in every walk of life."
2. As Lloyd Bitzer tells us, only a rhetorical audience can (or knows someone who can) resolve or address the exigence of the rhetorical situation (4). In rhetorical feminism, especially when both rhetor and audience are marginalized, the resolution may not be as important as the transaction itself. A rhetorical audience may be already resistant to the rhetor and the message and unwilling to listen rhetorically.
3. In *The Psychic Life of Power,* Butler explains, "Power not only *acts on* a subject, but in a transitive sense, *enacts* the subject into being" (13).
4. Spivak's purpose, however, has been to disturb the stability of the term *subaltern:* "What I'm interested in is seeing ourselves as namers of the subaltern. If the subaltern can speak, then, thank God, the subaltern is not the subaltern any more" ("Political Commitment" 283).
5. Jolie was promoted to the rank of Special Envoy to the High Commissioner, Filippo Grandi, and to the Office of the United Nations High Commissioner for Refugees at the diplomatic level, with a focus on major refugee crises.
6. See chapter 3 where I analyze the concept of *disidentification*, a strategy of resistance where a person outside the mainstream ideology adopts and then reappropriates that ideology for her own purposes, to her own advantage. Gloria Anzaldúa serves as a case in point.
7. It is important to note the gendered limits of Burke's work, as Kyle Jensen and Krista Ratcliffe so persuasively demonstrate in "Mythic Historiography: Refiguring Kenneth Burke's Deceitful Woman Trope." Identification with Burke's truthful, speaking "man" is the universal move, for his woman is deceitful and silenced.
8. Like *belie, ravel, splice,* and *resign, cleave* is a binary word, a contronym, a word that holds within it contradictory or opposite meanings. For instance, *cleave* can mean merge or separate.
9. The category of *woman,* considered by movement leaders to be inclusive, was actually *ex*clusive, easily lending itself to a hierarchy of women with white middle-class heterosexuals at the top and everyone else below or in the margins. Any stable group identification, then, was faulty.

    Any definition of *woman* will miss its mark, but Jack Halberstam's definition of *lesbian* might work well to describe *woman*: "the term we affix to the pleasurable and cumbersome intersections of embodiments, practices, and roles that historical processes have winnowed down to the

precise specifications of an identity" (50). And in *Gender Trouble,* Judith Butler argues for an "inessential" woman, one whose identity is constructed by repetitive acts and is constituted by discourse (25, 136).
10. At the 2017 Women's March on Washington, I saw one sign that read, "I'll see you nice white ladies at the next #BlackLivesMatter march, right?"
11. Their feminist rhetorical statement clearly outlines a theory that Crenshaw would coin as *intersectionality.*
12. Butler writes that "certain forms of acknowledged fragmentation might facilitate coalitional action precisely because the 'unity' of the category of women is neither presupposed nor desired" (*Gender* 15).
13. In her 1980 "Age, Race, Class, and Sex: Women Redefining Difference," Lorde writes,

> Certainly, there are very real differences between us of race, age, and sex. But it is not those differences between us that are separating us. It is rather our refusal to recognize those differences, and to examine the distortions which result from our misnaming them and their effects upon human behavior and expectation. (119)

14. In "What Does It Mean to Say That All White Feminists Are Racist?," feminist theologian Carol P. Christ writes about the way Lorde's open letter to Daly continues to shape feminist discourse. Christ notes the importance of "setting the record straight about Mary Daly" as "one step in retelling the history of feminism" in a more complex way. Perhaps she is right: all feminists—regardless of their material conditions, cultural-ethnic affiliation, and other identifying characteristics—should know that Daly wrote back with care and intelligence.
15. Nevertheless, as Christ writes,

> Racism exists. . . . Everyone in a racist culture is affected by racism and it lives in our collective unconscious in many and insidious ways. The structures of racism shape all of our lives and white people benefit from "white privilege." . . . At the same time, most of the white feminists I know are consciously anti-racist, have marched and voted against racism, have stuck their own academic necks out in meetings to speak against perceived racism from their colleagues and superiors, and have almost never included only white middle class . . . issues in their classes.

16. In her *Critique of Postcolonial Reason,* Spivak explores how major works of European metaphysics (for example, those by Kant and Hegel) not only tend to exclude subaltern subjects (brown people, all women) from their discussions but actively prevent non-Europeans from occupying positions as fully human subjects.
17. One crest of the third wave is postfeminism, which advocates the pleasure of "girl culture." Another is power feminism, which, according to Naomi Wolf, is based on the belief that "women deserve to feel that the qualities of starlets and queens, of sensuality and beauty, can be theirs . . ." (137–38). Clearly, third-wave feminism accounts for women's pleasures as well as their politics.

18. To that end, Alison Stone encourages a "rethinking of feminist politics as coalitional rather than unified ... as predicated not upon any shared set of feminine concerns but, rather, on overlaps and indirect connections within women's historical and cultural experience" (22). Caraway refers to such connections as "multicultural coalitions without domination" (201).
19. Gay reminds us, "Feminism is flawed because it is a movement powered by people and people are inherently flawed" ("Looking"). Given that the movement's goal is to create and sustain change, improvement, and hope for the future, "how do we reconcile the imperfections of feminism," Gay asks, "with all the good it can do?" ("Looking"). In fact, the work of moving the feminist rhetorical project forward will be richer, more ethical, and more effective if we do not all agree, if our work is the result of understanding rather than persuading one another. We cannot split up and give up.
20. Beverly Moss illuminates intersectional identities in her 1988 "Intersections of Race and Class in the Academy," as does Shirley Wilson Logan in her 1998 "'When and Where I Enter': Race, Gender, and Composition Studies." But Crenshaw seems to have coined the term in her 1989 essay "Demarginalizing the Intersection of Race and Sex: A Black Feminist Critique of Antidiscrimination Doctrine, Feminist Theory and Antiracist Politics." Crenshaw's open-ended, complex theory captured the imagination of a broad swath of academics and became an academic buzzword.
21. In *Mappings: Feminism and the Cultural Geographies of Encounter*, Susan Stanford Friedman polemically declares, "The time has come to ... reinvent a singular feminism that incorporates myriad and often conflicting cultural and political formations in a global context" (4).
22. As more and more feminists come to rhetorical feminism, they will learn to embrace dialogism and rhetorical transactions over monologism and rhetorical reaction. Such a move forward is always difficult. An act of courage—and hope.
23. This exchange between Shan and Gandy no longer appears in web searches and seems to have been removed from Twitter. Shan continues:

    > That's part of the privilege: the automatic benefit of living in a world that has been deliberately structured to be All About You, to the point where you don't even have to think about it. Hence, the difficulty with erasure and the sometimes pathological inability to just shut up and listen. (qtd. in Gandy, par. 3)

    For mainstream white feminists to understand their stance and its effects, they need "an understanding of structural power and racism, cultural differences and how they play out" (Ross 22). They need to do the hard work. Most do not have that understanding that comes with the work.
24. What is too often missing is a willingness to listen conscientiously, a demonstration of self-education, a serious consideration of self-critique, a willingness to change, a potential for rethinking the definition and politics of feminism, and making room for more nonwhite voices—what is missing is anything substantive that will enable her to reach and hear an outsider audience.
25. Despite the limitations to Burke's theory that I noted earlier in this chapter.
26. Jimmy Kimmel's regular feature "Mean Tweets" offers a case in point: famous people read aloud the mean tweets about themselves.

27. And as Mutz explains, people who remain surrounded only with people who think like they do will remain less aware of the legitimate arguments on the other side of political controversies, less aware that the controversy itself is legitimate (85). Such isolated groups may believe that if they keep their differences with others to themselves, they are more likely to keep the peace, preserve cordial relationships, and prevent painful contact, maybe even violent interaction, with people who identify in other ways.
28. After all, no single conception of feminism—or identity—will ever fit everyone, but together we can do the work necessary to help everyone: talking, listening, handing over power, giving up defensiveness, and reaching out to talk some more. Even as apologizing, forgiving, listening, and bridging personal rifts (in order to close political ones) can enhance the rhetorical transaction, STFUs never can.
29. Despite or maybe because of the fractures within feminism, many of us stay faithful to its proclaimed political purpose, even when each of us dares to admit: like Gay, I am "a fairly bad feminist, full of contradictions, but feminism is as much a part of who I am as . . . everything else that defines me" (par. 5). Whether we individual feminists believe that identities and differences should be challenged or affirmed, whether we believe that the feminist project should be fixed or shape-shifted in order to include us all, all of us feminists must do the work necessary for engaging in cross-difference communication.

3. Theories

1. Keith Lloyd works to untangle rhetoric's "unexamined mechanism opposed to new ideas, especially that challenge [rhetoric's] assumptions" (80). He describes mainstream rhetoric as a system of "dichoto-negation," which divides "an issue into an either/or choice which not only favors the [traditional] rhetor's thesis, but explicitly or implicitly, and most often unnecessarily, dismisses other arguments as irrational, defective, irresponsible—even dangerous" (80).

    In other words, despite the fact that some feminist rhetorical theorists reach out to mainstream rhetoricians, their efforts are rarely reciprocated, other than serving as a special feature in a syllabus or edited collection.
2. The perception and production of theory as pure knowledge has been limited to public arenas such as science and politics and to experts, most of whom have been men. In contrast, Karen A. Foss, Sonja K. Foss, and Cindy L. Griffin explain *theory* as

    > a way of framing an experience or event—an effort to understand and account for something and the way it functions in the world. . . . Individuals theorize when they try to figure out answers for, develop explanations about, and organize what is happening in their worlds. . . . [W]e do not believe that there is only one theory that correctly describes or captures any particular situation or activity. . . . We suggest that multiple —and sometimes contradictory—theories are possible and viable. (8)

3. Eve Sedgwick was one of the earliest scholars to use the term (1993), but Muñoz, her former student, specifically and effectively employed it in 1999.

4. This term has been troubled by a number of scholars, particularly Trinh, who rightly describe it as insulting, confusing, and hierarchical.
5. So which kind of rhetorical theory is actually more "universal," "humanitarian," and "eternal"? Not hegemonic rhetorical theory, that is for sure. Anzaldúa's 1980 "Letter" prefigures Barbara Christian's 1987 "Race for Theory," in which Christian disparages such mainstream academic discourse as "self-indulgent" and "disconnected" (51): "I am appalled by the sheer ugliness of the language" (56). For Christian, "theory has become a commodity" that elides most people rather than connecting with them and improving their everyday life (56).
6. For whatever reasons, Daly does not explicitly invoke women of color or other groups (though she does celebrate Lesbianism) who populate the subaltern in the foreground, a topic Lorde took up with her.
7. She and Jane Caputi define *Lesbian* as

    [a] Woman-loving woman; a woman who has broken the Terrible Taboo against Woman-Touching women on all levels; Woman-identified woman; one who has rejected false loyalties to men in every sphere.... Lesbian is capitalized to indicate Woman-identification. The word lesbian ... is used to refer to the degraded caricatures of Lesbian reality. (78)

8. This description of power-with could also be applied to dialogue, mutual understanding, rhetorical listening, and silence.
9. Trinh is her family name.
10. Or, "alternative facts," as President Trump's counselor Kellyanne Conway has taught us.
11. Foss and Griffin borrow from Starhawk to provide distinct transformative possibilities to the rhetorical transaction.
12. Addressing the resolution of conflict, Brigitte Mral is completing a monograph on "peace rhetoric" to counterbalance her previous work on "war rhetoric."
13. Sometimes, however, feminist rhetors decide to "fight." In "Feminism and Composition: The Case for Conflict," Susan Jarratt makes a compelling argument for the necessity of agonism, even antagonism in rhetorical and professional work. In "Taking Sides," Nancy Welch speaks of the power of confrontation in activism.
14. She is referring to critics who are usually powerful-in-some-way white men.
15. *Écriture féminine*, made popular by Hélène Cixous, Luce Irigaray, and Julia Kristeva, acknowledges the value of language for engaging in one's own woman's body, one's own otherness, and for inscribing woman's body into language—acts of rhetorical feminism, to be sure.
16. See, for instance, the scholarship of Adams, Bordelon, Enoch, Hallenbeck, Hogg, Jack, Mattingly, Ratcliffe, Sharer, Wood, and me.
17. Of course, "almost" is the operative term here, for logos has long reigned supreme in terms of its perceived power.
18. Lorde writes that "[a]s women, we have come to distrust that power which rises from our deepest and nonrational knowledge. We have been warned against it all our lives by the male world" ("Uses" 53).

19. Recent research into the role of reason has proved how very emotionally laden and unreliable it actually is, for impressions, beliefs, and incomplete understandings all function to invalidate logical reasoning. (See Mercier and Sperber; Sloman and Fernback.)
20. Contemporary neuroscience has shown we make decisions based on emotion, not on logos. (See Camp.)
21. Although it has taken me several years to fully appreciate the experience—and learn from it—I value the unsettling department review I did, a review in which I met with a cascade of very angry faculty. Some were so angry and scared that they could barely speak aloud. Their anger—their emotions—repelled me at the time. I could not see my way around them until my co-reviewer said, "Cheryl, you must stop focusing on their emotions as anger and see them as passion." She was right. Only now do I truly understand my experience—and the experiences of those faculty, many of whom felt besieged.
22. See Hickson, Stacks, and Amsbury. In various other publications, these scholars also ranked the research productivity of "Active Researchers," "Active Prolific Scholars in Communication," and "Administrator-Scholars in Speech Communication."
23. Of course, Gilligan's research findings might now be considered dated, as her work took place when men's and women's/masculine and feminine identities were more strongly demarcated. Still, Gilligan's was a feminist attempt to discover what the results might be when girl subjects replaced the all-boy subjects of Lawrence Kohlberg's, William Perry's, and Jean Piaget's studies of moral development. She arrived at markedly different conclusions.

4. Methods and Methodologies

1. Lorraine Code writes that the ideologies of objectivity and value-neutrality "sustain the 'myth of the neutral man' who is presumed to be able to represent everyone's interests with detached objectivity" ("How" 17). She continues:

    > Many of the research methods modelled on scientific methodology that govern conceptions of what counts as knowledge in the academic mainstream have yielded the consequence that women and other socially disadvantaged groups of people are not only invisible in the data from which conclusions are drawn, but can also find no way of making their experience count as informed or knowledgeable. (20)

2. Writing about online feminist research practices, Heidi A. McKee and James E. Porter echo the ethical awareness of Royster and Kirsch when outlining the key qualities of careful and respectful feminist research:

    > For feminist research the welfare and betterment of research participants ... is paramount, taking precedence over research findings, over methodological considerations, over disciplinary or institutional values.... Respect for participants means acknowledging their agency, heeding their wishes, consulting their wisdom. (155)

3. Forward-looking scholarship that immediately comes to mind includes Rebecca Dingo's *Networking Arguments*, Debra Hawhee and Christa Olson's "Pan-historiography," and Wendy S. Hesford and Wendy Kozol's *Just Advocacy?*
4. Such representative works include those by Stephen H. Browne; Lindal Buchanan and Kathleen J. Ryan; Jane Donawerth; Jessica Enoch and Cristina Ramirez; David Gold and Catherine Hobbs; Hildy Miller and Lillian Bridwell-Bowles; Brigitte Mral, Nicole Borg, and Philippe-Joseph Salazar; Joy Ritchie and Kate Ronald; Molly Meier Wertheimer; and Hui Wu. See also the titles in Southern Illinois University Press's Studies in Rhetorics and Feminisms series, found at the end of this book.
5. According to McKee and Porter, ethical feminist research methodology can be identified by its six key qualities, in that it is committed to social justice, careful and respectful, critically reflexive, flexible, dialogic, and transparent (155–56).

5. Teaching

1. Wendy Sharer makes the crucial point that most college instructors hold teaching-intensive positions in "institutions that do not place as much value on or expend as many resources in support of traditional . . . genres of scholarship" ("Opening"). In other words, most institutions actually prize teaching.
2. Denmark, Norway, Sweden, and Finland are among the nations spending the most money on education as a percentage of their gross domestic product, according to the World Bank (McPhillips).
3. According to Anthony P. Carnevale, director of the Georgetown University Center on Education and the Workforce, generosity of funding correlates positively with homogeneity. Therefore, in Scandinavian and Asian countries there is "broad public support for education" (qtd. in Carlson). He continues with the foreboding message that "[d]iversity is an impediment to the welfare state, of which education is a part" (qtd. in Carlson).
4. That these legislators have thus far responded to the regularity of school shootings with the singular idea that some teachers should be armed is beyond the pale.
5. In "The Great Shame of Our Profession," Kevin Birmingham writes that adjuncts are the "centerpiece of higher education. . . . Part-time adjuncts are now the majority of the professoriate and its fastest growing segment. Thirty-one percent of part-time faculty members live near or below the poverty line" (pars. 7, 8).
6. Funding is an issue, to be sure. Nationwide (state-by-state) cuts to the education budget and threats to tenure are led mostly by state legislators who have little, if any, experience with higher education, unaware that tenure is the earned privilege of practicing academic freedom—not an unearned, unfair perquisite guaranteeing a lifetime job.
7. Carnevale continues, "All the great advances in education [the Morrill Act that created land-grant colleges in 1862 and the GI Bill that has educated veterans since World War II] have come when there was a strong white majority" (qtd. in Carlson).

8. The average debt-at-graduation for a Penn State undergraduate student, for instance, is nearly $40,000.
9. "HBCUs disproportionately enroll low-income, first-generation, and underrepresented college students—precisely the students that the country most needs to obtain college degrees" ("About Us").
10. According to Charlayne Hunter-Gault, 80 percent of African American college students attended HBCUs in the 1970s; in the twenty-first century, only 9 percent do.
11. With student retention in the forefront of their concerns, the rhetoric and writing leaders at HBCUs are leading national conversations on the direct positive correlation between purposeful course planning and sequencing and the positive outcomes for student writers and their instructors (see D. Green's "Expanding" and "Raising"). Other initiatives focus on the value of considering students themselves as sources of knowledge, whether the course content involves linguistic, literate, and cultural pluralism (see D. Green); features history, theory, and praxis of hip-hop (Stone and Stewart); or invites feminist rhetorical approaches that offer "positive and affirming aspects of writing, such as self-discovery and self-recovery" (Spencer-Maor and Randolf 179, 180).
12. In *Home Girls Make Some Noise: Hip Hop Feminist Anthology,* editors Gwendolyn Pough, Elaine Richardson, Aisha Durham, and Rachel Raimist offer multigenre readings that extend all the pedagogical tactics of rhetorical feminism.
13. Frances Hoffman and Jayne Stake affirm the "legitimacy of students' personal experiences as the source of evidence and perspective" and connect that legitimacy to students' active participation in their own education, in their own construction of knowledge (80). (See Perryman-Clark; J. Green; Hoang; Kennedy, Middleton, and Ratcliffe; Pough; E. Richardson, *African American Literacies* and *PHD*; Ruiz; and Smitherman, *Black Talk, Talkin and Testifyin*, and *Talkin That Talk*.)
14. See Welch's "Taking Sides," which emphasizes the value of students' learning argument as preparation for their full participation in the workplace and in the world.
15. Carolyn Shrewsbury characterizes the feminist classroom as "persons connected in a net of relationships with people who care about each other's learning as well as their own" (8).
16. In *A Pedagogy of Possibility*, Kay Halasek maps out a writing course that leverages the hope of students and instructors alike, rooted as it is in helping students recognize the limitations they bring to the classroom, in strategies for overcoming those limitations, and in pathways for claiming their agency and coming to voice.

6. Mentoring

1. As Cheryl Dahle writes, "[A] senior male . . . would anoint a younger version of himself as his protégé . . . [and] steer the lower man toward career-enhancing projects or plum assignments." Given that the mentor and his protégé were to have a great deal in common (gender, race, and social class, for example), Others remained outsiders.

2. Writing decades before Heilbrun, Virginia Woolf questions how the women entering academia might reshape an institution that had, for too long, served as "the procession of sons of educated men" (*Three Guineas* 60).
3. Good reasons for same-sex mentoring are many, but people who know how still need to mentor those who want to know. The problems of cross-sex mentoring are also many, including being the "only" woman/black/Asian who must perform herself into the sphere of "exceptional" and the dangers of being the target of gossip.
4. Women who are mentored by a white man earn a higher annual income than those who are not (Dreher and Cox). Ironically, men mentors have a more positive impact on the careers of their women protégées than on those of their men protégés (Chandler 83)
5. Just as being associated with a powerful mentor can provide "reflected power" on the part of the student, mentors benefit from the power and visibility that come with developing students who carry on their work and serve as potential collaborators (McGuire and Reger 56–57).
6. Of the twenty-some women at all academic ranks and across the nation I asked about their mentoring experiences, about half responded.
7. Carol Gilligan describes an ethic of care as "grounded in voice and relationship," an ethic that "encourages the capacities that constitute our humanity" (*Joining* 175, 177). Suzanne Clark challenges us to rethink this ethic of care, which is "exploited," for "caring is far from natural: it takes time, it is learned, and it is associated with subordination" ("Argument" 95).
8. Pamela VanHaitsma and Steph Ceraso use the phrase "horizontal mentoring" to "accentuate its distinction from power-laden [hierarchical] mentoring dynamics" (211).
9. The feminist mentor "invites the mentee to engage with the world in feminist ways," writes a graduate student:

   > Instead of simply asking, "How can I help you succeed within the patriarchal societal structure of success?" the feminist mentor asks, "How can I help you succeed according to your definition of success, and how can I equip you to work within or to violate societal expectations as necessary in order to achieve that success?" (Anonymous 8)

10. Often, dual-career couples want to live together; parents of young children want access to the support that comes with living near family; and some young academics want to pursue teaching and advising more than research and publishing. Others want to work outside the academy. What makes mentoring "feminist" is far more than just its ostensible subject matter.
11. Coalescing with like-minded allies—if only temporarily—seems to be the most effective way to confront serious or enduring problems head-on. In chapter 7, I describe our faculty senate's attempt to reenvision our first-year speaking and writing courses and how six of us rhetoric faculty from across the campuses and departments successfully used group agency to address and ultimately resolve the issue.
12. "Socrates sometimes came to see her with his disciples, and his intimate friends brought their wives to her to hear her discourse . . . as a teacher of rhetoric" (Plutarch 200).

13. In Xenophon's *Oeconomicus*, Socrates ascribes to Aspasia good advice on marriage, and in the *Memorabilia*, good advice on successful, ethical matchmakers (2.36).
14. In "Networked Feminism: Mentoring in the New Economy," Roxanne Mountford and I describe our feminist mentoring network of graduate students, including our sisters-in-rhetoric Krista Ratcliffe, Becky Rickly, Susan Kates, and several other remarkable women.
15. Alexis Pauline Gumbs addresses her fellow aspiring black feminist scholars when she argues that "the more mentors we have, in more places, the better off we are" (par. 11). Julia Schmalz describes the work of Sister Mentors, who mentor low-income minority girls to develop their talents and minority doctoral students to complete their dissertations.
16. Gumbs encourages women to "[b]uild a base of badass mentors that take different risks, make different sacrifices for each other, work in different conditions and with different styles" (par. 13).
17. Some graduate programs now feature mentoring awards, as do organizations such as the Coalition of Feminist Scholars in the History of Rhetoric and Composition, which presented the inaugural Lisa Ede Mentoring Award in 2015.
18. The Coalition and the Rhetoric Society of America are among the professional organizations that have institutionalized mentoring sessions and relationships.

7. (Writing Program) Administration

1. Although surrounded by self-identified feminist activists such as Rich, Barbara Christian, June Jordan, Toni Cade Bambara, and her good friend Janet Emig, Shaughnessy was not—to my knowledge—a feminist. Those who worked with her on special projects during the 1970s—Andrea Lunsford and Dixie Goswami, for instance—knew of no connection between Shaughnessy and feminism. Shaughnessy biographer Jane Maher confirms that "Janet Emig has described Mina as 'breathtakingly nonfeminist,'" continuing with Rich's remembrance of Shaughnessy as "good-natured" about feminism, a movement she regarded as having no "possible relevancy . . . to her life and concerns" (144).
2. Bell hooks invokes such margins as "spaces for radical openness" (*Yearning* 145).
3. My sense is that "coordinator" is the term used most often, given that it registers so little power without diminishing the responsibility. Maybe it was just that thinking that motivated me to seek a title change from "coordinator" to "director" when I became a WPA.
4. Echoing Holbrook, Enos reminds us that doctoral programs tend to call themselves "rhetoric and writing" as a way to distinguish themselves from "composition," first-year service work. She goes on to say that "rhetoric is recognized as more of a discipline while composition is simply a service-oriented field with no accepted theory or methodology" (79).
5. Thus, Bloom carefully points out the perceived difference between "work" (that is, service) and "scholarly work": "I want a Writing Director who will not demand attention when I am preoccupied with my scholarly work, and

who will remain faithful to my needs so that I do not have to clutter up my intellectual life with administrative details" (177).
6. The authors replicated Linda Peterson's 1986 survey of the Council of Writing Program Administrators, which was entitled "The WPA's Progress."
7. Hooks translates the "politics of location" into a stance of re-vision, a realm of counterhegemony, a movement "out of one's place," a confrontation of choice and location (*Yearning* 145).
8. Such a map of my location, though, omits some of the most crucial markers—those of my relationships with friends, family, colleagues, and administrators, as well as the place of rhetoric and writing studies within those relationships.
9. My location is University Park, the main campus of Penn State. Many other Penn State campuses have impressive writing and rhetoric faculty, including Laurie Grobman, Kyle King, Catherine Latterell, Danielle Mitchell, Jennifer Nesbitt, and Christian Weisser.
10. Some 15,000 undergraduate students move through our writing and rhetoric courses each year, taught by over 60 graduate students and approximately 150 fixed-term teaching faculty. Throughout, I work to distinguish among the graduate students, teaching faculty, and faculty who constitute the cohort of writing "instructors."
11. Tenured faculty include Suresh Canagarajah, Rich Doyle, Rosa Eberly, Keith Gilyard, Debra Hawhee, Stuart Selber, Jack Selzer (emeritus), Xiaoye You, and myself. Untenured are Ebony Coletu, Ana Cooke, Jon Olson, and Dan Tripp.
12. Wilma Ebbitt (whose influence remains), Jeff Walker, Jack Selzer, Marie Secor, Margaret Lyday, Rich Doyle, Stuart Selber, and I have all taken turns.
13. Land grant also refers to funding mechanisms, with the state working to fund the land-grant university. But given that state funding hovers around 6.4 percent of Penn State's total budget, we rely on the land-grant ideology more than on the funding mechanism. At present, Penn State (along with the University of Michigan, the University of Connecticut, and Rutgers University, for example) is considered a public ivy, a publicly funded university considered to be providing a quality of education comparable to those of the Ivy League.
14. I have nearly phased out our noncredit development writing course and replaced it with a full-credit enhanced first-year writing course, which includes a smaller class size, the regular curriculum, weekly tutorials with a graduate student, and assignment-specific tutorials in the writing center. Many of the other Penn State campuses are using the same model, just as they are using our same model of guided self-placement into our first-year courses (developmental, "regular," and honors).
15. The two-course sequence, Rhetoric and Civic Life (RCL), constitutes a collaboration between the rhetoric faculty in communications arts and sciences and in English, with graduate students and teaching faculty from both departments teaching in the program. This course is limited to honors students and aspiring honors students.
16. We offer upper-division rhetoric courses in history, theory, and translingualism as well as courses in cross-cultural, digital, collaborative, feminist, cultural-ethnic, and writing-center-focused rhetorics.

17. The administrative staff in English believes that the backlog would have been dislodged already if Smeal students had been willing to take sections of business writing that met on times and days *other* than Tuesdays and Thursdays between 10 a.m. and 2 p.m.
18. Penn State is what I describe as "centrally isolated." The pool of experienced writing teachers is small, relative to that of an urban center.
19. My department head, my associate dean, and I managed negotiations with the dean of business, dean of liberal arts, and provost to underwrite these three positions for two years (thinking that we could widen the bottleneck in those two years), despite my arguments for hiring only two assistant professors for three years, on the grounds that two years is not enough.
20. Although the teaching load is the same for these new hires as for the visiting assistant professors, the salaries are lower—but the terms are longer. I was not included in these negotiations, and both my department head and I were surprised when we were informed we could make these hires. He and I worked closely together to write the job ads. I interviewed candidates with the associate head and another member of the teaching faculty. All of these collaborations could be considered feminist as they were all strategic, respectful, and, ultimately, productive. Of course, some will consider these collaborations unsuccessful since they did not lead to tenure-track or visiting professor positions.
21. In other words, the number of students registered for our courses determines the number of sections we will offer and, therefore, the number of writing instructors we can hire. As director of the PWR, I work closely with the associate head in the hiring, evaluation, and renewal of our fixed-term instructors. Penn State is a system of strong deans, so our dean hands down her decisions for us to carry out, which we do with various levels of pleasure.
22. Our dean may or may not decide to fund tenure lines, regardless of departmental votes and priority rankings.
23. It has never been up to any rhetoric, literature, or theory group to hire in its field. We submit our wishes to the department for discussion, the department head carries the full department's rankings to the dean, and they (or just the dean) make the decision.
24. Several members of the English department did, however, respond to the proposed gen ed changes, chiding members of this faculty senate committee that the process was too fast to result in quality decisions and that their "themes and clusters" were akin to the "majors and minors" the committee so wanted to displace. They also spoke out against the proposed themes for first-year writing, which (as rumor had it) included the themes of "life and death," "love and sex," and "a continent." On the surface, the theme idea was so ridiculous that it served as an easy target, even when members of the committee replied that it was "just one idea." By the time of this writing, the gen ed review seems to have been slowed down to the point that proposed curricular changes seem to be considered, even interesting. And so far, first-year writing has been pretty much left alone, save for the greater emphasis on rhetoric.

25. Our then associate dean happened to be leading part of the gen ed review and, by some fortunate sequence of events, began collaborating on the writing and speaking requirements. When he asked me whom I would like to work with, I quickly named campus-wide leaders in rhetoric, writing, and speech communication, including Laurie Grobman, Michele Kennerly, Danielle Mitchell, Molly Meijer Wertheimer, and Mary Miles. We held just two hour-long meetings, during which we managed to dispatch a set of disciplinary-based criteria that were approved by faculty senate. Our dean was impressed.
26. My so-far-unsuccessful argument is to offer more (not fewer) writing and speaking requirements.
27. *Rhetorical knowledge* is the ability to analyze contexts and audiences and then to act on that analysis by determining appropriate lines of inquiry and creating a range of written and oral responses. Writers and speakers develop and apply rhetorical knowledge by negotiating purpose, audience, context, genre, and conventions as they explore, compose, and deliver a variety of texts for ever-evolving situations and media.

    Critical thinking is the ability to analyze, synthesize, interpret, and evaluate ideas, information, situations, and texts. When writers and speakers think critically about the materials they use—whether print texts, photographs, data sets, videos, speeches, or other materials—they separate assertion from evidence, evaluate both sources and supporting evidence, recognize and evaluate underlying assumptions, read across texts for connections and patterns, identify and evaluate chains of reasoning, and compose appropriately qualified and developed claims and generalizations. These intellectual practices serve as the foundation of advanced academic writing and speaking.

    Writers and speakers use multiple strategies, or *composing processes*, to conceptualize, develop, and finalize projects. Composing processes are seldom linear: a writer or speaker may research a topic before drafting, then conduct additional research while revising or after consulting a colleague. Composing processes are also flexible: successful writers and speakers can adapt their composing processes to different contexts, audiences, and occasions.

    Conventions are the formal rules and informal guidelines that define genres and, in so doing, shape perceptions of correctness or appropriateness. Most obviously, conventions govern such things as mechanics, usage, spelling, pronunciation, and citation practices. But they also influence features of content, style, arrangement/organization, graphics, delivery (or presentation), and design. Conventions are not universal, however; they vary by genre (conventions for lab notebooks and discussion-board exchanges differ); by discipline (conventional moves in psychology literature reviews differ from those in English); and by occasion (meeting minutes and executive summaries, extemporaneous remarks and official addresses use different registers). A writer's or speaker's grasp of conventions in one context does not mean a firm grasp in another. Successful writers and speakers understand, analyze, and negotiate the conventions associated with different purposes, audiences, contexts, and genres as they analyze, compose, and deliver messages in a range of written, oral, and digital media.

28. Penn State's PWR recently introduced a small number of sections of first-year writing for international students who are not enrolled in ESL courses. These sections are taught by one of our international graduate students—and to great success. We have also added one section of ESL business writing, which is taught by a member of the teaching faculty with ESL expertise, as well as one section of ESL technical writing.

8. This Thing Called Hope

1. Unfortunately, the United States and too many governments around the globe offer specific examples of wasted talent, foolish if not deadly identity politics, and refusals to collaborate, let alone coalesce.
2. On the Saturday after the 2016 presidential election, *Saturday Night Live*'s Kate McKinnon opened the show by impersonating Clinton. "Clinton," dressed all in white as the early suffragists had done, played piano and sang Leonard Cohen's moving "Hallelujah." McKinnon's performance captured the zeitgeist perfectly, as she sang his haunting lyrics:

   > I did my best, it wasn't much
   > I couldn't feel, so I tried to touch
   > I've told the truth I didn't come to fool ya
   > And even though it all went wrong
   > I'll stand before the Lord of Song
   > With nothing on my tongue but Hallelujah.

   McKinnon's Clinton exquisitely conveyed the struggles and hope that constitute rhetorical feminism.
3. Donald J. Trump statement on preventing Muslim immigration, *DonaldJTrump.com*, 7 Dec. 2015, http://www.donaldjtrump.com/press-releases/donald-j.-trump-statement-on-preventing-muslim-immigration (accessed 30 Aug. 2016). The statement was deleted 10 May 2017.
4. Michelle Ye Hee Lee, "Donald Trump's False Comments Connecting Mexican Immigrants and Crime," *Fact Checker*, 16 June 2015, https://www.washingtonpost.com/news/fact-checker/wp/2015/07/08/donald-trumps-false-comments-connecting-mexican-immigrants-and-crime/ (accessed 30 Aug. 2016).
5. Jim Holt, "Donald Trump: I Would Build a Great, Great Wall on Our Southern Border and Make Mexico Pay for It," *Gateway Pundit*, 16 June 2015, http://www.thegatewaypundit.com/2015/06/donald-trump-i-would-build-a-great-great-wall-on-our-southern-border-i-would-make-mexico-pay-for-it-video/ (accessed 30 Aug. 2016).
6. Euan McKirdy, "Trump and Clinton Battle over Isis," *CNN*, 11 Aug. 2016, http://www.cnn.com/2016/08/11/politics/trump-obama-isis/ (accessed 30 Aug. 2016).
7. Eli Watkins, "Trump Tweet Angers Survivors of Parkland Shooting," *CNN*, 17 Feb. 2018, https://www.cnn.com/2018/02/18/politics/donald-trump-florida-shooting-twitter/index.html (accessed 20 Feb. 2018).
8. We live in an age of post-truth politics, where media run with stories they *think* are true (later to apologize and correct), and politicians, wanting to enhance their mediated performances, too often go with ideas they *wish*

were true (but are not supported by fact), a concept called "truthiness" by brilliant political analyst Stephen Colbert.
9. Alexander Burns and Nick Corasanti, "Donald Trump's Other Campaign Foe: The 'Lowest Form of Life' News Media," *New York Times*, 12 Aug. 2016, https://www.nytimes.com/2016/08/13/us/politics/donald-trump-obama-isis.html (accessed 30 Aug. 2016).
10. "Trump: I Could Stand in the Middle of Fifth Avenue and Shoot Somebody and I Wouldn't Lose Any Voters," *Real Clear Politics*, 23 Jan. 2016, http://www.realclearpolitics.com/video/2016/01/23/trump_i_could_stand_in_the_middle_of_fifth_avenue_and_shoot_somebody_and_i_wouldnt_lose_any_voters.html (accessed 30 Aug. 2016).
11. The forthcoming *Norton Anthology of Rhetoric and Writing*, coedited by Andrea Lunsford and Susan Jarratt, with its global reach, cultural-ethnic sensitivity, and feminist stance, will transform our collective understanding of rhetorical histories, practices, and actions.
12. Among the earliest contributors to the coalition were Nan Johnson, Winifred Horner, C. Jan Swearingen, Kathleen Welch, and Marjorie Curry Woods. They were soon joined by Lisa Ede, Catherine Hobbs, Gesa Kirsch, Shirley Wilson Logan, Andrea Lunsford, Joyce Middleton, Krista Ratcliffe, Jacqueline Jones Royster, and me, among others.
13. Taken directly from the Coalition of Feminist Scholars in the History of Rhetoric and Composition website.
14. As Malea Powell and many others have pointed out, marginalized rhetorics that do not nod to "the" tradition are often quickly dismissed, if not ignored altogether by mainstream rhetoricians. And feminist rhetoricians, too, have built up a high intolerance for those theories, praxes, and histories that do not meet the criteria for what Hallenbeck calls the feminist "sanctioned narrative" ("Toward" 9), the inclination to focus on historical women whose actions and beliefs most easily align with our own twenty-first-century ones.
15. I am not arguing for the absorption of feminist rhetoric into "traditional" rhetoric; rather, I am arguing for ways that feminist rhetoric might be better understood and appreciated. Powell's scholarship has helped me understand the value of rhetorical alliances and the power of rhetorical sovereignty—and the wisdom of knowing which one to implement, when, where, and with whom. The wisdom is the hardest to develop, to be sure.
16. I am quoting from a reprint of Bell's initial explanation of his theory ("*Brown v. Board of Education* and the Interest-Convergence Dilemma," *Harvard Law Review*, vol. 93, no. 3, 1979–80, pp. 518–34):

> Although no such subordination is apparent in Brown [v. Board of Education], it is possible to discern in more recent school decisions the outline of a principle, applied without direct acknowledgment, that could serve as the positivistic expression of the neutral statement of general applicability. Its elements rely as much on political history as legal precedent and emphasize the world as it is rather than how we might want it to be. Translated from the judicial activity in racial cases both before and after Brown, this principle of

"interest convergence" provides: The interest of blacks in achieving racial equality will be accommodated only when it converges with the interests of whites. However, the Fourteenth Amendment [all citizens have equal protection under the law], standing alone, will not authorize a judicial remedy providing effective racial equality for blacks where the remedy sought threatens the superior societal status of middle and upper class whites. (Bell 35)

Bell argues that the post–World War II *Brown v. Board* decision declared to the world that equality and freedom, the values Americans fought for, were the order of the law at home. In particular, the decision refuted Communist claims that the United States formally subjugated black citizens.

17. Beyond historiography, though, feminist rhetorical scholar-teachers such as Dominic Dellicarpini, Jenn Fishman, Joyce Kinkead, Jesse Moore, and many others are seeing undergraduate students as researchers in their own right, teaching them the methods and methodologies that will enable them to make knowledge. (See, for example, the undergraduate research sections of *Xchanges*, the Naylor Workshop for Undergraduate Research at York College, the CCCC Committee on undergraduate research, and *Young Scholars in Writing*.)
18. Trump's pronouncement is true. In the United States alone, four thousand women are murdered by their husbands or partners every year (that is more than three a day), with battering the single major cause of injury to women (more than rapes, muggings, and auto accidents combined). Approximately 75 percent of women who are killed by their batterers are murdered when they attempt to leave or after they have left an abusive relationship. These statistics are from *DomesticShelters.org*, http://www.domesticshelters.org/national-global (accessed 9 Dec. 2016).

WORKS CITED AND CONSULTED

"About Us." *Thurgood Marshall College Fund*, 8 Mar. 2017, www.tmcf.org. Accessed Mar. 2017.
Adams, Heather Brook. "Institutional 'Protections,' Assumptions of Research, and the Challenges of Compliance: Opening a Conversation Space for Feminist Scholars Working with Participants." Enoch and Jack, forthcoming.
———. "Shame, Secrets, and Silences: The Rhetorical Legacy of Unwed Pregnancy in the United States, Since 1960." Manuscript.
———. "Visual Style and the Looking Subject: Nell Brinkley's Illustrations of Modern Womanhood." *Women's Studies in Communication*, vol. 37, no. 1, 2014, pp. 90–110.
Adams, Katherine, and Michael Keene. *Alice Paul and the Suffrage Campaign*. U of Illinois P, 2008.
Adewunmi, Bim. "Kimberlé Crenshaw on Intersectionality: 'I Wanted to Come Up with an Everyday Metaphor That Anyone Could Use.'" *NewStatesman*, 2 Apr. 2014, www.newstatesman.com/lifestyle/2014/04/kimberle-crenshaw-intersectionality-i-wanted-come-everyday-metaphor-anyone-could.
Adichie, Chimamanda Ngozi. *We Should All Be Feminists*. Anchor Books, 2012.
AEIR. Arnold-Ebbitt Interdisciplinary Rhetoricians at Penn State, https://sites.psu.edu/aeir/. Accessed 20 Feb. 2018.
Ahmed, Sara. *Feminist Attachments: The Cultural Politics of Emotion*. Routledge, 2004.
———. *Living a Feminist Life*. Duke UP, 2017.
Alcoff, Linda Martín. "The Problem of Speaking for Others." Roof and Wiegman, pp. 92–119.
Anonymous 1. "Feminist? Mentoring." Email received by author, 15 Apr. 2016.
Anonymous 3. "Feminist? Mentoring." Email received by author, 17 Apr. 2016.
Anonymous 4. "Feminist? Mentoring." Email received by author, 20 Apr. 2016.
Anonymous 5. "Feminist? Mentoring." Email received by author, 21 Apr. 2016.
Anonymous 8. "Feminist? Mentoring." Email received by author, 11 June 2016.
Anzaldúa, Gloria. *Borderlands/La Frontera: The New Mestiza*. Aunt Lute, 1987.
———. "Haciendo caras, una entrada." Anzaldúa, *Borderlands*, pp. xv–xxvii.
———. "How to Tame a Wild Tongue." Anzaldúa, *Borderlands*, pp. 75–86.
———. "Speaking in Tongues: A Letter to 3rd World Women Writers." *This Bridge Called My Back: Writings by Radical Women of Color*, edited by Cherríe Moraga and Gloria Anzaldúa, 1981. Kitchen Table P, 1983, pp. 165–73.

WORKS CITED AND CONSULTED

Arendt, Hannah. *The Human Condition.* U of Chicago P, 1958.

———. "Truth and Politics." *New Yorker,* 25 Dec. 1967, pp. 49+.

Aristotle. *Nicomachean Ethics.* Translated by J. A. K. Thomson, 1953. Penguin, 2004.

———. *Politics.* Translated by H. Rackham, Loeb/Harvard UP, 1977.

———. *The Rhetoric and Poetics of Aristotle.* Translated by W. Rhys Roberts and Ingram Bywater, Modern Library, 1984.

Arquette, Patricia. Academy Awards acceptance speech. *Bustle,* 22 Feb. 2015, https://bustle.com/articles/65843-transcript-of-patricia—Arquettes-acceptance-speech-shows-her-passionate-words-about-gender-inequality-video. Accessed 1 March 2015.

Athenaeus. *The Deipnosophists.* Translated by Charles Burton Gulick, Harvard UP, 1967.

"Background Facts on Contingent Faculty." American Association of University Professors, www.aaup.org/issues/contingency/background-facts. Accessed 30 Aug. 2015.

Bacon, Margaret Hope. *Mothers of Feminism: The Story of Quaker Women in America.* Harper and Row, 1986.

Ballif, Michelle, Diane Davis, and Roxanne Mountford. *Women's Ways of Making It.* Routledge, 2008.

Barr-Ebest, Sally. "Gender Differences in Writing Program Administration." *WPA: Writing Program Administration,* vol. 18, no. 3, 1995, pp. 53–73.

Bates, Laura. *Everyday Sexism.* St. Martin's Griffin, 2014.

Baumgardner, Jennifer. "Is There a Fourth Wave? Does It Matter?" *Feminist.com,* http://www.feminist.com/resources/artspeech/genwom/baumgardner2011.html. Accessed 21 Apr. 2016.

Baumgardner, Jennifer, and Amy Richards. *Manifesta: Young Women, Feminism, and the Future.* Farrar, Straus and Giroux, 2000.

———. "The Number One Question about Feminism." *Feminist Studies,* vol. 29, no. 2, 2003, pp. 448–52.

Belanoff, Pat. "Silence: Reflection, Literacy, Learning, and Teaching." *College Composition and Communication,* vol. 52, no. 3, 2001, pp. 399–428.

Belenky, Mary Field, Blythe McVicker Clinchy, Nancy Rule Goldberger, and Jill Mattuck Tarule. *Women's Ways of Knowing: The Development of Self, Voice, and Mind.* Basic, 1986.

Bell, Derrick. "*Board v. Board of Education* and the Interest-Convergence Dilemma." *The Derrick Bell Reader,* edited by Richard Delgado and Jean Stefancic, New York UP, 2005, pp. 33–39.

Bennett, Catherine. "To All the Little Girls Out There, Let 2017 Be a Better Year." *Guardian,* 13 Dec. 2016, www.the guardian.com/commentisfree/2017/jan/01/all-little-girls.

Bereano, Nancy K. Introduction. *Sister Outsider,* by Audre Lorde, Crossing P, 1984, pp. 7–12.

Bergson, Henri-Louis. *Time and Free Will: An Essay on the Immediate Data of Consciousness.* Translated by F. L. Pogson, 1889. Dover, 2001.

Berrett, Dan. "What Spurs Students to Stay in College and Learn? Good Teaching Practices and Diversity." *Chronicle of Higher Education,* 6 Nov. 2011, www.chronicle.com/article/What-Spurs-Students-to-Stay-in/129670/.

WORKS CITED AND CONSULTED

Bessette, Jean. *Retroactivism in the Lesbian Archives*. Southern Illinois UP, 2017.
Biesecker, Barbara. "Coming to Terms with Recent Attempts to Write Women into the History of Rhetoric." *Philosophy and Rhetoric*, vol. 25, no. 2, 1992, pp. 140–61.
———. "Of Historicity, Rhetoric: The Archive as Scene of Invention." *Rhetoric and Public Affairs*, vol. 9, no. 1, 2006, pp. 124–31.
———. "Towards a Transactional View of Rhetorical and Feminist Theory: Reading Hélène Cixous's 'The Laugh of the Medusa.'" *Southern Communication Journal*, vol. 25, no. 4, 1992, pp. 86–96.
Birmingham, Kevin. "The Great Shame of Our Profession: How the Humanities Survive on Exploitation." *Chronicle of Higher Education*, 12 Feb. 2017, https://www.chronicle.com/article/The-Great-Shame-of-Our/239148.
Bitzer, Lloyd. "The Rhetorical Situation." *Philosophy and Rhetoric*, vol. 1, 1968, pp. 1–14.
Bizzell, Patricia. "Feminist Methods of Research in the History of Rhetoric: What Difference Do They Make?" *Rhetoric Society Quarterly*, vol. 30, no. 4, 2004, pp. 5–17.
———. "Opportunities for Feminist Research in the History of Rhetoric." *Rhetoric Review*, vol. 11, no. 3, 1992, pp. 50–58.
Bizzell, Patricia, and Bruce Herzberg. *The Rhetorical Tradition*. Bedford/St. Martin's, 1990.
Blair, Carole. "Contested Histories of Rhetoric: The Politics of Preservation, Progress, and Change." *Quarterly Journal of Speech*, vol. 78, no. 4, 1992, pp. 403–28.
Blair, Carole, Julie R. Brown, and Leslie A. Baxter. "Disciplining the Feminine." *Quarterly Journal of Speech*, vol. 80, no. 4, 1994, pp. 383–409.
Bloom, Lynn Z. "I Want a Writing Director." *College Composition and Communication*, vol. 43, no. 2, 1992, pp. 176–78.
Bordelon, Suzanne. *A Feminist Legacy: The Rhetoric and Pedagogy of Gertrude Buck*. Southern Illinois UP, 2007.
Bordo, Susan. *The Destruction of Hillary Clinton*. Melville House, 2017.
Brettell, Caroline B., editor. *When They Read What We Write: The Politics of Ethnography*. Bergin and Garvey, 1993.
Briskin, Linda. "Activist Feminist Pedagogies: Privileging Agency in Troubled Times." *Feminist Pedagogy in Higher Education: Critical Theory and Practice*, edited by Tracy Penny Light, Jane Nicholas, and Renée Bondy, Laurier, 2015, pp. 57–86.
Brooks, David. "No, Not Trump, Not Ever." *New York Times*, 18 Mar. 2016, http://nyti.ms/1XzyN39.
Brown, Iemanjá, Stefania Heim, erica kaufman, Kristin Moriah, Conor Tomás Reed, Talia Shalev, Wendy Tronrud, and Ammiel Alcalay, editors. "'What We Are Part Of' Teaching at CUNY: 1968–1974. Adrienne Rich Part II." *Lost and Found*, edited by Conor Tomás Reed, series 4, no. 3, part 2, 2013, pp. 36–65.
Brown, Wendy. "The 'Jewish Question' and the 'Woman Question.'" *Going Public: Feminism and the Shifting Boundaries of the Private Sphere*, edited by Joan Wallach Scott and Debra Keates, U of Illinois P, 2004, pp. 15–42.

WORKS CITED AND CONSULTED

Browne, Stephen H. *Angelina Grimké: Rhetoric, Identity, and the Radical Imagination*. Michigan State UP, 1999.
Brueggemann, Brenda. *Deaf Subjects: Between Identities and Places*. New York UP, 2009.
———. *Lend Me Your Ear*. Gallaudet UP, 1999.
Buchanan, Lindal. *Motherhood: Rhetorics and Representations*. Southern Illinois UP, 2013.
———. *Regendering Delivery: The Fifth Canon and Antebellum Women Rhetors*. Southern Illinois UP, 2005.
Buchanan, Lindal, and Kathleen J. Ryan, editors. *Walking and Talking Feminist Rhetorics: Landmark Essays and Controversies*. Parlor, 2010.
Bunch, Charlotte. "Not by Degrees: Feminist Theory and Education." *Quest: A Feminist Quarterly*, vol. 5, no. 1, 1979, pp. 248–60.
Burke, Kenneth. *Language as Symbolic Action*. U of California P, 1966.
———. *Permanence and Change: An Anatomy of Purpose*. 3rd ed., U of California P, 1984.
———. *Philosophy of Literary Form*. 3rd ed., U of California P, 1974.
———. "Poem." *The Legacy of Kenneth Burke*, edited by Herbert W. Simons and Trevor Melia, U of Wisconsin P, 1989, p. 263.
———. *A Rhetoric of Motives*. 1950. U of California P, 1969.
———. *The Rhetoric of Religion*. 1961. U of California P, 1970.
Burton, Vicki Tolar. *Spiritual Literacy in John Wesley's Methodism: Reading, Writing, and Speaking to Believe*. Baylor, 2008.
Butler, Judith. *Gender Trouble: Feminism and the Subversion of Identity*. Routledge, 1990.
———. *The Psychic Life of Power*. Stanford UP, 1997.
Cain, Susan. *Quiet: The Power of Introverts in a World That Can't Stop Talking*. Crown, 2012.
Camp, Jim. "Decisions Are Emotional, Not Logical: The Neurosciences behind Decision Making." *Bigthink.com*, http://bigthink.com/experts-corner/decisions-are-emotional-not-logical-the-neuroscience-behind-decision-making. Accessed 4 Jan. 2017.
Campbell, Karlyn Kohrs. "Biesecker Cannot Speak for Her Either." *Philosophy and Rhetoric*, vol. 26, no. 2, 1993, pp. 153–59.
———. *Man Cannot Speak for Her: A Critical Study of Early Feminist Rhetoric*. Vol. 1, Greenwood P, 1989.
———, editor. *Man Cannot Speak for Her: Key Texts of the Early Feminists*. Vol. 2, Praeger, 1989.
———. "The Rhetoric of Women's Liberation: An Oxymoron." 1971. Repr. in *Communication Studies*, vol. 50, no. 2, 1999, pp. 125–37.
———. "'The Rhetoric of Women's Liberation: An Oxymoron,' Revisited." *Communication Studies*, vol. 50, no. 2, 1999, pp. 138–42.
———. "What Really Distinguishes and/or Ought to Distinguish Feminist Scholarship in Communication Studies?" *Women's Studies in Communication*, vol. 11, no. 1, 1988, pp. 4–5.
Caraway, Nancie. *Segregated Sisterhood: Racism and the Politics of American Feminism*. Tennessee UP, 1991.

WORKS CITED AND CONSULTED

Carlson, Scott. "When College Was a Public Good." *Chronicle of Higher Education*, 27 Nov. 2016, www.chronicle.com/article/When-College-Was-a-Public-Good/238501.

Certeau, Michel de. *The Writing of History*. Translated by Thomas Conley, 1975. Columbia UP, 1988.

Chandler, Christy. "Mentoring and Women in Academia: Reevaluating the Traditional Model." *NWSA Journal*, vol. 8, no. 3, 1996, pp. 79–100.

Charland, Maurice. "The Constitution of Rhetoric's Tradition." *Philosophy and Rhetoric*, vol. 36, no. 2, 2003, pp. 119–34.

Charlton, Jonikka, and Shirley K Rose. "Twenty More Years in the WPA's Progress." *Writing Program Administration*, vol. 33, nos. 1–2, 2009, pp. 114–45.

Chen, Tina. "Towards an Ethics of Knowledge." *Melus*, vol. 30, no. 2, 2004, pp. 157–73.

Chira, Susan. "Feminism Lost. Now What?" *New York Times*, 30 Dec. 2016, http://nyti.ms.2iLe2TR.

Christ, Carol P. "What Does It Mean to Say That All White Feminists Are Racist? (Questions Posed to White Women/Myself about Our Part in the Dialogue with Women of Color)." *Feminism and Religion*, 7 Oct. 2011, www.feminismandreligion.com/2011/10/07/what-does-it-mean-to-say-that-all-white-feminists-are-racist-questions-posed-to-white-womenmyself-about-our-part-in-the-dialogue-with-women-of-color-by-carol-p-christ/.

Christian, Barbara. "The Race for Theory." "The Nature and Context of Minority Discourse," edited by Abdul R. JanMohamed and David Lloyd, special issue, *Cultural Critique*, no. 6, Spring 1987, pp. 51–63.

Cicero. *De Inventione, De Optimo Genere, Oratorum, Topica*. Translated by H. M. Hubbell, Harvard UP, 1976.

———. *De Oratore*. Translated by E. W. Sutton, Harvard UP, 1979. 2 vols.

Cixous, Hélène. *"Coming to Writing" and Other Essays*. Harvard UP, 1992.

———. "Laugh of the Medusa." *New French Feminisms*, edited by Elaine Maimon and Isabelle de Courtivron, Schocken, 1981, pp. 245–64.

Clark, Suzanne. "Argument and Composition." Jarratt and Worsham, pp. 94–99.

———. "Julia Kristeva: Rhetoric and the Woman as Stranger." *Reclaiming Rhetorica: Women in the Rhetorical Tradition*, edited by Andrea A. Lunsford, U of Pittsburgh P, pp. 305–17.

Clark, Suzanne, and Lisa Ede. "Collaboration, Resistance, and the Teaching of Writing." *The Right to Literacy*, edited by Andrea A. Lunsford, Helene Moglen, and James Slevin, Modern Language Association, 1990, pp. 276–87.

Clinton, Hillary Rodham. Concession speech. *CNN*, 9 Nov. 2016, https://www.cnn.com/2016/11/09/politics/hillary-clinton-concession-speech/index.html.

Cocks, Joan. *The Oppositional Imagination*. Routledge, 2012.

Code, Lorraine. "How Do We Know? Questions of Method in Feminine Practice." *Changing Methods: Feminists Transforming Practice*, edited by Sandra Burt and Lorraine Code, Broadview, 1995, pp. 13–44.

WORKS CITED AND CONSULTED

———. *What Can She Know? Feminist Theory and the Construction of Knowledge*. Cornell UP, 1991.

Collins, Patricia Hill. *Black Feminist Thought*. 2nd ed., Routledge, 2000.

Combahee River Collective. "The Combahee River Collective Statement: A Black Feminist Statement." 1977. *All the Women Are White, All the Blacks Are Men, but Some of Us Are Brave*, edited by Gloria T. Hull, Patricia Bell Scott, and Barbara Smith, Feminist Press at City U of New York P, 1982, pp. 13–22.

Condon, Frankie. "On Campus Mental Health." *Words in Place*, 27 Apr. 2017, https://englishatwaterloo.wordpress.com. Accessed 7 May 2017.

Condon, Frankie, and Vershawn Ashanti Young, editors. *Performing Antiracist Pedagogy in Rhetoric, Writing, and Communication*. Colorado State UP, 2017.

Conley, Thomas. *Rhetoric in the European Tradition*. U of Chicago P, 1994.

Corbett, Edward P. J. *Classical Rhetoric for the Modern Student*. Oxford UP, 1971.

———. "The Rhetoric of the Open Hand and the Closed Fist." *Selected Essays of Edward P. J. Corbett*, edited by Robert J. Connors, Southern Illinois UP, 1989, pp. 98–113.

Crenshaw, Kimberlé. "Demarginalizing the Intersection of Race and Sex: A Black Feminist Critique of Antidiscrimination Doctrine, Feminist Theory and Antiracist Politics." *University of Chicago Legal Forum*, vol. 1989, article 8, 1989, pp. 139–67.

Cuomo, Chris J. "Feminist Sex at Century's End: On Justice and Joy." *On Feminist Ethics and Politics*, edited by Claudia Card, U of Kansas P, 1999, pp. 269–87.

Dahle, Cheryl. "Women's Ways of Mentoring." *FastCompany*, 31 Aug. 1998, www.fastcompany.com/34854/womens-ways-mentoring.

Dalke, Anne French. *Teaching to Learn, Learning to Teach: Meditations on the Classroom*. Lang, 2002.

Daly, Mary. *Gyn/Ecology: The Metaethics of Radical Feminism*. Beacon, 1978.

———. Letter to Audre Lorde, http://feminismandreligion.files.wordpress.com/2011/10/mary-daly-to-audre-lorde00012.pdf. Accessed 15 Oct. 2016.

Daly, Mary, in cahoots with Jane Caputi. *Websters' First New Intergalactic Wickedary of the English Language*. Beacon, 1987.

Daniell, Beth, and Letizia Guglielmo. "Changing Audience, Changing Ethos." *Rethinking Ethos: A Feminist Ecological Approach to Rhetoric*, edited by Kathleen J. Ryan, Nancy Myers, and Rebecca Jones, Southern Illinois UP, 2016, pp. 89–109.

Denny, Harry. *Facing the Center: Toward an Identity Politics of One-to-One Mentoring*. Utah State UP, 2010.

Derrida, Jacques. "Freud and the Scene of Writing." *Writing and Difference*, translated by Alan Bass, U of Chicago P, 1978, pp. 196–231.

Dicker, Rory, and Alison Piepmeier, editors. *Catching a Wave: Reclaiming Feminism for the Twenty-First Century*. Northeastern UP, 2003.

Dickinson, Emily. "Hope Is the Thing with Feathers—254." Franklin, p. 333.

———. "I dwell in Possibility—466." Franklin, pp. 483–84.

Dickson, Marcia. "Directing without Power: Adventures in Constructing a Model of Feminist Writing Program Administration." *Writing Ourselves into the Story: Unheard Voices from Composition Studies*, edited by Sheryl I. Fontaine and Susan Hunter, Southern Illinois UP, 1993, pp. 140–53.

Dingo, Rebecca. *Networking Arguments: Rhetoric, Transnational Feminism, and Public Policy Writing*. U of Pittsburg P, 2012.

@django_paris (Django Paris). "#JustTeacherSyllabus." *Twitter*, 2 Sept. 2016, 11:30 a.m., www.twitter.com/@django_paris/.

Donahue, Patricia, and Gretchen Flesher Moon, editors. *Local Histories: Reading the Archives of Composition*. U of Pittsburg P, 2007.

Donawerth, Jane. *Conversational Rhetoric: The Rise and Fall of a Women's Tradition, 1600–1900*. Southern Illinois UP, 2011.

———, editor. *Rhetorical Theory by Women before 1900*. Rowman and Littlefield, 2002.

Douglass, Frederick. *Woman's Journal*, 14 Apr. 1888. *BlackPast.org*. http://blackpast.org/1888-frederick—douglass-woman-suffrage. Accessed 3 May 2017.

———. "Woman's Rights Convention." *North Star*, 14 July 1848, *Frederick Douglass: In Progress*, leighfought.blogspot.com/2015/07/womans-rights-convention-north-star-14-html. Accessed 3 May 2017.

Dow, Bonnie J. "Feminism, Difference(s), and Rhetorical Studies." *Communication Studies*, vol. 46, no. 1–2, 1995, pp. 106–17.

Dow, Bonnie J., and Mari Boor Tonn. "'Feminine Style' and Political Judgment in the Rhetoric of Ann Richards." *Quarterly Journal of Speech*, vol. 79, no. 3, 1993, pp. 286–302.

Dreher, George F., and Taylor H. Cox Jr. "Race, Gender, and Opportunity: A Study of Compensation, Attainment, and the Establishment of Mentoring Relationships." *Journal of Applied Psychology*, vol. 81, no. 3, 1996, pp. 297–308.

DuBois, Ellen Carol. *Feminism and Suffrage: The Emergence of an Independent Women's Movement in America, 1848–1869*. Cornell UP, 1978.

Duffy, John. "Post-truth and First-Year Writing." *Inside Higher Education*, 8 May 2017, https:// www.insidehigheredu.com/news/2017/05/08/first-yearwriting. Accessed 8 May 2017.

Eagly, Alice H., and Linda L. Carli. *Through the Labyrinth: The Truth about How Women Become Leaders*. Harvard Business School P, 2007.

Eble, Michelle F., and Lynée Lewis Gaillet, editors. *Stories of Mentoring: Theory and Praxis*. Parlor, 2008.

Ede, Lisa, Cheryl Glenn, and Andrea Lunsford. "Border Crossings: Intersections of Rhetoric and Feminism." *Rhetorica: A Journal of the History of Rhetoric*, vol. 13, no. 4, 1995, pp. 401–41.

Ede, Lisa, and Andrea Lunsford. "Audience Addressed/Audience Invoked: The Role of Audience in Composition Theory and Pedagogy." *College Composition and Communication*, vol. 35, no. 2, 1984, pp. 155–71.

———. *Singular Texts, Plural Authors*. Southern Illinois UP, 1992.

Eichhorn, Jill. "Women's Bodies in the College Writing Classroom: The Threat of Feeling Exposed." *College Composition and Communication*, vol. 43, no. 3, 1992, pp. 308–11.

WORKS CITED AND CONSULTED

Eichhorn, Jill, Sara Farris, Karen Hayes, Adriana Hernández, Susan C. Jarratt, Karen Power-Stubbs, and Marian M. Sciachitano. "A Symposium on Feminist Experiences in the Composition Classroom." *College Composition and Communication*, vol. 43, no. 3, 1992, pp. 297–322.

Eisler, Rianne. *The Chalice and the Blade*. Harper, 1987.

Elshtain, Jean Bethke. "Feminist Discourse and Its Discontents: Language, Power, and Meaning." *Signs*, vol. 7, no. 3, 1982, pp. 603–21.

———. *Public Man, Private Woman*. Princeton UP, 1987.

Enoch, Jessica. *Refiguring Rhetorical Education: Women Teaching African American, Native American, and Chicano/a Students, 1865–1911*. Southern Illinois UP, 2008.

———. "There's No Place Like the Childcare Center: A Feminist Analysis of <Home> in the World War II Era." *Rhetoric Review*, vol. 31, no. 4, 2012, pp. 422–42.

Enoch, Jessica, and Jordynn Jack, editors. *Retelling: Fulfilling the Dream of a Feminist Rhetoric*. Southern Illinois UP, forthcoming.

Enoch, Jessica, and Cristina Ramirez, editors. *Mestiza Rhetorics: An Anthology of Mexican Activism in the Spanish Language Press*. Southern Illinois UP, forthcoming.

Enos, Theresa. *Gender Roles and Faculty Lives in Rhetoric and Composition*. Southern Illinois UP, 1996.

Fallowes, James. "Despair and Hope in Trump's America." *Atlantic*, Jan. 2017, www.theatlantic.com/magazine/archive/2017/01/despair-and-hope. Accessed 20 Jan. 2017.

Farris, Sara. "'What's in It for Me?' Two Students' Responses to a Feminist Pedagogy." *College Composition and Communication*, vol. 43, no. 3, 1992, pp. 304–07.

Fitch, Suzanne Pullon. "Sojourner Truth (1797?–1883), Legendary Anti-slavery and Woman's Rights Agitator." *Women Public Speakers in the United States, 1800–1925: A Bio-critical Sourcebook*, edited by Karlyn Kohrs Campbell, Greenwood, 1993, pp. 421–33.

Flynn, Elizabeth A. "Composing as a Woman." *College Composition and Communication*, vol. 39, no. 4, 1988, pp. 423–35.

Foss, Karen A., Sonja K. Foss, and Cindy L. Griffin. *Feminist Rhetorical Theories*. Sage, 1999.

Foss, Sonja K., and Cindy L. Griffin. "Beyond Persuasion: A Proposal for an Invitational Rhetoric." *Communication Monographs*, vol. 62, 1995, pp. 2–18.

———. "A Feminist Perspective on Rhetorical Theory: Toward a Classification of Boundaries." *Western Journal of Communication*, vol. 56, 1992, pp. 330–49.

Foucault, Michel. *Power/Knowledge: Selected Interviews and Other Writings*, edited by Colin Gordon, translated by Colin Gordon, Leo Marshall, John Mepham, and Kate Soper, Pantheon, 1980.

Franklin, Ralph W., editor. *The Poems of Emily Dickinson*. Belknap–Harvard UP, 1998.

Freire, Paulo. *Pedagogy of Hope: Reliving Pedagogy of the Oppressed*. Translated by Robert R. Barr, 1992. Bloomsbury, 2014.

WORKS CITED AND CONSULTED

———. *Pedagogy of the Heart*. Translated by Donaldo Macedo and Alexandrea Oliveria, Continuum, 1998.
Friedan, Betty. *The Fountain of Age*. Simon and Schuster, 1993.
Friedman, Megan, and Michael Sebastian. "Fourteen Ways Women Still Aren't Equal to Men." *Marie Claire*, 26 Aug. 2015, www.marieclaire.com/politics/news/a15652/gender-inequality-stats/.
Friedman, Susan Stanford. *Mappings: Feminism and the Cultural Geographies of Encounter*. Princeton UP, 1998.
Frost-Knappman, Elizabeth, and Kathryn Cullen-DuPont. *Women's Suffrage in America*. 1992. Updated ed., Facts on File, 2005.
Gaillet, Lynée Lewis, Helen Diane Eidson, and Don Gammil Jr., editors. *On Archival Research*. Routledge, 2015.
Gale, Xin Lu. "Historical Studies and Postmodernism: Rereading Aspasia of Miletus." *College English*, vol. 62, no. 3, 2000, pp. 361–86.
———. "Xin Lu Gale Responds." *College English*, vol. 63, no. 1, 2000, pp. 105–07.
Garner, Shirley Nelson. "Mentoring Lessons." *Women's Studies Quarterly*, vol. 22, no. 1/2, 1994, pp. 6–13.
Gay, Roxane. *Bad Feminist*. Harper, 2014.
———. "Looking for a Better Feminism." *NPR*, 23 Aug. 2013, www.npr.org/sections/codeswitch/2013/08/22/214525023/twitter-sparks-a-serious-discussion-about-race-and-feminism.
Gayathri, Amrutha. "US 17th in Global Education Ranking: Finland, South Korea Claim Top Spots." *International Business Times*, 27 Nov. 2012, www.ibtimes.com/us-17th-global-education-ranking-finland-south-korea-claim-top-spots-901538.
Gearhart, Sally Miller. "Notes from a Recovering Activist." *Sojourner: The Women's Forum*, vol. 21, no. 1, 1995, pp. 8–11.
———. "Sally Miller Gearhart." *Readings in Feminist Rhetorical Theory*, edited by Karen A. Foss, Sonja K. Foss, and Cindy L. Griffin, Waveland P, 2004, pp. 239–70.
———. "The Womanization of Rhetoric." *Women's Studies International Quarterly*, vol. 2, no. 2, 1979, pp. 195–201.
Gere, Anne Ruggles. "Revealing Silence: Rethinking Personal Writing." *College Composition and Communication*, vol. 53, no. 2, 2001, pp. 203–23.
Gilley, Jennifer. "Writings of the Third Wave: Young Feminists in Conversation." *Reference and User Services Quarterly*, vol. 44, no. 3, 2005, pp. 187–98.
Gilligan, Carol. *In a Different Voice*. Harvard UP, 1982.
———. *Joining the Resistance*. Polity, 2011.
Gillis, Stacy, Gillian Howie, and Rebecca Munford, editors. *Third Wave Feminism: A Critical Exploration*. 2004. 2nd ed., Palgrave Macmillan, 2007.
Glenn, Cheryl. "Comment: Truth, Lies, and Method: Revisiting Feminist Historiography." *College English*, vol. 62, no. 3, 2000, pp. 387–89.
———. "Remapping Rhetorical Territory." *Rhetoric Review*, vol. 13, no. 2, 1995, pp. 287–303.
———. *Rhetoric Retold: Regendering the Tradition from Antiquity through the Renaissance*. Southern Illinois UP, 1997.

WORKS CITED AND CONSULTED

———. "sex, lies, and manuscript: Refiguring Aspasia in the History of Rhetoric." *College Composition and Communication*, vol. 45, no. 2, 1994, pp. 180–99.

———. *Unspoken: A Rhetoric of Silence*. Southern Illinois UP, 2004.

Glenn, Cheryl, and Jessica Enoch. "Drama in the Archives: Rereading Methods, Rewriting History." *College Composition and Communication*, vol. 61, no. 2, 2009, pp. 321–42.

Glenn, Cheryl, and Andrea A. Lunsford, editors. *Landmark Essays on Rhetoric and Feminism, 1973–2000*. Routledge, 2015.

Glenn, Cheryl, and Krista Ratcliffe, editors. *Silence and Listening as Rhetorical Arts*. Southern Illinois UP, 2011.

Godbee, Beth, and Julia C. Novotny. "Asserting the Right to Belong: Feminist Co-mentoring among Graduate Student Women." *Feminist Teacher*, vol. 23, no. 3, 2013, pp. 177–95.

Gold, David, and Jessica Enoch, editors. *Women at Work: Rhetorics of Gender and Labor in the US, 1830–1950*. Southern Illinois UP, forthcoming.

Gold, David, and Catherine Hobbs. *Educating the New Southern Woman: Speech, Writing, and Race, 1884–1945*. Southern Illinois UP, 2013.

———, editors. *Rhetoric, History, and Women's Oratorical Education: American Women Learn to Speak*. Routledge, 2013.

Goodburn, Amy, and Carrie Shively Leverenz. "Feminist Writing Program Administration: Resisting the Bureaucrat Within." Jarratt and Worsham, pp. 276–90.

Gorsevski, Ellen W. *Peaceful Persuasion: The Geopolitics of Nonviolent Rhetoric*. State U of New York P, 2004.

Goswami, Dixie. "Feminism!" Email received by author, 7 May 2015.

Green, David F., Jr. "Expanding the Dialogue on Writing Assessment at HBCUs: Foundational Assessment Concepts and Legacies of Historically Black Colleges and Universities." *College English*, vol. 79, no. 2, 2016, pp. 153–73.

———. "Raising Game." *Composition Studies*, vol. 44, no. 2, 2016, pp. 162–66.

Green, Joyce, editor. *Making Space for Indigenous Feminism*. Zed Books, 2007.

Greenberg, David. "Are Clinton and Trump the Biggest Liars Ever to Run for President?" *Politico Magazine*, 2016, http://www.politico.com/magazine/story/2016/07/2016-donald-trump-hillary-clinton-us-history-presidents-liars-dishonest-fabulists-214024.

Gubar, Susan. *Rooms of Our Own*. U of Illinois P, 2006.

Gumbs, Alexis Pauline. "Off-the-Hook Black Feminist Mentorship: An Anti-capitalist Re-evaluation." *The Feminist Wire*, 21 Dec. 2011, www.thefeministwire.com/2011/12/off-the-hook-black-feminist-mentorship-an-anti-capitalist-re-evaluation. Accessed 15 Nov. 2016.

Gunner, Jeanne. "Decentering the WPA." *WPA: Writing Program Administration*, vol. 18, no. 1–2, 1994, pp. 8–15.

Halasek, Kay. *A Pedagogy of Possibility*. Southern Illinois UP, 1999.

Halberstam, J. Jack. *Female Masculinity*. Duke UP, 1998.

Hallenbeck, Sarah. *Claiming the Bicycle: Women, Rhetoric, and Technology in Late Nineteenth-Century America*. Southern Illinois UP, 2016.

———. "Toward a Posthuman Perspective: Feminist Rhetorical Methodologies and Everyday Practices." *Advances in the History of Rhetoric*, vol. 15, no. 1, 2012, pp. 9–27.
Haran, Joan. "Redefining Hope as Praxis." *Hope and Feminist Theory*, edited by Rebecca Coleman and Debra Ferreday, Routledge, 2011, pp. 81–96.
Harding, Sandra. *Whose Science? Whose Knowledge? Thinking from Women's Lives*. Cornell UP, 1991.
Hartsock, Nancy. *The Feminist Standpoint and Other Essays*. Basic Books, 1999.
Hawhee, Debra. *Bodily Arts: Rhetoric and Athletics in Ancient Greece*. U of Texas P, 2004.
Hawhee, Debra, and Christa Olson. "Pan-historiography: The Challenges of Writing History across Time and Space." *Theorizing Histories of Rhetoric*, edited by Michelle Ballif, Southern Illinois UP, 2013, pp. 90–105.
Hayden, Wendy. *R/Evolutionary Rhetoric: Sex, Science, and Free Love in Nineteenth-Century Feminism*. Southern Illinois UP, 2013.
Hayes, Karen. "Creating Space for Difference in the Composition Class." *College Composition and Communication*, vol. 43, no. 3, 1992, pp. 300–04.
Hedge, Radha S. "Narratives of Silence: Rethinking Gender, Agency, and Power from the Communication Experiences of Battered Women in South India." *Communication Studies*, vol. 47, no. 4, 1996, pp. 303–17.
Heilbrun, Carolyn. *When Men Were the Only Models We Had*. U of Pennsylvania P, 2002.
Helle, Anita, editor. *The Unraveling Archive: Essays on Sylvia Plath*. U of Michigan P, 2007.
Herrick, James. "From *topoi* to Tweets: What Ancient Rhetoricians Can Teach Digital Natives." *Perspectives on Academic and Professional Writing in an Age of Accountability*, edited by Shirley Wilson Logan and Wayne Slater, Southern Illinois UP, forthcoming.
———. "From *topoi* to Tweets: What Ancient Rhetoricians Can Teach Digital Natives." 2014 Maryland Conference on Academic and Professional Writing, 10–11 Oct. 2014. Lecture.
Hesford, Wendy S. *Spectacular Rhetorics: Human Rights, Transnationalism, and the Politics of Representation*. Rutgers UP, 2005.
Hesford, Wendy S., and Wendy Kozol, editors. *Just Advocacy? Women's Human Rights, Transnationalism, and the Politics of Representation*. Rutgers UP, 2005.
Hickson, Mark, III, Don W. Stacks, and Jonathan H. Amsbury. "Active Prolific Female Scholars in Communication: An Analysis of Research Productivity, II." *Communication Quarterly*, vol. 40, 1992, pp. 350–56.
Hoang, Haivan V. *Writing against Racial Injury: The Politics of Asian American Student Rhetoric*. U of Pittsburgh P, 2015.
Hobbs, Catherine, and David Gold. *Educating the New Southern Woman: Speech, Writing, and Race at the Public Women's Colleges, 1884–1945*. Southern Illinois UP, 2014.
Hoffmann, Frances L., and Jayne E. Stake. "Feminist Pedagogy in Theory and Practice: An Empirical Investigation." *NWSC (National Women's Studies Association) Journal*, vol. 10, no. 1, 1998, pp. 79–97.

WORKS CITED AND CONSULTED

Hogg, Charlotte. *From the Garden Club: Rural Women Writing Community*. U of Nebraska P, 2006.
Holbrook, Sue Ellen. "Women's Work: The Feminization of Composition." *Rhetoric Review*, vol. 9, no. 2, 1991, pp. 201–29.
Homer. *The Odyssey*. Translated by Barry B. Powell, Oxford UP, 2014.
hooks, bell. "Critical Reflections." *Artforum International*, vol. 33, no. 3, 1994, pp. 64–65, 100.
———. *Talking Back: Thinking Feminist, Thinking Black*. South End P, 1989.
———. *Teaching to Transgress: Education as the Practice of Freedom*. Routledge, 1994.
———. *Yearning: Race, Gender, and Cultural Politics*. South End P, 1990.
Houston, Marsha, and Cheris Kramarae. "Speaking from Silence: Methods of Silencing and of Resistance." *Discourse and Society*, vol. 2, no. 4, 1991, pp. 387–99.
Hult, Christine, David Joliffe, Kathleen Kelly, Dana Mead, and Charles Schuster. "'The Portland Resolution': Guidelines for Writing Program Administrator Positions." *WPA: Writing Program Administrators*, vol. 16, no. 1–2, 1992, pp. 88–94.
Hunter-Gault, Charlayne. "Hard Times at Howard U." *New York Times*, 4 Feb. 2016, hppt://nyti.ms/Ls80eb. Accessed 3 March 2017.
Inoue, Asao. *Antiracist Assessment Ecologies: Teaching and Assessing for a Socially Just Future*. Parlor P, 2015.
Inoue, Asao, and Mya Poe, editors. *Race and Writing Assessment*. Peter Lang, 2012.
Irigaray, Luce. *Speculum of the Other Woman*. Cornell UP, 1985.
———. *This Sex Which Is Not One*. Cornell UP, 1985.
Jack, Jordynn. *Autism and Gender: From Refrigerator Mothers to Computer Geeks*. U of Illinois P, 2014.
———. *Science on the Home Front: American Women Scientists in World War II*. U of Illinois P, 2009.
Jaggar, Alison M. *Feminist Politics and Human Nature*. Rowman and Allanheld, 1983.
———. "Love and Knowledge: Emotion in Feminist Epistemology." *Inquiry: An Interdisciplinary Journal of Philosophy*, vol. 32, no. 2, 1989, pp. 151–76.
Jarratt, Susan C. "Comment: Rhetoric and Feminism: Together Again." *College English*, vol. 62, no. 3, 2000, pp. 390–93.
———. "Feminism and Composition: The Case for Conflict." *Contending with Words: Composition and Rhetoric in a Postmodern Age*, edited by Patricia Harkin and John Schilb, MLA, 1991, pp. 105–23.
———. "Feminist Pedagogy." *A Guide to Composition Pedagogies*, edited by Gary Tate, Amy Rupiper, and Kurt Schick, Oxford UP, 2001, pp. 113–31.
———. "Teaching across and within Differences." *College Composition and Communication*, vol. 43, no. 3, 1992, pp. 315–18.
Jarratt, Susan C., and Rory Ong. "Aspasia: Rhetoric, Gender, and Colonial Ideology." Lunsford, *Reclaiming*, pp. 9–24.
Jarratt, Susan C., and Lynn Worsham. *Feminism and Composition Studies: In Other Words*. Modern Language Association, 1998.

WORKS CITED AND CONSULTED

Jensen, Kelly, editor. *Here We Are: Feminism for the Real World*. Algonquin, 2017.
Jensen, Kyle, and Krista Ratcliffe. "Mythic Historiography: Refiguring Kenneth Burke's Deceitful Woman Trope." *Rhetoric Society Quarterly*, vol. 48, no. 1, 2017, pp. 1–20.
Johnson, Nan. "A Rhetorical Model of Social Change." Women/Writing/Rhetoric Conference, 7 Apr. 2017, University of Maryland, College Park. Lecture.
Johnson, Sonia. *Going Out of Our Minds: The Metaphysics of Liberation*. Crossing, 1987.
Jordan, June. *Technical Difficulties*. Beacon, 1994.
Jung, Julie. *Revisionary Rhetoric, Feminist Pedagogy, and Multigenre Texts*. Southern Illinois UP, 2005.
Kalamaras, George. *Reclaiming the Tacit Dimension: Symbolic Forms in the Rhetoric of Silence*. State U of New York P, 1994.
Kelly, Joan. *Women, History, and Theory: The Essays of Joan Kelly*. U of Chicago P, 1984.
Kelly, Shalonda, and John H. Schweitzer. "Mentoring within a Graduate School Setting." *College Student Journal*, vol. 33, no. 1, 1999, pp. 130–48.
Kendall, Mikki. "#SolidarityIsForWhiteWomen: Women of Color's Issue with Digital Feminism." *Guardian*, 14 Aug. 2013, https://www.theguardian.com/commentisfree/2013/aug/14/solidarityisforwhitewomen-hashtag-feminism. Accessed 25 Feb. 2015.
Kennedy, George. *Classical Rhetoric and Its Christian and Secular Tradition from Ancient to Modern Times*. U of North Carolina P, 1980.
Kennedy, Tammie, Joyce Irene Middleton, and Krista Ratcliffe, editors. *Rhetorics of Whiteness*. Southern Illinois UP, 2017.
Kezar, Adrianna, and Daniel Maxey. "The Changing Academic Workforce." *Association of Governing Boards*, May/June 2013, www.agb.org/trusteeship/2013/5/changing-academic-workforce.
Kirsch, Gesa. *Ethical Dilemmas in Feminist Research: The Politics of Location, Interpretation, and Publication*. State U of New York P, 1999.
Kirsch, Gesa E., and Liz Rohan. *Beyond the Archives: Research as Lived Process*. Southern Illinois UP, 2008.
Kirsch, Gesa E., and Jacqueline J. Royster. "Feminist Rhetorical Practices: In Search of Excellence." *College Composition and Communication*, vol. 61, no. 4, 2010, pp. 640–72.
Knoblauch, A. Abby. "In Theory and Practice: Constructing an Embodied Feminist Rhetorical Pedagogy." Enoch and Jack, forthcoming.
Kohlberg, Lawrence. *The Philosophy of Moral Development*. Harper and Row, 1981.
Kramarae, Cheris. "Feminist Theories of Communication." *International Encyclopedia of Communication*, vol. 2, edited by Erik Barnouw, Oxford UP, 1989, pp. 157–60.
Kristeva, Julia. *The Kristeva Reader*. Edited by Toril Moi, Columbia UP, 1986.
———. *Revolution in Poetic Language*. Columbia UP, 1984.
Kristof, Nicholas D. "The Value of Teachers." *New York Times*, 12 Jan. 2012, p. A21.

WORKS CITED AND CONSULTED

LaCapra, Dominick. *History and Criticism*. Cornell UP, 1985.
Lakritz, Andrew. "Identification and Difference: Structures of Privilege in Cultural Criticism." Roof and Wiegman, pp. 3–29.
Lamb, Catherine E. "Beyond Argument in Feminist Composition." *College Composition and Communication*, vol. 42, no. 1, 1991, pp. 11–24.
Lather, Patti, and Chris Smithie. *Troubling the Angels: Women Living with HIV/AIDS*. Westview, 1997.
Latterell, Catherine G. "Decentering Student-Centeredness: Rethinking Tutor Authority in Writing Centers." *Stories from the Center: Connecting Narrative and Theory in the Writing Center*, edited by Lynn Craigue Briggs and Meg Woolbright. NCTE, 2000, pp. 104–20.
Lerner, Gerda. *The Grimké Sisters from South Carolina: Pioneers for Women's Rights and Abolition*. Schocken, 1967.
Letherby, Gayle. *Feminist Research in Theory and Practice*. Open UP, 2003.
Lewin, Tamar. "Most College Students Don't Earn a Degree in 4 Years, Study Finds." *New York Times*, 1 Dec. 2014, www.nytimes.com/2014/12/02/education/most-college-students-dont-earn-degree-in-4-years-study-finds.html.
Lilla, Mark. "The End of Identity Liberalism." *New York Times*, 18 Nov. 2016, www.nytimes.com/2016/11/20/opinion/sunday/the-end-of-identity-liberalism.html.
Lipari, Lisbeth. *Listening, Thinking, Being: Toward an Ethics of Attunement*. Penn State UP, 2014.
Lippe, Berit von der. "Philanthropic War Narratives and Spectacular Protection Scenarios." Enoch and Jack, forthcoming.
Lloyd, Keith. "Beyond 'Dichotonegative' Rhetoric: Interpreting Field Reactions to Feminist Critiques of Academic Rhetoric through an Alternate Multivalent Rhetoric." *Rhetorica*, vol. 34, no. 1, 2016, pp. 78–105.
Logan, Shirley Wilson. *Liberating Language: Sites of Rhetorical Education in Nineteenth-Century Black America*. Southern Illinois UP, 2008.
———. "Re: I Know You're Buried." Email received by author, 22 Apr. 2017.
———. *We Are Coming: The Persuasive Discourse of Nineteenth-Century Black America*. Southern Illinois UP, 1999.
———. "'When and Where I Enter': Race, Gender, and Composition Studies." Jarratt and Worsham, pp. 45–57.
———, editor. *With Pen and Voice: A Critical Anthology of Nineteenth-Century African-American Women*. Southern Illinois UP, 1995.
Logan, Shirley Wilson, and Wayne Slater, editors. *Perspectives on Academic and Professional Writing in an Age of Accountability*. Southern Illinois UP, 2018.
Lorde, Audre. "Age, Race, Class, and Sex: Women Redefining Difference." 1980. Lorde, *Sister Outsider*, pp. 114–23.
———. *Black Unicorn: Poems*. W. W. Norton, 1995.
———. "The Master's Tools Will Never Dismantle the Master's House." Lorde, *Sister Outsider*, pp. 110–13.
———. "An Open Letter to Mary Daly." Lorde, *Sister Outsider*, pp. 66–71.
———. "Poetry Is Not a Luxury." Lorde, *Sister Outsider*, pp. 36–39.
———. *Sister Outsider: Essays and Speeches by Audre Lorde*. Crossing, 1984.

———. "Uses of Erotic: The Erotic as Power." Lorde, *Sister Outsider*, pp. 53–59.
Lunsford, Andrea A., editor. *Reclaiming Rhetorica: Women in the Rhetorical Tradition*. U of Pittsburgh P, 1995.
———. *Writing Matters: Rhetoric in Public and Private Lives*. U of Georgia P, 2007.
Lunsford, Andrea A., and Lisa Ede. "Crimes of Writing and Reading." Ronald and Ritchie, pp. 13–30.
Lunsford, Andrea A., and Susan C. Jarratt, general editors. *The Norton Anthology of Rhetoric and Writing*. W. W. Norton, forthcoming.
Maher, Jane. *Mina P. Shaughnessy: Her Life and Work*. NCTE, 1997.
Mathieu, Paula. *Tactics of Hope: The Public Turn in English Composition*. Heinemann, 2005.
Mattingly, Carol. *Appropriate[ing] Dress: Women's Rhetorical Style in Nineteenth-Century America*. Southern Illinois UP, 2002.
———. *Secret Habits: Catholic Literacy Education for Women in the Early Nineteenth Century*. Southern Illinois UP, 2016.
———. "Telling Evidence: Rethinking What Counts in Rhetoric." *Rhetoric Society Quarterly*, vol. 32, no. 1, 2002, pp. 99–108.
McGuire, Gail M., and Jo Reger. "Feminist Co-mentoring: A Model for Academic Professional Development." *NWSA Journal*, vol. 15, no. 1, 2003, pp. 54–72.
McKee, Heidi A., and James E. Porter. "Rhetorica Online: Feminist Research Practices in Cyberspace." *Rhetorica in Motion: Feminist Rhetorical Methods and Methodologies*, edited by Eileen Schell and K. J. Rawson, U of Pittsburgh P, 2010, pp. 152–72.
McLeod, Susan H. *Notes on the Heart: Affective Issues in the Writing Classroom*. Southern Illinois UP, 1997.
McPhillips, Deidre. "Best Countries for Education." *US News*, 7 Mar. 2017, https://www.usnews.com/news/best-countries-best-education. Accessed 5 May 2017.
Mercier, Hugo, and Dan Sperber. *The Enigma of Reason*. Harvard UP, 2017.
Micciche, Laura R. *Doing Emotion: Rhetoric, Writing, Teaching*. Boynton/Cook, 2007.
———. "More Than a Feeling: Disappointment and WPA Work." *College English*, vol. 64, no. 4, 2002, pp. 432–58.
Miller, Alice. "The Essential Role of an Enlightened Witness in Society." *Alice Miller: Child Abuse and Mistreatment*, 1 Jan. 1997, www.alice-miller.com/en/the-essential-role-of-an-enlightened-witness-in-society.
Miller, Hildy. "Postmasculinist Directions in Writing Program Administration." *WPA: Writing Program Administration*, vol. 20, no. 1/2, 1996, pp. 49–61.
Miller, Hildy, and Lillian Bridwell-Bowles, editors. *Rhetorical Women: Roles and Representations*. U of Alabama P, 2005.
Miller, Susan P. *Textual Carnivals: The Politics of Composition*. Southern Illinois UP, 1991.
———. *Trust in Texts: A Different History of Rhetoric*. Southern Illinois UP, 2007.

WORKS CITED AND CONSULTED

Miller, Thomas P. "Reinventing Rhetorical Traditions." *Learning from the Histories of Rhetoric: Essays in Honor of Winifred Bryan Horner*, edited by Theresa Enos, Southern Illinois UP, 1993, pp. 26–41.

Milstein, Sarah. "Five Ways White Feminists Can Address Our Own Racism." *Huffington Post*, 24 Sept. 2013, www.huffingtonpost.com/sarah-milstein/5-ways-white-feminists-can-address-our-own-racism_b_3955065.html.

Mohanty, Satya P. "The Epistemic Status of Cultural Identity." *Reclaiming Identity: Realist Theory and the Predicament of Postmodernism*, edited by Paula M. L. Moya and Michael R. Hames-García, U of California P, 2000, pp. 29–66.

Morrison, Toni. *The Bluest Eye*. Chatto, 1979.

Mortensen, Peter, and Gesa E. Kirsch. *Ethics and Representation in Qualitative Studies of Literacy*. NCTE, 1996.

Moss, Beverly J. *A Community Text Arises*. Hampton P, 2002.

———. "Intersections of Race and Class in the Academy." *Coming to Class: Pedagogy and the Social Class of Teachers*, edited by Alan Shepard, John McMillan, and Gary Tate, Heinemann, 1988, pp. 157–69.

———. "'Phenomenal Women,' Collaborative Literacies and Community Texts in Alternative 'Sista' Spaces." *Community Literacy Journal*, vol. 5, no. 1, 2010–11, pp. 1–24.

Mott, Lucretia. *Discourse on Woman: Delivered at the Assembly Buildings, December 17, 1849. Being a Full Phonographic Report, Revised by the Author*. Peterson, 1850.

Mouffe, Chantal, and Ernesto Laclau. "Hope, Passion, Politics." *Hope: New Philosophies for Change*, edited by Mary Zournazi, Routledge, 2002, pp. 122–48.

Mountford, Roxanne, and Cheryl Glenn. "Networked Feminism: Mentoring in the New Economy." *Rhetoric and Writing Studies in the New Century: Historiography, Pedagogy, and Politics*, edited by Cheryl Glenn and Roxanne Mountford, Southern Illinois UP, 2017, pp. 175–91.

Moya, Paula M. L. *Learning from Experience*. U of California P, 2002.

Moya, Paula M. L., and Michael R. Hames-García, editors. *Reclaiming Identity: Realist Theory and the Predicament of Postmodernism*. U of California P, 2000.

Mral, Brigitte. *Talande Kvinnor: Kvinnliga retoriker från Aspasia till Ellen Key*. [*Women Speaking: Female Rhetoricians from Aspasia to Ellen Key*.] Nya Doxa, 1999.

———. *"We're a Peaceful Nation": War Rhetoric after September 11*. Swedish Emergency Management, 2004.

Mral, Brigitte, Nicole Borg, and Philippe-Joseph Salazar, editors. *Women's Rhetoric: Argumentative Strategies of Women in Public Life, Sweden and South Africa*. Retorikförlaget, 2009.

Muñoz, José Esteban. *Disidentifications: Queers of Color and the Performance of Politics*. U of Minnesota P, 1999.

Mutz, Diana C. *Hearing the Other Side: Deliberative versus Participatory Democracy*. Cambridge UP, 2006.

National Center for Education Statistics. "Graduate Rates." *Institute of Education Sciences*, 2015, www.nces.ed.gov/fastfacts/display.asp?id=40. Accessed 20 Sept. 2015.

Nordell, Jessica. "Millions of Women Voted This Election. They Have the Iroquois to Thank." *Washington Post*, 24 Nov. 2016, https://washingtonpost.com/posteverything/wp/2016. Accessed 3 Mar. 2017.

Obama, Barack. "State of the Union 2012." *Washington Post*, 24 Jan. 2012, www.washingtonpost.com/politics/state-of-the-union-2012-obama-speech-full-text/2012/01/24/gIQA9D3QOQ_story.html.

Obama, Michelle. Interview with Oprah Winfrey. CBS, 16 Dec. 2016.

O'Brien, Sara Ashley. "Girls Who Code to Give $1 Million to Underprivileged Girls." *CNN*, 19 Jan. 2016, money.cnn.com/2016/01/19/technology/girls-who-code-1-million-in-scholarships/.

Okawa, Gail Y. "Diving for Pearls: Mentoring as Cultural and Activist Practice among Academics of Color." *College Composition and Communication*, vol. 53, no. 3, 2002, pp. 507–32.

Olson, Gary A., and Evelyn Ashton-Jones. "*Doing* Gender: (En)Gendering Academic Mentoring." *Journal of Education*, vol. 174, no. 3, 1992, pp. 114–27.

Owens, Kimberly Hensley. *Writing Childbirth: Women's Rhetorical Agency in Labor and Online*. Southern Illinois UP, 2016.

Palczewski, Catherine Helen. "Bodies, Borders, and Letters: Gloria Anzaldúa's 'Speaking in Tongues: A Letter to 3rd World Women Writers.'" *Southern Communication Journal*, vol. 62, no. 1, 1996, pp. 1–16.

———. "The Male Madonna and the Feminine Uncle Sam: Visual Argument, Icons, and Ideographs in 1909 Anti-woman Suffrage Postcards." *Quarterly Journal of Speech*, vol. 91, no. 4, 2005, pp. 365–94.

Parmar, Pratibha. "Woman, Native, Other: Pratibha Parmar Interviews Trinh T. Minh-ha." *Feminist Review*, vol. 36, 1990, pp. 65–74.

Penley, Constance, and Andrew Ross. "Interview with Trinh T. Minh-ha." *Camera Obscura*, vol. 13–14, 1985, pp. 86–103.

Perelman, Chaim, and Lucie Olbrechts-Tyteca. *The New Rhetoric: A Treatise on Argumentation*. 1958. Translated by John Wilkinson and Purcell Weaver, U of Notre Dame P, 1982.

Perry, William. *Forms of Intellectual and Ethical Development in the College Years*. Holt, Rinehart, and Winston, 1968.

Perryman-Clark, Staci. *Afrocentric Teacher Research: Rethinking Appropriateness and Inclusion*. Peter Lang, 2017.

Peterson, Linda. "The WPA's Progress: A Survey, Story, and Commentary on the Career Patterns of Writing Program Administrators." *WPA: Writing Program Administration*, vol. 10, no. 3, 1987, pp. 11–18.

Piaget, Jean. *The Moral Judgment of the Child*. 1932. Free Press, 1985.

Plato. *Euthyphro, Apology, Crito, Phaedo, Phaedrus*. Translated by H. N. Fowler, Harvard UP, 1977.

———. *Protagoras, Philebus, Gorgias*. Prometheus Books, 1996.

Plutarch. *The Lives of the Nobel Grecians and Romans*. Translated by John Dryden, revised by Arthur Hugh Clough, Modern Library, 1932.

WORKS CITED AND CONSULTED

Poe, Mya, Asao Inoue, and Norbert Elliot, editors. *Writing Assessment, Social Justice, and the Advancement of Opportunity*. WAC Clearinghouse, 2018.

Pough, Gwendolyn D. *Check It While I Wreck It: Black Womanhood, Hip-Hop Culture, and the Public Sphere*. Northeastern UP, 2004.

Pough, Gwendolyn D., Elaine Richardson, Aisha Durham, and Rachel Raimist, editors. *Home Girls Make Some Noise: Hip Hop Feminism Anthology*. Parker, 2007.

Powell, Malea. "Princess Sarah, the Civilized Indian: The Rhetoric of Cultural Literacies in Sarah Winnemucca Hopkins' *Life among the Piutes*." *Rhetorical Women: Roles and Representations*, edited by Hildy Miller and Lillian Bridwell-Bowles, U of Alabama P, 2005, pp. 63–80.

———. "Stories Take Place: A Performance in One Act." 2012 CCCC Chair's Address. *College Composition and Communication*, vol. 64, no. 2, 2012, pp. 383–406.

Power-Stubbs, Karen. "Watching Ourselves: Feminist Teachers and Authority." *College Composition and Communication*, vol. 43, no. 3, 1992, pp. 311–15.

Quintilian. *The Institutio Oratoria*. Translated by H. E. Butler, Heinemann, 1969. 4 vols.

Raine, Kathleen. *The Collected Poems of Kathleen Raine*. Counterpoint, 2001.

Ramsey, Alexis E., Wendy Sharer, Barbara L'Eplattenier, and Lisa S. Mastrangelo. *Working in the Archives: Practical Research Methods for Rhetoric and Composition*. Southern Illinois UP, 2010.

Ratcliffe, Krista. *Anglo-American Challenges to the Rhetorical Traditions: Virginia Woolf, Mary Daly, and Adrienne Rich*. Southern Illinois UP, 1996.

———. "Coming Out: Or, How Adrienne Rich's Feminist Theory Complicates Intersections of Rhetoric and Composition Studies, Cultural Studies, and Writing Program Administration." Ronald and Ritchie, pp. 31–47.

———. "Eavesdropping: A Tactic for Listening to Scholarly Discourses." *Rhetorical Listening: Identification, Gender, Whiteness*, by Krista Ratcliffe, Southern Illinois UP, 2005, pp. 101–32.

———. *Rhetorical Listening: Identification, Gender, Whiteness*. Southern Illinois UP, 2005.

Ratcliffe, Krista, and Rebecca Rickly, editors. *Performing Feminism and Administration in Rhetoric and Composition Studies*. Hampton, 2010.

Reda, Mary M. *Between Speaking and Silence: A Study of Quiet Students*. State U of New York P, 2009.

Reynolds, Nedra. "Interrupting Our Way to Agency: Feminist Cultural Studies and Composition." Jarratt and Worsham, pp. 58–73.

Rheineck, Jane E., and Catherine B. Roland. "The Developmental Mentoring Relationship between Academic Women." *Adultspan Journal*, vol. 7, no. 2, 2008, pp. 80–93.

Rhodes, Jacqueline. *Radical Feminism, Writing, and Critical Agency: From Manifesto to Modern*. State U of New York P, 2005.

Rich, Adrienne. "Arts of the Possible." Rich, *Arts of the Possible*, pp. 146–68.

———. *Arts of the Possible: Essays and Conversations*. Norton, 2001.
———. *Blood, Bread, and Poetry: Selected Prose*. 1986. Norton, 1994.
———. "Cartographies of Silence." Rich, *Collected*, pp. 455–60.
———. "Claiming an Education (1977)." Rich, *On Lies*, pp. 231–36.
———. *Collected Poems: 1950–2012*. Introduction by Claudia Rankine, Norton, 2016.
———. "Compulsory Heterosexuality and the Lesbian Existence." Rich, *Blood*, pp. 23–76.
———. "Contradictions: Tracking Poems, Poem 29." Rich, *Collected*, p. 656.
———. "Divisions of Labor." Rich, *Collected*, p. 693.
———. "Letters: March 1969." Rich, *Collected*, pp. 317–20.
———. "Notes toward a Politics of Location (1984)." Rich, *Blood*, pp. 210–32.
———. *On Lies, Secrets, and Silence: Selected Prose, 1966–1978*. Norton, 1979.
———. "Sources, IV." *Your Native Land, Your Life*, Norton, 1986, p. 6.
———. "Split at the Root." Rich, *Blood*, pp. 100–23.
———. "Taking Women Students Seriously." Rich, *On Lies*, pp. 237–45.
———. "Teaching Language in Open Admissions (1972)." Rich, *On Lies*, pp. 51–68.
———. "Terza Rima." Rich, *Collected*, pp. 877–85.
———. "Toward a Woman-Centered University." Rich, *On Lies*, pp. 125–55.
———. "Upper Broadway," Rich, *Collected*, p. 480.
———. "What Does a Woman Need to Know?" Rich, *Blood*, p. 3.
———. "What Is Possible." Rich, *Collected*, p. 537.
Richards, Ann. "Democratic National Convention Address." *Gifts of Speech*, 18 July 1988, gos.sbc.edu/r/richards.html.
Richardson, Elaine. *African American Literacies*. Routledge, 2002.
———. *PHD to Ph.D.: How Education Saved My Life*. New City Community, 2013.
Richardson, Marilyn, editor. *Maria W. Stewart, America's First Black Woman Political Writer: Essays and Speeches*. Indiana UP, 1987.
Ritchie, Joy, and Kate Ronald, editors. *Available Means: An Anthology of Women's Rhetorics*. U of Pittsburgh P, 2001.
Robbins, James S. "Hillary's Not Bad, OK Job." *USA Today*, 6. Feb. 2013, p. 9A.
Ronald, Kate, Cristy Beemer, and Lisa Shaver. "'Where Else Should Feminist Rhetoricians Be?' Leading a WAC Initiative in a School of Business." Ratcliffe and Rickly, pp. 159–69.
Ronald, Kate, and Joy Ritchie. *Teaching Rhetorica: Theory, Pedagogy, Practice*. Boynton/Cook, 2006.
Roof, Judith, and Robyn Wiegman, editors. *Who Can Speak? Authority and Critical Identity*. U of Illinois P, 1995.
Rorty, Richard. "The Historiography of Philosophy: Four Genres." *Philosophy in History: Essays on the Historiography of Philosophy*, edited by Richard Rorty, J. N. Schneewind, and Quentin Skinner, Cambridge UP, 1984, pp. 49–75.
Ross, Theodore. "Mikki Kendall and Her Online Beefs with White Feminists." *Vice*, 29 May 2014, www.vice.com/en_us/article/their-eyes-were-watching-twitter-0000317-v21n5.
Rowe, Aimee Carrillo. "Be Longing: Toward a Feminist Politics of Relation." *NWSA Journal*, vol. 17, no. 2, 2005, pp. 15–46.

WORKS CITED AND CONSULTED

Royster, Jacqueline Jones. "Disciplinary Landscaping, or Contemporary Challenges in the History of Rhetoric." *Philosophy and Rhetoric*, vol. 36, no. 2, 2003, pp. 148–67.

———. *Southern Horrors and Other Writings: The Anti-lynching Campaign of Ida B. Wells, 1892–1900*. Bedford, 1997.

———. *Traces of a Stream: Literacy and Social Change among African American Women*. U of Pittsburgh P, 2000.

———. "When the First Voice You Hear Is Not Your Own." *College Composition and Communication*, vol. 47, no. 1, 1996, pp. 29–40.

Royster, Jacqueline Jones, and Gesa E. Kirsch. *Feminist Rhetorical Practices: New Horizons for Rhetoric, Composition, and Literacy Studies*. Southern Illinois UP, 2012.

Ruiz, Iris. *Reclaiming Composition for Chicano/as and Other Ethnic Minorities: A Critical History and Pedagogy*. Palgrave Macmillan, 2016.

Ruti, Mari. *Reinventing the Soul: Posthumanist Theory and Psychic Life*. Other, 2006.

Ryan, Kathleen J., Nancy Myers, and Rebecca Jones, editors. *Rethinking Ethos: A Feminist Ecological Approach to Rhetoric*. Southern Illinois UP, 2016.

Sanders, Lise Shapiro. "'Feminists Love a Utopia': Collaboration, Conflict and the Futures of Feminism." Gillis, Howie, and Munford, pp. 3–15.

Sappho: Poems and Fragments. Translated by Josephine Balmer, Meadowland Books, 1984.

Schell, Eileen. *Gypsy Academics and Mother-Teachers: Gender, Contingent Labor, and Writing Instruction*. Boynton, 1998.

Schell, Eileen, and K. J. Rawson, editors. *Rhetorica in Motion: Feminist Rhetorical Methods and Methodologies*. U of Pittsburgh P, 2010.

Schmalz, Julie. "Nurturing 'the Next Generation of Women-of-Color Leaders.'" *Chronicle of Higher Education*, 13 Dec. 2016, www.chronicle.com.ezaccess.libraries.psu.edu/article/Nurturing. Accessed 21 Mar. 2017.

Schneider, Jack. "America's World Education Ranking Is No Reason to Panic." *TakePart*, 22 Jan. 2014, www.takepart.com/article/2014/01/22/united-states-world-education-rankings.

Schniedewind, Nancy. "Feminist Values: Guidelines for Teaching Methodology in Women's Studies." *Learning Our Ways: Essays in Feminist Education*, edited by Charlotte Bunch and Sandra Pollack, Crossing P, 1983, pp. 261–71.

Schultz, Katherine. *Listening: A Framework for Teaching across Differences*. Teachers College P, 2003.

———. *Rethinking Classroom Participation: Listening to Silent Voices*. Teachers College P, 2009.

Schuster, Charles. Foreword. *Resituating Writing: Constructing and Administering Writing Programs*, edited by Joseph Janangelo and Kristine Hansen, Boynton, 1995, pp. ix–xiv.

Sciachitano, Marian M. "Introduction: Feminist Sophistics Pedagogy Group." *College Composition and Communication*, vol. 43, no. 3, 1992, pp. 297–300.

Scott, Joan Wallach. *The Fantasy of Feminist History*. Duke UP, 2011.

Sedgwick, Eve Kosofsky. *Tendencies*. Duke UP, 1993.
Selzer, Jack. *Kenneth Burke in Greenwich Village: Conversing with the Moderns, 1915–1931*. U of Wisconsin P, 1996.
Sharer, Wendy. "Opening the Conversation." Enoch and Jack, forthcoming.
———. *Vote and Voice: Women's Organizations and Political Literacy, 1915–1930*. Southern Illinois UP, 2004.
Shaughnessy, Mina P. *Errors and Expectations: A Guide for Basic Writing Teachers*. Oxford UP, 1977.
Shrewsbury, Carolyn M. "What Is Feminist Pedagogy?" *Women's Studies Quarterly*, vol. 15, no. 3/4, 1987, pp. 6–14.
Skinner, Carolyn. *Women Physicians and Professional Ethos in Nineteenth-Century Feminism*. Southern Illinois UP, 2014.
Sloman, Steven, and Philip Fernback. *The Knowledge Illusion: Why We Never Think Alone*. Riverhead Books, 2017.
Smith, Anna Deavere. *Letters to a Young Artist*. Anchor, 2006.
Smith, Zadie. "On Optimism and Despair." *New York Review of Books*, 22 Dec. 2016, www.nybooks.com/articles/2016/12/22/on-optimism-and-despair. Accessed 2 Jan. 2017.
Smitherman, Geneva. *Black Talk: Words and Phrases from the Hood to the Amen Corner*. Houghton Mifflin, 1994.
———. *Talkin and Testifyin: The Language of Black America*. Wayne State UP, 1997.
———. *Talkin That Talk: Language, Culture, and Education in African America*. Routledge, 2000.
Solnit, Rebecca. *Hope in the Dark: Untold Histories, Wild Possibilities*. 3rd ed., Haymarket Books, 2016.
Solomon, Akiba. "On Patricia Arquette, Coded Language and the Hotness of 'Intersectionality.'" *Color Lines*, 23 Feb. 2015, www.colorlines.com/articles/patricia-arquette-coded-language-and-hotness-intersectionality.
Spencer-Maor, Faye, and Robert E. Randolph, Jr. "Shifting the Talk: Writing Studies, Rhetoric, and Feminisms at HBCUs." *Composition Studies*, vol. 44, no. 2, 2016, pp. 179–82.
Spitzack, Carole, and Kathryn Carter. "Women in Communication Studies: A Typology for Revision." *Quarterly Journal of Speech*, vol. 73, no. 4, 1987, pp. 401–23.
Spivak, Gayatri Chakravorty. "Can the Subaltern Speak?" *Wedge*, no. 7/8, 1985, pp. 120–30. Repr. in *Marxism and the Interpretation of Culture*, edited by Cary Nelson and Lawrence Grossberg, U of Illinois P, 1988, pp. 271–313.
———. *A Critique of Postcolonial Reason: Toward a History of the Vanishing Present*. Harvard UP, 1999.
———. "Political Commitment and the Postmodern Critic." *The New Historicism*, edited by Harold Aram Veeser, Routledge, 1989, pp. 277–92.
Stallybrass, Peter, and Allon White. *The Politics and Poetics of Transgression*. Cornell UP, 1986.
Stanton, Elizabeth Cady, Susan B. Anthony, and Matilda Joselyn Gage. *History of Woman Suffrage, 1848–1861*. Vol. 1, Fowler and Wills, 1881.
———. *History of Woman Suffrage, 1861–1876*. Vol. 2, Charles Mann, 1881.

WORKS CITED AND CONSULTED

Starhawk. *Dreaming the Dark: Magic, Sex and Politics*. 1982. Beacon, 1988.

———. *Truth or Dare: Encounters with Power, Authority, and Mystery*. Harper and Row, 1987.

Steinem, Gloria. Foreword. *To Be Real: Telling the Truth and Changing the Face of Feminism*, edited by Rebecca Walker, Anchor, 1995, pp. xiii–xxiii.

———. *Moving Beyond Words*. Simon and Schuster, 1994.

———. "Sisterhood." *New York Magazine*, 20 Dec. 1971, p. 49.

Still, William. *The Underground Railroad*. Porter and Coates, 1872.

Stone, Alison. "On the Genealogy of Women: A Defence of Anti-essentialism." Gillis, Howie, and Munford, pp. 16–29.

Stone, Brian J., and Shawanda Stewart. "HBCUs and Writing Programs: Critical Hip Hop Language Pedagogy and First-Year Student Success." *Composition Studies*, vol. 44, no. 2, 2016, 183–86.

Sullivan, Patricia A. "Feminism and Methodology in Composition Studies." *Methods and Methodology in Composition Research*, edited by Gesa Kirsch and Patricia A. Sullivan, Southern Illinois UP, 1992, pp. 37–61.

Swers, Michele L. *The Difference Women Make: The Policy Impact of Women in Congress*. U of Chicago P, 2002.

Syfers, Judy. "I Want a Wife." *Ms. Magazine*, 31 Dec. 1971, p. 13.

Tasker, Elizabeth, and Frances B. Holt-Underwood. "Feminist Rhetorical Methodologies in Historic Rhetoric and Composition: From the 1970s to the Present." *Rhetoric Review*, vol. 21, no. 1, 2008, pp. 54–71.

Terrell, Mary Church. *Progress of Colored Women*. 1898. Qontro Historical Reprints, 2009.

Tomkins, Jane. "Me and My Shadow." *New Literary History: A Journal of Theory and Interpretation*, vol. 19, no. 1, 1987, pp. 169–78.

Tomlinson, Barbara. *Feminism and Affect at the Scene of Argument: Beyond the Trope of the Angry Feminist*. Temple UP, 2010.

Trinh, Minh-ha T. "Difference: 'A Special Third World Women Issue.'" *Feminist Review*, no. 25, 1987, pp. 5–22.

———. *When the Moon Waxes Red: Representation, Gender and Cultural Politics*. Routledge, 1991.

———. *Woman, Native, Other*. Indiana UP, 1989.

Truth, Sojourner. "Address to the First Annual Meeting of the American Equal Rights Association," New York, 9 May 1867. *Documenting Modern World History*, https://bcc-cuny.digication.com/MWHreader/Truth_Speeches_1851_1867. Accessed 20 Feb. 2018.

Tuana, Nancy. "Conceptualizing Moral Literacy." *Journal of Educational Administration*, vol. 45, no. 4, 2007, pp. 364–78.

"Twitter, Feminism, and Race: A Roundtable." *NPR*, 26 Aug. 2013, www.npr.org/sections/codeswitch/2013/08/26/215804045/twitter-feminism-and-race-a-roundtable.

"Twitter, Feminism, and Race: Who Gets a Seat at the Table?" *NPR*, 5 Sept. 2013, www.npr.org/sections/codeswitch/2013/09/05/219278156/twitter-feminism-and-race-who-gets-a-seat-at-the-table.

"Twitter Sparks a Serious Discussion about Race and Feminism." *NPR*, 23 Aug. 2013, www.npr.org/sections/codeswitch/2013/08/22/214525023/twitter-sparks-a-serious-discussion-about-race-and-feminism.

WORKS CITED AND CONSULTED

VanHaitsma, Pamela, and Steph Ceraso. "'Making It' in the Academy through Horizontal Mentoring." *Peitho Journal*, vol. 19, no. 2, 2017, pp. 210–33.

Veblen, Thorstein. *The Instinct of Workmanship and the State of the Industrial Arts*. Macmillan, 1914.

Waite, Stacy. *Teaching Queer: Radical Possibilities for Writing and Knowing*. U of Pittsburgh P, 2017.

Walker, Rebecca. "Becoming the Third Wave." *Ms. Magazine*, vol. 2, no. 4, 1992, pp. 39–41.

———, editor. *To Be Real: Telling the Truth and Changing the Face of Feminism*. Anchor, 1995.

Wang, Bo. "Rethinking Feminist Rhetoric and Historiography in a Global Context: A Cross-Cultural Perspective." *Advances in the History of Rhetoric*, vol. 15, no. 1, 2012, pp. 28–52.

———. "Writing to Connect Minds: Bing Xin as a Feminist Rhetorician." *College Composition and Communication*, vol. 60, no. 4, 2009, pp. W66–76.

Weiler, Kathleen, editor. *Feminist Engagements*. Routledge, 2001.

———. *Women Teaching for Change: Gender, Class, and Power*. Bergin, 1998.

Weis, Lois, and Michelle Fine. *Beyond Silenced Voices: Class, Race, and Gender in the United States Schools, Revised Edition*. State U of New York P, 2005.

Welch, Nancy. "Taking Sides." Ronald and Ritchie, pp. 147–59.

Wells, H. G. *The Outline of History: Being a Plain History of Life and Mankind*. 3rd ed., Macmillan, 1921.

Wertheimer, Molly Meier, editor. *Listening to Their Voices: The Rhetorical Activities of Historical Women*. U of South Carolina P, 1997.

West, Cornel. "Hope." Performed by Anna Deavere Smith. *Twilight: Los Angeles 1992*, Dramatist Play Service, Inc., 2003, pp. 105–06.

West, Lindy. *Shrill: Notes from a Loud Woman*. Hachette, 2016.

Wolf, Naomi. *Fire with Fire: The New Female Power and How to Use It*. Fawcett, 1998.

"Women in National Parliaments." *Inter-Parliamentary Union*, 2017, www.ipu.org/wmn-e/classif.htm. Accessed 7 Dec. 2016.

"Women in Parliaments: World Classification." *Inter-Parliamentary Union*, 1 Nov. 2016, www.ipu.org/wmn-e/classif.htm. Accessed 10 Dec. 2016.

"Women in Politics." *Women's Campaign Fund Foundation*, www.wcffoundation.org/pages/research/women-in-politics-statistics. Accessed 6 Sept. 2011.

Wood, Henrietta Rix. *Praising Girls: The Rhetoric of Young Women, 1895–1930*. Southern Illinois UP, 2016.

Woolbright, Meg. "The Politics of Tutoring: Feminism within the Patriarchy." *Writing Center Journal*, vol. 13, no. 1, 1992, pp. 16–30.

Woolf, Virginia. *A Room of One's Own*. 1929. Harvest-HBJ, 1957.

———. *Three Guineas*. 1938. Harcourt, 1966.

"The World's Most Powerful People." *Forbes*, 2016, www.forbes.com/wealth/powerful-people/list. Accessed 7 Dec. 2016.

"The World's 100 Most Powerful Women." *Forbes*, 2016, www.forbes.com/wealth/power-women. Accessed 7 Dec. 2016.

WORKS CITED AND CONSULTED

Wu, Hui. "A Comment on 'Historical Studies and Postmodernism: Rereading Aspasia.'" *College English*, vol. 63, no. 1, 2000, pp. 102–05.

———. *Once Iron Girls: Essays on Gender by Post-Mao Chinese Literary Women*. Lexington, 2009.

Xenophon. *Memorabilia and Oeconomicus*. Translated by E. C. Marchant, Harvard UP, 1988.

Yancey, Kathleen Blake. "Defining Moments: The Role of Institutional Departure in the Work of a (Feminist) WPA." Ratcliffe and Rickly, pp. 143–58.

INDEX

abolitionism, 10–13, 16, 18–20
academic discourse, as hegemonic, 52–56, 65–66, 91–92, 145
academic hierarchy, 179
accessibility, 58, 70, 153. *See also* vernacular
accountability logic, 82
action, 134–36, 164–65, 174
"Active Prolific Female Scholars" (*Communication Quarterly*), 91–92
activism, 5–23; abolitionism, 18–20; current, 20–23; legal rights, 7–9; suffrage, 9–20, 216n9
actor-network theory, 81
Adams, Heather Brook, 120–21
Adams, Katherine, 20
advocacy, 85
affective labor, 160, 170–72
affirmative action approach, 107
African American women's clubs, 16
ageism, 207–8
agency, 4, 26–27, 46, 208; comparative, 29; delivery and, 80–81; encouragement of, 57–58; ethos and, 84; of marginalized writer, 53; power-from-within, 62–63; teaching and, 135–36; of third-world women writers, 55–56
aging, 206–8
Ahmed, Sara, 198, 203
Albrecht, Lisa, 199
Albright, Madeleine, 8, 211
Alcoff, Linda Martín, 28, 29, 131, 186
Alice Paul and the Suffrage Campaign (Adams and Keene), 20

Amendments to the Constitution: Fifteenth, 18–19; Fourteenth, 18; Nineteenth, 7, 11, 20
American Equal Rights Association, 19–20, 37, 218nn28, 30
angry feminist, trope of, 77, 88, 225n21
antiwar activism, 22
Anzaldúa, Gloria, 51, 64, 86, 103, 147, 201
apologizing, 41, 223n28
appropriation, 101
archives, 97–98, 115–16, 208
Arendt, Hannah, 155
"Aren't I a Woman" (Truth), 16–17
argument: culture of, 74–75; scene of, 70, 74–79; student learning of, 227n14
Aristotle, 79, 84, 88, 137, 164–65
Arquette, Patricia, 38–39
"Arts of the Possible" (Rich), 1, 174, 190, 198
Ashton-Jones, Evelyn, 154
"Aspasia: Rhetoric, Gender, and Colonial Ideology" (Jarratt and Ong), 110–14
Aspasia of Miletus, 110, 165, 228n12, 229n13
Athena-as-Mentor, 149, 163
Athenians, 8
audience, 25, 26–29; as consumer, 68; ethical concerns and, 117; ethos and, 84–85; marginalized, 50–51, 220n2; meaning and, 67–68; persuasion, challenge to, 71; rhetorical feminism and, 50–51; third-world women writers, 53–54
authority, 26–27; teaching and, 135–36

INDEX

Background, 60–62
Ballif, Michelle, 156
Barr-Ebest, Sally, 178
Baxter, Leslie A., 91–92, 102
becoming, politics of, 151–55
being, mentoring and, 155–58
Belenky, Mary Field, 94
Bell, Derrick, 205–6, 234–35n16
belonging, ethics of, 163–66
Bennett, Catherine, 211
Bergson, Henri-Louis, 197
Berrett, Dan, 129–30
"Beyond Argument in Feminist Composition" (Lamb), 74
biblical references, leveraging of, 12–13, 15, 17
Biesecker, Barbara, 106–9, 201–2
"Biesecker Cannot Speak for Her Either" (Campbell), 108–9
Bizzell, Patricia, 51, 96
black feminists, 31–33
"Black feminist" statement (Combahee River Collective), 31–32
Black Liberation, 32
Black Lives Matter, 22
Black Sash movement (South Africa), 22
black women, free, 1–13, 6, 7, 16–17, 218n28; abolitionists, 10
Blair, Carole, 91–92, 102, 114
Bloom, Lynn Z., 178, 229–30n5
body, writing, 80
"Border Crossings: Intersections of Rhetoric and Feminism" (Ede, Lunsford, and Glenn), 2
Bridwell-Bowles, Lillian, 199
Brooks, David, 196
Brown, Julie R., 91–92, 102
Brown, Wendy, 8
Brown v. Board of Education, 205, 234–35n16
Bunch, Charlotte, 133–34
Burke, Kenneth, 1, 25, 29, 62, 204
Burton, Vicki Tolar, 97, 115–16
Butler, Judith, 27, 220n3, 221nn9, 12

Campbell, Karlyn Kohrs, 72–74, 85–86, 105; Biesecker, controversy with, 106–9; on commonalities, 201
canons, rhetorical, 79
"Can the Subaltern Speak?" (Spivak), 27
Caputi, Jane, 61
care, ethic of, 94, 157, 228n7
caring, 94
Cato the Elder, 79, 163
center-margin metaphor, 52, 56, 191
Chandler, Christy, 155
Charland, Maurice, 50
Charlton, Jonikka, 178–79
Chen, Tina, 137
Chira, Susan, 204
Christ, Carol P., 221nn14, 15
Christian, Barbara, 55, 56, 58
church, nineteenth-century, 10
Cicero, 20, 79, 165–66, 205
citizen, as category, 30
City College of New York, 140–41, 174
Civil War, 18, 19
Cixous, Hélène, 103
claims, 82, 135–36, 209
clarity, 56, 66, 67
Clark, Suzanne, 130–31, 202, 228n7
Clinchy, Blythe McVicker, 94
Clinton, Hillary Rodham, 8, 20–22, 80, 194, 196, 216nn5–7, 219nn34–39; "Listening Campaign," 21
clubs and societies, 16
Coalition of Women (Feminist) Scholars in the History of Rhetoric and Composition, 199, 228n17
Cocks, Joan, 104, 113
Code, Lorraine, 131, 225n1
Code Pink, 22
Cohen, Leonard, 233n2
collective hope, 198–200
collectivist perspectives, 75–76
colonies, North American, 9
Combahee River Collective, 31–32
"Comment: Rhetoric and Feminism: Together Again" (Jarratt), 112

commonalities, identifications across, 44, 82
communication: as academic discipline, 91–92; cross-cutting conversation, 44, 82; online, 43
Communication Quarterly report, 91–92
communication studies, 106–7
A Community Text Arises (Moss), 118–20
"Composing as a Woman" (Flynn), 143
composition studies, 143–48, 229–30n5, 229n4; feminization of, 176; process, focus on, 146. *See also* writing program administration (WPA)
Condon, Frankie, 209
contemplation. *See* strategic contemplation
control, 80–81
coordinator, as term, 229n3
Council of Writing Program Administrators, 179, 189, 230n6
courtroom practices, 78–79
Crenshaw, Kimberlé, 25, 38–39, 203–4
critical engagement, 133–35
critical imagination, 100–102, 190
critical thinking, 134, 189, 232n27
Cullors, Patrisse, 22

Daly, Mary, 33–35, 37, 51, 221n14, 224nn6, 7; *Works: Gyn/Ecology*, 33–34, 60–62; *Websters' First New Intergalactic Wickedary of the English Language*, 61
Dana, Richard Henry, Sr., 15
Davis, Diane, 156
Declaration of Independence, 9, 11
Declaration of Sentiments (Woman's Rights Convention), 11, 216n11
decorum, breach of, 74
delivery: alternative systems, 4, 50, 51, 203–4; emotion and, 88; feminist resistance to traditional, 80–81; rhetorical feminism at scene of, 79–84;

silence and listening as, 81–84; stylistic conventions, 79–80
democratic debate, 112–13
democratic equality, 8
demonstrating, 23
Demosthenes, 79
demystification, 56, 61
Denny, Harry, 134
Derrida, Jacques, 108
dialogic rhetoric, 53–54, 202
Dickinson, Emily, 198
difference, 48, 68, 201; ethical stance toward, 137–40; power and, 33, 39; reification of, 27
disappointment, emotion of, 93
disciplinary expertise, 208
"Disciplining the Feminine" (Blair, Brown, and Baxter), 91–92
discourse, possibilities of, 145–48
"Discourse on Woman" (Mott), 15
disidentification, 4, 5, 12, 13, 49–50; by black women, 16; center-margin metaphor countered, 52, 56; Clinton campaigns and, 21; feminine style(s) and, 85–87; feminist rhetoric and, 31–33; of feminist rhetoric from traditional masculinist practices, 73; with master discourse, 67; mentoring and, 150, 158–59; separation from power, 55–56; spiritual approaches, 62–64; theory and, 51–64; in third-world women's writings, 51–57; vernacular and, 58–60; with/in foreground, 60–62
disruption, 65
distributed administrative model, 186, 187
diversity, 44, 220n1, 226n3
doing, technologies of, 92–93
Doing Emotion: Rhetoric, Writing, Teaching (Micciche), 92–93
"*Doing* Gender: (En)Gendering Academic Mentoring" (Olson and Ashton-Jones), 154
domestic violence, 78–79, 81–82

dominant ideology, 47; academic hegemony, 52–56, 65–66
Douglass, Frederick, 11, 217n12
Dow, Bonnie J., 85–87, 104–5, 201
Dreaming the Dark (Starhawk), 62–64
DuBois, Ellen Carol, 10
Duffy, John, 138–39

Ebbitt, Wilma, 192
Eble, Michelle, 150, 210
écriture feminine, 80, 224n15
Ede, Lisa, 2, 49, 54, 130–31, 199
education. *See* teaching
Eichhorn, Jill, 132, 137–39
emotions, 225n19, 21; as analytic tool, 91; hope, 93; intersectionality and, 43; mentoring and, 150–51; "outlaw," 90–91; rhetorical feminism and, 87–93; rhetorical feminist leveraging of, 5, 12, 13, 51
enlightened witness, 158
Enoch, Jessica, 157
Enos, Theresa, 177, 229n4
Ensler, Eve, 22
epistemic resources, 26, 46–48
epistolary form, 53–54
eponymous theories, 203
equality, 216n8; democratic, 8; in feminist rhetoric, 72–73; intersectional concerns, 42; social, 8–9
Equal Rights Amendment (ERA), 7, 30–31, 37
Erdoğan, Recep Tayyip, 211
essentialism, 30, 108; strategic, 25–26, 35–37, 204
estrangement, 63
Ethical Dilemmas in Feminist Research (Kirsch), 117
ethics, 117; of belonging, 163–66; mentoring and, 166–72; stance toward difference, 137–40
Ethics and Representation in Qualitative Studies of Literacy (Mortensen and Kirsch), 117

ethos, 84–85, 150
eudaemonia, 5, 23, 164–66, 190
evaluation, emotion and, 89–90, 93
exclusion, feminist messages of, 44–45
experience: as basis for theory, 58–60, 75; delivery and, 79–80; intersectionality and, 43; leveraging of, 5, 10, 12, 22; mentoring and, 151; social and theoretical construction of, 46

Fallowes, James, 194
familiarity, 44
"Farewell Address to Her Friends in the City of Boston" (Stewart), 12
Farris, Sara, 137–39
feminine style, 85–87
feminism: as academic discipline, 1–2; communication failures, 40–41; first-wave, 6, 30; fissures within, 26, 29–45, 72, 107–14, 200–203, 222nn18, 19, 223nn28, 29; forefront, women in, 42; fourth-wave, 36, 37; global political moment and, 6; group identification, 29–30; nonmainstream, 30–31; power feminism, 36, 221n17; second-wave, 30–31, 72; third-wave, 32–33, 36, 221n17; "waves" of, 25
Feminism and Affect at the Scene of Argument (Tomlinson), 76–79
"Feminism Lost. Now What?" (Chira), 204
Feminism(s) and Rhetoric(s) Conference (FemRhets), 199
feminist pedagogy, 126, 130–31; critical engagement, 133–35; rhetorical, 136–43; of Rich, 140–43. *See also* teaching
feminist rhetoric: abolitionist, 11; disidentification and, 31–33; established practices, 5; feminist responses to, 93–95; as oxymoron, 72–73, 77; possibilities for future, 206–10; possibility of integrated rhetorical theories and praxis, 200–206; rhetorical recovery

work, 2–3; as term, 3; theoretical divisions, 201–6. *See also* rhetorical feminism; *individual methods and methodologies*
"Feminist Rhetorical Methodologies in Historic Rhetoric and Composition" (Tasker and Holt-Underwood), 122
"Feminist Rhetorical Practices: In Search of Excellence" (Kirsch and Royster), 99
Feminist Rhetorical Practices: New Horizons for Rhetoric, Composition, and Literacy Studies (Royster and Kirsch), 100–103, 118, 121, 122
feminist scholarship, goal of, 49
"Feminist Writing Program Administration: Resisting the Bureaucrat Within" (Goodburn and Leverenz), 175–76
Fifteenth Amendment, 18–19
Filipovic, Jill, 43
"Five Ways White Feminists Can Address Our Own Racism" (Milstein), 41
Flynn, Elizabeth, 143
foreground, 60–62
Foss, Karen, 43, 45
Foss, Sonja K., 43, 45, 49, 68–70, 74, 145
Foucault, Michel, 108
Fourteenth Amendment, 18
Freire, Paulo, 131, 136
French feminists, 80, 102, 224n15
Friedan, Betty, 30, 31
From the Garden Club: Rural Women Writing Community (Hogg), 97

Gage, Matilda Joslyn, 11
Gaillet, Lynée, 150, 210
Gale, Xin Lu, 110–14
Garza, Alicia, 22
Gay, Roxanne, 38, 39–40, 45, 222n19
Gearhart, Sally Miller, 70–72, 74, 145
"Gender Differences in Writing Program Administration" (Barr-Ebest), 178

Gender Roles and Faculty Lives in Rhetoric and Composition (Enos), 177
Gillespie, Cynthia K., 78
Gilligan, Carol, 94, 225n23, 228n7
Girls Who Code, 22, 220n43
Glenn, Cheryl, 51–57, 82; Gale-Glenn-Jarratt-Ong-Wu exchange, 110–14; "Networked Mentoring" (with Mountford), 171–72; "sex, lies, and manuscript: Refiguring Aspasia in the History of Rhetoric," 110; *Works*: "Border Crossings: Intersections of Rhetoric and Feminism" (Ede, Lunsford, and Glenn), 2; "sex, lies, and manuscript: Refiguring Aspasia in the History of Rhetoric," 110; *Silence and Listening as Rhetorical Arts* (with Ratcliffe), 83; *Unspoken: A Rhetoric of Silence*, 82
globalization, as feminist rhetorical practice, 100, 103, 190, 191
global political moment, 6
Goddess, 63
goddess images, 33–34
gods, 61
Goldberger, Nancy Rule, 94
Goodburn, Amy, 175–76
Gorsevski, Ellen W., 74–76
"great women speakers," 107–9
Greeks, 110
Greenberg, David, 196
Griffin, Cindy, 43, 45, 49, 68–70, 74, 145
Grimké, Angelina, 11, 13–14
Grimké, Sarah, 14
group identification, 29–30
Gubar, Susan, 187
Gumbs, Alexis Pauline, 169, 228n15
Gunner, Jeanne, 186
Gyn/Ecology (Daly), 33–34, 60–62
Gypsy Academics and Mother-Teachers (Schell), 177

Hags and Crones, 60–62
Haran, Joan, 123

INDEX

Harper, Frances, 19, 218–19n32
Hayes, Karen, 137–39
Hearing the Other Side (Mutz), 43–44
Hedge, Radha S., 80–81
hegemony, 4, 5, 16, 60, 75–76, 94; of academic discourse, 52–56, 65–66; of language, 65; persuasion, 39, 64, 69
Heilbrun, Carolyn, 150, 151
Hernández, Adriana, 137–39
Herrick, James, 189
hierarchy, 37, 45, 62, 126, 220n9; mentoring and, 151–55, 168
historically black colleges and universities (HBCUs), 128, 227n11
historiography, 103–14; controversies, 106–7; postmodern, 110–11; as rhetorical, 114. *See also* methods and methodologies
History of Woman Suffrage, 19
Hogg, Charlotte, 97
Holbrook, Sue Ellen, 176
Holt-Underwood, Frances B., 122
Homer, 149
hooks, bell, 40, 51, 57–60, 102, 125, 129, 133, 180
hope, 93, 147–48, 193–212; collective, 198–200; mentoring and, 172–73; possibility of integrated rhetorical theories and praxis, 200–206; of reimagining, 211–12; Rich's work, 140–43; teaching and, 129–36, 227n16
"Hope, Passion, Politics" (Mouffe and Laclau), 123
Houston, Marsha, 82
humility topos, 12

identification, 25, 29, 42, 204, 220n7
identity/ies, 24–48; black feminist, 31–32; cleaving, 29–31, 229n8; communication failures, 40–41; created in presence of Others, 48; diversity-in-identity, 36; as epistemic resources, 26, 46–48; experiential knowledge, 25; feminist options for bridge building, 41–46; generative capacity, 25; intersectionality, 38–40; knowledge-accruing location of, 48; meriting a rhetorical audience, 26–29; speaking for others, 33–35
identity politics, 27, 194, 204
identity studies, 46
immanence, 63–64
individualism, ideology of, 108–9
"Institutional 'Protections,' Assumptions of Research, and the Challenges of Compliance: Opening a Conversation Space for Feminist Scholars Working with Participants" (Adams), 120–21
Institutional Review Board (IRB), 120–21
instrumentality, 66–67
intellectual contact, 42
interest-convergence theory, 204–6, 234–35n16
interest-group politics, 205
interpretation, 104–5
interruption, 85, 156
intersectionality, 19, 25, 30–31, 38–40, 198, 221n11; fourth-wave feminism and, 37; as legal concept, 39; possibilities of, 203–4; teaching and, 130–33
invitational rhetoric, 34, 42–45, 68–70, 145
Iroquois Confederacy, 11, 217n13
"I Want a Wife" (Syfers), 178
"I Want a Writing Director" (Bloom), 178, 229–30n5

Jaggar, Alison M., 89–91, 102
Jarratt, Susan, 110–14, 137–39, 145–46
Johnson, Nan, 138, 179
Jolie, Angelina, 28, 29, 220n5
Jones, Rebecca, 85
Jordan, June, 33

Keene, Michael, 20
Kelly, Joan, 153
Kendall, Mikki, 38, 41, 42, 45

Kirsch, Gesa, 83, 99–103, 117, 190; Works: *Ethical Dilemmas in Feminist Research*, 117; *Ethics and Representation in Qualitative Studies of Literacy* (with Mortensen), 117; "Feminist Rhetorical Practices: In Search of Excellence" (with Royster), 99; *Feminist Rhetorical Practices: New Horizons for Rhetoric, Composition, and Literacy Studies* (with Royster), 100–103, 118, 121, 122
Knoblauch, A. Abby, 130
knowing, women's ways of, 94
knowledge: constructed, 94; rhetorical, 28, 189, 205, 232n27
Kramarae, Cheris, 82

Laclau, Ernesto, 123
Lakritz, Andrew, 26
Lamb, Catherine E., 74, 76
language: as hegemonic, 65; instrumentality of, 66–67
Lather, Patti, 117
Latterell, Catherine G., 144
Leadsom, Andrea, 211
"Lecture Delivered at Franklin Hall" (Stewart), 12
legal rights, 7–9, 216n10
Lesbos, 163–64
Letherby, Gayle, 122
Leverenz, Carrie Shively, 175–76
Liberian Mass Action for Peace, 22
Liberian Women in White, 22
Lilla, Mark, 204
Lipari, Lisbeth, 83–84
listening, 25, 26–29; asking questions, 188; dismissed as feminine or passive, 60; racism and, 222nn23, 24; recognition of other, 83–84; understanding as goal, 82; white women's inability, 59–60
Lloyd, Keith, 202, 223n1
location, politics of, 151–52, 175, 230nn7, 8

Logan, Shirley Wilson, 106, 132–33, 200
logos, 4, 67, 74–75, 88–90
Lorde, Audre, 33–35, 37, 57, 154, 221nn13, 14, 224n18
Lunsford, Andrea, 2, 49, 54, 162, 210

Madres de la Plaza de Mayo (Argentina), 22
Man Cannot Speak for Her (Campbell), 105, 107
marginalized groups, 3; attention to, 5, 10, 12; as audience, 50–51; feminist rhetorical studies as, 200; Fifteenth Amendment and, 18–19; mentees and, 156; purposeful marginality, 53
marginal rhetorics, 203–5, 234n14
marriage, loss of legal rights, 9–10
masculinist frames, 110; of delivery, 80–81, 91–92; methods and methodologies, 96–97; research as, 177. *See also* persuasion
master-apprentice model, 149–50
maternalism, 86
Mathieu, Paula, 129, 147
May, Theresa, 211
McKee, Heidi A., 117, 225n2
McKinnon, Kate, 233n2
McLeod, Susan H., 180
meaning, 67–68
mentoring, 149–73, 209–10; affective labor as investment, 170–72; benefits to mentor, 228n5; capacity building, 162–63, 168–69; cultural prodding, 160–62; disidentification and, 150, 158–59; ethics of belonging and, 163–66; "everything else," 158–63, 228nn7–11; expectations, and ethical/intellectual contract, 166–72; gender and, 153, 228nn3, 4; hope and, 172–73; intersectionality and, 150; master-apprentice model, 149–50; multiple mentors, time, and energy, 168–70, 228nn15, 16; mutuality and, 152–55; networks, 155; politics of

INDEX

mentoring (continued)
    becoming and, 151–55; politics of feminist, 153–54; rhetorical feminism and, 150, 153; rhizomic feminist, 167; taking mentees seriously, 155–58
methods and methodologies, 96–123, 210; archival research, 97–98, 114–16, 208; Biesecker-Campbell exchange, 107–9; critical imagination, 100–102; Gale-Glenn-Jarratt-Ong-Wu exchange, 110–14; historiography, 103–14; Institutional Review Board (IRB), 120–21; for invigorating historical inquiry, 114; for naturalistic research, 117–21; objectivity, critique of, 96–97, 225n1; possibilities, 121–23, 145–48; recovery and recuperation, 107; research routes, 97–98; research subjects, 97, 100, 102, 117–24; in search of excellence, 99–103; taxonomy of researchers, 102; value-laden research, 96–97
Micciche, Laura R., 92, 186, 189
Miller, Alice, 158
Miller, Hildy, 183, 187
Miller, Susan, 176–77
Miller, Thomas P., 105
Milstein, Sarah, 41
Minh-ha, Trinh T., 51, 65–68, 103, 106
misogyny, 84–85
Mohanty, Satya P., 47
monologic argument, 74, 75
moral development, 94, 225n23
More, Thomas, 193–94
Morrill Land Grant Act (1862), 182, 226n7
Mortensen, Peter, 117
Moss, Beverly, 118
Mott, Lucretia, 11, 12, 217–18n21, 218n23
Mouffe, Chantal, 123
Mountford, Roxanne, 156, 171–72
Moya, Paula, 48, 169
Muñoz, José Estaban, 52
mutual aid societies, 16

mutuality, 45; mentoring and, 152–55; teaching and, 144–45, 147
Mutz, Diana C., 43–44, 223n27
Myers, Nancy, 85
mystery, 56, 61

National Association of Colored Women's Clubs, 16, 149, 218n28
Native Americans, voting rights and, 9
naturalistic research, 117–21
naturalization of feminist rhetoric, 2
"Networked Mentoring" (Mountford and Glenn), 171–72
network theory, 81
Nicomachean Ethics (Aristotle), 165
Nineteenth Amendment, 7, 11, 20
nonviolent rhetoric, 74–76
normalization of women's issues, 14, 60
North Star, 11
"Notes from a Recovering Activist" (Gearhart), 71

Obama, Barack, 124–25, 196
Obama, Michelle, 193
objectivity, 65–66, 90, 96–97, 225n1
Odyssey (Homer), 149
Okawa, Gail, 170
Olbrechts-Tyteca, Lucie, 42
Olson, Gary, 154
One Billion [Women] Rising, 22
Ong, Rory, 110–14
online communications, 43
"An Open Letter to Mary Daly" (Lorde), 33–34
openness, white stance of, 40
oppositional identity politics, 27
optimism, 195
Oregon State University, 199
Others: cultural prodding and, 160–62; education and, 136–43; feminist research and, 121–23; identity created in presence of, 48; listening and recognition of, 83–84; non-normative subjects and arenas, 203; persuasion

violates goals of, 71; power-with-others, 63–64; second-wave feminism and, 30–31; speaking for, 33–35; as term, 3; voting rights and, 9

Palczewski, Catherine Helen, 218n29
Pascarella, Ernest, 129–30
pathos, 87–89, 150
patriarchal rhetoric, 61–62, 69, 113–14
Paul, Alice, 7, 20
Peaceful Persuasion: The Geopolitics of Nonviolent Rhetoric (Gorsevski), 74–76
Penn State University, 175, 181–83, 230nn9–16, 231nn17–24, 232nn25–26; general education review, 187–90
Perelman, Chaim, 42
Performing Feminism and Administration in Rhetoric and Composition Studies (Ratcliffe and Rickly), 179
personal as political, 178
persuasion, 39, 69; challenges to, 70–72, 83; definitions, 69, 84, 189; emotion and, 88; ethos and, 84–85; feminist pedagogy and, 145; hegemony and, 39, 64, 69; identification, 25, 29, 42, 204; moral development and, 94; peaceful, 75; as violence, 70, 74
Phenomenal Women, Inc., 118–20
Plato, 88, 146
Politics (Aristotle), 164–65
politics, women in, 7–8, 20; 2017, 20. *See also* Clinton, Hillary Rodham
politics of relation, 151
Porter, James E., 117, 225n2
"Portland Resolution," 182
positionality, 131–33, 140, 144–45; location, politics of, 151–52; WPA and, 180
positivist stances, 89–90
possibilities: of discourse, 145–48; for future feminist rhetorical work, 206–10; integrated rhetorical theories and praxis, 200–206; of

intersectionality, 203–4; methods and methodologies, 121–23, 145–48
postfeminism, 221n17
postmodernism, 110–11
poststructuralism, 108
"Post-truth and First-Year Writing" (Duffy), 138–39
post-truth politics (truthiness), 233–34n8
Powell, Malea, 202, 234nn14, 15
power, 27; difference and, 33, 39; ethos and, 84–85; exclusion from theory, 55–56; hidden imbalances, 77–78; patriarchal, 113; of teacher, 133
power feminism, 36, 221n17
power-from-within, 63–64
power-over, 27, 62, 75
Power-Stubbs, Karen, 137–39
power-with-others, 63–64
presidential campaign, 2016, 194–95
private sphere, 15
privilege, 34, 40–41
"The Problem of Speaking for Others" (Alcoff), 28
promiscuous audience, 11, 12–13
public and private spheres, concept of, 15
public sphere, 15, 80, 134, 215n2 (ch 2); angry feminist, trope of, 77; feminine style(s) and, 85–87
publishing, 161–62

Quakers. *See* Religious Society of Friends (Quakers)
Quintilian, 125

racism, 204, 221nn14, 15, 222n23; betrayal, nonwhite women's sense of, 59–60; interest-group politics, 205; listening and, 222nn23, 24; in white women's movement, 31–33, 59
Raine, Kathleen, 148
Ratcliffe, Krista, 43, 44, 45, 82–85, 140
Rawson, K. J., 99

INDEX

"real feminist," 40
reason, 88–89, 225n19
Reinventing the Soul (Ruti), 196–97
relating, 85
religion, 61
Religious Society of Friends (Quakers), 10, 13–14
replicability, 90
research, as term, 177. *See also* methods and methodologies
research subjects, 97, 100, 102, 117–24
resistance, silence as tool of, 81–82
re-sourcement, 74
responsibility, 68
Rethinking Ethos: A Feminist Ecological Approach to Rhetoric (Ryan, Myers and Jones), 85
Reynolds, Nedra, 156
rhetoric, 1–5; goals of traditional, 71, 76; hegemonic, 4, 5, 16, 56, 60, 75–76, 94; monologic, 68; transformation of discipline, 72–74; women in masculinist culture, 73. *See also* feminist rhetoric; rhetorical feminism
Rhetoric (Aristotle), 164–65
rhetorical feminism: church as venue, 10; conceptual actions, 51; countering of academic writing, 52–53; emotion, leveraging of, 5, 12, 13, 29; goals, 56–57, 74; mentoring and, 150, 153; at scene of delivery, 79–84; at the scene of the argument, 74–79; teaching and, 130; as term, 3–4; theorizing and, 50–51. *See also* feminist rhetoric
rhetorical knowledge, 28, 189, 205, 232n27
rhetorical recovery work, 2–3
rhetorical studies, democratization of, 49
"The Rhetoric of Women's Liberation: An Oxymoron" (Campbell), 72–74, 107
"'The Rhetoric of Women's Liberation: An Oxymoron' Revisited" (Campbell), 73

Rice, Condoleezza, 8
Rich, Adrienne: on claiming education, 135–36, 168; feminist pedagogy of, 140–43, 166–67; on mentoring, 158; politics of location, 151–52, 175; *Works*: "Arts of the Possible," 1, 174, 190, 198; "Cartographies of Silence," 200; "Letters: March 1969," 206; "Teaching Language in Open Admissions," 141; "What Is Possible," 64
Richards, Ann, 86–87
Rogers, Hester Ann, 98
Roof, Judith, 26
Rorty, Richard, 112
Rose, Shirley K, 178–79
Rowe, Aimee Carrillo, 151
Royster, Jacqueline Jones, 26, 51, 83, 99–103, 190; Afracentric methodological approach, 117; non-normative subjects and arenas, 203; on rhetorical history, 104; *Works: Feminist Rhetorical Practices* (with Kirsch), 100–103, 118, 121; "Feminist Rhetorical Practices: In Search of Excellence" (with Kirsch), 99; "When the First Voice You Hear Is Not Your Own," 101
Ruti, Mari, 196–97
Ryan, Kathleen J., 85

Sanders, Bernie, 194
Sanders, Lise Shapiro, 37
Sappho, 163–64
Saujani, Rehma, 22
Schell, Eileen, 99, 177
Schmalz, Julia, 229n15
Schniedewind, Nancy, 134–35
school shootings, 195, 196
Schuster, Charles, 190
Schwartz, Robert, 199
Sciachitano, Marian M., 137–39
Scott, Joan Wallach, 8, 113
second-wave feminism, 30–31

270

SEEK (Search for Education, Elevation, and Knowledge) program, 140–43, 144, 174
"sex, lies, and manuscript: Refiguring Aspasia in the History of Rhetoric" (Glenn), 110
Sharer, Wendy, 97, 226n1
Shaughnessy, Mina P., 174, 175, 229n1
Shepherd, Gregory J., 69
silence: Clinton campaigns and, 21–22; listening and, 5, 10, 11, 26, 44, 51, 94; privileged feminists and, 42; as rhetorical delivery, 81–84; as rhetorical tactic, 188
Silence and Listening as Rhetorical Arts (Glenn and Ratcliffe), 83
silencing, 81–82, 84–85
Sister Mentors, 229n15
Smith, Zadie, 211–12
Smitherman, Geneva, 157, 167
Smithies, Chris, 117
social circulation, 100, 102–3, 190, 191
social equality, 8–9
social positioning, 36, 46–48, 73
#SolidarityIsForWhiteWomen campaign, 38
Solnit, Rebecca, 197
Solomon, Akiba, 39
Southern Illinois University Press, 200
speaker: audience, relationship with, 28; feminist options, 41–42
"Speaking in Tongues: A Letter to 3rd World Women Writers" (Anzaldúa), 51–57
Spinsters, 60–62
spiritual approaches, 62–63
Spiritual Literacy in John Wesley's Methodism: Reading, Writing, and Speaking to Believe (Burton), 97
Spivak, Gayatri, 3, 21n16, 38, 53, 108, 220n4; "Can the Subaltern Speak?," 27; strategic essentialism, 25–26, 35–37, 204
Stallybrass, Peter, 176

Stanton, Elizabeth Cady, 11
Starhawk, 51, 62–64
Steinem, Gloria, 5, 31
Stewart, Maria W. Miller, 11, 12–13, 20
Stories of Mentoring (Eble and Gaillet), 150
strategic contemplation, 83, 95, 100, 102, 190–91
strategic essentialism, 25–26, 35–37, 204
Studies in Rhetorics and Feminisms series, 200
subaltern, 3, 27–28, 35–37, 204–5, 220n4; silence and listening as rhetorical arts, 83; as woman, 35–36
suffrage, 7–20, 216n8, 216n9; Fourteenth and Fifteenth Amendments, 18
Sullivan, Patricia A., 143
Syfers, Judy, 178
"A Symposium on Feminist Experiences in the Composition Classroom" (Eichhorn, Farris, Hayes, Hernández, Jarratt, Power-Stubbs, and Sciachitano), 137–39

"Taking Sides" (Welch), 146
Tarule, Jill Mattuck, 94
Tasker, Elizabeth, 122
teaching, 124–48, 227nn11–16; adjuncts, 128, 226n5; agency, authority, and action, 135–36; body of teacher, 132–33; composition studies and, 143–48; critical engagement, 133–35; cross-cultural issues, 131–32; current state of American education, 126–29; discourse, possibilities of, 145–48; effective feminist teachers, 130–31; feminist pedagogy, 126; feminist rhetorical pedagogy, 136–43; historically black colleges and universities (HBCUs), 128; hope and, 129–36, 227n16; lawmaker influence on, 127–28; mutual learning, 144–45, 147; peer tutors, 134–35; positionality

INDEX

teaching (*continued*)
(and intersectionality), 131–33, 140, 144–45; rhetorical feminism and, 130; six-dimension scale, 130; student loan concerns, 127–28, 227n8. *See also* feminist pedagogy
Teaching to Transgress: Education as the Practice of Freedom (hooks), 58
tenure, 186
Terenzini, Patrick, 129–30
terministic screens, 1
Textual Carnivals (Miller), 176–77
theory, 49–95, 223n2; Background vs. foreground, 60–62; disidentification and, 51–64; divisions, 201–6; experience as basis for, 58–60; feminine, rhetorical feminism and, 84–93; feminist responses to feminist rhetoric, 93–95; interest-convergence, 204–6; invitational rhetoric, 68–70; marginal rhetorics, 203–5, 234n14; power-from-within and power-with, 62–63; "race for," 55, 224n5; rhetorical feminism and, 50–51; rhetorical feminism at the scene of argument, 70, 74–79; spiritual approaches, 62–64; third-world women's writing, 51–57; transformations and transactions, 64–74, 95; vernacular writing in, 58–60, 70, 86–87
third-wave feminism, 32–33, 36, 221n17
third-world women's writing, 51–57
Tometi, Opal, 22
Tomlinson, Barbara, 76–79, 88
Tonn, Mari Boor, 85–87
tradition narrative, 50, 104–5
trained incapacities, 17, 84, 97, 217n21
transactions, rhetorical, 66–67, 70, 95
transformation, 43, 51, 64–74; Campbell, 72–74; Foss and Griffin, 68–70; Gearhart, 70–72; Minh-ha, 65–68; Trinh, 65–68
transparency, 117

Troubling the Angels: Women Living with HIV/AIDS (Lather and Smithies), 117
Trump, Donald, 23, 44, 80, 211, 235n18
Trump presidency, 194–98
truth, 28, 67–68, 233–34n8
Truth, Sojourner, 12, 16–18, 37, 80, 217n15
Tuana, Nancy, 129
"Twenty More Years in the WPA's Progress" (Charlton and Rose), 178
"Twitter, Feminism, and Race: Who Gets a Seat at the Table?" (Kendall), 42

understanding, as rhetorical goal, 42, 47–48, 75, 152
United States, gender discrimination, 8
University of Minnesota, 199
Unspoken: A Rhetoric of Silence (Glenn), 82
US Constitution, 8, 11
Utopia (More), 193–94

value-laden research, 96–97
vernacular, 4, 5, 16, 54–55, 180; feminine style and, 86–87; mentoring and, 150; in theoretical writing, 58–60, 70, 86–87
violence: domestic, 78–79, 81–82; persuasion as, 70, 74
vita activa, 20
Vote and Voice: Women's Organization and Political Literacy, 1915–1930 (Sharer), 97
voting rights. *See* suffrage

Walker, Rebecca, 36
Wang, Bo, 113
Warren, Elizabeth, 21
Websters' First New Intergalactic Wickedary of the English Language (Daly), 61
Weiler, Kathleen, 144–45

272

Welch, Nancy, 146
Well, H. G., 126
Wesley, John, 115–16
West, Cornel, 195
"What Spurs Students to Stay in College and Learn?" (Berrett), 129–30
"When and Where I Enter: Race, Gender, and Composition Studies" (Logan), 132–33
"When the First Voice You Hear Is Not Your Own" (Royster), 101
When They Read What We Write: The Politics of Ethnography (Brettell), 117
white privilege, 34, 40
white women: intersectionality and, 38–39; middle-class white heterosexual, 30–31; openness, stance of, 40; racism in white women's movement, 31–33, 59
Who Can Speak? Authority and Critical Identity (Roof and Wiegman), 26
Wiegman, Robyn, 26
Wilson, Woodrow, 20
woman: second-wave framing of, 30–31; subaltern as, 35–36; as term used by feminist rhetors, 15–16, 220–21n9; as term used by free black women, 16–17; as term used by men, 14–15
"The Womanization of Rhetoric" (Gearhart), 70–72
woman president, 197–98
Woman's Rights Convention, Akron, Ohio, 1851, 16–18, 80, 217n15
Woman's Rights Convention, Seneca Falls, New York, 1848, 11
Woman Suffrage Party, 19–20

Women in Black, 22
"Women's Bodies in the College Writing Classroom" (Eichhorn), 132
Women's March on Washington, 23, 221n10
Women's Ways of Knowing: The Development of Self, Voice, and Mind (Belenky, Clinchy, Goldberger, and Tarule), 94
"Women's Work" (Holbrook), 176
Woolbright, Meg, 135, 136
Woolf, Virginia, 181, 228n2
World War I, 19
writing center interactions, 144
Writing in Business
Writing in Business course (Penn State University), 184–85
writing program administration (WPA), 93, 174–92; across the nation, 175–80; budgetary concerns, 185–86; distributed administrative model, 186, 187; "female ghettos," 177; feminist models, 184–87; feminization of composition, 176; four feminist research practices and, 190–91; future prospects, 187–90; location and, 180–81; as mesosystem, 180, 183–84; Penn State University, 175, 181–83; respect, salary, and promotion, 178. *See also* composition studies
Wu, Hui, 110–14

Xenophon, 165–66

Yancey, Kathleen Blake, 180, 185
Yousafzai, Malala, 28–29

Cheryl Glenn is Distinguished Professor of English at the Pennsylvania State University, the director of the Program in Writing and Rhetoric there, and a coeditor of the Studies in Rhetorics and Feminisms series of books. Her publications include *Rhetoric Retold: Regendering the Tradition from Antiquity Through the Renaissance*; *Unspoken: A Rhetoric of Silence*; *Silence and Listening as Rhetorical Arts*; and *Rhetoric and Writing Studies in the New Century: Historiography, Pedagogy, and Politics* (all published by Southern Illinois University Press).

Studies in Rhetorics and Feminisms

Studies in Rhetorics and Feminisms seeks to address the interdisciplinarity that rhetorics and feminisms represent. Rhetorical and feminist scholars connect rhetorical inquiry with contemporary academic and social concerns, exploring rhetoric's relevance to current issues of opportunity and diversity. This interdisciplinarity is transforming the rhetorical tradition as we have known it (upper-class, agonistic, public, and male) into regendered, inclusionary rhetorics (democratic, dialogic, collaborative, cultural, and private). Our intellectual advancements depend on such ongoing transformation.

Rhetoric, whether ancient, contemporary, or futuristic, always inscribes the relation of language and power at a particular moment, indicating who may speak, who may listen, and what can be said. The only way we can displace the traditional rhetoric of masculine-only, public performance is to replace it with rhetorics that are recognized as being better suited to our present needs. We must understand more fully the rhetorics of the non-Western tradition, of women, of a variety of cultural and ethnic groups. Therefore, Studies in Rhetorics and Feminisms espouses a theoretical position of openness and expansion, a place for rhetorics to grow and thrive in a symbiotic relationship with all that feminisms have to offer, particularly when these two fields intersect with philosophical, sociological, religious, psychological, pedagogical, and literary issues.

The series seeks scholarly works that both examine and extend rhetoric, works that span the sexes, disciplines, cultures, ethnicities, and sociocultural practices as they intersect with the rhetorical tradition. After all, the recent resurgence of rhetorical studies has been not so much a discovery of new rhetorics as a recognition of existing rhetorical activities and practices, of our newfound ability and willingness to listen to previously untold stories.

The series editors seek both high-quality traditional and cutting-edge scholarly work that extends the significant relationship between rhetoric and feminism within various genres, cultural contexts, historical periods, methodologies, theoretical positions, and methods of delivery (e.g., film and hypertext to elocution and preaching).

Studies in Rhetorics and Feminisms / Queries and Submissions

Professor Emerita Shirley Wilson Logan
University of Maryland
Email: slogan@umd.edu

Professor Cheryl Glenn
Penn State University
Department of English
402 Burrowes Bldg.
Penn State University
University Park, PA 16802-6200
Email: cjg6@psu.edu

Other Books in the Studies in Rhetorics and Feminisms Series

Retroactivism in the Lesbian Archives: Composing Pasts and Futures
Jean Bessette

Feminist Rhetorical Science Studies: Human Bodies, Posthumanist Worlds
Edited by Amanda K. Booher and Julie Jung

A Feminist Legacy: The Rhetoric and Pedagogy of Gertrude Buck
Suzanne Bordelon

Regendering Delivery: The Fifth Canon and Antebellum Women Rhetors
Lindal Buchanan

Rhetorics of Motherhood
Lindal Buchanan

Conversational Rhetoric: The Rise and Fall of a Women's Tradition, 1600–1900
Jane Donawerth

Feminism beyond Modernism
Elizabeth A. Flynn

Women and Rhetoric between the Wars
Edited by Ann George, M. Elizabeth Weiser, and Janet Zepernick

Educating the New Southern Woman: Speech, Writing, and Race at the Public Women's Colleges, 1884–1945
David Gold and Catherine L. Hobbs

Food, Feminisms, Rhetorics
Edited by Melissa A. Goldthwaite

Women's Irony: Rewriting Feminist Rhetorical Histories
Tarez Samra Graban

Claiming the Bicycle: Women, Rhetoric, and Technology in Nineteenth-Century America
Sarah Hallenbeck

The Rhetoric of Rebel Women: Civil War Diaries and Confederate Persuasion
Kimberly Harrison

Evolutionary Rhetoric: Sex, Science, and Free Love in Nineteenth-Century Feminism
Wendy Hayden

Liberating Voices: Writing at the Bryn Mawr Summer School for Women Workers
Karyn L. Hollis

*Gender and Rhetorical Space
in American Life, 1866–1910*
Nan Johnson

*Antebellum American
Women's Poetry:
A Rhetoric of Sentiment*
Wendy Dasler Johnson

*Appropriate[ing] Dress:
Women's Rhetorical Style in
Nineteenth-Century America*
Carol Mattingly

*The Gendered Pulpit:
Preaching in American
Protestant Spaces*
Roxanne Mountford

*Writing Childbirth:
Women's Rhetorical Agency
in Labor and Online*
Kim Hensley Owens

*Rhetorical Listening:
Identification, Gender, Whiteness*
Krista Ratcliffe

*Feminist Rhetorical Practices:
New Horizons for Rhetoric,
Composition, and Literacy Studies*
Jacqueline J. Royster and
Gesa E. Kirsch

*Rethinking Ethos:
A Feminist Ecological
Approach to Rhetoric*
Edited by Kathleen J. Ryan, Nancy
Myers, and Rebecca Jones

*Vote and Voice:
Women's Organizations and
Political Literacy, 1915–1930*
Wendy B. Sharer

*Women Physicians and Professional
Ethos in Nineteenth-Century America*
Carolyn Skinner

*Praising Girls:
The Rhetoric of Young
Women, 1895–1930*
Henrietta Rix Wood